Deathworlds to Lifeworlds

Deathworlds to Lifeworlds

Collaboration with Strangers for Personal,
Social and Ecological Transformation

Edited by
Valerie Malhotra Bentz
James Marlatt

DE GRUYTER

ISBN 978-3-11-126197-3
e-ISBN (PDF) 978-3-11-069181-8
e-ISBN (EPUB) 978-3-11-069186-3

Library of Congress Control Number: 2021941380

Bibliographic information published by the Deutsche Nationalbibliothek
The Deutsche Nationalbibliothek lists this publication in the Deutsche Nationalbibliografie;
detailed bibliographic data are available on the Internet at http://dnb.dnb.de.

© 2023 Walter de Gruyter GmbH, Berlin/Boston
This volume is text- and page-identical with the hardback published in 2021.
Cover image: Ben Goode/iStock/Getty Images Plus
Typesetting: Integra Software Services Pvt. Ltd.
Printing and binding: CPI books GmbH, Leck

www.degruyter.com

To the continued positive transformation of the 100 students and colleagues who participated in learning phenomenology.

To the continued transformation of Deathworlds into Lifeworlds.

To the Great Spirit within each of us that is One.

Acknowledgements

Thanks to Professor Krzysztof Konecki for inviting me to teach and research transformative phenomenology at the University of Łódź, Poland, Winter 2019 and for his presence as a co-learner in our doctoral seminar there. Also, the support of Professors Anna Kacperczyk and Anna Kubczak, and Dr. Rafal Matera, Dean of the Faculty at the University of Łódź. Much gratitude to Dr. James Maddirala, Provost at the University of Virgin Islands, who changed the course schedule for the Doctoral students in Creative Leadership so that they could be co-participants in the research. Special thanks to Associate Provost for Research, Kathryn McGraw, and to Fielding Graduate University Office of Research, which provided financial support for the project, and to Provost Monique Snowden and Program Director Patrice Rosenthal for releasing time from some faculty obligations. Doctoral research assistants Carol Estrada (Fielding), Eion Maison (University of the Virgin Islands), Natalia Martini (Jagiallonian University), and Łucja Lange (University of Łódź) were critically important to the success of the project. Without the partnership of co-editor and Fielding alumnus, Dr. Jim Marlatt, this project would not have been possible. Jim served as overall Research Coordinator of the project and designed the Basecamp website to organize the hundreds of documents and on-going communications. Fielding alumnus, Dr. Bart Buechner, was an essential partner, both as co-teacher and overall coordinator of the Somatics, Phenomenology and Communicative Leadership Community of Practice (SPCL). Dr. David Haddad, alumnus and phenomenologist, not only wrote chapters, but organized and analyzed protocols in a sensitive and insightful manner. Thanks especially to my spouse, Dr. S.K. Figler, for support from home when I was in Łódź, while he was recovering from major back surgery, as well for his keen editorial eye at crucial times. Heartfelt appreciation for the astute editing and formatting assistance of Anna Haefele of True Bloom Cooperative. Thanks to Steve and Rita Wrolstad, who fostered puppy "Kali," my lab-heeler partner, while I was away doing this research. Much appreciation also for the continued spiritual support from my guru, Swami Sarvadevanada, Head of the Vedanta Society of Southern California. Finally, great appreciation to founding thinkers of phenomenology, especially Edmund Husserl, Alfred Schütz and Helmut Wagner.

Without the sterling support of Christoph Schirmer, Mara Weber, and Suruthi Manogarane of De Gruyter this book would not have been possible.

Foreword

Four Arrows

The Foreword of a book, when written by an invited guest, usually proffers why the text is being written *now*. If I were to try to accomplish this in one sentence, I might say something like: "This book is about how Transformative Phenomenology can be a methodology and a way to bring forth life-affirming cultures to replace or overshadow death-affirming ones that currently have us at the edge of extinction." Such a single sentence, however, would not do justice to the chapters that follow. For transformational learning to take place on the scale the editors and contributors intend, one sentence could never convey the goals and urgency of this text's editors and contributors. They are too complex, holistic, intuitive, and too mystical for a single sentence. So, I will continue writing for a while.

I'm not the first to suggest alignment between phenomenology and mysticism, and I am guessing one reason I was invited to write this Foreword relates to my own mystical orientation as an Indigenous-based scholar. If we define a mystic as one who believes in the spiritual apprehension of truths that are beyond the intellect, then this well describes the Indigenous worldview that umbrellas the great diversity of place-based knowledge traditional First Nation wisdom keepers may possess:

> Mysticism, although differently expressed in particular Indigenous lifeways, manifests the intimate relatedness of person, community, spirits and ecosystem. This interactive quaternity is ritually embedded in Indigenous lifeways and symbolically unfolded in cosmological narratives. (Grim 2020, p. 114)

Valerie Bentz, and others associated with this book, have recognized the power of traditional Indigenous wisdom and spirituality. She was especially interested by my assertion that there are only two worldviews (Four Arrows 2016) – the Indigenous that guided us for 99% of human history, and the Dominant one that has essentially guided us for the past 1%, or approximately 9,000 years, with the Americas suffering the most during the past 600 years or so. The father of social-anthropology, Robert Redfield, proposed this idea in the 1940s (Redfield 1952, 1956). He also felt that the new worldview's oppression and disregard for the Indigenous worldview would prove to be one of the great human tragedies. Perhaps he was among the first academics to notice Deathworlds within Lifeworlds and Deathworlds overtaking Lifeworlds. Genocide and culturecide against Indigenous Peoples continues today.

This brief history implies that, rather than reinventing the proverbial wheel from scratch, Collaborative Transformative Phenomenology might utilize Indigenous worldview precepts in its various explorations on behalf of eradicating the Deathworlds all around us. Indeed, one might merely look at the contrasting and potentially complementary dualities that exist between dominant and Indigenous consciousness and lifeways. This can be done by peeking at the list of 40 pairings printed in Chapter One of this book that I have shared from my book *The Red Road: Linking Diversity and Inclusion Initiatives to Indigenous Worldview* (2020). It does not take much consideration to realize connections between Deathworlds and adherence to personal and institutional assumptions and policies based on such characteristics of the Dominant Worldview as:

- dualistic thinking without seeking complementarity
- acceptance of rigid hierarchies
- fear-based thoughts and behaviors
- living without a strong social purpose
- primarily selfish goals for personal gain
- rigid and discriminatory gender stereotypes
- uncritical acceptance of materialism
- anthropocentric and not honoring the Earth as Sentient and Sacred
- unfamiliarity with an alternative consciousness
- disregarding holistic interconnectedness
- emphasis on theory and rhetoric versus action
- acceptability of dishonesty and deception
- seeing ceremony as a rote phenomenon
- autonomy not connected to the group

Although the contributors to this text may or may not refer directly to Indigenous worldview in each chapter, the reader might imagine how approaches to Lifeworld and Deathworld applications can be further enriched by noting which worldviews in the list may apply here or there. In other words, aspects of consciousness, experience and transformation relating to Lifeworlds versus Deathwords might be also seen as relating to the inability of people to notice the proverbial water in which we swim I describe as "worldview." At the same time, one might easily align the dominant worldview side of the list with the cultivation and preservation of Deathworlds. Moreover, with the deep insights that phenomenology can evoke, the worldview precepts can be used to help with metacognitive transformations or at least recognizing possibilities for complementarity between opposing views.

Note that, at least as relates to ecological harmony, claims about the importance of such worldview reflection are increasingly being acknowledged. The largest study ever done, the United Nations Biodiversity and Extinction Rate Report released in May of 2019, using 450 researchers from 50 countries going over more than 15,000 peer-reviewed papers, revealed that where Indigenous worldview operates, extinction rates are absent or minimal (Four Arrows 2019). Yet it may be that in order for enough people to come to terms with this, they must collectively engage in reflection, storytelling, and dialogue about the phenomenon of worldview and its relationship to Life- and Deathworlds. If the reader is able to learn from these chapters about phenomenology accordingly, this book and its timeliness will serve as a culminating event that builds on the work of Edmund Husserl and his 1936 text, *The Crisis of European Sciences and Transcendental Phenomenology*. Referring to *Lifeworld* as a contextual context for phenomenology, he reveals a concern about declining moral, political and scientific integrity. More than 50 years later, Jürgen Habermas went a little further, explaining how Lifeworld can be distorted by unjustifiable authority and human rationalization of colonization (1981). In 2003, Achille Mbembe wrote about "the creation of death-worlds, new and unique forms of social existence in which vast populations are subjected to conditions of life conferring upon them the status of living dead" (p. 14). Five years later, Rehorick and Bentz write a book about "transformative phenomenology" and how it can be used to change our Lifeworlds (2008). A decade later, Bentz, Rehorick, Marlatt, Nishii and Estrada published a piece in a research journal about how "transformative phenomenology" can be an antidote to Deathworld-making (2018).

And now, Collaborative Transformative Phenomenology, in joining with the Indigenous Worldview, may have finally come to realize the most invisible source – worldview – and its role in using phenomenological awareness to bring our world back into harmony.

References

Bentz, Valerie/Marlatt, James/Nishi, Ayumi/Estrada, Carol (2018): "Transformative Phenomenology as an Antidote to Technological Deathworlds". In: *Schutzian Research* 10, pp.189–220.

Four Arrows (2016): *Point of Departure: Returning to Our More Authentic worldview for Education and Survival*. Charlottesville: Information Age Publishing.

Four Arrows (2019): "The Media Have Missed a Crucial Message of the UN's Biodiversity Report". Retrieved from https://www.thenation.com/article/archive/biodiversity-un-report-indigenous-worldview/, visited October 13, 2020.

Grim, John (2020): "Cosmology and Native North American Mystical Traditions". In: *Theologique* 1, pp. 113–142.

Habermas, Jürgen (1985): *The Theory of Communicative Action: Lifeworld and System, A Critique of Functionalist Reason* (T. McCarthy, Trans.). Boston: Beacon.
Mbembe, Joseph-Achille (2003): "Necropolitics." In: *Public Culture* 15. No.1, pp. 11–40.
Redfield, Robert (1952): *The Primitive World View. Proceedings of the American Philosophical Society* 96. No.1, pp. 30–36.
Redfield, Robert (1956): *Peasant Society and Culture: An Anthropological Approach to Civilization*. Chicago: University of Chicago Press.
Rehorick, David/Bentz, Valerie (Eds.) (2008): *Transformative Phenomenology: Changing Ourselves, Lifeworlds and Professional Practice*. New York: Lexington.

Contents

Acknowledgements —— VII

Foreword —— IX

Part I: Lifeworlds in Deathworlds in Łódź, Poland

Valerie Malhotra Bentz and James Marlatt
Chapter 1   From Deathworlds to Lifeworlds Through Collaborative Transformative Phenomenology —— 3

Krzysztof T. Konecki
Chapter 2   Deathworld of the City of Łódź: Insider Experience —— 27

Valerie Malhotra Bentz
Chapter 3   Deathworld of the City of Łódź: Outsider Lived Experiences —— 45

Anna Kacperczyk
Chapter 4   Phenomenology of Trash —— 63

Natalia Martini
Chapter 5   Walking with Homeless Persons in Kraków and Łódź —— 91

Łucja Lange
Chapter 6   The Experience of Precognition —— 102

David Haddad and Łucja Lange
Chapter 7   Personal Discovery and Transformation Through the Study of Lived-Experience —— 117

Part II: Experiences of Lifeworlds and Deathworlds

David Haddad and James Marlatt
Chapter 8 Restoring Lifeworlds Through Phenomenological Writing, Reflection and Collaboration —— 135

Carol Estrada
Chapter 9 Be-*ing* with Dying: A Personal Experience with the Death of a Young Person —— 150

Tetyana Azarova
Chapter 10 Inspiration in Times of Personal Challenge: A Mindful Inquiry —— 163

Lorraine Crockford
Chapter 11 The Deathworld of First Responders: Being a Stranger to Oneself —— 180

Part III: Lifeworlds and Deathworlds in We-Relationships

Whitney P. Strohmayr and David R. Jones
Chapter 12 Grief and Unraveling in Romantic We-Relationships —— 195

Lori Davidson, Jennifer Decker, and Dagmara Tarasiuk
Chapter 13 Overcoming Deathworlds of Addiction, Self-Injury, and Stress —— 205

Michelle Elias and Darlene Cockayne
Chapter 14 Military Wife and Mother: Lifeworlds and Deathworlds Surrounding Military Life —— 225

Barton Buechner, Ann Ritter, and Rik Spann
Chapter 15 Embracing Endless Liminality: Improvisation and the "Practical Mystic" —— 242

Part IV: Deathworlds and the Indigenous

Debra Irene Opland
Chapter 16 Indigenous Worldview and the Vision of a Peace Educator —— 263

Tsolmontuya Myagmarjav
Chapter 17 Colonization of the Lifeworld of Sheepherder Communities of Mongolia —— 280

Małgorzata Burchard-Dziubińska
Chapter 18 Deathworld Encroachments on the Amazon Rainforest —— 289

Valerie C. Grossman
Chapter 19 Sustaining Lifeworlds in the Face of Famine, Water Shortages, and Malaria —— 296

Part V: Transformative Phenomenology Practice

Valerie Malhotra Bentz, David Rehorick, James Marlatt, Ayumi Nishii, and Carol Estrada
Chapter 20 Transformative Phenomenology as an Antidote to Technological Deathworlds —— 319

James Marlatt and Valerie Malhotra Bentz
Epilogue: The Essence of Collaborative Transformative Phenomenology —— 349

About the Authors —— 353

About the Editors —— 359

Endorsements —— 361

Index —— 365

Part I: **Lifeworlds in Deathworlds in Łódź, Poland**

> The stranger discerns, frequently with a grievous clear-sightedness, the rising of a crisis which may menace the whole foundation of the "relatively natural conception of the world," while all those symptoms pass unnoticed by the members of the in-group, who rely on the continuance of their customary way of life.
>
> – Alfred Schütz, "The Stranger," in *Collected Papers Vol II*.

Valerie Malhotra Bentz and James Marlatt
Chapter 1
From Deathworlds to Lifeworlds Through Collaborative Transformative Phenomenology

Abstract: This collaborative action research based on *Transformative Phenomenology* highlights the increase in Deathworlds globally and fosters collaboration among strangers as a Lifeworld-making Antidote. Researchers engaged 78 participants from three universities and 14 countries in phenomenological writing to expand their awareness of experiences of significance in their lives. They connected via face-to-face communication and computer platforms. Recognizing and sharing emotional challenges, participants revealed Deathworlds within their Lifeworlds that included traumatic echoes of war, genocide, oppression, and practices that contribute to illness, community decline, and climate change. Participants and researchers collaborated on chapters including grief, death, addiction, environmental devastations, suicide attempts, and impacts of disasters. The participants developed reflective qualities of being such as open-mindedness, a sense of "wonder" and embodied awareness. These are among the Ten Qualities of Transformative Phenomenologists discovered from prior research. Deathworlds to Lifeworlds will appeal to those looking for practical ways to expand consciousness and promote collaboration for personal, social, and environmental transformation. The Dominant Worldview promotes Deathworlds at an exponential rate. A return to the Indigenous Worldview is essential. Collaborative Transformative Phenomenology provides a roadmap back.

Keywords: Transformative Phenomenology, Lifeworlds, Deathworlds, Indigenous Worldview, action research

Introduction

What is the place and relevance of *Transformative Phenomenology* in transforming consciousness for a livable world? What is the value of "teaching" phenomenology by introducing different ways-of-knowing through "writing phenomenology"?

What is it like to be a "stranger" collaborating with others in a global community? Can Transformative Phenomenology act as an antidote to Deathworlds that pervade our Lifeworlds? These are some of the questions that we posed in the context of a multi-national and multi-institutional participatory action research project (2019) on the phenomenon of being a "stranger" while building relationships across cultures – phenomenological research that builds upon over two decades of doctoral study experience at Fielding Graduate University.

In this chapter, we discuss: (1) our research project design, and the process of "writing phenomenology" as a way of supporting consciousness-raising; (2) how engaging with Transformative Phenomenology revealed Deathworlds in the Lifeworlds of our students; (3) how today's common, *Deathworldy*, Dominant Worldview contrasts with the Lifeworldly Indigenous Worldview; and (4) how collaborative somatic phenomenology offers a way back. We conclude the chapter with a short description of the individual and collaborative contributions from our authors, that include doctoral students, alumni, and professors.

Our research project focused on understanding and developing approaches to raising consciousness founded on the principles of Transformative Phenomenology – a somatic-hermeneutic-phenomenology put into action in the Lifeworld that was developed during 20 years of "teaching" doctoral students at Fielding by Professors David Rehorick and Valerie Malhotra Bentz (2008, 2017). Rehorick and Bentz call this evolving era the "Silver Age of Phenomenology at Fielding" (Bentz et al. 2019). The practice of Transformative Phenomenology is founded on the essence-based phenomenology of Edmund Husserl, the social phenomenology of Alfred Schütz, the embodied phenomenology of Maurice Merleau-Ponty, the ontologic-existential phenomenology of Martin Heidegger, and the reflective interpretative hermeneutic methods of Hans-Georg Gadamer (Marlatt et al. 2020).

The research involved 78 doctoral students and alumni from Fielding Graduate University, the University of the Virgin Islands (including participants from the Marshall Islands), and the University of Łódź, Poland, including visiting undergraduate students from the Erasmus Institute (Figure 1). During ten weeks of learning and applying Transformative Phenomenology, students developed rich descriptions of lived experience (*protocols*) and reflective commentaries through their collaborations that were used as information for the research. The research involved the recording and collection of information founded on the methodologies and methods of phenomenological inquiry – including Husserlian eidetic and Schützian social phenomenology.

The project was designed to replicate research which highlighted the ten phenomenological qualities of Transformative Phenomenologists as a foundation for consciousness-raising that graduates of Fielding obtained through the study and practice of phenomenologically based contemplative social research (Rehorick/Bentz 2017; Bentz/Giorgino 2016). Our focus was on *co-learning* through "teaching" that was based upon the principles of participation, empowerment, and change. As participatory action researchers, we acted in facilitative roles in the process of inquiry aimed at consciousness-raising. As well, our work supported the continued emergence of a Fielding based community-of-practice (Wenger 1998) supporting social and ecological justice.

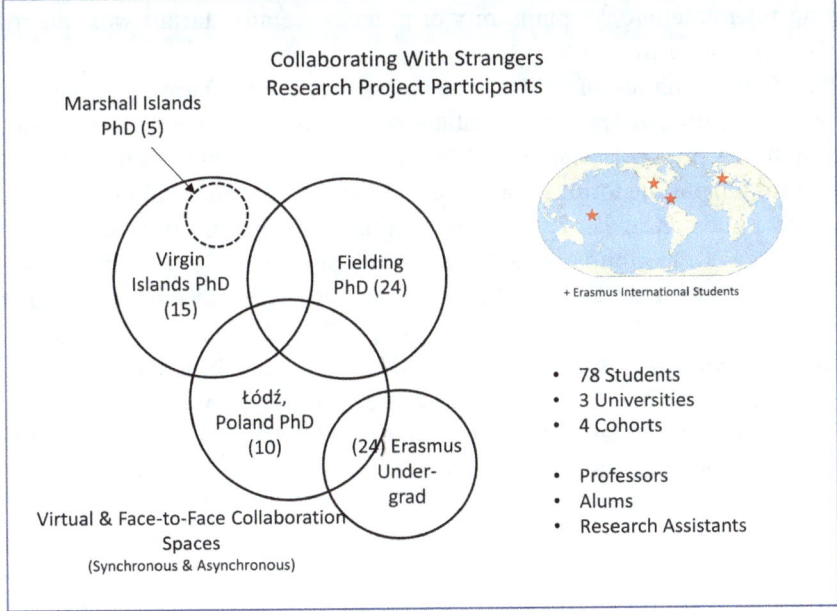

Figure 1: Our research project participants.
Image by authors, Valerie Bentz and James Marlatt.

Transformative Phenomenology with Strangers

Professor Krzystof Konecki invited me (Bentz) to come to the University of Łódź to teach Transformative Phenomenology and conduct research. He suggested an overall theme of collaboration among strangers.[1] Doctoral students from The University of the Virgin Islands (UVI) participated via a course taught in parallel by Bentz and Dr. Barton Buechner. Doctoral students in Human Development from Fielding Graduate University (Fielding) were enrolled in a course in writing phenomenology with Bentz. Undergraduates from the Erasmus Institute program for students from various European countries also participated in a course at Łódź initially taught by Bentz, and later by research assistant Łucja Lange. Also participating were alumni and colleagues connected with the Fielding phenomenology community-of-practice. James Marlatt was our research project coordinator.[2]

Based on techniques of writing phenomenology I (Bentz) used in a class for over a decade, the participants simultaneously wrote six to eight phenomenologically-based protocols and shared them within and across programs. They shared through on-line forums (Basecamp and Moodle), conversations on Zoom calls, and in-person in Łódź. Most of the students were strangers before the course. Three of the groups were doctoral students in sociology or applied social sciences. The Fielding and UVI students had little or no face-to-face contact as these were primarily virtual learning groups. The UVI students worked in a cohort model with classes on Zoom. The Łódź students met face to face in classroom settings. Bentz and Buechner and research assistants embraced a teaching model that promoted "learning together" (*leregogy*)[3] (Rehorick/Taylor 1995). We choose to de-academize the term by calling it "co-learning."

---

[1] As principle researcher I was a stranger at the University of Łódź, having contact with Krzysztof only from one conference in Krakov in 2016 where he had invited me to give a Keynote address at the European Sociological Association.

[2] The research project was made possible by a grant from Fielding Graduate University Office of Research. The grant allowed Fielding students, alumni, and faculty to participate in the project as research associates or assistants and to collaborate on the resulting publications.

[3] David Rehorick describes the neologism "leregogy" as a "term coined to bridge the indomitable severing of roles between teacher and learner. It implies a transactional and shifting set of 'roles' wherein both people are, at various times and sometimes synchronously, both teachers and learners. It also avoids the accepted term for adult learning (andragogy) which has its linguistic roots on maleness; and the authoritarian role-sets implied by the term pedagogy" (Rehorick/Taylor 1995).

Design of Protocols

Husserlian Essential Protocols

The phenomenological protocols are designed so that students may deeply explore an experience of importance to each of them using Husserlian-based essential phenomenology. These protocols focus on the writer's most poignant experience, the earliest memory of that experience, and protocols using phenomenological techniques such as *imaginative variation, bracketing,* and *horizontalization*. Additional protocols focus on descriptions of the opposite of the experience or when the experience was not present. The exploration leads to the identification of the resulting *essential structure*s of the experience itself.

When asked to describe an experience of importance in their lives, students will often tell a story. Storytelling has a long history as a social glue as well as a way of motivating listeners to empathize with the storyteller and to take action. Stories have a typical structure in which an emotion is raised as a problem. A crisis is reached followed by some kind of resolution.

We coached the participants to get underneath the story, back to recalling the experience as it occurred, which does not usually take the form of a story. Stories are told in retrospect. Our direct experience as written in a phenomenological protocol does not necessarily have any purpose, or if so, we may not know what it is. It is a jumble of sensations, bodily feelings, and impulses. Phenomenological protocols can bring our bodily feelings and our emotions into focus. Sometimes this is a challenge for those of us brought up in the *Dominant Worldview* which devalues our bodies (Four Arrows/Narvaez 2019; Berman 2015). Writing protocols through the lens of Max van Manen's Lifeworld existentials (spatiality, corporeality, temporality, and relationality) helped the writers to focus inward (van Manen 1997).

Phenomenological protocol writing, through the technique of *bracketing,* teaches us that we are capable of re-seeing an experience by setting parts of it aside. We become aware that we contain *multiple realities*. By *horizontalizing*, we may see that something we thought was tangential is very important. For example, the calm waters of the sea out my window are really central to the peaceful experience we have while peeling potatoes at the sink. If we learn the phenomenological technique of *imaginative variations*, we can start to see what could have been different. This allows us to see our *intentionality* in our life's journey.

In sharing, we find companions who have had similar experiences. Since our expressions of them are authentic, others can relate to our differences. We can realize that someone in conversation with us may have a different *vantage point*.

The phenomenological description has a parallel path to transcendental meditation (Mare 2017). It evokes awareness of our deeper selves, or *Atman* because it requires us to observe our thoughts, therefore it brings to our awareness that we exist beyond our thoughts and that they are changing. We learn that our higher *Self* can serve as a coachman to control our senses and our minds becoming aware that we are spiritual beings (Śaṅkarācārya/Nikhilananda 1974). This is vital to human essence, but centuries of mind-body-soul splitting scientism has stripped this from our awareness, perhaps especially in the social "sciences" (Porpora 2016).

Schützian Lifeworld Protocols

Following in Schütz' footsteps but extending Lifeworld to include the other life forms, Bentz and Shapiro define Lifeworld as:

> The lived experiences of human beings and other living creatures as formed into more or less coherent grounds for their existence. This consists of the whole system of interactions with others and objects in an environment that is fused with meaning and language and that sustains the life of all creatures from birth through death. It is the fundamental ground of all experience for human beings. (Bentz/Shapiro 1998)

We asked the students to situate their chosen phenomenon in the Lifeworld in two protocols using concepts from Schütz, such as *relevance, typifications, multiple realities, vantage points, because and in-order-to-motives,* highlighting how we experience events (Wagner 1970, 1983). Participants constructed *types* or *puppets* which occupy their Lifeworld. Finally, we asked the doctoral students to explore their experience from a motivational perspective in using Kenneth Burke's pentad based on the communicative theory of social dramatism: act, scene, agent, agency, and purpose (Burke 1969).

The sequence of phenomenological protocol topics that we asked our students to follow is presented in Table 1.

Co-Learning

Sharing experiences that matter in a supportive environment allowed participants to break through from a private world into the community of co-learners. As opposed to secretive sharing of "trauma" diagnosed by "experts" as various forms of illness needing "expert" treatment, sharing meaningful events, on a spectrum from suffering to joyful, lends itself toward moving forward together

Table 1: The Sequence of Phenomenological Protocol Topics (rich descriptions of lived experience). Copyright (2020) by Valerie Bentz and James Marlatt, Used with Permission, Original Tabulation.

Protocol	Focus
1	Write a phenomenological protocol (lived-experience description) of your most poignant memory of the experience of a phenomenon of interest.
2	Referring to Lifeworld existentials (spatiality, corporeality, temporality, and relationality), describe your earliest memory of the phenomenon you wrote about in the first session (van Manen, 1997).
3	Write about an experience of either the opposite of the one you are focusing on or one where the phenomenon was not present. Consider and use several of the phenomenological writing techniques of bracketing and horizontalization. Look at the words you are using to describe your phenomenon and their sources and what they mean (etymology). Is there an embodied (somatic) connection?
4	Based on your protocols and others you may have found in literature, popular media, etc., write a short essential structure of the experience. What must be present in the experience for it to be the one in question? Also, what must not be present to be the experience in question? Refer to the protocols you recently wrote and distill the essence of the experience of your phenomenon. As you work with this, you may continue to use phenomenological techniques, such as imaginative variations, horizontalization, and bracketing.
5	Describe aspects of a Lifeworld in which your chosen experience or phenomenon occurs. Use Schütz's concepts of typifications, relevances, levels of awareness, "because" and "in-order-to" motivations; biographical determinants, we-relationships, and others.
6	Continue amplifying your description of the structures of the Lifeworld in which the phenomenon occurs or explore another typical Lifeworld. Use concepts like stocks of knowledge, multiple realities, paramount reality, precessors, contemporaries, and successors.
7	Write a short essay considering second-order constructs in the Lifeworld from the perspective of your phenomenon: Schützian "puppets," logical forces, moral code, and ways that patterns and archetypes can act to create both "Lifeworlds" and "Deathworlds." This essay allows you to explore ways that the awareness of such constructs, including the formation of shared moral code, may help to explain – and perhaps change – unwanted patterns. Think about Schützian "puppets" and other related concepts from our readings to consider how your phenomenon may be part of, and to some extent shaped or controlled by, a larger system, or a pattern of behavior driven by outside contextual forces.

Table 1 (continued)

Protocol	Focus
8	Describe the Lifeworld in which your phenomenon occurs using the five parts of Burke's dramatist pentad: act, scene, agent, agency, and purpose. Investigate whether there is a primary or guiding aspect of the pentad. The dramatistic pentad is an instrument used as a set of relational or functional principles that could help us understand what he calls the 'cycle cluster of terms' that people use to attribute motive.

for healing and change (McCown 2016). Consequently, we had intended to include a somatic retreat and sharing session in Łódź for all students from all three universities. There is a "special something," an energetic uplifting, that occurs in this shared space that helps us move forward together fearlessly (Elliott 2020).

David Rehorick and I (Bentz) reviewed over 75 doctoral dissertations that we supervised over twenty years of teaching at Fielding that were phenomenologically based, informed, or inspired (Rehorick/Bentz 2017). We identified ten qualities of phenomenological scholar-practitioners (Figure 2). Transformative phenomenologists seek to transcend the reality of everyday lived experience in service of generating common understanding. The transformative phenomenologist-in-action exhibits phenomenological qualities and attitudes of *leregogic* co-learning that promotes reflection and enhanced consciousness (Rehorick/Taylor 1995). Some of these qualities and attitudes are listed below after Rehorick and Bentz (2017):

- experiencing phenomenology as a way of being
- embracing embodied ways of knowing
- approaching life and practice with the "sparkle" of wonder and authenticity
- being open and mindful of learning from and within relationship
- seeking mutual enhanced understanding and understanding that Lifeworlds are constructed through patterns of communication
- looking beyond the taken for granted, with a practical focus on recognizing the natural attitude in the reality of everyday life
- seeking the "whatness" of experience
- embracing doubt and chaos and tolerating incoherence when encountering new situations
- staying open to immediate experience
- further development of new theory by combining unique experiences with embracing the deep thinkers who laid the groundwork.

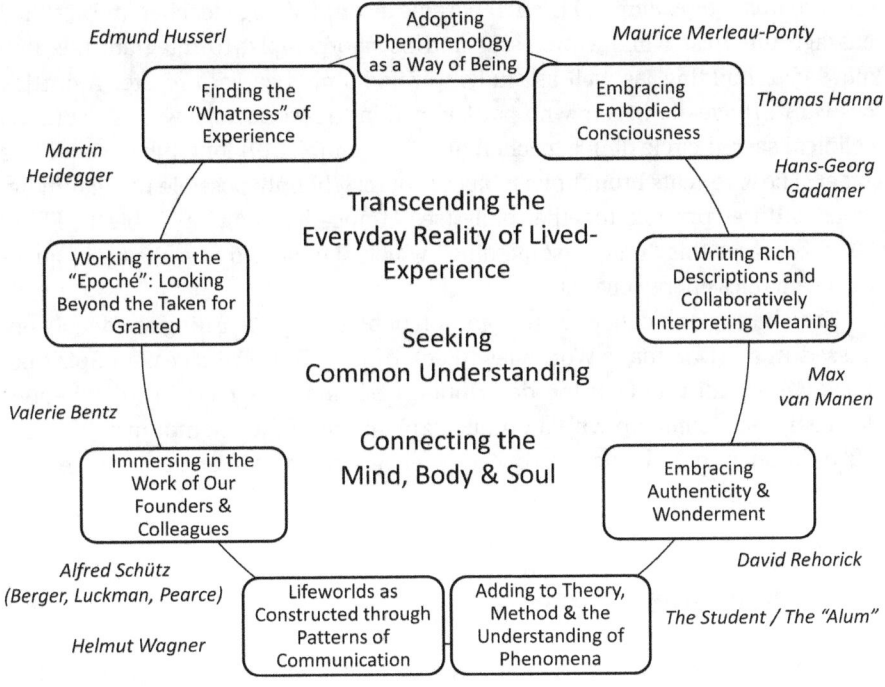

Figure 2: Ten Qualities of Transformative Phenomenologists with Influential Philosophers and Practitioners.
Copyright (2020) by Valerie Bentz and James Marlatt, Used with Permission, Original Artwork.

Expanding the Meaning of Embodiment to Shared Somatic Practices

Along with phenomenological writing and sharing, we developed somatic learning and practice and demonstrated them to our students. It was not enough for us with a scholar-practitioner model to simply learn about the somatic theory and scholarship (Merleau-Ponty 1962). Across disciplines, social scientists had over several decades begun to incorporate neuroscience (Damasio 1999), psychological somatics (Hanna 1988), and social somatics (Brennan 2004; Oliver 2004). But we also needed to take somatics out of books and into practice through somatic forms of learning from within.

Over the past ten years, we offered three-day somatics intensives where we use Kundali yoga, guided meditation, sacred circle dance, and drum circles along with sharing and processing to integrate embodied knowing into practice and research. For example, I (Bentz) became a certified yoga teacher and certified massage therapist while a professor and psychotherapist to integrate this into knowledge building, as well as studying Kundalini yoga with master Amrit Joy for over thirty years. Others who participated in the workshops were Beck (2017) a clinical sacred circle dance teacher; and Bolognini (2019) long-time drum circle leader. These retreats brought us moments of insight only possible in what Indigenous cultures practice together daily (see "trance learning" in Table 1). Elliott (2020) explores this "unique something" which she located in a theory of quantum mechanics energy change.

The sharing and collective recognition of body-spirit learning are deeply oppressed in the Dominant Worldview. Each of us has direct access to Spirit because we are all one (see the description of Chapter 18 later in this chapter) However, most come up with a unique explanation if they do not just "shake it off" or happen to find a deep knowledge recognition of it in ancient sources like Indigenous communities.

What the Writing Revealed

Soon after our participatory action research began with students from Fielding and Łódź, the opportunity to include another cohort of students from UVI emerged. Our project had evolved organically. Seventy-eight students representing four cohorts from three universities, joined our project, including participants from the USA, Virgin Islands, Marshal Islands, Mongolia, China, Poland, Europe, Canada – scattered across different time zones from around the world. We adopted online technologies to support our face-to-face and distance-learning project of writing phenomenology and collaborative reflection (Blackboard, Moodle, BaseCamp, and Zoom.) Together the research team engaged with students and alums, in co-learning phenomenology. Over the following weeks, we collected approximately 600 phenomenological protocols relating to 80 phenomena, and over 100 scripts describing experiences of collaborating with strangers and engaging with the qualities of transformative phenomenologists were created by the students. Video conferencing call transcripts provided additional information. Finally, about twenty participants in the research project engaged in phenomenologically inspired collaborative writing projects that appear in this volume, on a wide range of phenomena. All of our students form part of an evolving Transformative Phenomenology community-of-practice.

Through our work over the past two decades, we have observed that students engaging with phenomenology writing for the first time often encounter the push-pull, and attraction-repulsion, experiences of coming to an unfamiliar domain of inquiry, and the methodologies and methods of phenomenology (Rehorick/Bentz 2008). We guide students through the process of writing protocols with this in mind and engage through co-learning, offering sensitive, unobtrusive, nonjudgmental feedback. We encourage students to openly and authentically share what are often deeply personal protocols, creating the opportunity for offering trusted feedback and support to each other on their learning journey.

For our project, we observed that such sharing through Moodle (virtual asynchronous) was particularly evident from the Fielding cohort and considered a significant factor in supporting learning and collaboration. UVI students appeared to prefer real-time collaboration through videoconference as a mode of feedback and collaboration. On-line feedback with fellow UVI students was rare. We attributed this, in part, to the limited capability of the on-line platform (Blackboard before the transition to BaseCamp). Łódź doctoral and undergraduate students did not easily collaborate in class, face-to-face, and to an even lesser degree (at least initially) through the Moodle and BaseCamp online platforms. Language barriers (English was their second language), individualistic world view, challenges of communication between time zones, asynchronous and face-to-face teaching modalities, availability of reading material, and virtual communication platform technologies appear to be factors that have impacted the delivery of the "writing phenomenology" program.

A key element in our program of writing phenomenology is the opportunity for students to select a unique, personal, and poignant phenomenon for exploration through writing rich phenomenological descriptions of their lived experience. We believe that this freedom-of-choice offers an opening for a deeper self-exploration, to see things in different ways, with the possibility of raising consciousness. For some, this led toward a renewed, positive, way of seeing and being in their world. The range of phenomena selected by the student was vast and the students' protocols provided many insights into the essential nature of the phenomena in the social world. Examples of the poignant phenomenon that each student explored are presented in Table 2.

We "walked" with the students in we-relationships as they wrote and shared their protocols. And observed that many were recognizing and sharing emotional challenges that were for some lifelong, or rooted in childhood, relationships, health, the environment, and more. And on a grander scale, we recognized that many of our students were revealing Deathworlds within their Lifeworlds that included traumatic echoes of war, genocide, oppression, and practices that contribute to illness, community decline, and climate change. The protocol writing and sharing revealed the way suffering pervades the Lifeworlds of humans and other creatures.

Table 2: Examples of Poignant Phenomena.
Copyright (2020) by Valerie Bentz and James Marlatt, Used with Permission, Original Tabulation.

Phenomena Selected by Students for Protocol Writing		
Anxiety	Pressure	Women Taking Health Risks
Trash	Being a Parent	Lack of Control
Otherness	Aboutness of Pain	Power
Hatha-Yoga	Self-Discovery	Waiting
Spirituality	Fear	Disaster Experience
Walking with Homeless	Strangers and Collaborators	Being a Mom of a Soldier
Epilepsy	Waiting	Body Self-Image
Self-Determination	Destiny	The Knot in My Stomach
Emotional Regulation	Unraveling	Domestic Violence
Immigration	Teaching Reading	Friendship
Balance & Self-Discovery	Grief	Failure
First Love	Healing	Resilience
Tropical Storms	Living with Fibroids	Freedom
Technology	Relocating	Teenage Pregnancy
Hitting Rock Bottom	Studiousness	Panic
Bereavement	Decisions	Solitude
Accidents	Hurricanes	Pressure
Otherness	Flashes of Intuition	Precognition

What are Deathworlds?

The "Lifeworld is the lived experience of human beings and other living creatures as formed into more or less coherent grounds for their existence . . . that sustains the life of all creatures from birth through death" (Bentz/Shapiro 1998, p. 171).

Alfred Schütz devoted his scholarly life to delineating in elegant precision the structures of the "Lifeworld". The Lifeworld is more fundamental than social scientists' concepts of social life, such as "culture" and "society." The Lifeworld is the way persons experience their life from within, and the way that they navigate within it. The everyday Lifeworld is linked to planning for the future: hoping, anticipating, and sustaining.

Schütz (1970, p. 245) explored "multiple realities" within the Lifeworld as "provinces of meaning" or worlds among worlds. For example, Schütz viewed the world of "working" as the "paramount" reality – involving the taken-for-granted, common-sense style that we adopt when engaging/doing in the world of everyday life. He referred to other worlds within the Lifeworld as "finite provinces of meaning," such as the world of art, sports, scientific theorizing, and religion. We engage each "province of meaning" with different cognitive styles and relevances that are imposed and those that are chosen. We transit between these different worlds when we experience a "shock" such as when we are interrupted while engrossed in work or play, by an unexpected phone call, a loud machine out the window, an earthquake. Schütz wrote of the "fundamental anxiety: that humans know they will die and fear death" (Wagner 1983, pp. 174–175). Typically, this death anxiety is suppressed or ignored. It is awakened only when confronted with an unexpected shock of death, accident, or illness – a type of Deathworld province of meaning.

There has been an exponential increase of deadly shocks on earth. Due to global communications, we are aware of them. In the face of these, we posit the concept of Deathworlds (Chapter 20) to position us to be more awake to the collective and individual dangers we face. We experience Deathworlds as we are increasingly aware of the climate crisis, social disruption, and ecological destruction. We are witnesses to increased rates of suicide, depression, addiction, and violence. 37 million persons were displaced because of U.S. wars since the 9/11 terrorist attacks (Watson Institute 2020). Due to the climate crisis over a million species are destined to go extinct in the next decade. Much of the food supply is causing pollution and disease through chemical sprays and fertilizers or inhumane factory farms. We wrote this book before the worldwide onslaught of COVID-19 which as of this writing has caused over 1,000,000 deaths so far with more than 34,000,000 cases reported. We must stop being in denial and face up to the Deathworlds in which we live, and which are increasing across our planet. It is time we acknowledge the unnecessary encroachment of Deathworlds and Deathworld-making within our Lifeworlds.

We define *Deathworld* as a space in which the forces that work against life can cause physical, mental, social, and ecological decline. "Deathworld-making" are activities that contribute to the degradation, sickness, or death of places, persons, and other creatures. While Deathworld-making may produce monetary wealth, it is an ultimately destructive process. Every community has a continuum of Lifeworld-sustaining and Deathworld-making elements.

Gebser (1985) presented humanity with the dangers of self-destruction through the valorization of rationality and quantification over all aspects of life and experience:

> In everyday life, few are aware that the motorization, mechanization, and technologization impose quantification conditions on man that lead to an immeasurable loss of freedom. Machines, films, press, radio lead not only to mediocrity and a dependency relationship but also to an increasing de-individuation and atomization of the individual. (p. 537)

Gen Kida, Heidegger scholar, also put this succinctly:

> Technologies are exhausting the planet's resources, destroying the environment, and exposing humanity to the constant threat of annihilation. Technology is unambiguously a double-edged sword. The question is: are we capable enough to exploit the possibilities of this dangerous weapon we call technology without destroying ourselves in the process.
> (Kida n.d., p. 49)

Four Arrows points to crises of humanity:

> The threatened state of all life on earth that the agricultural, industrial and information revolutions are moving us towards an unsustainable world. The rise of a global market, and the triumph of the military industrial complex have made war a pervasive, and perverse system bringing great wealth to a few and death, homelessness and destitution to millions expelled from their lands. (Four Arrows 2020)

Derrida writes about the future as a future of Death unless humans "let the earth be, let the other come, letting life live on" (Lynes 2018, p. 119). After many arduous arguments, Lynes concludes that capitalism depends upon an ever-growing population and economic processes based on the exploitation of the earth's resources and brings life itself "into confrontation with death" (p. 191). He ends by concluding that humans and the planet are leading to self-extinction unless we change radically to "biocultural sustainability" (p. 212). Ethologist Frans De Waal attests to the common emotions shared by all mammals. Dominant Worldview institutions whitewash the horrendous treatment that animals receive via factory farming (De Waal 2019, pp. 233–236).

The decline of the extended family and advocacy of the "nuclear" family has failed to sustain most persons. "The nuclear family was a mistake" writes Brooks (2020). Before this, extended families allowed for generations to sustain each other in a local network. Today, research shows that only 19% (Vanorman/Jacobsen 2020) of Americans live in a nuclear family (mother, father, and children). The emphasis in the nuclear family was on the economic success of the individual member in competition with everyone else. Millions of the elderly are alone or in age-segregated facilities and millions of young people are left on their own at age 18 to either amass large debts for college or struggle for jobs in a limited job market (Brooks 2020, pp. 54–72).

The radical change in consciousness that Gebser called for may not mean an evolution ahead but rather a return from what Four Arrows called The Dominant Worldview to the Indigenous Worldview. It has become clear over the past decade that the forces of the Dominant Worldview are causing Dead Zones or Deathworlds throughout the earth (Sassen 2014). The Indigenous Worldview is exemplified by an empathetic, non-materialistic, collaborative, and socially purposeful life that is respectful of the natural world as our teacher (Table 3).

Table 3: Dominant Worldview and Indigenous Worldview.
Copyright (2020) by Four Arrows. Reprinted with Permission.

Common Dominant Worldview Manifestations	Common Indigenous Worldview Manifestations
Acceptance of rigid hierarchies	Use of egalitarian and reverse dominance
Fear-based thoughts and behaviors	Courage and fearless trust in the universe
Living without strong social purpose Primarily selfish goals for personal gain Unawareness of white privilege in the world Rigid and discriminatory gender stereotypes	Socially purposeful life Emphasis on generosity and future generations Historical awareness of white colonialism Respect for gender fluidity
Uncritical acceptance of materialism	Non-materialistic, barter and gift economics
Not honoring the Earth as Sacred	Sees all life forms as sacred and sentient
More head than the heart	More heart than head
Competition as way to feel superior	Useful to maximize survival & cooperation
Lacking empathy	Empathetic
Anthropocentric	Animals, insects, plants, water are our teachers
Using words to deceive self or others	Words are sacred vibrations
Truth is determined and absolute	Truth is multifaceted
Rigid boundaries	Flexible boundaries
Unfamiliarity with alternative consciousness	Use of trance continually for highest potential
Disbelief in spiritual energies	Recognition of spiritual energies
Disregarding holistic interconnectedness	Continually honoring holistic interconnectedness
Minimal contact with others	High interpersonal engagement, touching

Table 3 (continued)

Common Dominant Worldview Manifestations	Common Indigenous Worldview Manifestations
Emphasis on theory, rhetoric versus action	Inseparability of knowledge and action
Blindness to hegemony	Hegemonic awareness and resistance to it
Seeing time as linear	Time as cyclical
Dualistic thinking	Complementary duality
Mainstream acceptance of injustice	Collective and organized resistance to injustice
Not supporting Indigenous rights	Against all odds continual striving for rights
Fighting is highest expression of courage	Generosity is highest expression of courage
Seeing ceremony as rote phenomenon	Ceremony seen as life-sustaining
Learning as didactic	Learning as experiential and collaborative
Trance is dangerous or stemming from evil	Trance-based learning as natural and essential
Human nature is corrupt or evil	Human nature is malleable
Dishonesty and deception are acceptable	Dishonesty and deception are unacceptable
Humor as entertainment	Humor as essential tool for coping
Conflict mitigated via revenge & punishment	Conflict resolution as return to community
Learning is broadly contextualized	Place-based learning and responsibility is key
Personal health and fitness minimal	Personal vitality is essential
Social laws of society are primary	Seeing laws of nature as highest rules for living
Self-knowledge less important	Self-knowledge is most important
Individualism not connected to group	Autonomy connected to group
Nature is dangerous	Nature is benevolent
Nature is not sentient	Nature is sentient

Challenges of Collaboration in Dominant Worldview

The Dominant Worldview posits individualism as the way of being, whereas the Indigenous Worldview posits collaboration as a norm (Four Arrows 2020). Students at all three schools shared the Dominant Worldview of individualism, making collaboration a challenge. They differ in the extent to which the Dominant Worldview holds sway. For example, the role of faculty is reflected in different levels of formality. At Fielding, I was known as "Valerie." Slightly more formal, students at UVI address the faculty members as "Dr." At the University of Łódź, I was known as "Professor Bentz."

Fielding Graduate University has a stated ethos of student-centered learning and a mission of social and ecological justice. Also, as a scholar-practitioner program geared for seasoned adult learners, Fielding students are encouraged to collaborate across cultural and geographic, racial, and gender identity issues.

Students from the Virgin Islands tend to be socially oriented. UVI is a historically Black university. As a territory of the United States, the Virgin Islands history as a colonized Indigenous culture continues beneath the surface. UVI students exhibit more social openness and a sense of humor than the students at Fielding or Łódź. UVI students stay together as a cohort throughout their program.

Students at the University of Łódź are endowed with privileged status. They are a homogenous culture of Whites who nevertheless suffered historically from being a battleground with shifting boundaries between Russia and Germany. They also suffered from the Holocaust, where 300,000 Jews in Łódź alone were killed in the nearby Auschwitz concentration camp. They suffered post World War II under Soviet occupation for over 30 years. As newcomers to neo-liberal Western economics, entering the European Union, they were swiftly indoctrinated with ultra-capitalist ideologies.

The original research design included a week-long somatics retreat and conference that was to include the doctoral students from the participating universities. We were to spend several days face to face in somatic learning and sharing. This involved kundalini yoga, meditation, and sacred circle dance. Following this, the students would have shared the results of their phenomenological writing and discuss ways of putting their newly discovered insights into practice. Essentially, community-building practices are akin to Indigenous ways of being.

The students and faculty in Łódź seemed to be too pressured to produce research articles for prestigious journals in order to obtain and maintain employment. While this pressure was highest at Łódź, Fielding and UVI also demonstrated this mentality. The Łódź Erasmus students, though from different cultures, all reflected the Dominant Worldview and shared various kinds of Lifeworldly and Deathworldly experiences from a culture that did not foster personal and collaborative elements in an educational setting.

After several weeks of teaching in Łódź, it became clear to me (Bentz) that the planned somatics retreat and conference in Łódź was not going to work out. Bringing somatic practice into a Dominant Worldview-based university system presented a continued challenge. Although Professor Konecki had begun to teach hatha yoga to the students in a class designed to combat stress in the business environment, this was not a typical practice. Generally, it did not seem that doctoral students understood the value of somatics in the context of university programs.

Although they were strangers, the majority of the students from all three schools took for granted the Dominant Worldview of competitive individualism. However, the UVI students, including some from the Marshall Islands, understood what it was like to live in a post-colonial society. The Virgin Islands had recently experienced a devastating hurricane without receiving adequate support from the U.S. Government under which they were still considered a territory.

Also of importance is the related Lifeworld concept of *insidedness* and *outsidedness* (Seaman 2018). I was an "outsider" to Łódź. The students were outsiders to the academic world to varying degrees and outsiders to the world of Ph.D. academics and scholar-practitioners. The students found themselves feeling more like insiders as they began to collaborate. They revealed outsidedness within their home environments as well.

Phenomenologist David Seaman explores the relationship to place as outsidedness and insidedness. Living creatures exist in *place* which is a recognizable space where one exists necessarily with others in an ecosystem usually in more or less permanent physical arrangements. "Insideness" is the degree to which a person or group belongs to or identifies with a place . . . he or she feels comfortable, safe, at ease (2018, p. 54). Outsideness is when a person feels difference, separation, or even alienation from a place. As later illustrated in Chapters 2 and 3, the same place, in this case, Łódź, Poland was experienced very differently by Konecki, the insider who lived in the area all of his life, and Bentz, the outsider/stranger.

The outsider/insider distinction can also help us understand how one can be existentially an outsider in one's own home, such as in the case of the person exposed to violence or abuse:

> The victim's experience should not be interpreted as a lack of at-homeness but, rather, as one mode of existential outsidedness, which in relation to one's most intimate place – the home – is particularly undermining and potentially life-shattering. (Seaman 2018, p. 57)

In our terms, the situation for the victims of domestic violence is living a Deathworld within their Lifeworld. Seaman goes on to ask how these victims may be helped to regain existential insidedness, and what forces are present in a society where homes are places of despair and pain for so many.

Gebser's historical research covered the change in human consciousness from the archaic, through the magic, mythical and mental, to the integral. The move in consciousness away from the "magical" (his term for "Indigenous") to the mental age has been a move towards the destruction of not only humankind but millions of lifeforms on planet earth. The integral level transcends time and space and sees the unity of all through the powers of intuition. Vedantic thought calls this the Atman, which supersedes the mind, or the mental "stuff." The Atman attains bliss through its inherent oneness with Brahman, the Supreme Reality (Nikhilananda 1974, pp. 221–222). We have seen that the processes of Transformative Phenomenology are a way to transform consciousness into a life-affirming worldview parallel to the Indigenous Worldview which revered and sustained life.

The Roadmap Back

As we discovered, Transformative Phenomenology is, in many ways, similar to the Indigenous Worldview, and therefore, it comes as no surprise that the Dominant Worldview demonstrated by participants would be, in some ways, antagonistic to elements of our research. As we progressed through the project, it became clear that there were many parallels between the 10 qualities of phenomenologists and the Indigenous worldview described by Four Arrows. Together, Transformative Phenomenology and somatic community building can move humans toward an Indigenous way of living – a moral Lifeworld (See Narvaez 2019). As these similarities emerged, we realized that adopting phenomenological principles and progressing towards consciousness-raising were one and the same with integrating Indigenous Worldview, long rejected from daily Western life. Transformative Phenomenology made it possible to bridge the divide between the diametrically opposed viewpoints and explore the Dominant Worldview from an outside perspective – that of a stranger.

The Chapters

In the following chapters, our authors explore the essence of lived experience and the Lifeworlds in which it is situated. In the process, they reveal elements of Deathworlds within their Lifeworlds and the way back through Transformative Phenomenology.

Part I: The Study in Łódź, Poland

Chapters 2 and 3: Dr. Krzysztof Konecki and Professor at Łódź became intrigued by the Deathworlds concept and suggested that he and Bentz write about the

Deathworld of the City of Łódź, he as an insider and Valerie Bentz as an outsider. Our chapters together elucidate how Deathworlds remain deeply obscure and hidden for insiders whose systems of relevances require emotional and perceptual disengagement from them. As an outsider, Bentz felt the Deathworldly layers more keenly.

Chapter 4: Anna Kacperczyk, Professor of Sociology at Łódź, provides deep insight into the experience of encounters with trash based on her phenomenological protocols.

Chapter 5: Natalia Martini, Doctoral Candidate and student in the writing phenomenology seminar shares her experience of walking with the homeless in Łódź, raising questions about what it means to walk with someone who has very different relevances and needs.

Chapter 6: Łucja Lange, doctoral student and research assistant at Łódź brought to light her experiences as a clairvoyant perceiver. She moved from seeing these perceptions as a dark gothic force within, to understanding them as a normal capacity, connecting humans to energetic presences.

Chapter 7: Łucja Lange and David Haddad, Independent Research Collaborator, recount the awakening of the Erasmus undergraduate students to self-understanding and collaborative sharing through writing and sharing phenomenological protocols.

Part II: Experiences of Deathworlds to Lifeworlds

Chapter 8: David Haddad and James Marlatt interpret the protocols of the doctoral student participants from the Virgin Islands revealing their transformation from Deathworldly experiences using phenomenological writing and sharing.

Chapter 9: Graduate Research Assistant Carol Estrada recounts the Lifeworld/Deathworld experience of being with her young son who died of cancer.

Chapter 10: Tetyana Azarova Fielding alumna, describes how inspiration allows one to illuminate higher consciousness states, which can guide personal growth, and provide a roadmap for development.

Chapter 11: Lorraine Crockford, Fielding alumna, presents her work with first responders to disasters of a life and death nature. Through a Lifeworld analysis, she uncovers the zombie-like existence they have, as they cannot separate from their work lives where they face death.

Part III: Sharing Deathworlds

Chapter 12: Fielding doctoral students David Jones and Whitney Strohmayr explore experiences of grief and abuse in romantic relationships via a shared phenomenon of raveling and unraveling.

Chapter 13: Fielding doctoral students Lori Davidson, Jennifer Decker, and Łódź doctoral student Dagmara Tarasiuk address overcoming the Deathworld of addiction using weightlifting, how older women injure themselves in exercise, and ways of dealing with academic pressure through yoga.

Chapter 14: Fielding doctoral students Michelle Elias and Darlene Cockayne moved from being strangers to collaborators as military family members. Cockayne describes dealing with the aftermath of war through her life with her suicidal veteran husband, and Elias with fear and anxiety due to her son being called to active duty in Iraq.

Chapter 15: A collaborative effort between Ann Ritter, Barton Buechner, Fielding alumni, and musicologist Rik Spann on the experience of liminality, which is a frequent Deathworldly condition under the Dominant worldview. Yet it may become far more a pervasive state of being as climate crises continue.

Part IV: Indigenous Deathworlds

Chapter 16: Debra Opland, a Fielding Doctoral Candidate and a teacher among the Lakota Nation explores the Deathworld that colonialism and Dominant Worldview has made of these Indigenous communities.

Chapter 17: Tuulmontoya Myagmarjav, a doctoral student in economics at Łódź, from Mongolia, presents her research on her Indigenous culture where nomadic herder people have been driven from their homes by the activities of mining companies.

Chapter 18: Małgorzata Burchard-Dziubińska, Professor of Economics at Łódź, describes research on Indigenous Amazonia people affected by the destructive social and environmental impact of uncontrolled economic development.

Chapter 19: Valerie Grossman, Fielding alumna, explains the way phenomenological openness allowed her to combat the Deathworlds of famine for the people of Mizoram, India, and drought in remote communities in Nepal. At the same time she was suffering from undiagnosed malaria, only discovered and cured while she was in Tanzania building a hospital.

Part V: Combatting Deathworlds

Chapter 20: Bentz, Rehorick, Marlatt, Nishi, and Carol Estrada collaborate to illustrate the power of Transformative Phenomenology in action as an antidote to Deathworlds.

Epilogue: Marlatt and Bentz discuss the current world crises and building awareness through the Deathworld Mapping Project of the SPCL, Somatics, Phenomenology and Communicative Leadership Community of Action.

References

Beck, Evelyn Torton (2017): "The Experience of Sacred Circle Dance in a Wheelchair: A Somatic Phenomenological Case Study: 'She's Barbara. She's Not "Just" a Woman in a Wheelchair'". *Annual Conference*, Society for Phenomenology and Human Sciences, Memphis.

Bentz, Valerie/Shapiro, Jeremy (1998): *Mindful inquiry in social research.* Thousand Oaks: Sage Publications.

Bentz, Valerie Malhotra/Giorgino, Vincenzo M. B. (Eds.) (2016): *Contemplative social research: Caring for Self, Being, and Lifeworld.* Santa Barbara: Fielding University Press.

Bentz, Valerie/Rehorick, David/Marlatt, James/Nishii, Ayumi/Estrada, Carol/Buechner, Bart (2019): "The Silver Age of Phenomenology at Fielding Graduate University". In: Rogers, Katrina S./Snowden, Monique L. (Eds.): *The Fielding Scholar Practitioner: Voices from 45 years of Fielding Graduate University.* Santa Barbara: Fielding Press, (pp. 179–204).

Berman, Morris (2015): *Coming to Our Senses: Body and Spirit in the Hidden History of the West.* Brattleboro: Echo Point Books & Media, LLC.

Bolognini, Francesca (2019). "Drum Circle Magic" (Unpublished paper). *Somatics Retreat 2019*, Fielding Graduate University, Cambria.

Brennan, Theresa (2004): *The Transmission of Affect.* Ithaca: Cornell University Press.

Brooks, David (2020): "The Nuclear Family was a Mistake". In: *The Atlantic* 325. No. 2, pp. 54–72.

Burke, Kenneth (1969): *A Grammer of Motives.* London: University of California Press.

Damasio, Antonio (1999): *The Feeling of What Happens: Body and Emotion in the Making of Consciousness.* New York, San Diego, London: Harcourt Brace & Company.

Elliott, Carolyn (2020): *Somatic Phenomenology Leadership Development Model Explained Using Quantum Mechanics: A Case Study* (Doctoral dissertation). Fielding Graduate University.

Four Arrows/Narvaez, Darcia (2019): "Reclaiming our Indigenous Worldview: A More Authentic Baseline for Social/Ecological Justice Work in Education". In: Narvaez, Darcia/Halton, Eugene/ Collier, Brian S./Enderle, Georges (Eds.): *Indigenous Sustainable Wisdom.* Bern: Peter Lang.

Four Arrows (2020): *The Red Road: Linking Diversity and Inclusion Programs to Indigenous Worldviews.* Charlotte: Information Age Publishing.

Gebser, Jean (1985): *The Ever-present Origin.* Athens: Ohio University Press.

Hanna, Thomas (1988): *Somatics: Reawakening the Mind's Control of Movement, Flexibility, and Health.* Cambridge: Da Capo Press.

Husserl, Edmund (1970): *The Crisis of European Sciences and Transcendental Phenomenology: An Introduction to Phenomenological Philosophy* (D. Carr, Trans.). Evanston: Northwestern University Press. (Original work published in 1954)

Kida, Gen (n.d.): In: *The True Nature of Technology* (M. Emmerich, Trans.). Tokyo: Deco Press.

Mare, Christopher E. (2016): "Designing for Consciousness: Outline of a Neurophenomenological Research Program". In: Bentz, Valerie/Giorgino, Vincenzo: *Contemplative Social Research: Caring for Self, Being, and Lifeworld*. Santa Barbara: Fielding University Press, pp. 300–334.

Marlatt, James/Rehorick, David/Bentz, Valerie (2020): "Transformative Phenomenology". In: Possamai, Adam/ Blasi, Anthony J. (Eds.): *SAGE Encyclopedia of Sociology of Religion*. Thousand Oaks: SAGE.

McCown, Doug Donald (2016): "Inside-Out: Mindfulness-based Interventions as a Model for Community Building". In: Bentz, Valerie/Giorgino, Vincenzo: *Contemplative Social Research: Caring for Self, Being, and Lifeworld*. Santa Barbara: Fielding University Press, pp. 98–128.

Merleau-Ponty, Maurice (1962): *Phenomenology of Perception* (C. Smith, Trans.). London: Routledge & Keegan, Paul.

Oliver, Kelly (2004): *The Colonization of Psychic Space: A Psychoanalytic Social Theory of Oppression*. Minneapolis: University of Minnesota Press.

Pearce, W. Barnett (2007): *Making Social Worlds: A Communication Perspective*. Singapore: COS Printers Pte Ltd.

Porpora, Doug (2016): "Critical Reason and Spirituality". In: Bentz, Valerie/Giorgino, Vincenzo: *Contemplative Social Research: Caring for Self, Being, and Lifeworld*. Santa Barbara: Fielding University Press, pp. 80–97.

Rehorick, David A./Taylor, Gail (1995): "Thoughtful Incoherence: First Encounters with the Phenomenological-hermeneutical Domain". In: *Human Studies: A Journal for Philosophy and Social Sciences* 18. No.4, pp. 389–414.

Rehorick, David A./Bentz, Valerie (Eds.) (2008): *Transformative Phenomenology: Changing Ourselves, Lifeworlds, and Professional Practice*. Lanham: Lexington Books.

Rehorick, David/Bentz, Valerie (Eds.) (2017): *Expressions of Phenomenological Research: Consciousness and Lifeworld Studies*. Santa Barbara: Fielding University Press.

Śaṅkarācārya/Nikhilananda, Swami (1974): *Self-knowledge (Atmabodha): an English Translation of Sankarāchārya's Ātmabodha with Notes, Comments, and Introduction*. New York: Ramakrishna-Vivekananda Center.

Sassen, Saskia (2014): *Expulsions: Brutality and Complexity in the Global Economy*. USA: Harvard University Press.

Schütz, Alfred (1970): "Transcendences and Multiple Realities". In: Helmut R. Wagner (Ed.): *Alfred Schütz on Phenomenology and Social Relations*. Chicago: University of Chicago Press, pp. 245–264.

Seaman, David (2018): *Life Takes Place: Phenomenology, Lifeworlds, and Place Making*. New York: Routledge.

van Manen, Max (1997): *Researching Lived Experience: Human Science for an Action Sensitive Pedagogy*. London, Ontario: Althouse Press.

Vanorman, Alicia/Jacobsen, Linda A. (2020): "U.S. Household Composition Shifts as the Population Grows Older; More Young Adults Live With Parents". Population Reference Bureau. Retrieved from https://www.prb.org/u-s-household-composition-shifts-as-the-population-grows-older-more-young-adults-live-with-parents/, visited on October 27, 2020.

Wagner, Helmut R. (1983): *Phenomenology of Consciousness and Sociology of the Life-world: An Introductory Study.* Edmonton: The University of Alberta Press.

Wagner, Helmut R. (Ed.) (1970): *Alfred Schütz: On Phenomenology and Social Relations.* Chicago: The University of Chicago Press.

Watson Institute (2020): "Costs of War". Retrieved from https://watson.brown.edu/costsofwar/, visited on October 09, 2020.

Wenger, Étienne (1998): *Communities of Practice: Learning, Meaning, and Identity.* Cambridge: Cambridge University Press.

Krzysztof T. Konecki
Chapter 2
Deathworld of the City of Łódź: Insider Experience

Abstract: The chapter explains the lived experiences of the city of Łódź from an insider, Konecki, who has lived in Łódź for most of his life. Valerie Bentz, outsider, who was visiting professor and principal researcher on the project of collaboration among strangers describes her lived experiences in the City of Łódź in the next chapter. The paper is based on the concepts of *Lifeworld* (Schütz 1962) and *Deathworld* (Bentz et al. 2018) as the sensitizing concepts (Blumer 1969) that led the analysis. The problems of pollution, the dirt, the danger of living in the city but also the positive sides of living in the city (the tradition, beautiful secession architecture, the development of the city) and the issue of awareness of Lifeworld and ontological anxiety will be considered from a phenomenological perspective. The strategies of dealing with the anxiety will be described from the first-person perspective, as using the *natural attitude epoché*, "others do the same," "nothing happened so far," "do not worry," "I soon leave this place," "let's practice yoga," "the air in the city is good for nature's allergic sufferers," etc. The problem of a *death zone* close to the city will be also presented (in photos) and reflectively considered in the paper. A reflection on the relationship of the everyday Lifeworld and Deathworld from the point of view of the concept of *finite province of meaning* will also be addressed.

Keywords: Deathworld, Lifeworld, lived experiences, phenomenology, Alfred Schütz, contemplation

> There was someone every day here.
> There is the city,
> I see the blooming trees
> and magpies are still around
> No calls, no calls
> No coughing
> The dust covers longing
> – Poem for Valerie from Łódź, by Krzysztof T. Konecki

Introduction

Husserl (1954/1970, p.103) posited the "Lifeworld as the fundamental ground for all human action." Bentz and Shapiro defined the *Lifeworld* as:

> The lived experiences of human beings and other living creatures as formed into more or less coherent grounds for their existence. This consists of the whole system of interactions with others and objects in an environment that is fused with meaning and language and that sustains the life of all creatures from birth through death. It is the fundamental ground of all experience for human beings. (1998, p. 172)

Schütz delineated the elements of Lifeworlds, which mostly are taken for granted as humans pursue their tasks. Today we are faced with environmental and social crises related to the ability of humans to destroy Lifeworlds and exist in and expand *Deathworlds* to the point where life on planet earth is endangered (Bentz et al. 2018).

I will focus particularly on Schütz' (1975, p. 116) concepts of *relevances* and *taken for granted, natural attitude* and *epoché* as we explore the Lifeworld and Deathworld of the city of Łódź, Poland. Other Schützian concepts include *homunculi* or *puppets* and *typifications*.

From Krzystof Konecki: The City of Łódź, Insider Perspective

The problem of Deathworlds in our everyday life is connected with not noticing the obvious and taken for granted (Bentz et al. 2018; Zerubavel 2018). We try to isolate ourselves from Deathworlds. It is the natural attitude epoché, that we use to avoid keeping in mind the fundamental anxiety, that is, being aware of death.

There is a semiotic asymmetry between the conceptual pair of "life" and "death" in everyday life discourse (Zerubavel 2018, pp. 10–11). The term "death" is less marked and rarely conspicuous, in contrast to the use of the term "life."[1] The marked and unmarked regions of our phenomenal world indicate the relevance not only of the words but also of our selective attention to perceive the world. The pollution of the air is taken for granted; it does not often appear in our

---

[1] A Google search on August 20, 2019 for the English terms death and life yield 3,020,000,000 and 11,690,000,000 results, respectively; in the Polish language the results are 84,100,000 and 291,000,000.

attentional landscape.² It is sometimes marked in the media, but in my natural perspective, I must overcome it, forget it and proceed in the world of work (the "paramount reality" [Schütz 1975, p. 253]). I must still breathe; I cannot stop it. So, the natural attitude allows me to survive emotionally. I should ignore the obvious things to deal with life. I must ignore the Deathworld to immerse in the Lifeworld. The Lifeworld is a background of my perception that I do not question. The anxiety appears when something wrong happens, when I am pressed to be awakened from "the peaceful dream of everyday life," for example, when I am sick or have had an accident.

Deathworlds have institutional backgrounds. There are some organizations and institutions that support killing. I mention only a few types of such organizations, the hunting associations, and breeders' associations and meat cattle producers.³ Killing is accepted by the statutes of the organizations and the members of the organizations. The killing of animals by hunting associations is not mentioned on their websites (Polish Hunting Association 2012a); rather, it is shooting not killing (*odstrzał zwierząt* in Polish). The animals are shot off, not killed. There are also criteria for shooting off that are settled by the hunting council, so that everything is legal and according to social norms (Polish Hunting Association 2012b). The killing becomes legal.

Killing is accepted by the statutes of the organizations and the members of the organizations. The killing of animals. The anthropocentric perspective dominates and makes the distinctions between typifications of human living beings and non-human living beings. Some human beings can be killed under some conditions. Non-humans can be killed; there is no sin, no punishment if you kill the animals for eating in so-called "humane conditions." These conditions make this kind of Deathworld legitimate and the mood of killing can be spread and gain acceptance in society. The legislation and formal regulations approve it and legitimize it, so there is nothing wrong with the killing of some animals. The animals can be killed during hunting and also in slaughterhouses. This creates the mood of killing and the generalized permission to kill.

---

2 In a Google search on August 20, 2019, we found the frequency of appearance of the term of *clean air* – 1,190,000,000; *polluted air* – 24,500,000.
3 See: Polish Breeders Association and Meat Cattle Producers (2018). On the web page of the association there is no information about killing and death of the animals. The information is about working life of the producers. There is not one word about how it is possible to produce meat. What happened before the meat arrived on the table? Technicalities and legislation cover the trajectory of the animal's pathway to become the meat for consumption.

Location of the Deathworld: Cycling to Work

Below is a note from cycling to work by professor of sociology Krzysztof T. Konecki (the author of the chapter), dated April 19, 2019. I use Schütz' concept of types or "puppets" (Schütz 1962, p. 41) as a way to locate the way, as a cyclist, that I may be looked upon by automobile drivers as a *Culprit*, and how drivers may be looked upon as *Grim Reapers* by cyclists. When I am on the street, I am no longer a professor, only a cyclist and the potential Culprit. I have to go across the Deathworld of the City of Łódź in order to meet professor Valerie Bentz at the University:

> When I go outside in the morning, I feel the smell of gasoline and smoke. Sometimes I feel it as a reek of something really strong. I notice it for a while, I feel it, and I have no reflection on it. I am leaving this warning. And I cycle to work. No problem. Nothing happened. Everything is normal, as usual, as every day, I feel it so the odor does not surprise me. I accept it. I take a bicycle and go to work. Every minute I feel the smell of the smoke from gasoline. I feel the dust from renovated roads and buildings. A lot of old cars with smog escaping from tailpipes chase me, to give the polluted air into my lungs. But it is normal, others also inhale the same air, so why I should bother? I take it for granted. Reflection on it does not bother me so much. I want to cycle, I want to work, I want to earn money.
>
> I do not protest, I do not write letters to the mayor of the city. I bracket what I feel. It is normal, it is not important. Almost nobody notices it. I should get to work now, fast. I train my muscles. My bicycle allows me to avoid traffic jams. Great! I am a smart guy.
>
> I cycle and I see how people drive. Their driving is rather dangerous for me, they do not notice the cyclist, even on the bicycle path. I am invisible to them, they do not look at me at the crossroads, they look at the other cars, the cyclist is invisible. I feel in danger all the time when I approach the crossroad, on the bicycle path. *I am a potential Culprit (puppet)*. I feel it, anything can happen during my travel to work. I feel some excitement because of the danger. And I construct the justification: by cycling, I do not produce smog; I am more healthy and stronger, I am in close contact with the world.
>
> However, the drivers are potential *Grim Reapers (homunculi)*. They can kill me at any moment if I am not careful enough. They have the power behind the steering wheel. I feel defenseless. I feel like a potential Culprit. However, when I change from riding my bicycle to my car, and I drive, I become the potential Grim Reaper. I only change the mask, but I am still in the same Deathworld nested so deeply in everyday Lifeworld that I do not see it. I am the potential Culprit and the Reaper at the same time. Double identity. Life and Death, Death and Life. I see a lot of potential Grim Reapers around. When I stop and contemplate for a while, everywhere I see the angels of death chasing Culprits. But after a while I forget it, I set aside the Grim Reaper type, I do not want to look behind and see him with a scythe. To forget means to live but not necessarily survive.
>
> ***
>
> Another day, I am cycling with my son to wonderful places around Łódź. We are looking for the beautiful natural landscapes, lakes, and forests. We look for something original and traditional, like buildings. We find them and admire the beauty of nature and an old water mill. However, we also find the trash, and suddenly I feel the pain in my chest, I cannot understand how it happened that there is so much rubbish thrown out into the

water. I am sad and I do not want to break the wonderful feeling of seeing the glamor of nature, especially because I am with my son and I want to share the same common perspective with him. When I take a picture of *beautiful objects,* I usually adopt something like the natural epoché; I try to avoid the ugliness of human waste and take wonderful photographs of esthetic and attractive views. My camera avoids unlovely objects. Natural choice. It is unconscious. I understand it now when I write. Do I cheat myself or defend my Lifeworld taking in pictures in such a way?

I take more photos of picturesque views, not the horrible objects like trash or destroyed objects. (K. Konecki, self-observation, April 19, 2019)

The Visual Representation and Interpretation of Lifeworld and Deathworld

The photographer sees the world as his system of relevancies (Schütz 1962) which allows him to see some objects and ignore others (Konecki 2019). When the photographer is on a relaxing trip on a bicycle, as I was, she or he is especially sensitive when some objects do not fit with his expectation to see beautiful sceneries and views. The Deathworld could emerge in perception: beauty with near romantic awe, and ugliness with almost physical pain on the other side. When I expect to see only beauty the sudden view of dangerous and ugly objects redirects my attention. What was not noticed is noticed, what was unmarked becomes marked.

Beauty and Lifeworld views and objects are adjacent to the Deathworld views and objects. From one side of the road are houses and everything is clean; on the other side of the road there is the rubbish. I have to make a big effort to see and take the picture of the second ones. The ugliness and dirt work against my desire to see the optimistic features of the Lifeworld where people take care of nature and their Lifeworld landscapes. The Deathworld is located in the Lifeworld but rarely noticed.

The pictures shown in Figures 1–10 are from bicycle trips by Krzysztof T. Konecki with his son around the city of Łódź. They are visual stories of my perception, surprises, and experiences. The visual sensory system was supported by olfactory sensing. Sometimes I had sensed the beautiful smell of the poppies and cornflowers but sometimes the smell of gasoline and grease emerging from rivers and ponds. The contemplation of nature is supported by photographing it. It is a moment when we can stop our mind working and contemplate the *here and now* (Konecki 2018).

Figure 1: Lifeworld view, in front of water mill (almost perfect beauty).
Photo by the author, Krzysztof.T. Konecki, April 19, 2019.

We can see both sides of *the anthropized nature*. The Lifeworld and Deathworld are so close and they are two sides of the same coin. The street divides them visually. The human mind recognizes the distinction. Humans and nature, we and they, beauty and ugliness. But beauty belongs usually to my view, ugliness belongs to others. The distinctions create the conditions for the Deathworld to start to dominate our existence but usually without seeing it.

***

Below are pictures from another bicycle excursion around the city of Łódź. The place is where the chemical and metal waste is stored and where reclamation was supposed to be done and the terrain to be cleaned up. But it has not happened so far. On the terrain that belonged to the chemical factory Boruta, 200,000 barrels with toxic materials are stored. They are deposited under the ground and the metal barrels are corroded. The toxins leak out and pollute the ground and the air. The temperature around the barrels under the ground exceeds 100 C. and

Figure 2: Behind the Lifeworld is the Deathworld. The trash (bottles) at the watermill. The picture was taken from the same place as the picture above, no 1 (no epoché here, two views of the same river in the same place; catching the truth?) During the taking of these pictures I sensed the smell of the grease and I almost felt a physical pain in my body.
Photo by the author, Krzysztof T. Konecki, April 19, 2019.

toxic gases escape from below the surface.[4] There are about 200 dangerous substances in the ground. For example, there is benzene that is cancerous and mutagenic. Around the toxic places are located companies where people work (one is the big power plant) and even houses where the people live.

In May 2018, there was a big fire on the waste heap.[5] That produced a huge amount of smoke going around the cities of Zgierz and Łódź. It was difficult to

---

4 See: "Zgierz – Polish Chernobyl. Residents live near an ecological bomb" (POLSAT News 2019). The journalists and ecologists are marking the problem and show in the media what is covered and not noticed by the citizens, although a lot of them have seen the place.
5 See: "Zgierz. Landfill fire" (TVN24 2018).

Figure 3: Lifeworld. The view from one side of the road. *Isn't it romantic? A beautiful and relaxing view, that is what I expected from my trips.*
Photo by the author, Krzysztof T. Konecki, April 19, 2019.

see the sky because the smoke was so intense. Authorities assured the public that no harm was done.

The place is surrounded by a beautiful forest and ponds. Everything looks normal, but there is a Deathworld that is not officially acknowledged by the local governments in Zgierz and Łódź and even the local citizens. Only the ecologists and some journalists want to uncover the death zone and mark it to make it more apparent to the public. For some, this is seen as *whistleblowing* but more generally it should be treated as *silence breaking* for the community of Zgierz and Łódź. The elephant in the room could be actively noticed; what was in the background turning into a "figure" of explicit attention (Zerubavel 2015, pp. 64–65; 2018).

What is the social structure of relevance (Schütz 1962) of the problem for many social actors here? We can see that it could be the interests of the companies that want to keep the terrain for their operations and continue business there. The local government can avoid the topic for public relations reasons, ignoring the problem. And citizens in the natural attitude do not focus on the

Figure 4: The Deathworld is coming. Focusing on the trash.
Photo by the author, Krzysztof T. Konecki, April 19, 2019.

Deathworld aspects of the Lifeworld, due to ontological anxiety. Many of the citizens live in houses close to the Deathworld. The knowledge and feelings could be unpleasant, that they live on an ecological bomb that could explode, but when it is leaking slowly, the danger is not so vivid, so it could be avoided and the Deathworld could be safely kept in silence. The emotional dynamics of avoiding looking at the difficult truth (the figure of death) seem to be included in individual decision to keep silent, which becomes the collective conspiracy.

The visualization of the ignored phenomena is important in urging us to turn our eyes on unnoticed phenomena. The Deathworld is around us and in our Lifeworld. The death zones as this one in Zgierz (10 miles from the University in Łódź and Revolution 1905 street referred to in the next section) is ignored socially, although it was announced as a problem in media. It was discussed and commented on by government officials and politicians. So, it was noticed and marked. But after that, nothing happened. The poison and destruction moved to the background once again. This could be perceived as a sad and depressing phenomenon of not noticing the obvious. What should be done to make the

Figure 5: The trash heaps. The trash after the fire is still visible and very painful for the viewer. Photo by the author, Krzysztof T. Konecki, June 6, 2019.

ignored or irrelevant phenomena noticed and relevant at the same time? How may we make the transformation of the perception more permanent? At the time of writing, a Google search of Boruta chemicals said nothing about the fire or the dangerous toxins.

***

There are paradoxes of living in a polluted city. When I was a teenager I lived in the countryside and I was sick from asthma. I was allergic to hay, dust, pollens from grass and trees. I was allergic to almost everything that I encountered in the village. I was sick all the time with strong asthma attacks.

As a child, I worked on a farm and at the field helping my parents and often barely breathing. However, I moved to the city when I was nineteen years old and suddenly my attacks vanished. The smell was pleasant for me. I liked the smell of gasoline and the smoke from the coal. I felt the smoke, gasoline and grease in the air, and it was a smell of salvation for me. Finally, I had no asthma, I could breathe.

Figure 6: Chemical waste landfill.
Photo by the author, Krzysztof T. Konecki, June 6, 2019.

However, I am breathing toxins through my lungs slowly. And it is poisonous air that makes us wonder "When" as in the poem by Ewa Lipska (2019, p. 38):

> When death
> begins to breathe
> fear arises
> of the dead.

However, it has not happened in my case. The air that kills also could be considered clean and safe from rural pollens for the sufferers of nature allergies, but for how long?

Figure 7: The trash heap around the devastated buildings of the past chemical company Boruta. Photo by the author, Krzysztof T. Konecki, June 6, 2019.

Insider Interpretation After Theoretical Contemplation

To defray our anxiety, we bracket out the Deathworld that is nested in the Lifeworld. If I am a living being I want to live, although the Deathworld is ingrained in the everyday life, I want to live with the people alive around me and they are my others that I take into consideration when I make projects and act (Mead 1934). When I am active, and I am in action. My mind is located in interaction with others, so minding is social (Mead 1934). But the Deathworld is present and I sometimes feel it in my lungs, back, legs or when I am touched by passing cars while cycling or when the drivers shout at me and curse me, and finally when they hit the cyclist. However, the Lifeworld gives me hope and without any rational reason the certainty that I will never die. This is an effect of the natural epoché, that we make during our everyday life. Sometimes the fundamental anxiety comes back, however, I have a ready tool to defend myself against it: the natural attitude epoché. However, to hide a part of myself does not mean to survive. The Deathworld resides around us and in us. Yet, the

Figure 8: Residential buildings around the trash heap.
Photo by the author, Krzysztof T. Konecki, June 6, 2019.

attention a la vie is not directed on death but on life. And it could be misleading. Human *potestativity* (agency) is located in the Lifeworld; we have there projects and plans, intentions and future, and we can choose a line of action among many possibilities (Benţa 2014, p. 93). There is temporality in our perception of the world, and we locate our projects on a timeline. However, there is no time, no projects, no future in the Deathworld. It is an anti-world which we have no direct access to (Schütz 1962, pp. 207–259), where we have no direct access to, but we can create phantasms about it (there is eternity or nothingness) and homunculi (Reapers, ghosts, angels, souls and gods). However, the Lifeworld is only our world, it is so tangible we feel safe. The ontological security is needed, but not necessarily included, in the Lifeworld of contemporary western, industrialized cities.

We can be aware of global warming and destruction of nature (it is in our stock of knowledge) but we do not take it seriously in our life (Norgaard 2006, p. 373). There are uncomfortable feelings with the knowledge about nature's destruction that participants want to liquidate by emotion management (Hochschild 1983). There could be even the collective practices of distancing to the problems,

Figure 9: The companies still at work around the poisoned area.
Photo by the author, Krzysztof T. Konecki, June 6, 2019.

the social organization of denial (Young/Coutinho 2013; Zerubavel 1997, 2002; Zerubavel as cited in Norgaard 2006, p. 374). Even if we see in Poland the changes in climate and high pollution in the winter in cities because of coal use (the Polish economy is based on coal) generally we do not want to act against it. We have some protests but they are not massive.[6] The state media belittle the dangers of the use of coal for health and for climate warming. The media and politicians name coal the national treasure (Zerubavel 2015, p. 6).[7] Our attention is filtered so we can focus on treasure and ignore pollution. We filter the information; our attention is selective, and it helps us to survive emotionally by ignoring some stimuli and attending only to those that are relevant to keep a good mood (Zerubavel 2015, pp. 6, 50).

---

6 See the title of the paper: "No coal burning in Warsaw? There is a petition to the city authorities" (Chelmiński 2019).
7 See title of the papers: "This is our national treasure: coal! Poland is building large energy blocks!" (Republika 2017), "ZPGWK conference: coal with our national wealth" (netTG.pl 2011), and "Prime Minister: Coal is our national treasure" (GOSC.PL 2013).

Figure 10: The fire of the trash heap in Zgierz in May of 2018.
Adapted from "Several hours of firefighting. Landfill fire," 2018 (https://www.tvn24.pl/wiadomosci-z-kraju,3/zgierz-pozar-skladowiska-odpadow,840181.html, visited August 23, 2019). Copyright 2018 by TVN24.

Everybody knows, but almost nobody acts.[8] Fundamental anxiety is so strong that it is somehow suppressed, refused. We do not want to think about our premature death because of the pollution and do not want to think about the future generations not having clean air, water and food to live healthily or to live at all. We shift our attention from negative predictions to pleasant things here and now. The attention becomes selective and the construction of irrelevance starts (Zerubavel 2015).[9] My mind is social, it is located in interactions, so if there are blind spots in society, they are also in my mind (Mead 1934). I am taking the roles of others in also not noticing. "It is by means of reflexiveness, the turning-back of the

---

[8] This is well shown in the Icelandic-Ukrainian movie "Woman at War" (Erlingsson 2018), when control of the information and emotions in media was aimed at nationalistic and consumption goals. The attention is redirected to threats to the peaceful and still affluent society when one woman protested violently against the destructive system of collusive cooperation of state and corporations that destroy nature (summary available at https://www.womanatwar.film, visited on August 22, 2019).
[9] "The selective nature of our attention is evident not only in the organization of our sensory experience but also in the remarkably similar organization of the way we think about as well as remember things. It is likewise evident in the cognitive organization of our moral concerns, as any given set of moral considerations effectively 'goes out of focus' whenever a competing one 'comes into focus.' Given the striking similarity between the ways in which we focus our attention perceptually and conceptually, we thus often fail to notice things that are 'right in front of us' not only literally but also figuratively" (Zerubavel 2015, p. 5–6).

experience of the individual upon himself that the whole social process is thus brought into the experience of the individuals involved in it" (Mead 1934, p. 134). There are the norms of attention in society, supported by the state media that distribute the stock of three social narratives: Concentration on economic growth, increased affluence for society, and diversion of responsibility to others (Brussels means European Union, or Germany and Russia, etc.) (Norgaard 2006). The effectiveness of these attentional strategies depends on our *intentional ignorance*. Here are the challenge and the answer to the question: "How to make the transformation of the perception more permanent?" We should take responsibility for not seeing the Deathworld agency around. This is the moral responsibility that should be taken in each moment when we think and act in interaction with others and with nature. When the individual gives an indication to himself (Blumer 1969, p. 80) there is a short moment before the indication, a moment at which we can stop and adopt the *other attitude* process. This breaks the process when we do not want to see things because others do not want to see. We can notice the process, see the meanings of the objects that we accept because others accept them. And at this moment, we can free ourselves from the collective blindness and take personal responsibility for seeing the socially unseen phenomena.

We have also the attentional communities that have their attentional traditions (Norgaard 2006, p. 8). The farmers observe and put attention to nature as the object for exploitation and making profits. They also have *the attentional habit* to observe the weather and its consequences to the harvest result. Although they probably see the relationship between their work for profits with the use of chemicals as fertilizers and observable destruction of nature, and the changing of the climate that is happening in their place of work (e.g. lack of water), they do nothing. In this case, they should act against the destruction and stop distancing from the observable destruction of nature and climate warming. The perception becomes the ethical choice.

References

Benţa, Marius Ion (2014): *The Multiple Reality: A Critical Study on Alfred Schütz's Sociology of the Finite Provinces of Meaning*. Cork: University College Cork.
Bentz, Valerie/Shapiro, Jeremy (1998): *Mindful inquiry in Social Research*. Thousand Oaks: Sage.
Bentz, Valerie/Rehorick, David/Marlatt, James/Nishii, Ayumi/Estrada, Carol (2018): "Transformative Phenomenology as an Antidote to Technological Deathworlds". In: *Schützian Research* 10, pp. 189–220.

Blumer, Herbert (1969): *Symbolic Interactionism. Perspective and Method*. Berkeley: University of California Press.

Chelmiński, Jakub (2019): "No coal burning in Warsaw? There is a petition to the city authorities." Translated from Polish. Retrieved from http://warszawa.wyborcza.pl/warszawa/7,54420,24764441,zakaz-spalania-wegla-w-warszawie-jest-petycja-do-wladz-miasta.html, visited on August 22, 2019.

Erlingsson, Benedikt (Producer/Director)/Leblanc, Carine (Producer)/Slot, Marianne (Producer) (2018): *Woman at War* [Motion picture]. Iceland, France, Ukraine: Magnolia Studios.

GOSC.PL (2013): "Prime Minister: Coal is our National Treasure." Translated from Polish. Retrieved from https://katowice.gosc.pl/doc/1801559.Premier-Wegiel-to-nasz-narodowy-skarb, visited on August 22, 2019.

Hochschild, Arlie (1983): The Managed Heart: Commercialization of Human Feeling, Berkeley: University of California Press.

Husserl, Edmund (1970): *The Crisis of European Sciences and Transcendental Phenomenology: An introduction to Phenomenological Philosophy* (D. Carr, Trans.). Evanston: Northwestern University Press. (Original work published in 1954)

Konecki, Krzysztof T. (2018): *Advances in Contemplative Social Research*. Łódź: Łódź University Press/Kraków: Jagiellonian University Press.

Konecki, Krzysztof T. (2019): "Visual Images and Grounded Theory Methodology". In: Bryant, Tony/Charmaz, Kathy (Eds.): *Current Developments in Grounded Theory*. Los Angeles: Sage, pp. 352–373.

Lipska, Ewa (2019): *Miłość w trybie awaryjnym* [Love in a Safe Mode]. Kraków: Wydawnictwo Literackie.

Mead, George H. (1934): *Mind Self and Society from the Standpoint of a Social Behaviorist*. Charles W. Morris (Ed.). Chicago: University of Chicago.

netTG.pl (2011): "ZPGWK conference: coal with our national Wealth." Translated from Polish. Retrieved from http://nettg.pl/news/22462/konferencja-zpgwk-wegiel-naszym-narodowym-bogactwem, visited on August 22, 2019.

Norgaard, Kari Marie (2006): "'We don't really want to know' environmental justice and socially organized denial of global warming in Norway". In: *Organization & Environment* 19. No. 3, pp. 347–370.

Polish Association of Beef Cattle Breeders and Producers (2018): "Goals and Tasks". Translated from Polish. Retrieved from http://bydlo.com.pl/cele-i-zadania/, visited on August 20, 2019.

Polish Hunting Association (2012a): "Home". Translated from Polish. Retrieved from http://pzl.przemysl.pl/, visited on August 20, 2019.

Polish Hunting Association (2012b): "Hunting Criteria". Translated from Polish. Retrieved from http://pzl.przemysl.pl/2019/02/26/kryteria-odstrzalu/, visited on August 20, 2019.

POLSAT News (2019): "Zgierz – Polish Chernobyl. Residents live near an ecological bomb". Retrieved from https://www.polsatnews.pl/wiadomosc/2019-06-30/zgierz-polski-czarnobyl-mieszkancy-zyja-nieopodal-ekologicznej-bomby/, visited on August 23, 2019.

Republika (2017): "This is our national treasure: coal! Poland is building large energy blocks!" Translated from Polish. Retrieved from ved from https://telewizjarepublika.pl/ütz, Anarodowy-wegiel-polska-buduje-duze-bloki-energetyczne,44061.html, visited August 22, 2019.

Schütz, Alfred (1962): *Collected Papers I, The Problem of Social Reality.* Maurice Natanson (Ed.). The Hague: Martinus Nijhoff.
Schütz, Alfred (1975): *Alfred Schütz on Phenomenology and Social Relations.* Helmut R. Wagner (Ed.). Chicago: The University of Chicago Press.
TVN 24 (2018): "Several hours of firefighting. Landfill fire". Photo captured from video. Retrieved from https://www.tvn24.pl/wiadomosci-z-kraju,3/zgierz-pozar-skladowiska-odpadow,840181.html, visited on August 23, 2019.
Young, Nathan/Coutinho, Aline (2013): "Government, Anti-Reflexivity, and the Construction of Public Ignorance about Climate Change: Australia and Canada Compared".
In: *Global Environmental Politics* 13. No. 2, pp. 89–108. DOI:10.1162/GLEP_a_00168.
Zerubavel, Eviatar (1997): *Social Mindscapes: An Invitation to Cognitive Sociology.* Cambridge: Harvard University Press
Zerubavel, Eviatar (2002): "The Elephant in the Room: Notes on the Social Organization of Denial". In: Cerulo, Karen (Ed.): *Culture in Mind: Toward a Sociology of Culture and Cognition.* New York: Routledge, pp. 21–27.
Zerubavel, Eviatar (2015): *Hidden in Plain Sight: The Social Structure of Irrelevance.* Oxford, New York: Oxford University Press.
Zerubavel, Eviatar (2018): *Taken for Granted: The Remarkable Power of the Unremarkable.* Oxfordshire: Princeton University Press.

Valerie Malhotra Bentz
Chapter 3
Deathworld of the City of Łódź: Outsider Lived Experiences

Abstract: Using the concepts of *Lifeworld, the "Stranger"* (Schütz 1976, pp. 91–105) and *Deathworld* (Bentz et al. 2018), I explore experiences of the city of Łódź, Poland, where I served as Visiting Professor and principal researcher on the project of collaboration among strangers. I experienced a sense of profound desolation, despite the conscientiousness of host colleagues. I expand the Schützian *habitual type* of *Normal Foreign Visiting Professor* to the *characterological*: Elderly Foreign Woman Professor Recovering from Pneumonia with Driving Trauma and PTSD. This highlights the differences in experiences of Lifeworlds and Deathworlds between strangers and residents, as well as unique aspects of my own vantage point.

Keywords: Deathworld, Lifeworld, lived experience, Stranger, phenomenology, A. Schütz

Outsider/Stranger's Perspective – From One Deathworld to Another

At the invitation of Professor Krzysztof Konecki, I received a teaching and research fellowship with the School of Economics and Sociology Faculty at the University of Łódź, Poland, I arrived in March 2019, to teach a doctoral seminar on transformative phenomenology and an undergraduate course with Erasmus Institute students on embodied communication in organizations. Both courses involved readings on phenomenology and writing protocols about an experience of significance to the students. They shared their writing in an online Basecamp with other students and had the opportunity to discuss them in class and online. As well, they were working in parallel with students at the Fielding Graduate University and University of the Virgin Islands (Chapter 1). The design was to include a week-long intensive with the students from the Virgin Islands and Fielding coming to Łódź, Poland, to build collaboration face-to-face. We reluctantly cancelled this part of the design. The Dominant World View (Table 3, Chapter 1) based on competitive individualism was too strongly engrained in the university culture in Łódź to embrace this aspect of the project. Nevertheless, meaningful collaboration developed because of the project and settled around the theme of Deathworlds and Lifeworlds.

Before making the trip to Łódź, I had recently experienced five evacuations due to the Thomas Fire and its aftermath in Santa Barbara county.

Deathworlds surrounded our town. Constant noise from the ongoing construction of freeways, the rapid development of cannabis agribusiness emitting a skunk-like odor, and the spraying of chemicals pervaded the area. Oil spills and leakages, a nearby nuclear power plant built on known earthquake faultlines, water shortage, and tech companies thriving from war-based production are obvious signs of Deathworld-infused life in Central Coast California.

I had many apprehensions about the trip to Łódź, leaving all that was familiar, especially for an extended time, on my own, and not knowing the Polish language. These fears were tempered by the wonderful experience keynoting at a sociology conference in Kraków two years prior, also at Krzystof Konecki's invitation (Bentz 2016).

The persistent and cumulative effect of being in Łódź led me to an experience of desolation which I had not previously felt or even imagined. Unique aspects of Łódź included the following: the apartment and its immediate surroundings; the street, Revolution 1905; the university environment, both physical and social; and City of Łódź with layers of history of the Deathworlds of war, the holocaust, the Soviet occupation, and the rapid demolishing and reconstruction.

I perceived these aspects of a courageous city emerging from the effects of world wars, the holocaust and the soviet occupation in a particular way due to my *characterological type*.

Schützian Types: Habitual and Characterological

Schütz distinguishes two *Ideal types* which apply in my situation. The first is the *Habitual Type*, which typifies me in the system of expectations and *relevancies* of my hosts in Łódź, from their *insider* perspective. The Habitual Type was: *The Normal Foreign University Professor*.

The Normal Foreign University Professor: What at the time seemed like a Kafkaesque nightmare in retrospect was what any traveler going alone to a place in Eastern Europe might have expected. A "normal" university researcher may have looked upon the situation as a stimulating experience full of opportunities to expand and deepen awareness and knowledge. This indeed was also the case for me there.

Schütz refines the Ideal Type Model in what he calls the *Characterological Type* which, on the other hand, "refers to a real person whom I could meet face to face" (1975, p. 288).

Below I define my own Characterological Type which colored and focused my experience of Łódź. My "stock of knowledge" (Schütz 1975, p. 319) and the experience was colored by my being a woman who would at once become aware of the streets in the immediate vicinity as likely places to be raped or mugged. An *Elderly Foreign Woman Professor* was a more precarious type in the situation.

My type became even more refined: *Elderly Foreign Woman Professor with Driving Trauma*. My original PTSD (Post Traumatic Stress Disorder) came from surviving a car crash in 1995. Because of this I would not even consider driving in a foreign country. Since most places of interest required either walking through the marginal neighborhood or driving, I felt largely trapped in the apartment especially at night.

The life-threatening conditions from the Thomas Fire reactivated my PTSD. My characterological type coming to Łódź became: *Elderly Foreign Woman Professor with Driving Trauma and PTSD*. This experience allowed me to realize what a challenge it is to live post-trauma and in continued danger and exacerbated by being an old woman.

At the time, I was also recently recovered from pneumonia induced by the Thomas Fire. I had a cough from January 2018 until one month before traveling to Łódź, so my role in Łódź was *Elderly Foreign Woman Professor Recovering from Pneumonia with Driving Trauma and PTSD*.

By now, in retrospect, I see a humorous side to my situation! Almost like the 1930s comic movies of Laurel and Hardy getting deeper and deeper into situations that go O.K. for most folks but not for them.

The Situation Provided an Epoché of My "Natural Attitude"

Epoché is a technique used by phenomenologists to set aside or *bracket* aspects of their normal everyday way of experiencing life (*natural attitude*). In this way, the essential aspects of direct experience can be recovered and more deeply felt. This includes learned ways of seeing, such as through the sciences, as well as everyday awareness.

It is challenging for phenomenologists to learn to recognize the aspects of Lifeworlds that are taken for granted, so that they may set them aside or bracket them to see more clearly what is really there. We normally set aside observations of Deathworldly aspects of our ordinary lives. We are already taught as children ways of being safe, such as my grandmother saying about streets in Milwaukee that looked rather like 1905 Revolution Street in Łódź:

> "Cookie, don't ever go on such a street," and, "Cookie, do not go out alone after dark."

In the situation of being alone and not speaking the language there was a near total Epoché. Heidegger said, "Language is the House of Being." My "Being" was as an English speaker in a city of mostly Polish speakers with all the signs in Polish and with Uber and cab drivers not understanding English. I felt like I had lost my Being and lost my bearings, lost my *House of Being* (Heidegger 1982).

The Deathworld of the City of Łódź as Seen from my Elderly Foreign Woman Professor Recovering from Pneumonia with Driving Trauma and PTSD State of Being

I could not appreciate the tremendous accomplishment the City of Łódź was making in building a new city amidst and around the centuries of trauma. That they were doing this very rapidly was a source of pride on the part of city leaders. However, rapid construction takes its toll on the residents everywhere in the world as the destruction of old buildings and roads produces toxic dust and waste. It causes large scale disruption and necessarily destroys the fragile Lifeworlds that residents had managed to develop before these changes were thrust upon them by governments and other powerful interests.

Schütz described that "thinking as usual" does not work in his famous essay on "The Stranger":

> The discovery that things in his new surrounding look quite different from what he expected them to be at home is frequently the first shock to the stranger's confidence . . . Not only the picture which the stranger has brought along of the cultural pattern of the approached group but the whole hitherto unquestioned scheme of interpretation current within the home group becomes invalidated. It cannot be used as a scheme of orientation within the new social surroundings.   (Schütz 1976, p. 99)

The Stranger inherently carried both more *objectivity* about the place visited and *doubtful loyalty*. The insiders "do not understand that the stranger . . . does not consider the new community" as a "protecting shelter at all but as a labyrinth in which he has lost all sense of his bearings" (Schütz 1976, p. 104–105). In what follows I describe my experience as a stranger and outsider whose viewpoint was colored and focused by my characterological type: Elderly Foreign Woman Professor Recovering from Pneumonia with Driving Trauma and PTSD State of Being.

Arrival

It was early March 2019, when I flew from Munich to Łódź to begin my visiting professor and research fellow position at the University of Łódź. The passengers on this small propeller plane were businessmen who I later found out commuted daily to a razor factory in this long-time industrial city. There was only one other woman passenger. At near sunset, the forested landscape below changed from hilly to flat with few trees. Farmhouses were replaced by large warehouses. There were rows of large five or six story apartment buildings below. The Łódź airport was nearly deserted as its one café was closed. Krzysztof was waiting behind the baggage claim. We stopped at a large chain grocery store on the way to the apartment where Krzysztof helped me select supplies and essentials.

The Apartment at 48 Revolution 1905 Street

There were ice patches on the sidewalk in front of the apartment at Revolution 1905 Street. The door was right up to the sidewalk, with a step leading in. I had to hold an electronic device to the doorway to be buzzed in. A single hanging lightbulb lit the split hallway.

Everything in the apartment was coated with a thick layer of dust. On the walls there were photographic prints of famous buildings in Łódź mounted behind plastic sheets on pea green paper. All are austere buildings of the wealthy that had been maintained, converted from the huge slave labor factories in the two-hundred-year heyday of textile manufacturing in Łódź.

Despite updated appliances, the apartment held a series of annoyances: an ultramodern stove that seemed to flash lights at random; a dilapidated desk lamp with a burned out bulb; a water heater for tea which was corroded with a loose top; a sporadic and frequently failing internet connection which I depended upon for my continued teaching using Zoom at Fielding Graduate University and University of Virgin Islands. Doctoral students were co-participants in the research, most of it late at night in Łódź.

The back yard of the apartment was a long alley with five story apartments on one side and a row of long single-story units on the other behind a large section of trash containers. Just behind them was a bulldozer that worked daily tearing down a structure behind it. Cars were parked along both sides of this alley.

Figure 1: Entryway to 48 Revolution 1905 Street. Photo by the author, Valerie Bentz, 2019.

At the end of the alley there was a red umbrella standing in front of stairs leading to a basement unit. It announced Mammy's Food, open 5:30 to 8:30 daily. The restaurant was cheerfully painted with colorful oilcloth covered tables and a buffet of casseroles and salads. A young woman behind the counter announced that for 20 złotych (about eight U.S. dollars) one could have all one could eat. I was the only diner. As I was hungry, I gave it a try. When I returned the next week with a group of students, they were serving the same dishes. Several of us fell ill the next day.

The saving grace of the apartment were two large trees that remained in a tiny square of a garden, one of which was the home for two magpies.

Revolution 1905 Street

The apartment was on Revolution 1905 Street conveniently located only in that it was across the street from the University of Economics and Sociology classroom and office building. The street is narrow and busy and about two miles long between a busy thoroughfare on one side and, on the other, the famous Piotrkowska

Figure 2: Alley behind 48 Revolution 1905 Street.
Photo by the author, Valerie Bentz, 2019.

Street (a street that was called Adolph Hitler Strasse during the Nazi occupation). An old synagogue is barely visible and falling into ruin, echoing the slaughter of 300,000 Jews who were herded there before going to their deaths in Auschwitz. Cars are small and park halfway on the sidewalk. Once, when I accidentally touched the top of such a car to balance myself after having tripped over debris on the sidewalk, the car suddenly pulled away.

The following aspects of Revolution 1905 Street contributed to its foreboding qualities:
- new buildings in harsh ultra-modern style
- absence of trees and plants
- vacant buildings with raggedly dressed people peering out of windows or standing in front
- windows curtained with dusty shrouds of disintegrating cloth
- trash littering small courtyards where mothers play with children while smoking.
- the sidewalks cracked and littered with pipes, broken cement, dust and cigarette butts

Figure 3: Tree with magpies behind apartment.
Photo by the author, Valerie Bentz, 2019.

- pedestrians walking hunched over pulling shopping carts do not smile or notice each other
- young men gathered in the streets smoking
- the design on the back of a young man's jacket reading "I HATE LIFE" – a Deathworld jacket

Figure 4: Dust pile on Revolution 1905 Street.
Photo by the author, Valerie Bentz, 2019.

A Saving Grace: For a While

Down the block from the apartment, past a lovely old castle-like building standing boldly among a pile of debris and a bulldozer was a lovely small coffee shop. There was a darling life-sized cut out poster of a witch pointing to the coffee shop. One had to climb over some debris on the way, but it was worth it to find such a welcoming atmosphere. It was only open 9:00 am to 5:00 pm on weekdays but was like an oasis when it was open.

It had two levels, and a small counter with a fresh bakery. Young women students home cooked pancakes with vegetables and meat inside and salads along with coffees and teas. The sunken room had a table with some familiar games, such as Rummy Cube, Chess and Chinese checkers. Usually one or two persons were working on their computers and drinking wonderful fresh roasted coffee.

Figure 5: Inside of café.
Photo by the author, Valerie Bentz, 2019.

Figure 6: Café, post-demolition.
Photo by the author, Valerie Bentz, 2019.

On my way there one afternoon in late March, I found the poster was lying on the ground, and the entire coffee shop had been bulldozed to the ground.

The University

The University of Łódź Economics and Sociology Faculty was both physically and socially foreboding. Challenging aspects of the physical structures included:
- There were locked gates and a guardhouse around the parking lot of the university building.
- There were booths where faculty must sign in and out for office keys and also for keys to all classrooms.
- My office space was actually a room for copy machines and supplies. The computers in it could not be used for printing.
- Floors and offices connect in a complicated manner, like a maze (Konecki 2017).
- Parts of the building were under construction or remodeling at all times.
- There was lots of dust in the air from construction.
- Classrooms were not amenable to seminar format.

In addition to the physical challenges, there were social challenges. The first colleague I met was a visiting professor from Germany. However, he had just been released from the hospital after three weeks having broken his leg falling on the icy sidewalk in front of the building. He was in a wheelchair. He was a congenial fellow who I anticipated I may have stimulating conversations with. However, the next week he was no longer in his office. I was told he had left. Other social challenges were:
- fast-paced and reserved university culture worked against informal interactions;
- challenges with technology;
- friendly international office personnel did their best to process lots of forms I had to sign;
- challenge in meeting faculty from other departments due to stressful faculty schedules;
- pressure for the individualized achievement of students and faculty resulted in a need to cancel the culminating conference between the three universities; and
- unfamiliar holiday schedule resulted in delayed research efforts.

Lifeworlds Built Over Deathworlds in Łódź

Łódź is proud of its history as a center of textile manufacturing for centuries. Although the factories are no longer operating due to globalization, they have been preserved and turned to other uses. The factories once provided jobs for thousands – under slave labor conditions for men, women and children. The places of interest in Łódź all had histories of oppression, death, genocide, slavery and environmental destruction. The current construction boom was heaping more destruction in order, presumably, to create a better Lifeworld in the future, or to create wealth for some.

The largest example is a huge mall which is now the equivalent of a city center, called Manufactura built with red bricks from the original factory. There is an art museum and a museum of the history of the factory in the mall. A part of the mall is new and much like a mall anywhere in the world with a variety of shops. The appliance store contains appliances more advanced than available in the U. S. and at lower prices.

Figure 7: Child laborers as high-end décor.
Photo by the author, Valerie Bentz, 2019.

A huge mansion sits at the edge of the Manufactura which once was the home of the factory owners. Israel Poznański was the founder of the factory in the XIX century. It is being refurbished but is partly a museum where concerts are held; we attended a piano recital there by a world class Polish musician on the occasion of a visit by the Japanese ambassador. Murals are to be found around the city. They were cries of the hope of art amid the squalor below.

The extravagantly elegant Herbst family home is now a museum. Above is a greenhouse coffee shop adjacent to the gardens. An elegant restaurant housed in a new five-star hotel near Manufactura integrates industrial equipment with its design and remembers the child laborers who once worked there in the photograph. However, just as in the past, this five-star hotel is mostly empty on weekends. The main customers are the wealthy businessmen such as I saw on the commuter plane on the way to the city. On a Saturday evening, most of the tables were empty.

The Kindness and Support of The Polish Colleagues

Professor Konecki and Professor Anna Kacperczyk offered kindness and generosity. Despite extremely demanding academic schedules (Professor Konecki was also Dean), they had worked with university offices to provide a convenient, recently updated apartment for me across the street from the faculty offices and classroom building.

Anna Kacperczyk, Krzysztof Konecki and Natalia Martini (graduate assistant) all attended my weekly seminars and fully participated in writing the phenomenological protocols. Regularly after our Friday afternoon seminar these colleagues would have dinner with me. On several weekends they organized tours to sites in Łódź or around the area such as the Herbst Palace museum, the Nieberów castle, Krzysztof's home village and church, and the Manufactura shopping mall built upon what was a once a huge textile factory.

From within my characterological point of view, all of the above seemed Deathworldly. Nevertheless, the creativity and Lifeworld-making energy of the people of Łódź is evident in the lovely artistry of what once were castles, and in the renovations, which offer hope and promise for the future.

Figure 8: Inside Nieborów Castle, a demonstration of opulence. Photo by the author, Valerie Bentz, 2019.

Trip to Krzysztof's Home Village: Stroniewice

We visited Krzysztof's home village. There, we saw clearly a Lifeworld that had become a Deathworld. The river he swam in and skated on as a boy had been drained. We met with his sister, still living in his childhood home. But a terrible stink reeked as we stood in front of his home. It was a dairy farm where cows are kept tied up twenty-four hours a day, seven days a week in a barn and never see the light of day. A cruel and inhumane way to make a living, one magnified in North America into huge factory farms. Krzysztof sent this poem to me in March of 2019 to express his lived experience concerning the changes in his village:

> From This River, When I Was a Child,
> I Used to Drink

But when I came back I found
that the body of the river was dying.
"Did it speak?"
Yes, it sang out the old songs, but faintly.
"What will you do?"
I will grieve of course, but that's nothing.
"What, precisely, will you grieve for?"
For the river. For myself, my lost
joyfulness. For the children who will not
know what a river can be – a friend, a
companion, a hint of heaven.
"Isn't this somewhat overplayed?"
I said: it can be a friend. A companion. A
hint of heaven."
              (Oliver 2009, p. 44)

Desolation: Absence of Normal Taken-For-Granted

The Lifeworld functions based upon a series of assumptions about the way things normally are; the "taken for granted." Being thrust on my own into a place where I was alone and did not know the language went beyond my initial fears.

After six weeks, I developed a severe sinus infection. Despite several visits from a doctor, prescriptions, inhaling machine, infrared heater, it only got worse. My doctor said I needed to leave the environment immediately for the sake of health. I asked the officials if I could be moved to an apartment in a different location away from all the construction dust. They said they had a contract for the entire time and could not change it and, in any case, there was no place in the city that was not loaded with dust. I requested that the university provide an air purifier for my apartment or reimburse me for one. The request was denied.

Reflections on Deathworlds

Universities tend to operate under political and economic webs of thought, where departments are separated, individual competition resounds, fear of loss of jobs is pervasive, administrative apparatus increases (Rowe 2014), and disconnection exists between the intellectual work and the communities they are supposedly serving.

Universities governed by *scientific ways of thinking* and disembodied norms of conduct will disregard the lived experiences of those who work there: administrators,

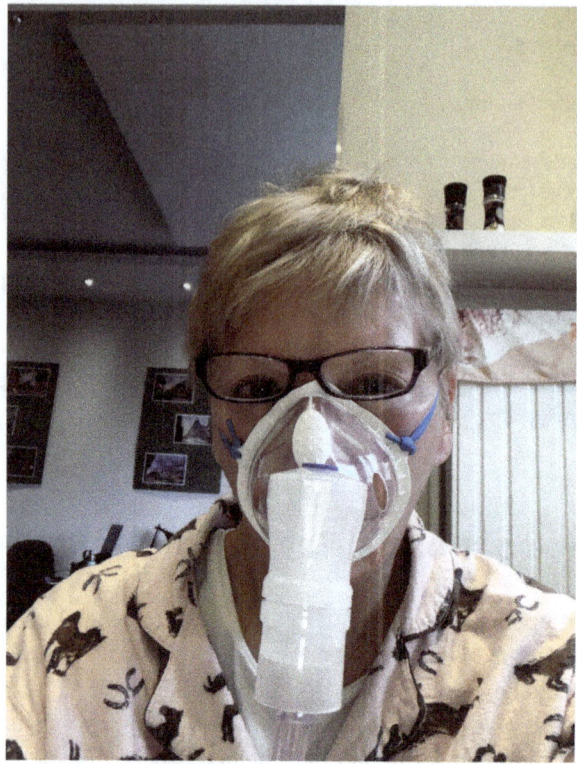

Figure 9: Sinus mask.
Photo by the author, Valerie Bentz, 2019.

staff, faculty and students (Four Arrows 2020). Students will be taught that it is "professional" to disregard their emotions, especially when it comes to processes that make money but may cause suffering to animals and the earth.

U.S. streets too are Deathworlds filled with the homeless and those desperate in their homes without medical care or adequate food, with increasingly polluted air. Even beautiful Santa Barbara produces Deathworlds there and elsewhere. The Raytheon company, a multi-billion-dollar defense company is in Goleta, just north of Santa Barbara. The bomb shells rained on Yemen aided by the U.S. military were made by Raytheon. There are 14 million Yemenis at risk of starvation and death from the war of Saudi Arabia backed by the U.S. in Yemen (United Nations Human Rights Watch 2019, par. 2). Today, the Amazon rain forest, a major source of oxygen globally, is being deliberately burnt, making a Deathworld of our whole planet. Millions of innocent creatures are being destroyed for the greed of a few miners and cattle and plantation farmers. There is now desolation for all life on earth through climate change. The current Covid 19 plague has by now affected millions worldwide. Fires are raging out of control in huge areas in Africa, South America, and North America (Fire Information for Resource Management System 2020).

A Note on Learning What to See and What Not to See

My natural attitude, despite being a phenomenologist, sociologist, psychotherapist, yoga teacher, initiated Vedantist, and social and environmental justice activist, was tuned to screen out the mixture of Deathworlds and Lifeworlds in my home country, particularly the Central and South coast of California. There, I learned not to see the realities of the relentless destruction of Lifeworlds by the pressures of population increase, exploitation by the oil and gas industries, agribusiness, highways, noise and light pollution, a war-based economy, relentless ocean pollution by plastics, deforestation by fires, and thought control by the media. The Deathworldly aspects in one's everyday Lifeworld are mitigated by what Schütz calls *finite provinces of meaning* (Schütz 1973). These are Lifeworlds within Lifeworlds, such as music and humor, which sooth the soul (Barber 2017). When my own finite provinces of meaning of the Vedanta temple, getting together with friends, walks on the beach, playing in a symphony, were all removed, the death world in Łódź was fully visible to all of my senses. At home in the California Deathworlds, it took a major catastrophe, the Thomas Fire and now Covid plague, to realize fully the dangers we are all in.

References

Barber, Michael (2017): *Religion and Humor as Emancipating Provinces of Meaning*. Dordrecht: Springer.
Bentz, Valerie Malhotra (2016): "Who is the Researcher? Soma, Contemplation and Lifeworld in 'Digitneyland'". *Qualitative Methods and Research Technologies*, European Sociological Association, Kraków, Poland.
Bentz, Valerie Malhotra/Rehorick, David Allen/Marlatt, James/Nishii, Ayumi/Estrada, Carol (2018): "Transformative Phenomenology as an Antidote to Technological Deathworlds". In: *Schützian Research* 10, pp. 189–220.
Fire Information for Resource Management System (2020): "Fires: Sep 12 2020 – Sep 13 2020". Retrieved from https://firms2.modaps.eosdis.nasa.gov/map/#t:adv;d:2020-09-12.2020-09-13;l:street;@-118.4,34.8,9z, visited on September 13, 2020.

Four Arrows (2020): "Hierarchy and Managerialism". In: *The Red Road: Linking Diversity and Inclusion Initiative to the Indigenous World View*. Charlottesville: Information Age Publishing.
Heidegger, Martin (1982): *On The Way to Language*. New York, Toronto: Harper & Roe.
Konecki, Krzysztof (2017): "How the University Organizational Culture is Being Experienced? Phenomenological Studies of Experiencing the Here and Now of the Organization". In: *Polish Sociological Review* 200, pp. 485–504.
Oliver, Mary (2009): *Red Bird*. Boston: Beacon Press.
Rowe, Stephen (2014): "Standing up to Managerialism". In: *Liberal Education* 100. No. 3, p. 56.
Schütz, Alfred (1973): "On Multiple Realities". In: Natanson, Maurice (Ed.): *Collected Papers I, The Problem of Social Reality*. The Hague: Martinus Nijhoff, pp. 207–259.
Schütz, Alfred (1975): *Alfred Schütz on Phenomenology and Social Relations*. Helmut R. Wagner (Ed.). Chicago: The University of Chicago Press.
Schütz, Alfred (1976): "The Stranger: An Essay in Social Psychology". In: Brodersen, Arvid (Ed.): *Collected Papers II, Studies in Social Theory*. The Hague: Martinus Nijhoff, pp. 91–105.
United Nations Human Rights Watch (2019): "Yemen: Events of 2018". Retrieved from https://www.hrw.org/world-report/2019/country-chapters/yemen, visited on February 27, 2020.

Anna Kacperczyk
Chapter 4
Phenomenology of Trash

Abstract: This chapter presents a study of trash as an object of human social practice and personal experiences. I position trash in the wider problem of environmental contamination and map the complexity of trash locations in everyday life. I begin from the very personal issue of my own contact with trash to generate a deep reflection of the issue of human practices toward trash. I use the Schützian concept of Lifeworlds, Max van Manen's advice on *Meaning-Giving Methods in Phenomenological Research and Writing* (2016) as well as the approach of *Transformative Phenomenology*[1] (Rehorick/Bentz 2008, 2017) to analyze trash in terms of Lifeworld phenomena. In our everyday life we may situate trash in various ways in our field of attention. It might be seen as a universe, a matter of life for those whose everyday experience is made by and within trash. It might be part of human action; the object of work and professional engagement like in the scrap industry and the world of solid waste management. It might also be a part of an overwhelming direct experience of the presence of unwanted waste in a neighborhood. And finally, it might be a shadow of our everyday activities that we tend to marginalize.

Keywords: trash, transformative phenomenology, Lifeworlds, animals, environment

Introduction: Litter Is Everywhere

Nine years ago, I visited Ecuador to participate in a research project aimed at studying the chance of a small Amazonian village in sustaining biodiversity and saving the richness of a local ecosystem around Laguna Limoncocha.[2] Apart

---

[1] This chapter is a result of a workshop delivered by Valerie Malhotra Bentz *From Strangers to Collaborators: Evaluating the Process of Transformative Phenomenology and Contemplative Research Across Cultures* held in Łódź University (Poland) from March to May 2019. The paper, "Phenomenology of Trash," was presented during the 9th Conference of the European Society for the Study of Symbolic Interaction, *The Interaction Order in the Global Village: Bridging the Atlantic in Symbolic Interaction Scholarship* in University of Iceland–Reykjavik, Iceland, July 3rd–6th, 2019.
[2] The project of Universidad Internacional SEK (Quito, Ecuador) and the Faculty of Economics and Sociology (University of Łódź, Poland) was titled: *Sustainable Development of the Local*

from the modern asphalt road leading through the middle of the jungle and the depressing view of the oil pipelines running hundreds of kilometers along this road and sucking the resources of the Amazon rainforest, the biggest surprise I experienced was the rubbish on the streets of the village.

Hand-painted boards with the inscriptions "Respect green" and "Clean up trash" came out from the bushes to meet us, but in the center of the village, the ground was literally encrusted with metal beer caps, plastic tops, and packaging for chocolate bars or shampoos. Absorbed in their daily affairs, the residents seemed not to notice the plastic-metal encrustations in their surroundings, just as they did not pay attention to the multi-meter processions of giant ants, crossing the pavements and disappearing somewhere in the brush.

This upsetting feeling of being surprised by the litter on the streets was probably created due to the idealized vision of the Amazon that I brought here with me. It was rooted in the deep assumption that the most beautiful and biodiverse part of the world should be clean, natural, and treated with mindfulness and care.

After returning to Poland, I was still thinking about it. Why did I expect those people to be more aware of the problem of plastic pollution and littering the environment than people in Europe, or my own country? Wandering around my city, I noticed that it is a huge problem in Poland too. And it has become clear that our own problems with garbage being left on the ground are much more serious and far exceeds the scale of littering in the Amazonian village.

We are literally drowning in trash. Our space is full of rubbish, small debris, and unlisted dumps. Litter is everywhere (Figure 1). Every patch of greenery is encrusted with bottle caps, plastic sticks, paper cups, and other human products. And of course, trash on the streets remains overlooked by the local inhabitants. During any walk in the forest, you can come across bags of rubble, parts from a broken-down car, the tube of an old TV, or even a sack of used diapers.

The ease with which people trash their environment and destroy places that could give them relaxation, a break from the surrounding concrete, remains truly confusing. So, too, is the absence of reflection that lies behind these practices of

---

Community of Limoncocha (2011–2012). Biodiversity and the research of the changes of economic, ecological and social attitudes of village residents. The project led to the publication of the book *The spirit of communitarianism and the cultural background of Limoncocha community in the context of sustainable development and environment protection* (Konecki et al., 2013).

leaving trash everywhere. After all, we share the space not only with other people but also with non-human animals. The lack of responsibility for common spaces raises real concern.

Figure 1: Garbage in a nearby forest in Łódź.
Photo by the author, Anna Kacperczyk, 2012.

"No-Places"

Leaving garbage in the forest may be seen as a form of vandalism. Litter changes natural features of the spot and destroys its previous biological and ecological functions. Animals and plants lose access to some ecosystem resources, and then the spot is somehow taken away from them. From a human point of view, the place loses its previous healing, esthetic, visual and landscape values. Dumps established in natural spots actually create *no-places*[3] that are excluded from "normal" use. The term "no-place" describes

---

[3] The term *no-place* generated on the basis of my field observations is used here in a different meaning than the one given by anthropologist Marc Augé (1995). His *non-places* (fr. *non-lieux*) are essentially forms of passages, spaces of movement, transit (like paths, highways, railway stations,

spaces deprived of their original function, since they are damaged by pollution and littering and this way became "uninhabitable," "un-co-exist-able" and somehow "in-actable." Their degraded status catches the eye. Turned into rubble, these places cease to fulfill their previous functions, and humans renounce them.

The extreme form of no-place would be a space extensively and willingly destroyed, which is labelled in environmental discourses as *ecocide*–the term coined by the American biologist Arthur W. Galston to label the massive damage and destruction of ecosystems caused by humans (Weisberg 1970, p. 4). Perhaps someday these spots will regain the status of *places*, and become a forest glade or just undergrowth once again, but now they are useless and cut off from their previous functions and the visual representations of the spot:

> I am visiting a nearby hillock in the city with my friend. Beneath the slope, I see the remains of disposable barbecues, some bricks, plastic rubbish, disposable cutlery and cups, mainly food packaging–everything scattered around the remnants of a bonfire–abandoned in the greenery close to the well-organized park. Seeing this damaged spot, I feel sad and a little surprised, since up to this place, everything around was quite clean and tidy. I take out my smartphone to take a picture, and then my friend says, "Don't you do this. Don't take pictures of rubbish–it's depressing." "I am doing this for the research," I answer taking some pictures. (A. Kacperczyk, field note, August 18, 2018)

People rarely photograph themselves against backgrounds filled with litter. The only exceptions are environmental activists willing to clean the spot by collecting rubbish or people who aim at raising the awareness of the garbage problem. They may visually present themselves as environmental heroes or concerned citizens against the background of destroyed or littered places. But usually framing their pictures, people focus their lenses on elements of untouched nature, and in this way try to erase garbage from the images taken of the landscape. This way trash becomes *visually absent* due to human visual practices. A specific form of bracketing takes place here.

However, the problem is not only that a damaged spot bothers us as spectators, but also that it creates a sense of loss caused by our fellow citizens with whom species ties bind us. Those invisible, anonymous people who have dared to litter the spot, in fact, received something valuable from us, the visitors of the place. And we instantly knew that "humans were here." Rubbish abandoned in the greenery not only reveals human practices or exposes how they

---

airports, malls)–hence places that are a stark contradiction to the idea of settlement. If we understand a place as a space to live, to stay in it, to enjoy it, or to use its affordances (Gibson 1977, 1979) and advantages to act, we may conversely define no-places as littered and ruined ones, visually excluded from the natural spot and making any action difficult or even impossible.

act, but additionally denudes the definition of natural habitat as a space that may be "erased" and destroyed without any regret.

This is Not Just an Esthetical Problem

But the problem is much more complicated if we assume that sometimes it is impossible to identify a particular person who performed a given action and to identify the guilty one because it results from the cumulated mass of actions of thousands of people living on this planet. I am thinking about plastic garbage patches and marine debris circulating in the oceans, about big landfills which are not just an esthetical, but a serious environmental problem.

I look at the photos of wildlife devastated by human activities. In one of the photographs, I see a stork that has become tangled in a plastic bag.[4] The picture is shocking. The bird stands on an old tire against the blue sky. The transparent blue foil covers its entire body. Only legs and beak stick out. The rest of the head is behind a foil curtain. The bird cannot free itself. It is not known if it can fly or whether it is able to eat. What is the chance of survival for the bird caught in such a trap? The scene captured in the frame turned out to be the last moment of his anguish, because the photographer managed to help him, and the bird was finally released. But not all animals are so lucky.

In the next photo, I see a duck that died of hunger because her beak was closed by a plastic ring from a regular bottle. I see a dead turtle photographed underwater entangled from the remains of abandoned fishing nets, which lost his life trapped in human garbage. In other photos I see turtles hunting for foil disposables floating in the water, which remind them of jellyfish, their natural food, and would become their last meal. These photographs just scream.

---

4 This picture made by John Cancalosi (2013) circulated the whole world, bringing its author numerous awards at photographic competitions devoted to wild nature. The photographer spent about a week at a huge garbage dump in Spain watching storks feeding there. One day he saw "a hapless stork, perched on a tire, trapped in a plastic bag. I was thrilled when I was able to drive my car close enough to take a series of photos as the stork struggled to release itself from its plastic prison. With sunset looming, I decided to try to help the bird. I left the car and started wading through the mess, edging toward the trapped bird. I was surprised that it didn't move away as I closed in. When I reached the bird's side, I was worried that it would lance me with its sword-like bill. I bent down to grab the bag at the stork's feet. It was a windy day and as I lifted the bag it filled with air and the stork suddenly flew up and was liberated! I will never forget how moved I felt as the snow-white stork rose up into the pure blue sky, free from the squalor below. The stork was given a second life."

And still new reports . . . an endless procession of images of animal tragedies that testify to their innocent suffering. In *The Guardian*, the story about attempts to rescue a whale stranded off the coast of Thailand. The animal noticed on Monday was kept alive by volunteers over the next days. With the help of buoys, they were holding him on the surface so that he could breathe and protected him from drying in the sun. During the rescue operation, the whale vomited five plastic bags. But it did not help. He died on Friday. Two pictures close the event with a buckle. In one the group of a dozen lifeguards leans over a whale in shallow water on a sunny bright day. The next one shows a room with a sectional table, around which two pathologists work. There is a lot of water on the floor, pools of blood, and the mass of dark plastic bags on the table and around it arranged on the floor–all drawn from the whale's stomach. The autopsy showed more than 80 plastic bags in the digestive system of a whale. Eight kilos of plastic prevented him from absorbing food and led to his death (The Guardian 2018).

It is hard to erase from memory a series of photos of Chris Jordan (2018) made as a part of the Midway Project. One can see in them albatrosses, which died many weeks ago, and the decomposition processes revealed the contents of their stomachs: plastic bottle caps, aglets, atomizers' parts, even plastic lighters. The albatross chicks are also dying, fed by their parents with plastic which they found in the sea and confused with food. A shocking ecological tragedy takes place there quietly and massively every day, as the adult albatrosses fill their children's throats with inedible rubbish. Thousands of young albatrosses are dead or dying in pain with stomachs filled with plastic on the Midway Atoll–the place furthest from civilization.

These images tear the heart apart. It is difficult to describe the feeling of regret, sadness, and depression at the sight of animals living among human garbage and dying because of it. As the members of the Midway Project write on working there:

> The experience was devastating, not only for what it meant for the suffering of the birds, but also for what it reflected back to us about the destructive power of our culture of mass consumption, and humanity's damaged relationship with the living world. (Jordan n.d., par. 1)

The category of *Deathworld* seems to be fully applicable here:

> With the decoupling of systems and Lifeworld the increasing destruction of living environments for humans and other creatures, the continued loss of species diversity, the planet is facing increased "Deathworlds" or socio-economic political systems which produce death and zones of death on the planet that can no longer support life. (Bentz et al. 2018, p. 6)

As Jürgen Habermas (1985) asserted, humans were destroying Lifeworlds having little awareness of the consequences of their acts. The predominance of rational thinking and the human obsession with effectiveness trigger insensate decisions and callous actions without empathy for other sentient beings, and finally for our own species too. Ultimately trash is a real ontological problem "resulting from our unsettled relation to nature" (Kennedy 2007; Konecki 2018).

Waste circulating in the ecosystem is not only a disturbance to the esthetics of the place but is a real threat to the sentient living beings with whom we share this planet. And the truth is, on this planet animals die because of human garbage. Is it a good enough reason to investigate the problem of trash?

Since man is the main agent of the mass destruction of the natural environment, one should look at how trash appears in human experience, how people understand and produce it, and what relations they establish with it. To analyze these very issues, I refer to *Transformative Phenomenology* (Rehorick/Bentz 2008, 2017).[5]

Trash in Personal Experience

To answer the question "How does trash appear in the human experience?" I will turn to personal accounts of my everyday contact with trash. The self-reports may be treated here as a form of exercise that helps to generate more deep reflection on the issue of human practices toward trash. They were created as part of the class conducted by Valerie Malhotra Bentz during her stay in Poland.[6]

---

5 In addition to the procedures of transformative phenomenology that I employed in my study, I used: (1) visual grounded theory (Konecki 2019; Glaser/Strauss 1967) to embrace visual aspects of trash production, sorting, disposal and processing; visualizations of the trash presence (or absence) in everyday life; (2) ethnography: interviews and observations comprising narratives on trash; reconstruction of symbolic, cognitive and reflexive processes related to trash; descriptions of behaviors, conducts and social practices related to trash; spatial and proxemic aspects of trash presence (or absence); (3) research walks with dumpster divers; tracking illegal waste dumps in the forests and parks; visiting spaces of trash storage and processing, transfer stations, landfills; and (4) autoethnography: self-observation of my own behaviors related to trash production, segregation, and disposal; self-observation of emotions and ways of thinking about trash; reporting on decisional problems of trash processing. Additionally, I use extant data sources on trash production, processing and management (like environmental statistics, journals of laws and dispositions, reports and so on).

6 These personal accounts have the form of protocols (descriptions of lived experience) prepared during classes and consist of six themes: (1) The most poignant experience with phenomenon; (2) Existentials and earliest memory; (3) Imaginative variations; (4) Essential structure; (5) Lifeworld basis of existence; and (6) Lifeworld structures and social construction of reality.

No Trash in the Traditional Zero-Waste World

I search in my memory to find my oldest experience with garbage and it turns out to be difficult to get something specific. I remember the last years and decades, when I lived in the city, but I cannot recall any scenes or experiences with garbage from my childhood spent in the village. I remember the mess that sometimes prevailing at home, the scenes of disorder in the backyard when things were in disarray, but I feel the difficulty in reaching the experiences related specifically to garbage and trash. I do not even remember that a dustbin was present in the house of my childhood.

In the central point of our rural house, built on a square plan and divided into four rooms, was a hallway or rather a porch, and in it, behind a separating curtain was a utility room, in which stood a coal furnace, next to it a bathtub and an electric boiler. There were buckets with hard coal, logs and wood slats, papers, used matches, and other items to be burnt at the stove. There was no need to have a garbage can in the house because trash was simply dropped into one of these buckets and then landed in the furnace. Materials, valuable things, were deposited on the shelves and covered up with dust until some kind hand could make something of them or made it into clothes. There was practically no plastic. Peelings from vegetables and leftovers from the kitchen were collected into one bucket, the contents of which were poured over compost behind a barn. Residues of food were put aside for pigs or hens. Garbage simply disappeared. There was no garbage anywhere. Things that were not burned were processed and reused. Objects wandered in the family–being passed from hand to hand. During communist times there was general scarcity, so practically no item was thrown away, but rather accumulated because: "Maybe it will be useful for something else."

It was years after when I could notice trash as an accumulated matter of crushed, smelly putrid objects being discarded and mixed up; when I saw overfilled dustbins, litter on the streets and stinking garbage chutes; when I started to recognize the sour odor of garbage containers, when I started to live in the city. (A. Kacperczyk, protocol March 20, 2019)

Everyday Decisions

Every day I have to deal with dozens of decisions related to the trash I have produced. *Used contact lenses*–should I throw them directly into the toilet or put them into the bin? What is better for the environment? *The packaging from the contact lenses*, which consists of plastic and aluminum foil–should they be separated into two categories or thrown together? Knowing that in my block of flats there are only three categories of garbage containers: "bio," "recyclable materials" and "others"–these two parts, plastic, and metal, will ultimately go together and will be separated later in the waste sorting plant. The remorse that accompanies me every time I throw out another packet. (A. Kacperczyk, self-observation, July 19, 2018)

Complicated Relationship with Things

Perhaps the deep personal motive to conduct this study is my complicated relationship with things. It is difficult for me to separate myself from some objects. Old toys, gadgets, empty perfume bottles, old jewelry, face cream boxes, boxes, books, ribbons, purses, handbags and shoes that I will never use again are still dotted around my flat. Even if I know I have too many things, I cannot throw away some old belongings. I am attached to some objects that I perceive as beautiful; they evoke pleasant memories or are simply traces of my experiences. I easily establish bonds with them. In effect, these are things that clutter my space. I know I should throw them away, but giving them too much meaning, I can't. I deceive myself that someday they may be useful again for someone or I will use them in some artistic project. But after four or five years they did not come in useful, and I still could not throw them away anyway. Claiming that 'I do not like to waste things' provides me with another reason to keep disused items *ad infinitum*. (A. Kacperczyk, self-observation, May 1, 2018)

What a Relief!

There is nothing more cleansing than getting rid of the rubbish. Discarding them, ruthlessly dealing with unnecessary, useless, broken or spoiled objects that clutter our space pushed in the corners, blur everyday paths of movement, and throttle the freedom of thinking. What a relief to throw away all these expendable things! To see simply clear space of own dwelling place. This is a way to gain clarity, the purity, the order, the tidiness of the spot.

All you need is just one determined decision–that "This is it!" "This is now." "This is enough!" that this is the right moment to do it. You have to grab the bin liner and put as much unnecessary stuff in it as you can. And you have to do it quickly; without hesitation. Whatever falls into your hands–throw to the trash bag. You must not think too long, because it evokes memories and hopes that something shall be useful someday. During such a "great purge" it is not allowed to recall memories of things or to plan its future application. These are definitely inappropriate mental processes, since they trigger cluttering and stocking the house–unfavorable from the point of view of cleaning the space from unnecessary things.

It is an emotion of great relief that accompanies the act of discarding. But usually I feel angry at the same time. My anger grown out of the accumulation of unnecessary things, gives me the energy to act very decisively and without hesitation. Throwing rubbish away seems to be stabilizing for the psyche, getting rid of trash means to abandon my own attachment to objects. And I feel like a "clearing agent."

When I clean the house I am thinking about a cell with its internal organelles and transformation processes–cellular respiration and excretion of waste products of the metabolism. Throwing out the bags full of waste I am thinking about the balance necessary to survive–the balance between what goes in and what goes out, what comes and what goes away. I perform this function in my home. I act like this kind of organelle in the cell, which is responsible for the excretion of unnecessary products–providing a flow of new energy, releasing and eliminating the metabolites outside. To sustain life every living being has to expel harmful and toxic substances of its own chemical transformations. And somehow I am doing this at my house. Getting rid of unnecessary things gives a cleaner feeling of freedom from useless objects and dirt. The practice of cleaning, throwing away what is unnecessary situates a cleaner in a sphere of cultural practice and cleansing rituals.

(A. Kacperczyk, protocol, March 27, 2019)

Being Thrown Away Like Trash

I was raised in the countryside. I used to play daily in the small yard in the property of my grandparents. The backyard was divided into two parts: the representative one–for people, and the other reserved for animals: hens, ducks, turkeys, sheep, who went there freely. Some pigs lived in the cowshed and rarely went out.

I was about three years old then. It would have been spring because hens with small chickens were already being released into the yard. That day I played in the backyard busy with my child affairs, when suddenly I saw a small yellow chicken under the fence–abandoned, clearly suffering, apparently ailing. I ran to him, took him in my hands–it was limp and very weak, but still alive. Despairing, I began to look for some rescue for the poor little one, and I was about to run to my mother when, to my joy, I saw my grandfather walking through the yard. I run to him. *Grandpa*–I called–*look, this chicken is sick, please help him*. I deeply believed that he would save the chicken. Grandfather took it in his hands, had just one quick look at a chicken and hurled him at the corner of the yard, saying that he would make nothing of it. I was totally shocked. I started shouting and yelling at him. I was calling him names and cussed him out. I ran to the chicken and picked it up again, lamenting his fate. I was shaken, distraught and furious with my grandfather. Tears are flooding my eyes. I cannot get a handle on what happened, and to understand how he could do it. Instantly, my grandfather lost everything in my eyes. All the trust and hope I placed in him, my childish confidence that he has the power to save a life . . . All this disappeared and in one moment transformed into disgust and hatred. Grandfather irretrievably fell off the pedestal of a half-god to become just a mean man. I still have this scene in front of my eyes. Why is it coming back to me?

Suffering sharpens the senses and promises a possible transformation. It is an open gate to change . . . But what change it is? What was shocking in this scene with a chicken was treating it as if it were trash. A living sentient being is not a thing! Being thrown like trash does not apply to animals, but . . . Is it really true in our world where animals' dead bodies or even live animals are thrown away like rubbish? One-day-old male chickens are ground alive as a side product of the fabrication process. When a plague is suspected the whole herds of pigs are buried alive. In our world animals are treated in this way–like trash, on a massive scale. The source of a child's shocking experience finds its vivid continuation and is still present in how our world works. (A. Kacperczyk, protocol, March 13, 2019)

Human Beings as Trash Creators

Trash is a shadow of any human activity. As William Rathje and Cullen Murphy emphasize, "the creation of garbage is an unequivocal sign of a human presence"

(Rathje/Murphy 1992, p. 10).[7] Every form of "doing" produces some waste as a side effect of the undertaken action. Hairdressing, shopping, eating, writing – in the majority of human activities, trash production to a greater or lesser extent is always involved. And usually in all of these situations trash is noticed not as a central trait of the activity but rather as its side effect, something unessential – and just because of this – expendable. Whatever you do, you will become part of waste-producing process. And probably you throw away dozens of items every day (Rathje/Murphy 1992).

The act of trash creating assumes throwing something away, which may be negatively appraised in the context of environmental contamination and *zero waste* ideology. But we must remember that getting rid of unnecessary or superfluous items remains a universal human practice that has also a strong ritual character and somehow plays an adaptive function as a way of coping with a surplus.

Another dimension of creating trash is fulfilling the social norm of purity and keeping order. Trash comes then from the process of cleaning and tidying up. People create it in the act of removing something dirty, greasy, rotten, rancid, mildewed, or decayed. All the means and cleaners being used during this process also become dirty and usually land in the garbage, which means that somehow dirt creates dirt. So, trash might be seen as a side effect of straightening up and an immediate product of cleaning practices, and more broadly as a by-product of the order creation. As Susan Strasser argues "we consider rotting and rancid organic material impure–though the line between rancid and not, edible and spoiled, pure and impure is a matter for cultural and personal debate" (Strasser 1999, p. 4).

In the culture of discardable things, many items that could be good and needed just a moment ago change their definition in one second after being used and become trash. Keeping the plastic cup in your hand, you know that in a minute it will land in the garbage.[8]

---

7 On this assumption the entire domain of garbage archaeology (garbology) is established. Complementary premises state that discarded items "are relics of specific human activities," and that garbage is not a concept nor an assertion but physical artifact that can testify about facts and events and this way set the record straight (Rathje/Murphy 1992, pp. 11–12; Pessel 2006).
8 It is estimated that the average amount of time that a plastic carrier bag is used is only 12 minutes (5Gyres n.d., par. 1). However Matt Wilkins in his article "More Recycling Won't Solve Plastic Pollution" (2018) states that blaming wasteful consumers for the plastic problem is wrong, since the real problem lays in the very idea of producing disposable plastic items which are used only for minutes "but can persist in the environment for half a millennium." He defines it as "an incredibly reckless abuse of technology" and states that "encouraging individuals to recycle more will never solve the problem of a massive production of single-use plastic that should have been avoided in the first place" (Wilkins 2018).

This mode of trash production is largely a matter of consumption patterns established in the Western World. The way people buy and use things in our culture creates situations where disposable items (like cups, straws, stirrers, spoons, forks, knives) seem to be a convenient option. *Time, comfort, relative cheapness* and *easiness* remain important dimensions of the practice of buying and discarding. In the society where mass production of disposable items is directly related to its mass consumption, people do not bother their minds by carrying extra packing, shopping bags, cutlery or vessels. In this case, to buy an item necessarily means creating trash just after the act of using. That pushes consumers to be an active part of the trash over-producing system. In this sense, the reason for excess waste is just excess buying. Vance Packard (1960) discussed the subject of planned obsolescence practices and "throwaway" products as early as 1960, warning that changes in product design and packaging would lead to a waste crisis.

Overproduction and overconsumption of the Western World generate both large landfills and the cluttering of the households. As Jeanne E. Arnold and collaborators Anthony P. Graesch, Enzo Ragazzini, and Elinor Ochs (2012) displayed in their visual anthropological study *Life at Home in the Twenty-First Century*, the western civilization is literally "overstuffed." The phenomenon of the *middle-class abundance* is about cluttering houses with things being used as signs of the social position and status. The term "stuffocation" coined by James Wallman (2013) to name the syndrome of being suffocated by things that people gather, indicates the process of accumulating objects that for sure will turn into garbage someday.

Summarizing, trash production is a complex social process. Regardless of whether it arises as a product of particular trade or activity, or as an immediate product of cleaning practices, or as a side effect of consumption or surplus, it remains an inherent human practice of everyday life that affects living conditions on Earth.

The Essence of Trash

What is and what is not trash? How is this object of the Lifeworld sensed and conceptualized by humans? Generally, "trash" describes things that people discard and throw away; things that they refuse and separate from the class of clean, useful and valuable items.

The interesting cognitive shift occurs at the moment when people re-define items being used in everyday life as having no value anymore and decide to throw them away. This seems to be the general rule of trash production: changing the definition of the object from a thing that is needed and useful into something that has no value.

One may use various terms that denote trash: rubbish, waste, refuse, litter, garbage, debris, junk, dross, detritus, sweepings, dregs, or remains. Those synonyms generally describe "matter thrown away or rejected as worthless". Trash is defined as "something worth little or nothing," "something in a crumbled or broken condition or mass"; "debris from pruning or processing plant material," but also "things that are no longer useful or wanted". Trash is also a noun designating a container where people put things that are being thrown away. We use the term trash for "something that has very low quality" or "something of little or no value". We also easily define something as trash when it's broken or loses its prime features when it is old, battered, shabby, or blown, and when the connection between the thing and its meaning for someone is missing. It denotes worthless things, abandoned, exposed to the impact of natural processes of decay and decomposition; unnecessary, useless, broken or spoiled objects (Merriam Webster Dictionary n.d.). The dividing line between *trash* and *no-trash* lies in the definition of the object that is constructed by an individual on the base of particular features of the object, human actions addressed to it, or the place where the object is located:

- Trash is defined based on the objects' features:
    - when the object irreversibly lost its primary features;
    - when it is old, battered, shabby, or blown;
    - when it is spoiled, crumbled, or broken;
    - when it is rotting and rancid;
    - when it is impure, dirty;
    - when it stinks;
    - when it is not edible anymore; and
    - when it is toxic or dangerous (hazard waste).
- Trash is defined based on ones' action:
    - trash are things that people discard and throw away;
    - things that people refuse; and
    - objects or organic matter that is separated from the class of clean, useful and valuable items.
- Trash is defined by the place where it is located ("trash-place"):
    - trash are things in the dustbins, litter bins, dumpsters, garbage containers, or landfills;
    - the matter that is being transporting to these places; but also
    - "matter out of place" (Reno 2014, p. 3) as a special category that includes objects that should go to the proper containers or landfills but finish up in the rivers, in the fields, greenery space or the forest instead (Figure 2, 3).

Thus, what defines something as trash is the physical condition of the object, the very act of discarding it, and the place where one can find a given object.

Usually, a thing becomes trash when the object lost its meaning in the eyes of the person who assessed it, when the object is defined by someone as being not needed anymore, when it lost its previous function for someone, is broken or works improperly, or when the connection between the thing and its significance for someone is missing. As Susan Strasser asserts, "what counts as trash depends on who's counting. Our daily experience suggests that trash is a dynamic category. Objects move in and out of it in many ways" (1999, p. 3).

The definition of a given object as trash is based on a human appraisal. As a form of decision making, this process has mental character but is always related to three indispensable dimensions: the materiality of discarded thing, activity of the person who creates trash, and spatial dimension of the displaced object. The appraisal of the physical features of an object, the decision where to place it and the very act of discarding or keeping the thing meet together and finally define an object as *trash* or *no-trash*.

Figure 2, 3: Textile waste left by someone in the field, Poland.
From "Portal informacyjny Gminy Brójce – Jest poważny problem ekologiczny!" 2019 (https://www.brojce.pl/art,396,jest-powazny-problem-ekologiczny, visited on June 5, 2019.). Licensed under CC BY 4.0.

In both cases interesting shifts take place. One is the *separation* of the object from the one who owned or kept it until this moment. Second is the loss of *ownership*: a given object loses relation with its owner and becomes "nobody's thing." Losing property is problematic when it happened unintentionally–for example when we threw an engagement ring into the trash bin by accident or by inattention. The diamond ring that fell into the trash loses the owner at the moment the cleaning service removes the garbage. If someone will find it and define it as a treasure it will, in turn, regain the status of a valuable item. The object may be re-defined again and again until it is annihilated.

Losing contact with the thing is also to resign from our own responsibility for it–which is problematic particularly in the case of "matter out of place" (Reno 2014, p. 3). Such an instance of garbage being left in the forest usually assumes intentional detachment of the abandoned matter from the owner to not take responsibility. Although in some rare cases it works out to re-connect the trash with its owners again and force them to face the consequences.

Regardless of whether it is possible to determine the owner, waste found in the forest or greenery always indicate human action.

Covers and Layers: The Way of Creating More Trash

I am opening a new packet of herbal tea. Fennel in express bags arranged in a cardboard package. Very ecological product, but . . . the whole paper bag is additionally covered with a thin plastic foil. *What for?* I think. Could it not be enough if it was limited to a cardboard package? Would something happen with the content if it did not have this foil? Well, dust or dirt could get inside. So the foil responds to our need for cleanliness. It tells me a lot about the human idea of what is clean and what is not; and introduces the modes of conduct how to keep it clean.

Much of my household garbage is created in the same way–the problematic object is encapsulated with foil and this way separated from my senses, confined, inactivated, incapacitated. Covers and layers separate my own body from things that are harmful, dirty or messy: latex gloves that I use when cleaning, washing the toilet, scrubbing with irritants, replanting flowers.

But the layers also work the other way, in the opposite direction: when I scan old photographs and clichés to the archive, I use the gloves to stop my body secretions from destroying or marking an old photograph.

Covers and layers that separate objects from external agents also protect the internal features. The foil is there to keep the scent of the tea–to stop evaporation and perhaps also to keep the product dry . . . to keep the quality of the content intact.

(A. Kacperczyk, self-observation, April 7, 2019)

Creating trash is entwined with our cultural beliefs about what is clean and sterile, concerns about purity and dirt, our ideas of how to keep something clean and untouched, and finally what is valuable (the scent or other qualities of the product). But it also brings some paradoxes when the technology that can prolong the quality of the product and keep it fresh at the same time creates an additional artificial cover – very problematic for the environment. There are photos of bananas in the basket just prepared for sale. Each of the fruit lies on a polystyrene tray foiled and labeled with a bar code. These photos circulate on the Internet with the sentence in English or Spanish: "If you asked me to define human stupidity in just one image". Another example is the case of pre-peeled oranges put into plastic boxes in the Whole Foods Market stores. Nathalie Gordon published such a photo on Twitter with the comment: "If only nature would find a way to cover these oranges so we didn't need to waste so much plastic on them" (2016). The post in a few days has gotten 100,000 reactions and raised questions if natural products really need to be shrouded in plastic.[9]

Lobbyists for the plastic industry and producers of to-go containers are implicated in initiating the problematic situation related to excess packaging.[10] But certainly, people who are ready to buy them are also involved. Thus, it turns out that the problem with garbage is strongly entangled with the issue of packaging and the very idea of wrapping.

Trash on the Margins of Human Attention

Every business, every industry, every action to a greater or lesser extent produces garbage and has to deal with it. However most often trash functions on the margin of human attention as things we usually tend to ignore as irrelevant (Zerubavel 1997, p. 37), since people are instead focused on other relevant activities and tend to disconnect themselves from the nasty content of trash bins and garbage itself. Trash-related facilities like street litter bins, baskets, garbage cans, and dumpsters constitute permanent elements of the urban scenery and create a well-organized system of waste distribution but are ignored or overlooked by bystanders. They are neither interesting nor eye-catching objects (Figure 4) unless someone plans to get rid of his garbage. Then, they become the center of attention but just for a short time.

> Pisa, Italy, the city center in the morning, about 8.00 a.m. I see an aesthetic, tidy dustbin neutrally implemented in the city scenery. A woman approaches it with a white plastic trash bag in her hand. She brings an electronic card to the card reader at the front of the

---

9 The issue addresses many dimensions: one related to work which is done by someone, and for which other people are willing to pay, another addresses problems of people with limited hand dexterity who wouldn't be able to peel the fruit on their own. The short discussion on this subject by Katie Herzog (2016), "Here's why Whole Foods' pre-peeled oranges might not be as absurd as they sound."

10 Louis Blumberg and Robert Gottlieb in their book *War on Waste: Can America Win Its Battle with Garbage?* indicate the critical role of advertising in restructuring the waste issue: "Advertising became responsible, in part for the system's tendency toward overproduction and the elevation of waste generation into an essential byproduct of economic activity . . . advertising and marketing activities was most pronounced in influencing the role of packaging in the production system" (1989, p. 11).

Figure 4: Waste containers in public city space in Pisa, Italy.
Photo by the author, Anna Kacperczyk, March 9, 2018.

container and presses a special pedal to make the dumpster open. She quickly throws the garbage inside and releases the pedal to close the container. She turns and walks away. In the city center, one can find many facilities like dustbins, garbage cans, and dumpsters. They comprise a network of units that allow people to easily throw away their garbage. The bigger dumpsters are closed. Their content is hidden (as something valuable or as something disgusting?). Here in Pisa, the inhabitants have to pay to get access to garbage and use special electronic cards to open the city's dumpsters. The special foot pedal enables the opening of the container in the way that people may do not even touch the rubbish while dumping their trash bags. There are professionals who operate the receptacles with the content – people who will regularly empty containers and cans and remove litter from the streets.   (A. Kacperczyk, field note, March 9, 2018)

Trash circulation is institutionalized and professionalized. Regularly taken by services of cleansing departments, trash seems to be under control and the way people interact with trash is normalized. In well-developed waste management systems, the personal activity of humans as waste producers is reduced to dumping trash bag into the proper dustbin (often after paying for the access). In effect, people may feel they are "clean" at the moment they close the dumpster cover.

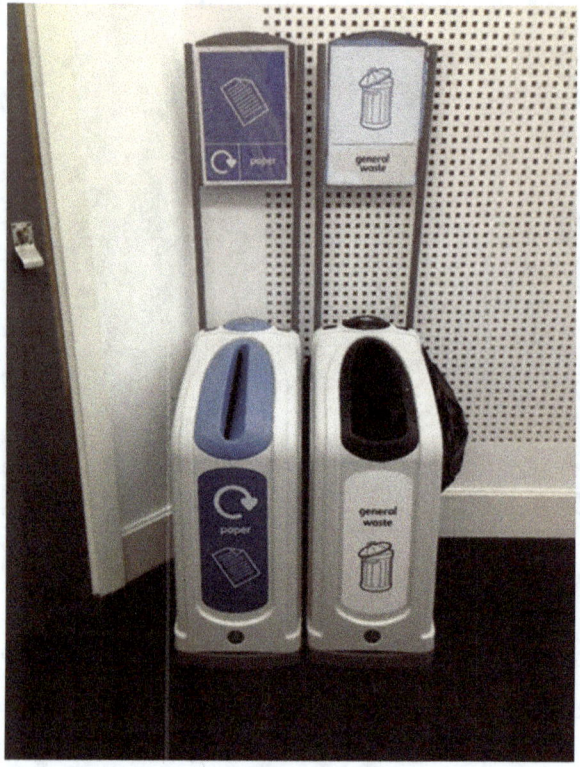

Figure 5: Aesthetic dustbins in the assembly hall at Lancaster University, Great Britain. Photo by the author, Anna Kacperczyk, July 5, 2018.

In this way, trash is effectively hidden in well-maintained public spaces, which may result in the tendency to marginalize environmental problems since people cannot see how much garbage they produce. Aesthetic bins (Figure 5) may help them easily disconnect their activities of trash production with the effects of these actions. The very fact that in the city the contents of the trash cans are not visible to bystanders – hidden from our view, nicely separated and encapsulated – may create an impression that the problem has been properly solved. Finally, garbage visually disappears. However, collecting waste in containers is only one step in the process of waste management, and the processing of trash itself remains not as effective as we would like to believe. Furthermore, in the city space we can easily observe reverse instances – litter bins overfilled with trash and surrounded by messy scattered waste.

Lifeworlds of Trash

Sometimes trash remains directly connected with the core of an activity and lie in the center of human perception. Usually, it happens when the activity requires taking trash into account or conscious decisions about trash is needed. There are realms of trash within the Lifeworld with their own relevances, the stocks of knowledge and vantage points brought by the members, with particular typifications and specific levels of awareness experienced and observed in the others.

Using a Schützian Lifeworld lens (Schütz 1962, 1975) one may distinguish many realms of trash Lifeworlds in which trash remains an object of attention: living and working in the landfill; the Lifeworld of dumpster divers; the world of waste management and scrap industries; the Lifeworld of illegal trash sellers or arsonist; the world of inhabitants trapped in the direct neighborhood of the trash-station. Also, the world of environmental activists committed to cleaning the planet, as well as the world of the garbage archaeologist (garbology world) for whom the landfill is the space of extensive investigation. In all of these situations, trash has to be taken into account and consciously processed during activity. The "mental processes of attending and ignoring" that are involved here are socially constructed and carried through social interaction (Zerubavel 1997, p. 11). "Attending something in a focused manner entails mentally disengaging it (as a 'figure') from its surrounding "ground," which we essentially ignored" (Zerubavel 1997, p. 35).

Living in the Landfill

There is the world of endless landfills and garbage dumps that create space for a source of life, nutrients, valuable objects of everyday use, a source of items that can be sold or re-used. This is a Lifeworld of millions of people in the world, the space of their lived experiences, everyday struggle and the very ground for their existence. It is estimated that around 15 million people around the globe live and work at garbage dumps, spending their lives within municipal rubbish tips "combing through trash every day for items of the slightest value to sell for a pittance" (England 2018). Rachel England in her article *Living in Landfill* describes the situation of these communities:

> Families–sometimes several at a time–live in shanties made from found wood and sheets of corrugated metal and plastic, with bricks and tires placed carefully on roofs to stop them blowing away. Surrounding these homes, stretching for as far as the eye can see and sometimes two or three stories high, are piles and piles of medical and electronic waste, used nappies and sanitary items, general household rubbish and broken glass, not to

mention dead animals and human feces. Under the burning sun the smell of these dumps is sickening, exacerbated by dark plumes of thick smoke billowing from piles of trash that have spontaneously combusted because of unstoppable rising methane gases. It is hell on earth, but trapped in an inescapable cycle of poverty, these people have no choice but to call it home.
(England 2018)

One can encounter a trash-picking community in the Philippines, India, Kenya, Cambodia, Brazil, and Ethiopia living on the fringes of society and at the heart of landfills. They live within and around the waste produced by others–the richer ones, better equipped and socially positioned. For trash-picking communities, the landfill is a Lifeworld. For people whose everyday experience is made by and within the trash, this is not just a place of dwelling, but a universe, a matter of life, and most often a place that defines them as irreversibly trapped:

> Waste pickers don't have access to hot water, or even running water, so there is always a smell, which makes it difficult for children to go to school or to then get jobs. And if they do get jobs–where they could earn up to 10 times as much as they do as a waste picker–it's still very difficult for them to make a break from the dump.
(England 2018)

The main relevances operating in the group comprise: surviving, getting food, feeding the family and animals, finding a shelter, finding valuable items. Sometimes: making a break out from the dump. Rarely: educating children, to give them a chance to avoid their parents' way of life.

The stocks of knowledge and vantage points brought by the members of these communities embrace the creation of the survival map of the landfill. People have to know where valuable goods can be found. But also, where dangerous spots are, and how to safely operate on the landfill. They must learn how to recognize safe and unsafe places while working to avoid deadly landslides when mountains of rubbish collapse. A garbage dump is a physically dynamic and unstable place where everything is changing day by day as tractors and trucks bring new layers of waste. The features of the landfill must be recognized to understand where it is dangerous, and where is safe. Kathleen M. Millar in her book *Reclaiming the Discarded: Life and Labor on Rio's Garbage Dump* describes hazardous situations to which *catadores* (people who collect and sell recyclables on the dump for a living) are exposed everyday:

> It was a tractor, Eva tells me. She had been collecting all night. By early morning, she was tired and her legs dragged, and she ended up slipping in front of a tractor that bulldozed a mound of garbage on top of her. She was buried. She couldn't breathe. The weight of all that garbage. The tractor driver did not see her fall, but luckily another catador noticed and grabbed her arm.
(Millar 2018, p. 2)

The other stocks of knowledge consist of information: how to construct a shelter, what is edible, and what is not, what is valuable, how to effectively work with garbage, whom to sell gathered goods, and who is in power? The typifications in operation in the group necessarily include "own people" and "strangers"; friends and allays or enemies, people in power, middleman, charity volunteers. Other subjects are community, recycling factories, social service and volunteer helpers, and sometimes social researchers or journalists.

Trash is the very matter of life here. It is what the world is made of. There is no escape outside the landfill. It feeds, gives maintenance, provides livelihood and, at the same time, kills. "The garbage dump thus appears as an end zone in a double sense: the burial grounds for unwanted things, the end of the line for urban poor" (Millar 2018, p. 4).

The World of Inhabitants Trapped in the Trash Neighborhood

There are other forms of trash occurrence, when people have to deal with the immediate vicinity of landfills or waste transfer stations: there is the suffocating and overwhelming stench of garbage, the toxic pollution of soil, water, and air, both from the garbage itself and from truck traffic. A documentary produced by members of Clean Up North Brooklyn shows how horrific the experience is for people living close to a waste transfer station. The inhabitants describe their neighborhood as "extremely disgusting and nasty," breathing in a "putrid, horrible smell," that is "overwhelming." "The smell is, is crazy. When in the morning you wake up, you can smell it. The smell is you lose the desire even to eat," says one resident. Another one asserts: "People don't realize how hard it is to live around here. The stink in the summer . . . you can't come outside your house" (Clean Up North Brooklyn 2015).

Toxic places like landfills, dumps, or places of garbage incineration that are institutionally created and controlled by garbage disposal companies represent the most unwanted form of space organization and planning–especially for their actual or potential neighbors. Residents do their best to avoid such a neighborhood, with its overwhelming stench, earth pollution, water contamination, inevitable toxic leaks, and ugliness. They would like to erase these places from their everyday life maps, but they cannot escape, and looking away is not enough.

The problem has many levels. First, it is obvious that the situation must affect the workers of these facilities too, as they have to work every day in these extremely difficult conditions doing dirty work for the rest of the community (Hughes 1962, p. 3). Second, it may be defined as environmental and racial injustice when some part of the city is overburden and has to deal with the waste from the more privileged parts (Bullard 1990; Cole/Foster 2001). "For decades, low-income communities and communities of color have handled a disproportionate burden of NYC's commercial waste" (Eddie Bautista, Executive Director of the New York City Environmental Justice Alliance as quoted in Diaz 2015). And this goes together with real health consequences for the disadvantaged residents who report "far higher rates of emergency room visits and hospitalizations for asthma than the rest of the borough and New York City" (Diaz 2015; Gibbs 1982).

At the local level, there is always the question of what to do with garbage, where to store it. Some groups with more resources and power may constitute a lobby which continually influences urban planning to remove the foul-smelling problem as far away from them as possible. Other disadvantaged groups must bear the burden and suffer "under a system in which only a few neighborhoods handle the vast majority of the entire city's garbage" (Diaz 2015; Bullard 1990; Cole/Foster 2001). So, this is another example of how trash exists in the human world and the meaning which is attached to trash–as toxic pollution and an environmental burden that indeed divides society (Saha/Mohai 2005, p. 618; Bryant 1995; Davy 1997).

What does oppression mean here? It relies on having sufficient financial, technical and legal resources to push unwanted garbage into the place where the inhabitants–people and animals–will not be able to effectively apply for their rights. This is how environmental injustice arises. And this is how the lack of empathy, understanding the position of others creates and sustains Deathworlds.

The World of Scrap Industry and Waste Management

Another realm is inhabited by agents and scrap dealers that belong to the wide world of the scrap industry and solid waste managers. There are appropriate technology and measures employed in the activity. This world of trash is just a part of lived experience, in so far as they are an object of work and professional engagement.

No one wants to have garbage on their land. However, the very fact that any entity needs to dispose of trash creates a supply-demand tension between those who want to get rid of it and those who are willing to accept it but for an adequate amount of money. If one can sell something, and someone is going to pay for it, then it has a measurable monetary value.

Hence the process of relocating trash starts, sending it via road or rail to landfill, to the garbage dump outside the city, out of the state, out of the country or even out of the continent. What becomes the subject of trading here is not the garbage itself but the service of its removal and storage, and, indirectly, the legal obligations toward trash management.

However, trash is also purchased.[11] The basic value of trash is the value of the material it is made of–plastic, paper, glass, copper, aluminum, and other metals that may be re-used as raw materials again–or the value of products that might be created from it–like biogas which, when burned, produces heat or electricity.

The recycling companies which are recipients and processors of industrial waste operate with bulky large dimension waste carried by big trucks. Waste is professionally prepared for further processing (Figure 6) and then sale as a commodity–a raw material:

> We are mainly focused on servicing, building and shaping waste management for our clients who are institutional ones–they are factories. All our plants are strongly focused on serving these clients in terms of the appropriate fractions that are emerging. Our core fractions, which we deal with it is paper and foil. So, for example, printing houses bring rolls of paper, or something is packed, or if we have logistics centers, these fractions are often together, they arise somewhere together. For example, we now have a large printing house that has 500 tons of waste of three different grades of paper a month, and 20 tons of foil. And for this we use baler-type machines and a sorting line . . . because the foil also splits. This white foil is a *positive fraction*. Well, there was once a color foil, that is, such admixtures of various types. Only now it is treated as a *negative faction*, where we already collect money from the client to take it from him, because it is very difficult to sort it. And besides, the types of this foil are very different in this. This is not pure PTE foil. There are still some customers who play in the production of this granulate for such a film, it is not known what color, and there you can get some little money for it, and then this is the negative fraction. On the other hand, we generally receive it for PLN 1, or if it is of terrible quality, it is not enough, as it will be dirty with some kind of meat, such as from meat plants, or something, then it is absolutely negative fraction.
>
> (manager and investor in waste management company, interview, July 19, 2019)

In this instance, waste is an object of work and professional engagement in the scrap industry, waste management, processing, and recycling. Waste has a countable value. A worker who guided me around the recycling plant and showed me bales of paper and foil just prepared for shipment and further processing affirmed with the deep conviction: "This is not trash–this is money."

---

11 As the Institute of Scrap Recycling Industries reports, in 2016, the United States "exported over 37 million metric tons of scrap commodities valued at $16.5 billion to 155 countries around the world" (ISRI 2017, par. 1). See also Adam Minter's *Junkyard Planet: Travels in the Billion-Dollar Trash Trade* (2013).

Figure 6: Compacted paper prepared for processing in the recycling station, Poland. Photo by the author, Anna Kacperczyk, July 19, 2019.

Being Part of the Problem

From the very beginning, my motivation to investigate trash wavered from having a very enthusiastic attitude or even an internal compulsion to deal with this topic, to surrender caused by the feeling of helplessness and the bleakness of the project in the face of the magnitude of the problem, its marginalization, and at the same time the banality of the studied activities and practices. In some way, these feelings reflect the essence of the matter of garbage.

Trash functions in the field of intersecting continua of visibility–invisibility, reflective reference–lack of reflection, banality–originality; the innocence of daily acts–and a sinister force destroying the planet. However, the most complicated issue of this study is the fact that each of these dimensions of treating trash concerns me personally. As a human being I am part of the problem–not just the one involved in the study, but the one that digests the planet.

Trash might be seen as too invisible, too banal, too marginal, or too intimate to be the object of serious research. But it is also difficult to write about problems that you are a part of, especially when it touches you personally and reveals how entangled you are in the matter. Research reflection on these problems arose in the course of my everyday practices and the continuing uncertainty about the correctness of my procedures with rubbish, but also from my relationships with objects.

Although my commitment to this project stems from a sense of responsibility for my own garbage and concern for the planet in the face of environmental contamination, it seems that despite all of the good intentions, I cannot cope with it on my own. The overflow of trash and the plastic pollution in the oceans need to be solved with global efforts and supranational decisions; this is a matter of the scale of the problem, which lies in a mass of events, not in individual actions. However, the importance of the issue and its ubiquity raises my research commitment; the conviction that I could do very little in this case somehow lowers my motivation. And it is small solace that it is not only me but all of us, our lifestyle, our daily activities and everyday conduct, that sustain the problem and are a significant part of it.

Another aspect that diminished my research enthusiasm was the tension between acting and knowledge-producing. This is, firstly, because stating the facts about littering does not exhaust the moral obligation that I feel. Should we make a map of the dumps in the forest instead of liquidating them? Does it make sense when action is needed? Of course, conducting the research is also a form of taking action, which indirectly can promote environmental awareness. But still, will this study serve the planet better than rolling up one's sleeves and cleaning up the spot? Such thoughts come to mind. And I still wonder whether it is better to write an article or if it would be more productive to go out and pick up some litter. To research or to act directly? I hope that searching for the answers through a sociological study and "being the change that we want to see in the world" are not mutually exclusive.

However, the most difficult moments of despair during the research process at hand appear with the feeling of uncertainty that we can still "save the Planet." Is there still a chance for that? And will we make it?

References

Arnold, Jeanne E./Graesch, Anthony P./Ragazzini, Enzo/Ochs, Elinor (2012): *Life at Home in the Twenty- First Century*. Los Angeles: The Cotsen Institute of Archaeology Press.
Augé, Marc (1995): *Non-Places: Introduction to an Anthropology of Supermodernity* (J. Howe, Trans.). New York, London: Verso.
Bentz, Valerie M./Rehorick, David/Marlatt, James/Nishii, Ayumi/Estrada, Carol (2018): "Transformative Phenomenology as an Antidote to Technological Deathworlds". In: *Schützian Research* 10, pp.189–220.
Blumberg, Louis/Gottlieb, Robert (1989): *War on Waste: Can America Win Its Battle with Garbage?* Washington DC, Covelo: Island Press.
Bryant, Bunyan (Ed.) (1995): *Environmental Justice: Issues, Policies, and Solutions*, Washington: Island Press.
Bullard, Robert D (1990): *Dumping in Dixie. Race, Class, and Environmental Quality*. Boulder: Westview Press.
Cancalosi, John (2013): "Stork in a bag". Retrieved from https://www.nature-photography.us/stork-in-a-bag/, visited on August 28, 2019.
Clean Up North Brooklyn (2015): *Brooklyn Transfer* [Video file]. Retrieved from https://vimeo.com/146860761, visited on July 1, 2018.
Cole, Luke W./Foster, Sheila R. (2001): *From the Ground Up: Environmental Racism and the Rise of the Environmental Justice Movement*. New York: New York University Press.
Davy, Benjamin (1997): *Essential Justice: When Legal Institutions Cannot Resolve Environmental and Land Use Disputes*. New York: Springer-Verlag Wien.
Diaz, Christina (2015): "Brooklyn Trash Problems". From *CUNY Academic Works*. Retrieved from https://academicworks.cuny.edu/gj_etds/80, visited on June 11, 2018.
England, Rachel (2018): "Living in Landfill". From *The Independent*, March 18, 2017. Retrieved from https://www.independent.co.uk/news/long_reads/living-in-landfill-a7632996.html, visited on April 11, 2019.
5Gyres (n.d.): "Plastic Bags." Retrieved from https://www.5gyres.org/plastic-bags/, visited on August 27, 2018.
Gibbs, Lois Marie (1982): *Love Canal: My Story*. Albany: State University of New York Press.
Gibson, James J. (1977): "The Theory of Affordances". In: Shaw, Robert/Bransford, John (Eds.): *Perceiving, Acting, and Knowing*. New York, Toronto: Lawrence Erlbaum Associates Publishers, pp. 67–82.
Gibson, James J. (1979): *The Ecological Approach to Visual Perception*. New York, Toronto: Lawrence Erlbaum Associates Publishers.
Glaser, Barney G./Strauss, Anselm L. (1967): *The Discovery of Grounded Theory: Strategies for Qualitative Research*. Chicago: Aldine Publishing CO.
Gordon, Nathalie [@awlilnaty] (2016): If only nature would find a way to cover these oranges so we didn't need to waste so much plastic on them. Tweet, March 3, 2016. Retrieved from https://twitter.com/awlilnaty/status/705375555030556672, visited on October 8, 2020.
Habermas, Jürgen. (1985): "The Theory of Communicative Action". Volume Two: Lifeworld and System: A Critique of Functionalist Reason, trans. Thomas McCarthy. Boston: Beacon Press.

Herzog, Katie (2016): "Here's why Whole Foods' pre-peeled oranges might not be as absurd as they sound". From *Grist*, March 7, 2016. Retrieved from https://grist.org/food/heres-why-whole-foods-pre-peeled-oranges-might-not-be-as-insane-as-they-sound/, visited on October 8, 2020.

Hughes, Everett C. (1962): "Good People and Dirty Work". In: *Social Problems* 10. No.1, pp. 3–11.

ISRI (2017): *Annual Report*. Online from Institute of Scrap Recycling Industries, Inc. Retrieved from http://www.isri.org/docs/default-source/default-document-library/2017annual-reportcb62f91e8fb866e3af13ff0000e99eee.pdf?sfvrsn=0, visited on September 18, 2018.

Jordan, Chris (2018): "The Midway Project". Retrieved from https://www.albatrossthefilm.com/, visited on August 28, 2019.

Jordan, Chris (n.d.): "Our Story". Retrieved from https://www.albatrossthefilm.com/ourstory, visited on August 29, 2019.

Kennedy, Greg (2007): *An Ontology of Trash. The Disposable and its Problematic Nature*. New York: State University of New York Press.

Konecki, Krzysztof T. (2018): "The Problem of Ontological Insecurity. What Can We Learn from Sociology Today? Some Zen Buddhist Inspirations". In: *Przegląd Socjologii Jakościowej* 14. No. 2, pp. 50–83.

Konecki, Krzysztof T. (2019): "Visual Images and Grounded Theory Methodology". In: Bryant, Tony/Charmaz, Kathy (Eds.): *Current Developments in Grounded Theory*. Los Angeles: Sage, pp. 352–373.

Konecki, Krzysztof T./Kacperczyk, Anna/Chomczyński, Piotr/Albarracín, Marco (2013): *The Spirit of Communitarianism and the Cultural Background of Limoncocha community in the Context of Sustainable Development and Environment Protection*, Quito: Universidad International SEK.

Merriam-Webster Dictionary (n.d.): "Trash". Retrieved from https://www.merriam-webster.com/dictionary/trash, visited on October 8, 2020.

Millar, Kathleen M. (2018): *Reclaiming the Discarded: Life and Labor on Rio's Garbage Dump*. Durham, London: Duke University Press.

Minter, Adam (2013): *Junkyard Planet: Travels in the Billion-Dollar Trash Trade*. New York, London, New Delhi, Sydney: Bloomsbury Press.

Packard, Vance (1960): *The Waste Makers*. New York: David McKay Company.

Pessel, Wlodzimierz K. (2006): "Rubbish as informants: a cultural contribution to Polish 'Garbeology'". From *Anthropology Matters Journal* 8. No. 1. Retrieved from https://www.anthropologymatters.com/index.php/anth_matters/article/view/79/284, visited on November 24, 2018.

"Portal informacyjny Gminy Brójce – Jest poważny problem ekologiczny!" (2019): Retrieved from https://www.brojce.pl/art,396,jest-powazny-problem-ekologiczny), visited on June 5, 2019.

Rathje, William/Murphy, Cullen (1992): *Rubbish! The Archaeology of Garbage*. New York: Harper Collins Publishers.

Rehorick, David Allan/Bentz, Valerie Malhotra (Eds.) (2008): *Transformative Phenomenology: Changing Ourselves, Lifeworlds, and Professional Practice*. New York: Lexington Books.

Rehorick, David/Bentz, Valerie (Eds.) (2017): *Expressions of Phenomenological Research: Consciousness and Lifeworld studies*. Santa Barbara: Fielding University Press.

Reno, Joshua Ozias (2014): "Toward a New Theory of Waste: From 'Matter out of Place' to Signs of Life". In: *Theory Culture Society* 31. No. 6, pp. 3–27.
Saha, Robin/Mohai, Paul (2005): "Historical Context and Hazardous Waste Facility Siting: Understanding Temporal Patterns in Michigan". In: *Social Problems* 52. No. 4, pp. 618–648.
Schütz, Alfred (1962): "On Multiple Realities". In: Natanson, Maurice (Ed.): *Collected Papers I, The Problem of Social Reality*. The Hague: Martinus Nijhoff, pp. 207–259.
Schütz, Alfred (1975): *Alfred Schütz on Phenomenology and Social Relations*. Helmut R. Wagner (Ed.). Chicago: The University of Chicago Press.
Strasser, Susan (1999): *Waste and Want: A Social History of Trash*. New York: Henry Holt and Company.
The Guardian (2018): "Whale dies from eating more than 80 plastic bags". Retrieved from https://www.theguardian.com/environment/2018/jun/03/whale-dies-from-eating-more-than-80-plastic-bags#img-1, visited on August 28, 2019.
van Manen, Max (2016): *Phenomenology of Practice. Meaning-Giving Methods in Phenomenological Research and Writing*. London, New York: Routledge.
Wallman, James (2013): *Stuffocation: Living More with Less*. United Kingdom: Penguin Books.
Weisberg, Barry (1970): *Ecocide in Indochina*. San Francisco: Canfield Press.
Wilkins, Matt (2018): "More Recycling Won't Solve Plastic Pollution". From *Scientific American*, July 6, 2018. Retrieved from https://blogs.scientificamerican.com/observations/more-recycling-wont-solve-plastic-pollution/, visited on August 27, 2018.
Zerubavel, Eviatar (1997): *Social Mindscapes: An Invitation to Cognitive Sociology*. Cambridge: Harvard University Press.

Natalia Martini
Chapter 5
Walking with Homeless Persons in Kraków and Łódź

Abstract: In this chapter, I reflect on the (im)possibilities of understanding the experiences of others. I ground my reflections through walking with homeless people as part of my doctoral research project with the aim of discovering how the city as a socio-material phenomenon manifests itself in the course of their everyday lives. I accompanied homeless urbanites along their habitual paths through the city with the assumption that through embodied and reflective immersion into their lived urban worlds I would get closer to the way in which they experience the city. In this chapter I discuss the challenges posed by the operationalization of this premise, focusing on, in particular, accessing and sharing the lived experiences while walking with others. I detail the process of overcoming these challenges through phenomenological writing which has helped me develop an enriched awareness of the nature of walking as a mode of experiencing and a way of knowing. In so doing, I comment on how to approach research walks with a phenomenological attitude and how this approach contributes to a better understanding of the method itself, as well as the insights it provides.

Keywords: research walks, urban homeless, phenomenological writing

> To experience is to learn.
> – Yi-Fu Tuan, *Space and Place: The Perspective of Experience*, 1977.

To Walk, to Walk With, and to Walk Through . . .

I frequently move around the city on foot. I walk from my apartment to a local farmers' market, or from my workplace to a nearby café. Walking serves me as a means of locomotion between different sites in the city. As an ordinary activity in my everyday life, I usually perform walking with "an absence of conscious attention" (Wunderlich 2008, p. 127). But walking is also one of my favorite leisure activities. I go for a walk when I need to unwind, or when I need to think. In this instance, walking "delineates a separable time-space that attains its own positivity" (Radley et al. 2010, p. 26). It becomes a chosen activity that I consciously perform. For relaxation. And for its own sake.

For homeless people too, walking is a way of getting around the city. They, too, perform recreational walking. They, too, walk for pleasure, or to pass the time. But walking that homeless people do is also defined by the condition of *placelessness* (Kawash 1998), a summative effect of various attempts to eradicate, or at least control, homeless people's presence in the city. From the establishment of the laws that "prohibit particular activities or behavior such as laying down or sitting in particular places, urinating, squeegeeing, panhandling" (Kawash 1998, pp. 326–327). Through forcible removal or physical harassment enacted by private security staff guarding semi-public spaces such as shopping malls, to design "innovations" such as "bum-proof" benches (Davis 1992). And, less blunt, but equally remarkably effective displays of social opprobrium and disgust (Mathews 2019). Thus, "for many people who live on the streets, walking becomes something of a way of life" (Radley et al. 2010, p. 36). An activity enforced by exclusion.

Despite differences, walking belongs to a set of routines that make up our (both mine and homeless dwellers') everyday urban lives. We walk. We move along by putting one foot in front of the other. We walk "to go to," "to get," and "to get to" (Radley et al. 2010). We traverse the city to pursue our daily lives. The sites where our activities take place are spread across this space. While doing this we also move from place to place, where place does not refer to location, but practical engagement with the urban environment. Through walking, we "immerse ourselves and dwell" in the city (Wunderlich 2008, p. 127). We experience it. Out of this recursive immersion grows our familiarity with the city. Not as a spatial unit, but as a spatiality (Heidegger 1996; Schatzki 2010), that is a lived-in environment. Along the paths of our routine daily walks, our experiences of the city as a Lifeworld accumulate, as well as our "practical wisdom" that comes from living through these experiences (van Manen 1984). Along these trails that delineate the urban milieu, which is experientially learned and known, the city manifests itself to us as a phenomenon.

I incorporated this philosophy that underpins walking as a Lifeworld activity (Wunderlich 2008), and its relation to the phenomenal constitution of the city, into my research practice. I was interested in the potential of walking as a method for yielding insights into how the city as a socio-material phenomenon manifests itself in the course of everyday lives of homeless dwellers. In taking walks with homeless urbanites I aimed at immersing myself in their Lifeworlds to better understand their lived experiences of the city. Between March 2018 and June 2019, I accompanied 36 homeless persons along their habitual paths in two Polish cities, Kraków and Łódź.[1]

---

[1] Research reported in this chapter was approved by the Ethics Committee of the Department of Philosophy of the Jagiellonian University and supported by the Polish National

In doing so, I not only walked *with* them, but also walked *through* with them, or rather was walked through the cities by them as my co-walkers were guiding me through their ways of navigating these urban environments. I framed these walks in terms of practical training in homeless urbanism–a way in which the city is both inhabited by homeless people and produced through that inhabiting (McFarlane 2011). The walks taught how to attend to the urban environment in a way that homeless dwellers do, so I could encounter the city as a phenomenon, as it presents itself in the experience. Not mine, but theirs.

In the remainder of this chapter I recount how this encounter between me, and the city experienced by the homeless, happened, and with what effect. As well as how a phenomenological attitude that emerged through phenomenological writing contributed to its happening (Sokolowski 2000; van Manen 1984). I do so through sharing and commenting on phenomenological protocols – experiential descriptions of my walks with homeless persons – written as part of the From Strangers to Collaborators project.[2]

Walking Through the Lived Experience . . .

In keeping with the methodological assumptions underpinning *walking with* in research practice, I relied on my own lived experience as a basis from which to learn empathetically about the experiences of homeless persons with whom I walked (Pink 2007). At first, I struggled with the "mechanics" of empathetic

---

Science Centre under grant no. 2016/23/N/HS6/00810. Detailed information about the research project can be retrieved from https://homelesscity.project.uj.edu.pl/, visited on October 12, 2020.

2 A multi-national and multi-institutional participatory action research project "From Strangers to Collaborators: Building a Community-of-Practice Through Transformative Phenomenology and Contemplative Research Across Cultures," led by Valerie Malhotra Bentz and James Marlatt, (Fielding Graduate University) and Krzysztof Konecki (University of Łódź), and included doctoral students from the University of the Virgin Islands. It ran between February and May 2019 with the aim of developing a community-of-practice focused on consciousness-raising for social and ecological justice through training in Transformative Phenomenology–a somatic-hermeneutic phenomenology, founded on the eidetic phenomenology of Edmund Husserl, the social phenomenology of Alfred Schütz, the embodied phenomenology of Maurice Merleau-Ponty, the ontologic-existential phenomenology of Martin Heidegger, and the reflective hermeneutic methods of Hans-Georg Gadamer, and put into action in the Lifeworld (Nishi/Marlatt 2018; Rehorick/Bentz 2008, 2017).

learning. In particular, I grappled with the operationalization of the assumption that *walking with* will lead to a shared set of lived experiences (Kusenbach 2003; O'Neill/Hubbard 2010; Pink 2007), that is a shared set of "direct feelings, thoughts, and bodily awareness" (Bentz/Rehorick 2008, p. 3) of the city. These concerns are reflected in the description of the first walk I completed:

> Protocol 1: The earliest experience of walking with homeless people
>
> I'm sitting with Sławek in a church. It's very quiet. Apart from us, there are maybe two other people here. We are behind the door, in the vestibule, sitting on a stone bench under which there is a radiator. We entered the church to rest a little. We had been walking around the neighborhood for over two hours. In the rain.
>
> I am (?), We are (?)–how do I know what he is experiencing?–soaked and cold. I'm wearing a winter jacket with a hood, a scarf and a hat. I've trekking boots on my feet. Even so, I'm a little bit cold. Sławek is wearing old dress shoes, thin tracksuit trousers and a jacket with a broken zip. He lost his hat somewhere. He has been swearing at it all day. Damn hat!
>
> Sławek pulls out a mineral water bottle, which he had been carrying around through the whole walk, and takes a sip. He asks me if I want one. I realize it's not mineral water that he's drinking. I recognize by the smell that it's vodka. No, thank you, I respond, I don't drink. This is not entirely true. After all, I will sometimes have a glass of wine at dinner, or a shot of "plum with lemon" in a pub. But this is a different kind of drinking. Compared with Sławek's, it's not drinking at all.
>
> I sit next to him on a bench in a church, I appreciate the heat emitted by a radiator. I relax my back muscles, which for most of the time are tense. They are part of a tense body, a body that stays alert. I smell the smell of old, damp clothes. I smell the smell of an unwashed body, and cheap, strong cigarettes. I notice that Sławek often scratches himself. Fleas? Scabies? Possible. I wonder how this affects his experience of this particular moment. How it is like for him to sit here, next to me.
>
> But I don't ask.

Phenomenologically speaking, through walking as a mode of experiencing the world around us, a "sensuous interrelationship of body-mind-environment" (Howes 2005, p. 7) is being established. Or to put it differently, "walking, ideally, is a state in which the mind, the body, and the world are aligned, as though they were three characters finally in conversation together, three notes suddenly making a chord" (Solnit 2001, p. 5). What if there are two minds, I was asking myself, two bodies, and two worlds? Is it possible for two different sets of three notes to suddenly make a chord? In other words, is it possible for my body-mind-environment interrelationship to align with the interrelationship of a homeless person with whom I am taking a walk? Is it possible for us to share a lived experience while walking together, while moving along on foot together, given that not only our minds and environments are different, but even our feet? Mine are of a relatively healthy, physically fit person, while some of my homeless co-walkers were affected by frostbite or neuropathy.

I gradually developed a way of experiencing walking together. Not by way of solely empathizing, but as a communicative activity. I connected to my co-walkers' lived experiences through a dialectical process that involved attentive attunement to my own lived experience (auto-observation), verbal articulation of what has been sensed, felt, and thought by me, and dialogical comparison of what it was like for them. In the case of the walk with Sławek, *I didn't ask*. I was skeptical about the possibility of consciously registering the manifold of the immediate sensations, subtle emotions, and fleeting reflections that make up a lived experience, and the possibility of putting them into words. But having intentionally focused my attention on various dimensions of lived experiences and describing them whilst writing phenomenological protocols, I had become more capable of doing that whilst walking.

Once I had become more capable of registering and articulating what I had been experiencing, *I started to ask*. Whether it was a physical sensation, like cold, an emotional state like the joy of eating instant noodles after a whole day of scavenging for empty bottles, or a complex situation like a street check, I would mindfully live through it and then deliberately reflect on it (Rehorick 1986). In dialogue with my co-walker, I entered a conversational process of meaning-making in which we would both assist each other in "overcoming the poverty of our language for describing subjective experience" (Petitmengin 2006, p. 253). At times I would have to pose an initial question that would propel the process of articulation and sense-making. At times the lived situations themselves would prompt narratives about what has been sensed, felt, and thought. An alcoholic epileptic seizure described in Protocol 2. was one of those experiences:

Protocol 2: The most poignant experience of walking with homeless people
I'm lying on a sofa in my apartment. My hair is still wet after a long, hot shower that I took right after coming back from the walk. I cover myself with a blanket. Not even for the warmth it gives, but for the feeling of being wrapped up. I'm tired, both physically and mentally. I had walked with Jadwiga and Tadeusz more than 11 kilometers within around 5 hours. My legs are numb from fatigue. I feel a burning in the quadriceps and glutes. I feel back pain. My eyes are dry and burning. This is how the body of a healthy physically fit 30-year-old, my body, was affected by one day in the homeless city. Not even the whole one. It was only a half a day of what is every day for Jadwiga and Tadeusz.
I go back in my thoughts to what I have experienced today. To the impressions from the visit to the vacant building, which Jadwiga and Tadeusz are living in. How I stand on an unfinished balcony with a view of the unfinished courtyard, which on the developer's advertising brochures is full of beautiful, happy people. How I sit in the Jadwiga's and Tadeusz's room immersed in the darkness. How I think about the sharp October sunshine that is behind the bricked-up window opening. How I try to forget about the stench of excrement. How, after an hour of sitting in their room, my jaw is numb from the cold. How while descending from the second floor, where their room is located, Jadwiga leads

me by the hand so that I wouldn't accidentally fall down an unsecured staircase. How I stick my back to the rough concrete wall and carefully take my steps.

I think back to circulating around the shopping mall and asking people for change. To this monotonous, ungrateful activity, in which I don't take part in order not to strike the job out for Jadwiga. Because I don't look like a homeless person. Both the homeless and the housed recognize it. Though not always. When we wander around the food court in the mall in search of a person who will buy us something to eat, I become an object of suspicious, controlling gaze of a security guard on an equal footing with Jadwiga and Tadeusz. On an equal footing with Jadwiga and Tadeusz I'm finally thrown out from the mall after we sat on sofas to rest for a while.

I come back to how we go around the mall again so that Jadwiga can gather enough change for beer, cigarettes, and candles. How we take 5 steps forward, 3 backward, 6 forward, 2 backward. How boring it is. How the wind begins to strongly blow and my head starts to hurt. How I want to enter the mall to hide from the wind, at least for a moment, but I know I can', because security is circling around inside. How, at some point, I begin to lose my patience and start to ask Jadwiga and Tadeusz "And now what? What's next? What's the plan? Where are we going?" And how in response they say "Maybe here, or maybe there . . . Maybe we will have dinner if someone will buy if for us."

I think back to how I sit with Jadwiga at a bus stop in front of a lunch bar and wait for Tadeusz, who went to arrange something to eat. How, at some point, Jadwiga shrinks within herself, says that she's feeling faint and landslides on the sidewalk. How I kneel on the sidewalk with her head on my knees, with my hands pressing her tiny convulsing body to the ground. How cars and buses pass by us. How people pass by us. And how we, in all that hustling and bustling, are trying to go through an alcoholic epileptic seizure. Me, a sociologist conducting a study on the city experienced by the homeless, and she, a homeless inhabitant of the city whose experiences I'm trying to apprehend.

Ad hoc explication (Petitmengin 2006) and dialogical sharing of lived experiences were not the only challenges I faced while walking with homeless urbanites. The multitude and the variety of experiences were also challenging. As depicted in Protocol 2, there was walking, and sitting, feeling hungry, and eating, earning, and buying, visiting vacant buildings, and window shopping, laughing, and swearing. And the list could go on. I was struggling with what to focus my attention on. The *whatness* of what to get at (Bentz/Rehorick 2008).

. . . And Making Sense of It

In the later stage of my research, after I stopped walking, I focused on how the walks made me experience the city differently. Writing about *walking* while contrasting it with *walking with* helped me to distill the essence of this difference was as illustrated by the excerpt from Protocol 3 and accompanying Figures 1–12.

Protocol 3: The phenomenon not present
   If I walked alone:
   I wouldn't comb through urban spaces in search of things I may use:

Figures 1, 2: Searching urban spaces.
Photo by the author, Natalia Martini, 2018.

I wouldn't know how (and how hard it is) to scavenge for empty bottles:

Figures 3, 4: Scavenging for bottles.
Photo by the author, Natalia Martini, 2018.

I wouldn't know the CCTV cameras' exact locations. I wouldn't even notice them:

Figures 5, 6: Looking for CCTV cameras.
Photo by the author, Natalia Martini, 2018.

I wouldn't know that through these doors those who are deemed "out-of-place" are being expelled from a certain shopping mall by security staff:

Figures 7, 8: Doors through which the homeless are expelled.
Photo by the author, Natalia Martini, 2018.

I wouldn't call this my favorite place:

Figures 9, 10: Unlikely favorite places.
Photo by the author, Natalia Martini, 2019.

Nor would I spend hours sitting there:

Figures 11, 12: Places I would not normally sit for long.
Photo by the author, Natalia Martini, 2019.

I wouldn't have to walk so much to meet my basic needs.
And I wouldn't cherish so much every moment when I wouldn't have to walk. . . .
I wouldn't focus on every detail of my environment.
I wouldn't feel tension in my body.
I wouldn't turn my fleeting perceptions into an object of my conscious attention.
I wouldn't feel overstimulated and overwhelmed.
I wouldn't articulate and discuss my lived experience of walking around the city, nor would I document it through photographing, note-taking, audio- and GPS-recording.

Reflecting on walking with homeless dwellers in such a manner, through employing polarities and reversals (Bentz/Rehorick 2008), illuminated the essential feature of my various encounters with the city as a socio-material phenomenon. It made me realize that in walking with homeless urbanites I experienced the city in an effortful way.

My way of experiencing the city while walking with homeless urbanites showed and required effort in two ways: as a lived method and a lived experience. First, it required physical and mental effort to overcome the natural attitude underlying walking as a routinely performed Lifeworld activity in order to transform it into a mode of knowing. It required, for instance, a stabilization of attention, heightened sensitivity of perception, articulation of sensations, emotions, reflections, and interpretation. As well as other activities, such as observing, interviewing, recording. That at the same time had to be skillfully kept in the background so as not to affect the natural unfolding of the events too much. The effort required by this transformation showed, for example, how walking as a lived method affected my body and bodily awareness, working almost like neurophysiological conditioning (Mare 2016). Second, my way of experiencing the city was effortful in a way in which it is for homeless dwellers. For it requires effort to maneuver through a matrix of social boundaries and material barriers (examples of which figure in the presented protocols). And this is what homeless dwellers do (though certainly not only) when they routinely walk around the city. They put an effort into what I conceptualized later on as "accomplishing place in the condition of placelessness" (Martini 2021).

This realization, achieved through phenomenological writing and further elaborated on through qualitative analysis, turned out to be crucial for my understanding of the city experienced by the homeless, as well as my awareness of how I have arrived at this understanding.

References

Bentz, Valerie M./Rehorick, David A. (2008): "Transformative Phenomenology: A Scholarly Scaffold for Practitioners". In: Rehorick, David A./Bentz, Valerie (Eds.): *Transformative Phenomenology: Changing Ourselves, Lifeworlds, and Professional Practice*. Lanham: Lexington Books, pp. 3–32.
Davis, Mike (1992): *City of Quartz: Excavating the Future in Los Angeles*. New York: Vintage.
Heidegger, Martin (1996): *Being and Time*. Albany: State University of New York Press.
Howes, David (2005): "Introduction". In: Howes, David (Ed.): *Empire of the Senses: The Sensual Culture Reader*. Oxford: Berg, pp. 1–17.
Kawash, Samira (1998): "The Homeless Body". In: *Public Culture* 10. No. 2, pp. 319–339.

Kusenbach, Margarethe (2003): "Street Phenomenology: The Go-Along as Eethnographic Research Tool". In: *Ethnography* 4. No. 3, pp. 455–485.
Mare, Christopher (2016): "Designing for Consciousness: Outline of a Neurophenomenological Research Program". In Bentz, Valerie/Giorgino, Vincenzo M. B. (Eds.): *Contemplative social research: Caring for Self, Being, and Lifeworld*. Santa Barbara: Fielding University Press, pp. 300–334.
Martini, Natalia (2021): Mooring in the Homeless City. A Practice Theoretical Account of Homeless Urban Dwelling and Emplacement". In: Qualitative Sociology Review 17. No. 3. Article Accepted for Publication.
Mathews, Vanessa (2019): "Reconfiguring the Breastfeeding Body in Urban Public Spaces". In: *Social & Cultural Geography* 20. No. 9, pp. 1266–1284.
McFarlane, Colin (2011): "The City as Assemblage: Dwelling and Urban Space". In: *Environment and Planning D: Society and Space* 29. No. 4, pp. 649–671.
Nishi, Ayumi/Marlatt, James (2018): "Transformative Phenomenology and us". E-Booklet. Retrieved from https://transformative-phenomenology-and-us.home.blog/, visited October 12, 2020.
O'Neill, Maggie/Hubbard, Phil (2010): "Walking, Sensing, Belonging: Ethno-mimesis as Performative Praxis". In: *Visual Studies* 25. No. 1, pp. 46–58.
Petitmengin, Claire (2006): "Describing One's Subjective Experience in the Second Person: An Interview Method for the Science of Consciousness". In: *Phenomenology and the Cognitive Sciences* 5. No. 3–4, pp. 229–269.
Pink, Sarah (2007): "Walking with video". In: *Visual Studies* 22. No. 3, pp. 240–252.
Radley, Alan/Chamberlain, Kerry/Hodgetts, Darrin/Stolte, Ottilie/Groot, Shiloh (2010): "From Means to Occasion: Walking in the Life of Homeless People". In: *Visual Studies* 25. No. 1, pp. 36–45.
Rehorick, David A. (1986): "Shaking the Foundations of Lifeworld: A Phenomenological Account of an Earthquake Experience". In: *Human Studies* 9. No. 4, pp. 379–391.
Rehorick, David A./Bentz, Valerie M. (Eds.) (2008): *Transformative Phenomenology: Changing Ourselves, Lifeworlds, and Professional Practice*. Lanham: Lexington Books.
Rehorick, David A./Bentz, Valerie M. (Eds.) (2017): *Expressions of Phenomenological research: Consciousness and Lifeworld Studies*. Santa Barbara: Fielding University Press.
Schatzki, Theodore (2010): *The Timespace of Human Activity: On Performance, Society, and History as Indeterminate Teleological Events*. Lanham: Lexington Books.
Sokolowski, Robert (2000): *Introduction to Phenomenology*. Cambridge: Cambridge University Press.
Solnit, Rebecca (2001): *Wanderlust: A History of Walking*. New York: Penguin Books.
Tuan, Yi-Fu. (1977): *Space and Place: The Perspective of Experience*. Minneapolis: University of Minnesota Press.
van Manen, Max (1984): "Practicing Phenomenological Writing". In: *Phenomenology + Pedagogy* 2. No. 1, pp. 36–69.
Wunderlich, F. Matos (2008): "Walking and Rhythmicity: Sensing Urban Space". In: *Journal of Urban Design* 13. No. 1, pp. 125–139.

Łucja Lange
Chapter 6
The Experience of Precognition

Abstract: The chapter presents the process of changing the understanding of the precognitive predictive awareness of death and birth through writing phenomenological protocols and sharing the story with students. Also, I show how I've moved from a dark gothic understanding of this ability, through a sense of solitude, to one of wholeness, using Max van Manen's advice on *Phenomenology of Practice: Meaning-Giving Methods in Phenomenological Research and Writing* (2016) as well as the approach of *Transformative Phenomenology* (Rehorick/Bentz 2008). The ability is somehow similar to an ouroboros in a metaphoric way – it reveals the cycle of life and death. In the process of discovering the meaning of the phenomena, I also compared the experience of other people, who share similar abilities – some of them accept them, others try to cope with them, but most deny their existence.

Keywords: precognitions, lived experience, Transformative Phenomenology

Introduction

In this chapter, I explore the experience of precognitions, showing how my perspective evolved during the phenomenological study based on Max van Manen's (1984, 2007, 2016, 2017) understanding of phenomenological research (lived experience, essence, attentive practice of thoughtfulness, search for what it means to be human, poetizing activity). I've noticed precognitions since I was about 18 years old. In my case, we discuss the ability to feel that a person (human and animal) will be dying soon (by illnesses, such as cancer or heart attack); that women will be pregnant soon (in the range of a year a child will be born); connecting to the death of people and animals in the sense that I can feel that someone died in a place or finding where the person was buried in the cemetery (without help and knowledge which direction to choose); or in feeling changes in my or someone else's life. In the beginning, I was not sure what has happened and what I should call it. I thought it would soon disappear. I have never liked this ability, and I was scared of it, but after one event I started to feel ashamed of being "not normal" and "not rational." I felt a bit strange. I started to isolate myself from people because when there are no people around, my phenomenon is not present. I have learned to live with it, but it can reappear at any time, and it turns my world upside down. My most poignant memory of the phenomenon blocked my research and caused me to take a break of several months. I have also tried to give that phenomenon a name and face – with the help of several photo sessions (done on my own) I managed to split myself, to accept the fact that I'm not only *me* (understood as a rational researcher, based in science) but also this phenomenon (understood as a paranormal or supernatural phenomenon based in nature and called the Black Queen). This "imaginative variation" about myself and the phenomenon helped me to shift from lack of acceptance for this uncomfortable ability and get a fresh and less judgmental perspective from a distance (Rehorick/Bentz 2008).

My goal is to show how my view on the concept of precognition was connected with negative feelings, other people's opinions, and Romantic Gothicism, and how it changed as I understood more about the roots of my opinion. I review the cultural and scientific understandings of the precognition to bracket it aside. This type of work gives me the possibility to see the experience, in the way Edmund Husserl (2001, p. 168) introduced as the "things themselves," how the phenomenon is given in the experience. The decision to explore this phenomenon led me through a spiritual experience – from something I could not feel good about to a transcendent feeling of liminality and solitude, the feeling of wholeness, and acceptance. I connected the phenomenon to a symbol – an ouroboros, and a state of mind – liminality. *Liminality* is Victor Turner's (1975, 1985, 1995) term referring to the rites of passage and the life-cycle ceremonies. But it is also the state "in-between" when a person is neither the same anymore, nor a new one. The *ouroboros* is an Ancient emblematic serpent eating its tail – a very popular alchemic symbol. "Ouroboros expresses the unity of all things, material and spiritual, which never disappear but perpetually change form in an eternal cycle of destruction and re-creation" (Britannica online n.d.).

The process of phenomenological writing has given me the possibility to dig into the precognitions and my feelings about them. I needed to rediscover and elucidate the way cultural and scientific views on precognitions preconditioned my understandings in order to get to the "essence" of the phenomenon. Husserl (1970) points out that human science is based almost exclusively on representations and formatted concepts. It means that the true essence of something stays behind the representations, and the adequate representations and knowledge we have is in our souls and bodies. It was not clear to me at the beginning how I felt in connection to them, but the first recollection brought me to an event which left me with two feelings: a) I was afraid because I felt something that I shouldn't feel; b) I was ashamed because of what I felt, and because it happened when my role was strictly scientific – I was a researcher in the field, interviewing someone important for my research. I wrote:

> I've stopped feeling my body. I started to feel afraid and wanted to run away. Not because I was in the same place where someone committed suicide, but because I felt that kind of strange and unpleasant energy. I was afraid of myself. I lost my balance for good. I lost my academic personality and switched to the other one, which I don't accept in the situations when I need to interact with other people, who probably don't understand and don't feel the same things I do. (L. Lange, protocol, 2019)

Writing descriptions of lived experience (*protocols*) made me more open. I could talk about this phenomenon, discuss it online, and face to face. I become more aware of it. I recalled all the events, when they happened, and how I felt. I realized and that it was with me as far as I could reach in my memories. The whole process enabled me to search for other people with similar abilities. That gave me the strength to dig even deeper and test my abilities consciously. I gained the last level of acceptance during the course with Erasmus students when I openly shared my phenomenon with them (Chapter 7). I answered their questions and felt, once and for all, at peace with this ability. I told the Erasmus students about my phenomenon as part of our routine sharing during the process of discovering their truths by writing about their lived experiences. It was a very enlightening experience that proved to me that there is nothing too strange or too shameful about my phenomenon. To my surprise, my openness made the students more curious about their phenomena and the reflective processes that they had started. I was not a separate being, not an isolated atom; I was as much a part of their cycle of understanding as they were part of mine.

Cultural Research on Precognitions

An important step in phenomenological research is to recognize the cultural and scholarly understandings that cloud and skew our direct experiences. I review what these were for me in this section.

I recall a bunch of old books from my childhood. They belonged to my grandmother and always inspired my imagination. Two of them were written by William Walker Atkinson – about exercising memory and mind powers, which were considered secret mental magic. There was also a book written by Rajnhard Karma – *Clairvoyance*. It was the most interesting to me. I was too young to read it, so I deduced what it was about. If a person could "see clear," it couldn't be bad. It has to be something marvelous, a bit magical. It may be naïve to believe that clairvoyance or the psychokinetic powers of the human mind could move a spoon, for example, only by thinking of it – everything was natural. And I was near nature, so I accepted its rules. I was like a hunter-gatherer from one side and a very religious little girl from the other. I worshipped nature and believed in ghosts; at the same time, I was very much into Christianity and the only God.

Magical Creatures?

If we could go quickly through human history and look at the cultural and folkloric understanding of precognitions, we would see that the supernatural source was always connected with it. Many authors (Coffey 2008; Guiley 1991; Wolff 2001) say that the pre-Neolithic and the Early Neolithic societies and cultures were linked to nature. But with the appearance of the monotheist religious traditions, the link was broken (Coffey 2008, pp. 19–20). It could be more or less accepted, sometimes banned and banished but always "not natural" in a sense that the source was a higher power, bad or good, but not "natural for the human being." The Greek mythological characters like Pythia oracle at Delphi, who had the chance of glancing into the future, were always connected with gods and it was the gods who made them "see." The future could be foreseen in dreams, by observing nature (the flight of birds, the sound of animals, the examination of the entrails of sacrificial creatures).

The nature of precognitions depended on a person who possessed the abilities. Some could answer almost every question about the future, others were answering in puzzles and the interpretation of such an answer was never clear. The ability was given or could be gained through meditation, herbal mixtures, dancing, chanting, ecstatic rituals, etc. Precognitions together with people who were the vessel for them were present in most cultures and societies in order to connect with the higher power (nature, gods, ghosts of ancestors).

Animals could also be seen as magical (or supernatural) if they could do something not possible for people to achieve. In time, it started to be clear that each creature is different and some – for example, dogs – have different abilities. But those abilities were not explained scientifically. One of them is knowing when the caretaker will come back home or "predicting death." Rupert Sheldrake (2011, p. 467) investigated not only dogs, but also cats, rabbits, parrots, and horses. In his book on the subject of "unexplained powers," he wrote: "The reactions of pets before the onset of illness are easily misunderstood, and their meaning becomes clear only in retrospect. The same is true of unusual behavior before sudden deaths." He also claims that:

> Some premonitions seem to depend on telepathy, as when animals know in advance when their people are coming home. In some instances, the animal may have detected odors, sounds, electrical changes, or other physical stimuli. But others may involve precognition, which literally means "knowing in advance," or presentiment, "feeling in advance."
>
> (2011, p. 441)

As for the aspect of detecting odors, Fernand Méry (1968, p. 144) was sure that the butyric acid is one very specific to an individual (animal or human) and it can be perceived by a dog from up to 300 feet. As I don't know the true nature of my abilities, I cannot say for sure that it is not some kind of "super perceptivity" or "super sensitivity" of one of my sensors.

The Romantic Gothicism of the 19th Century

Precognition is:

> Supernormal knowledge of future events, with emphasis not upon mentally causing events to occur, but upon predicting those, the occurrence of which the subject claims has already been determined.
>
> (Britannica n.d.)

When I started my phenomenological research into precognitions, I was looking for the right word to express my phenomenon. I used the word "spirituality." I recognized that precognition was connected with both a higher power (like that experienced by one of my interviewees, who is a believer) and with the noun "spiritualist," which in the etymological dictionary stands for "one who believes in the ability of the living to communicate with the dead via a medium" (Online Etymology Dictionary n.d.). At the end of writing the protocols, I was sure that the most appropriate word for my phenomenon would be the word "liminality." Being liminal means "of or pertaining to a threshold" (Online Etymology Dictionary n.d.).

What I didn't search for was "clairvoyance." It is funny because this was the only word that I had in my head from my childhood, but I couldn't identify what I was experiencing with that name. It was too magical. It was too distant. The etymology of the word means: "paranormal gift of seeing things out of sight" (Online Etymology Dictionary n.d.). *Britannica* offers a better explanation:

> Knowledge of information not necessarily known to any other person, not obtained by ordinary channels of perceiving or reasoning – thus a form of extrasensory perception (ESP). Spiritualists also use the term to mean seeing or hearing (clairaudience) the spirits of the dead that are said to surround the living.
>
> (n.d.)

Harper's Encyclopedia of Mystical & Paranormal Experience adds to those definitions that clairvoyance can be "experienced in different ways and degrees" (Guiley 1991, p. 111).

The very important phrase, which appears in many of the definitions, is *extrasensory perception (ESP)*. It is explained in the *Britannica* as:

> A perception that occurs independently of the known sensory processes. Usually included in this category of phenomena are telepathy, or thought transference between persons; clairvoyance, or supernormal awareness of objects or events not necessarily known to others; and precognition, or knowledge of the future. Scientific investigation of these and similar phenomena dates from the late 19th century, with most supporting evidence coming from experiments involving card guessing. (n.d.)

The history of communication with ghosts reaches back to the beginnings of human history. But the communicating spiritualists I had in mind were those from the 19th century. The Church has seen in them a kind of witchcraft worth condemnation. The practices were forbidden as an act of necromancy – communication with the deceased to learn about future events. The spiritualism was also inspiring for science and provoked the discipline of psychic research, which was to support or decline phenomena of mediumship and supernatural abilities. In the 20th century, spirituality like that was reborn within the New Age movement, where the mediums (here called "channelers") contacted entities and spiritual beings who not only helped them to see the future but also guided people to a better world and enabled the self-development process.

The Power of the Human Mind

Sheldrake (2015, pp. 15, 282–285) has stated that we tend to believe that in science we have almost all the answers to the fundamental questions. He sees ten dogmas in science that prevent us from free-thinking and researching – one of them is that the supernatural things are an illusion. Going further, the materialistic point of view uses the name of *normal* and *paranormal* activities. Everything is normal if science can explain it with the knowledge we have already gained. If something lays beyond that line of knowledge, it should be called paranormal. The term parapsychology stands for discipline that goes beyond psychology, into the realm of unknown. The classification of the events is made based on the existing theory of the mind which stays in the head (as the synonym of the brain). It seems that my early concerns that I cannot be a professional researcher if I have these abilities were connected with this classification.

Sheldrake also describes precognitions as something that should be considered as normal (not paranormal). He states that among his 842 cases of precognitions 70% were about the possibility of death or disaster, 25% were neutral, and 5% positive (2015, p. 305). In his opinion, the human (and animal) mind is something that can and should be researched not only by experimental methods, which for skeptics are not good enough to provide real answers. If we turn down this dogma and let psychotronic research happen freely and unconditionally, it may become that people feel more open to publicly talk about their experiences and are also willing to take part in such academic research. They wouldn't feel judged and stigmatized as much as they actually feel. He also sees potential in such studies: we could understand, deeper and better, human nature and the human mind, the nature of social bonds, time and causality (2015, p. 313–314).

Contemporary View on Precognitions

Maria Coffey refers to some research in the United States of America and the United Kingdom about the mystical and paranormal experiences:

> A 2005 Gallup poll showed that out of a thousand people interviewed, 47 percent believed in ESP (extrasensory perception), 32 percent in the existence of ghosts, 26 percent in clairvoyance, and 21 percent in the possibility of contact with the dead. In a similar survey done in the United Kingdom, 43 percent of interviewees believed they had been in contact with the dead, 71 percent believed in the existence of the soul, and 53 percent believed in some form of afterlife. In general, older people were more skeptical and women were more prone to such beliefs than men. (2008, pp. 18–19)

It shows clearly that the issue of precognition (extrasensory perception) is something real to 47% of the researched people in the U.S. But it also tells me that 53% neither accept it nor have an opinion about it. They also could be not willing to tell, as the subject is judged and stands against rational thinking and contemporary science, so we shouldn't declare our involvement in such things. I'm skeptical about the results of such a study, as the subject is something we don't talk about with researchers.

Either Culture or Nature

The biggest question of all is still about the source of precognitions. Do they come from culture or nature? Are they straight and clear or symbolic and puzzled? If they are clear and straight, and we can understand them without any use of cultural knowledge, then they could come from nature. But if we need a key to unlock the visions, it seems that they come from culture somehow, and are symbolic and metaphoric. But what is culture and what is nature anyway? Aren't they both part of the same realm? The split between those two is visible both in science and in common opinions on psychic abilities.

Sheldrake (1987) has a proposal for scientists – the hypothesis of formative causation. He explains that the motor field associated with the body depends on the physics and chemical states of the body. The:

> Subjective experience which is not directly concerned with the present environment or with immediate action – for example in dreams, reveries, and discursive thinking – need not necessarily bear any particularly close relationship to the energetic and formative causes acting on the brain. (1987, p. 205)

Pop Culture or Useful Crooks

Contemporary pop culture offers some visions of ESP. I'm going to mention a few of them represented in TV series, but I have chosen only those in which the main character has the abilities. In 2005, two series about ESP were launched – *Ghost Whisperer* (2005–2010) and *Medium* (2005–2011). The first was aired on CBS and followed the life of Melinda Gordon (played by Jennifer Love Hewitt), a lady who can communicate with ghosts. She sees them and tries to help them cross over. Not all of her tasks are easy (most of them are not) – she has to solve the mystery behind every apparition. Her gift is something that was in her family – this is her heritage. The second drama series was originally aired on NBC for five seasons, and on CBS for two more seasons. It shows the life of Allison DuBois (played by Patricia Arquette) who is a medium employed as a consultant for the district attorney's office in Phoenix, Arizona. Allison can see ghosts and solve criminal cases. Her character was based on the real experiences of medium Allison DuBois – mentioned also by Mary Roach (2009, pp. 231–232) in her book *Six Feet Over: Adventures in the afterlife*.

The DuBois' case is not solely in law enforcement – the people with ESP abilities are sometimes used by investigative teams in the search for missing or dead people (Swanson 2009, p. 43). It is also explored in the new series which has started (and ended) in 2019 on NBC – entitled *The InBetween*. The story is a little bit similar to the two shows already mentioned. It follows Cassie Bedford (played by Harriet Dyer), who was born with a gift of seeing ghosts. She can communicate with the dead, helping them with their unresolved issues. She also helps her father, Detective Tom Hackett, and his new partner, former FBI Agent Damien Asante. The three shows mostly use the motif of communication with ghosts. Also worth mention is *Proof,* aired on TNT in 2015. The series follows the life of Dr. Carolyn Tyler (played by Jennifer Beals) who experienced the death of her teenage son, a legal separation from her husband, and a rift with her daughter. She is persuaded by Ivan Turing, a tech inventor and billionaire with cancer, to investigate supernatural cases of reincarnation, near-death experiences, and hauntings, in hope of finding evidence that death is not final. She doesn't have any abilities – she is a true-blood scientist, who doesn't believe in "that kind of thing." But she is desperate and on the edge. With time, she connects with the other side. This series explores the whole range of knowledge about the afterlife – as described by Eben Alexander, M.D. (2012).

I have mentioned those TV series because they can be useful: they answer the viewers' inner need for "something out there," which Coffey defines as:

> The inexorable yearning for something beyond the mundane or the explainable runs deep in the human psyche. It arises from an urge to find meaning in existence, for something bigger than ourselves. It also comes from a need to belong, to experience life in terms of a harmonious interaction – with others, with nature, with God, with the universe. An interaction that was once part of the human condition. (2008, p. 19)

They create a realm which can help to launch scientific research into this subject. Sometimes, they are based on real stories and discoveries. They can help people who have such abilities to adapt and understand what is going on with them, and to understand that they are not alone and that they can be useful. The negative thing about the series is the stereotypical view: the medium is a woman; the gift is transferred from mother or grandmother; and they all see ghosts that are visible for viewers too, which can bring someone to a conclusion that he or she will experience similar things. It is important to portray every kind of psychic ability, as there are many opinions (not always false) that this kind of activity is a fraud and those who practice it trick people to earn money. Often the characters with the powers are portrayed as mentally ill, some even had an episode or two with mental health facility. It shows that "normal" people don't see ghosts, don't talk to dead people. Only a delusional person could see a ghost. Only a person with problems (depression, for example), could reach the afterlife.

I had to set aside all of these preunderstandings as I set out to get to my direct experience. My next goal was to interview some others who had similar abilities to mine.

Interviews with Others with Extrasensory Abilities

The question of how other people with similar abilities perceive this gift/curse was so strong for me, that I began to search for others. In a short time, I found three more: two women and one man. Both women were keen to meet me and tell me about their abilities; the man was not interested. My collaboration with strangers online and face-to-face gave me the strength to search for the answers, but also solved the issue of feeling shame. The collaboration with strangers who have similar abilities has opened another realm for me, leading to the identification of some different perspectives on the same problem. Facing others gave me the possibility to see myself and these abilities from a different perspective.

Three Not-So-Much Witches

The first woman I met, with the ability to feel the changes (mostly death) was a very open person. She is a believer in a higher power, which she doesn't name. She could be described as an artistic soul, very sensitive to Nature, and having a good connection with it. Our meeting took place in the woods on a picnic she organized for us. She accepts her gift and believes that she has it for a reason. That is why she helps people terminally ill to cross over (almost as a death doula), to finish their worldly existence and close this chapter. She had no problem exploring her gift. She gave me copies of her notes on the meditations she used to communicate with the other side.

The second woman met me in a vegan bar. She was demanding, but nice. Also open, but in a different way. She is also an artistic, sensitive soul. She works with people and helps them. She is a declared Catholic and her abilities are not accepted by her. After some events, which she didn't want to mention in detail, she decided to never use the abilities again. She rather thinks of them as a curse and something she doesn't want to have. She believes that it makes her life more complicated. She feels a bit ashamed before the eyes of God. And she is definitively scared that she could reveal too much of the future. She can sense all kinds of changes – death, pregnancy, and big life events.

I felt connected to both of them. I understood both of them. My connection to a divine power of nature was mirrored in the first meeting. My problem with the feelings of being ashamed and scared found itself in the second encounter. That is how I arrived at the continuum between acceptance and denial.

Using Imaginative Variations with my Own Experiences

As I felt divided most of the time, I have created The Black Queen, who was the true nature of my abilities – not me. In one of the protocols, when I was supposed to think about the situation where my phenomenon would not be present, I decided to imagine a different situation, when I described the phenomenon in visual form. I wrote:

> I have even given her face and have let her act through photography, but I have never let her be. So, let's imagine, I've accepted her. She took control once again and for good. She has the body and knowledge. She knows everything past and future. She is total and timeless. There is no feeling of being afraid, of not being understood. There is no feeling of being misjudged or taken for granted. There are no more opinions that are not true – because no words could get the essence of the Black Queen, so there is no use in taking care if someone is right or wrong if he or she understands. The Black Queen understands it for them. Being Black Queen is rather light and the main focus is on the "just knowing," not bragging about it. So once and for all: The Black Queen doesn't have to shout through me. She is the nature after all. She is everything. (L. Lange, protocol, 2019)

This exercise helped me to calm down. And as I was selecting pictures to attach to the protocol, I saw that this "persona" was also calm, as she "already knew" (Figures 1 and 2).

Figure 1: The Black Queen.
Photo from author's archives, 2009.

Figure 2: The Black Queen.
Photo from author's archives, 2009.

I shall refer here to the core of the phenomenological experience of precognitions' practice. We are not able to separate sensitive experience from spiritual consciousness or understanding. This is not new, and according to Saint Thomas, the "spiritual understanding is never disconnected from sensitive knowing" (Luijpen 1960, p. 120). The essential structure of the phenomenon evolved and gave me a new perspective, that enabled the acceptance of the gift – not a curse anymore.

The Names We Use

Beside "gift" or "curse" – which defines whether we accept the ability or not – we call it "phenomenon" or "ability." But also, we use more metaphorical names such as "a draft of wind" (*przeciąg* in Polish), which brings other realms to the mind. It may be called more theatrically, like a "curtain" which, when raised, reveals sometimes more than it should. And I feel that it is rather more like something that I would call "a clearance" (*prześwit* in Polish), which stands very near "clairvoyance". In English it does not have the same meaning – it is the "action of making clear." In Polish, it can also be considered from a transcendental point of view as "standing in the clearance of existence." This correct naming of the phenomenon was exactly the way leading to the Husserlian transcendental realm (Husserl 1970). This puts me in the continuum along with the name I use called "the feeling of liminality." I feel more of me when I am with animals. No pointing fingers. No aggression towards me. We are all in the process of discovering our purposes and what we can do, where our boundaries are, what is out of our reach. This is quite liberating: knowing that we are all (in the animal world) on the way. And it means that as we are on the way, we are not what we were before and not what we would be in the future. We are always liminal somehow. We may see things that for others are irrelevant, but for us mean something, and it is how we know more. As something natural and normal, I feel like being a part of the world. I may be in-between, but I am whole, maybe like a work-in-progress, like an unfinished painting just settling on canvas.

Being Alone, Lonely or Feeling the Solitude

If I could place on a timeline the appearance of the whole problem with my abilities, I should look for that one sentence that has blocked me. After one sentence and the transfer of someone's affect (Brennan 2004, pp. 1–23) toward my phenomenon, everything has changed. I had become scared by my abilities, even if they could be tamed. After that sentence, I couldn't move from the place it has left me, and work through the process of investigating my phenomenon. And all because one day someone, who I considered as important, told me: "I cannot be with you, because you have this darkness in you." Some people see me as a dark person, some people even fear me. But it is me who is afraid of others (because I can feel more?). That one sentence made me feel not only alone and lonely (Moustakas 2016, pp. 10–26) but also unlovable, disconnected, not worthy, strange, and . . . dark. Twelve years later I can finally see this and move on. I can feel that I accept myself and I understand more of my abilities. There are still many things that I don't know – but I can live with it because I have the ability to see more of the whole picture (I see the whole snake eating its tail, and I know the snake is endless). And I know that it is not the darkness after all. It is the light (as metaphorical knowledge, too).

Conclusions

It is interesting to understand from which event I started this voyage, how I understood my phenomenon, and where it brought me. The most horrifying feeling of someone who died in the flat I was having an interview with – it was my starting point. Next, I recalled the events, like premonitions of death, or a feeling of the near-death of a person. But I also was able to recall the funny situations with pregnancy (or rather children) premonitions. The next step was a recollection of my ability to find the burial places of people. And the last leads me to the one I had about my life – that it will change drastically.

So, I understood something that was a kind of a spiritual experience, something that can be discussed on philosophical and/or religious grounds (believing or not believing, being a part of a collective with common beliefs or not). The question of the nature of the precognition emerged – is it researchable or not, can a researcher be spiritual and not lose his or her authority? Is it normal or supernatural? Is a person with such abilities normal or crazy? I understood the psychological feeling of solitude and loneliness with its self-isolation (the need for membership, the relation to self and others), aggression, the misunderstanding and judgmental approach of others towards me, and me towards myself, and the stereotype and stigma. I stepped toward anthropological liminality, which I see as positive. It gives me a connection with nature and both sides – beginning and end. A connection with my animal side and the feeling of wholeness and empowerment.

References

Alexander, Eben (2012): *Proof of Heaven: A Neurosurgeon's Journey into the Afterlife*. New York: Simon & Schuster.
Brennan, Teresa (2004): *The Transmission of Affect*. Ithaca: Cornell University Press.
Britannica (n.d.): "Clairvoyance". Retrieved from https://www.britannica.com/topic/clairvoyance, visited on October 8, 2020.
Britannica (n.d.): "Extrasensory Perception". Retrieved from https://www.britannica.com/topic/extrasensory-perception, visited on October 8, 2020.
Britannica (n.d.): "Ouroboros". Retrieved from https://www.britannica.com/topic/Ouroboros, visited on October 8, 2020.
Britannica (n.d.): "Precognition". Retrieved from https://www.britannica.com/topic/precognition, visited on October 8, 2020.
Coffey, Maria (2008): *Explorers of the Infinite. The Secret Spiritual Lives of Extreme Athletes – And What They Reveal About Near-Death Experience, Psychic Communication, and Touching the Beyond*. New York: Jeremy P. Tarcher/Penguin.
Guiley, Rosemary Ellen (1991): *Harper's Encyclopedia of Mystical & Paranormal Experience*. San Fransisco: Harper San Francisco.
Husserl, Edmund (1970): *The Crisis of European Sciences and Transcendental Phenomenology: An Introduction to Phenomenological Philosophy* (D. Carr, Trans.). Evanston: Northwestern University Press.
Husserl, Edmund (2001): *Logical Investigations* (2nd ed.). Moran, Dermot (Ed.). London: Routledge.
Luijpen, Wilhelmus (1960): *Existential Phenomenology*. Pittsburgh: Duquesne University Press.
Méry, Fernand (1968): *The Life, History, and Magic of the Dog*. New York: Grosset & Dunlap.
Moustakas, Clark E. (2016): *Loneliness*. Auckland: Pickle Partners Publishing.

Online Etymology Dictionary (n.d.): "Clairvoyance". Retrieved from https://www.etymonline.com/word/clairvoyance, visited on October 8, 2020.
Online Etymology Dictionary (n.d.): "Liminal". Retrieved from https://www.etymonline.com/word/liminal, visited on October 8, 2020.
Online Etymology Dictionary (n.d.): "Spiritualist". Retrieved from https://www.etymonline.com/word/spiritualist, visited on October 8, 2020.
Rehorick, David/ Bentz, Valerie (2008): *Transformative Phenomenology: Changing Ourselves, Lifeworlds, and Professional Practice*. Lanham: Lexington Books.
Roach, Mary (2009): *Six Feet Over: The Adventures in the Afterlife*. Edinburgh: Canongate.
Sheldrake, Rupert (1987): *A New Science of Life: The Hypothesis of Formative Causation*. London: Paladin Grafton Books.
Sheldrake, Rupert (2011): *Dogs That Know When Their Owners Are Coming Home: And Other Unexplained Powers of Animals*. New York: Three Rivers Press.
Sheldrake, Rupert (2015): *The Science Delusion: Freeing the Spirit of Enquiry* (Polish ed., Maciej, M., Trans.). Wroclaw: Wydawnictwo Meandra.
Swanson, Claude (2009): *The Synchronized Universe: New Science of the Paranormal*. Tucson: Poseidia Press.
Turner, Victor (1975): *Dramas, Fields, and Metaphors: Symbolic Action in Human Society*. New York: Cornell University Press.
Turner, Victor (1985): "Liminality, Kabbalah, and the Media". In: *Religion* 15, pp. 205–217.
Turner, Victor (1995): *The Ritual Process: Structure and Anti-Structure*. Piscataway: Transaction Publishers.
van Manen, Max (1984): "Practicing Phenomenological Writing". In: *Phenomenology + Pedagogy* 2. No. 1, pp. 36–69.
van Manen, Max (2007): "Phenomenology of Practice". In: *Phenomenology & Practice* 1. No. 1, pp. 11–30.
van Manen, Max (2016): *Phenomenology of practice: meaning-giving methods in phenomenological research and writing*. Oxon, New York: Routledge.
van Manen, Max (2017): "Phenomenology in Its Original Sense". In: *Qualitative Health Research* 27. No. 6, pp. 810–825.
Wolff, Robert (2001) *Original Wisdom: Stories on an Ancient Way of Knowing*. Rochester: Inner Traditions.

David Haddad and Łucja Lange
Chapter 7
Personal Discovery and Transformation Through the Study of Lived-Experience

Abstract: Erasmus Institute university students from Europe and Asia participated in a "Collaboration Among Strangers" research project through a course at the University of Łódź titled "Communication in Organizations." Major themes revealed by the research included the notion of typification, as developed by Alfred Schütz (1973, pp. 13, 77), and the transformative effects of phenomenological writing. The notion of collaboration among students startled most of them, especially because they possessed different first languages and hailed from different cultures. Trepidation gave way to being pleasantly surprised when they found that, through engaging the course assignments, it was possible to collaborate with strangers and that those strangers were quickly on their way to becoming friends. This chapter samples their work by highlighting a variety of their topics and their potency.[1]

Keywords: Deathworld, Lifeworld, lived experience, stranger, phenomenology

Foreword: The Challenges of Collaboration Among Dominant World View Persons

Valerie Bentz

Those of us limited by the Dominant Worldview are not accustomed to phenomenological self-exploration or to collaborative sharing, common to the Indigeneous Worldview (Chapter 1, Table 3). This was apparent in teaching a course to a group of 40 undergraduate students, one of my two teaching assignments while I was at the University of Łódź. The Erasmus students came from a variety of countries, mostly Europe and the Near East. For all of them, English was a second language. I asked them to write and share online phenomenologically based protocols describing an experience of importance to them. We provided them with

---

[1] Lucja Lange participated in the research in Łódź and served as research assistant with the Erasmus students. David Haddad participated as a part of the community of practice in the Basecamp postings and many of the Zoom calls. Valerie Malhotra Bentz is the principal researcher for this project. Special acknowledgement to Dr. Alice Kitchel, Fielding alumna, for assisting with the collation of protocols.

access via a Basecamp site for posting their protocols and an internal University site to all the reading materials. Students typically did not read the material, and many had not written the assignments. Their attendance was inconsistent. During the classes, several of them were instead paying attention to their computers. Few volunteered to enter into the discussions. For the past decades, I had been teaching exclusively doctoral students who were an average age of 40 or older. I was not accustomed to working with unmotivated students. From other professors teaching classes for Erasmus students, I had heard comments like: "I wonder what I can do to keep them busy today . . ."

It was fortuitously beneficial to the students that for health reasons (Chapter 3) I had to leave Łódź early and that doctoral candidate Łucja Lange volunteered to take over the class in person with my presence via Zoom. Łucja was a student in my graduate class in *Transformative Phenomenology* and therefore was acquainted with the material. As a younger person with an artistic self-presentation with tattoos, the students related to her readily. Also, like them, English was Łucja's second language. Despite her tendency towards introversion (Chapter 6), Łucja taught the class with mastery. She shared her protocols about her precognition experiences with the students and found acceptance from them. She was dedicated to their learning and growth and put concentrated effort into reading each of their weekly postings and asking for rewrites until they "got it." This authoritative method of teaching was exactly what they were used to from their previous schooling. Her authentic self-disclosure freed them to follow her example and write about things they cared about. These students were not used to such deep self-examination or sharing. As the protocols described below demonstrate, it meant an opening up to collaboration and self-understanding.

Łucja as Teaching Assistant in the *Strangers to Collaborators* Project

The course, called "Communication in Organizations," initially presented students with communication issues typically found inside business and government organizations. Students took on challenging subjects, such as cultural differences as barriers to communication, gender differences, issues of age, social background, and learned communication skills. Coupled with this, students began to deepen their self-understanding as communicators through writing phenomenology (Rehorick/Bentz 2008, 2017).

During our first gathering, Bentz introduced students to the basic building blocks of writing phenomenology. The challenge for the students was selecting a personal poignant experience about which to write. She then outlined eight steps of the phenomenological protocol writing. Each step was used as a lens to focus the mind, to disentangle the dense fabric comprising their poignant experience, laying bare its multiple layers of rich hidden meaning Professor Bentz moved on to instruct them in managing vast stocks of knowledge locked within their experiences. The choice was left up to each student. They were to select an experience they found attractive and compelling, something each felt drawn to work on as a promising phenomenon.

Students were assigned the task of reflection and writing, a task that encompassed writing not one, but several, protocols, each one deepening their reflections on their experience (Table 1, Chapter 1). These protocols were:
- a rich experience about something you care about – a poignant experience;
- your earliest memory of the experience in terms of time, space, body, and emotions;
- an exploration of the experience using bracketing and imaginative variations;
- a description of the experience not present – its opposite;
- a description of the essence – the essential structure of the experience; and
- a description of the Lifeworld in which the experience occurs – typical actors, multiple realities, relevances, and points of view.

Students gained ground when they were later introduced to Professor Bart Beuchner, a Fielding alum who was instrumental in the overall research project and who spent a week in Łodz. Dr. Beuchner filled in more detail of what it means to learn through applied phenomenology, Burke's dramatistic communications theory, and how it promised to be helpful in their future work.

Deathworlds to Lifeworlds: An Emerging Theory

Though not emphasized as part of the syllabus, a surprising pattern emerged from the students' writing, a pattern illustrating the elaborate "Deathworlds-to-Lifeworlds" theory. "Deathworld," a term minted by Bentz, is conceived in contrast to one's Lifeworld. A Deathworld epitomizes the experience of destructive human acts such as cyber threats and security issues; economic stagnation and urban poverty; infrastructure decay; urban over-development; the threatening impact of climate change; unsustainable population growth; ocean pollution with plastics and human refuse; space junk; deforestation; abandoned ruins of defunct human civilization; pharmaceutical misuse; disease outbreak and pandemics; social turbulence; population displacement; information/communication hyperactivity, and war.

Lifeworld, a term invented by Edmund Husserl (1936, pp. 111–147) and developed by Alfred Schütz (1973, pp. 3–18), refers to the full range of unreflected naïve experience of everyday life, curious unsullied innocence, the intrinsic essence of one's basic orientation to life. Within everyone's Lifeworld are arrays of typifications. "Typification" speaks of perceiving the world and structuring it by means of types and typology, ready handles by which to negotiate daily life.

Typifications comprise the inherited multitude of cultural forms and meanings, constructs, typical ways of acting, and then interprets them. Interpretations are based on observations of others (socialization) assuming what are the typical underlying motivations. These gradually evolve one's patterns of thought, forming one's personality.

Phenomenological writing involved eight steps. Each student began by identifying a particularly poignant experience. That was followed by seven stages of an in-depth textual investigation. Taken together, these stages comprised the phenomenological protocol.

This is the heart of the project, the act of phenomenological writing. The task of the student researcher is to excavate multiple layers of sedimented thought, digging underneath taken-for-granted perceptions to arrive at the core, the essence of the lived experience (van Manen 2014, pp. 18–19; Moustakas 1994, p. 27). Essence can be described as an element of an experience that, if removed, would alter the very constitution of the experience itself, changing it, diminishing it, until what is left becomes something else altogether.

Second, students were encouraged to collaborate with their classmates who, until then, were strangers. We mark how successful (and surprising) that turned out to be. The third objective explored Schützian typifications, the mental constructs that prevent seeing through the taken-for-granted natural attitude built up by naïve acceptance of unexamined assumptions. To break through the natural attitude demands acquiring a phenomenological attitude through writing.

The students openly displayed reluctance to trust strangers. The pressures of enculturation by economic and political systems had, in the words of Jürgen Habermas (cited in Fleming 2002), "colonized" students' natural pre-reflective Lifeworlds. Only through their courageous communicative acts were they able to begin to reconstitute authentic Lifeworlds.

Through continued writing, they expanded their horizons, enabling them to better understand their phenomena. They seemed shocked that they, mere undergraduate students, could be a legitimate source of knowledge for each other.

Students began commenting on their classmates' protocols and lending support to one another, especially those who wrote about traumatic events. They discovered that they were not alone, that sharing their experiences wouldn't limit them; rather, sharing could take them further to become a new source of strength. The writing process opened a way through the cultural colonization of the mind to regain their Lifeworld as an ever-present fresh experience.

By setting aside the encroaching typifications inherited simply through the experience of growing up, they felt the transformative effects of seeing one another with new eyes, being freed to be spontaneous with one another. A phenomenon may have looked safe and easy to write about, but it soon became clear that writing brought hidden challenges. Dysfunctional education systems, demands of relatives, personal expectations, and challenging aspects of their chosen phenomena presented challenges.

Constant Surprises

The lack of awareness about the nature of the work required came as a surprise. While somewhat prepared for that, we hoped that some had prepared by immersing themselves in required reading. Even so, we did not entertain expectations that the majority would complete all of it. Ultimately, only one student who published his protocols online, got it right.

To stimulate a more vibrant learning environment and quietly demonstrate the effects of physical proximity, Łucja experimented with the classroom format by changing her physical distance from the students. European teachers typically stand far from students. Łucja began moving closer to them, standing nearby, asking questions about their phenomenon, and how they would develop the topic into the next protocols. Would this be easy or hard? How would they recognize progress? In case they were not able to make such decisions, Łucja opened the possibility that protocols already written contained promising ideas with unexplored avenues. They might choose from among them. Some may be easier to develop, others more difficult. Łucja did not press them to explore the more difficult ones. Some accepted her suggestions, some not. Nonetheless, the change in proximity helped. The discussions became stimulating and gave the students fresh ideas and new directions about how to tackle the remaining steps.

The second surprise was theirs. They didn't expect facilitators would actually read all their protocols and comment on them. They didn't expect they would help them to go further, to freely explore, to understand more. Some of them were sure that the stereotypic perspectives (typifications) they brought with them as they entered the program would remain unchanged. Students seemed to take for granted that their unexamined belief that they were all irreconcilably different was true, therefore they did not need to search further for any common ground. After receiving attribution as legitimate research participants, their surprise turned to respect. They realized their writing had been valued, regarded with seriousness by their instructor.

Between Discovery and Transformation

This section focuses on how transformation occurred, and the interplay of diversity and unity. At its deepest most durable levels, a transformation of mind occurs when one engages in a process that reveals and affirms latent potent new awareness of what is external and what is internal (Rehorick/Bentz 2008, pp. 5, 26). A new awareness of one's social surroundings and environment can be startling, discovering one's deep dynamic knowledge-making capabilities life-changing.

Practicing phenomenology activates and refines one's intentionality. It manifests transformative changes of mind through the elevation of awareness *if* one fully and textually engages the phenomenological protocol. Following a thorough textual engagement, a transformed mind experiences an intense new level of awareness, the apperception of structures of thought in fuller dimensions.

A transformed mind is evidenced through deepened self-awareness, adding layers of insight to critical decision making. It can manifest itself in a variety of creative acts such as dance or painting, sculpture or poetry, musical composition, or public performance (Haddad 2008).

This definition of transformation raises it well beyond simple "aha" moments; one transcends the ordinary, the mundane, the mind is raised to perceive changing strata governing complex relationships among diverse aspects of life. The innate persistent drive toward maturation is catalyzed to permanently stretch one's awareness, resulting in a flowering of consciousness rooted in one's unique inmost constitution.

Augmentation of thought to this level forestalls reverting to one's earlier under-developed frames of mind. Transformative augmentation endures. The mind is enlarged, stretched, endowed with enhanced capacity. An innate capacity that was latent is now awakened. The evidence for this is found in the writing itself, an articulation of dynamic new-found awareness in ways not previously possessed. Access to the phenomenological attitude frees one from the tyranny of the natural attitude.

Another way of describing transformation is in terms of being. One's intentional acts, the inmost source of one's consciousness, are directed toward a seemingly endless stream of objects, people, states of affairs. A mind exercised in the phenomenological protocol sharpens one's intentionality, rendering it with far fewer distortions, like wearing new prescription glasses. One sees without the inherited filtering bias accumulated by years of sedimented typifications, meanings handed down, and naïvely accepted. One's being, then, is free to directly connect to life's surround in all its manifestations.

One final point: learning in general—and learning phenomenology in particular—relies heavily on motivation. Deep learning does not occur by chance. The more self-directed the motivation, the more satisfying the outcome. Many of the students participating in Collaboration Among Strangers had little idea of what to expect. From the standpoint of surprise, many did experience a significant shift in their view of what an educational experience might be. A few took the opportunity to accomplish all eight steps of the phenomenological protocol.

Finally, our question is, "Among the student participants, who experienced transformation?" We look at the question in light of our themes: writing as a novice, Deathworlds to Lifeworlds, Collaboration Among Strangers, and Schützian typifications.

How Transformation Occurred

Many of our students reported that this project indeed led to a better understanding of others. Their reports highlighted the need for a safe learning environment where diversity and unity were in play. People, they said, who at first looked like strangers from different cultures may, in the end, "look just like us." They moved from an alienating Deathworld of "strangers" to a new Lifeworld of collaboration.

In this project, students came supposing they already knew what to expect. They arrived with a set of expectations, typifications, notions of "what will happen" while in their learning environment. Typically, they came more to be entertained by new ideas and meet new faces than to exert an unusual effort, one that could win them profound experiences of deep learning. And it wasn't just a question of whether they read the required material. Transformation depended on the courage to collaborate and, to a large extent, on a self-managed orientation to learning, that is, learning prompted by the *student's* initiative and responsibility, not the teacher's.

From Apprehension to Transformation

Was it reasonable to think undergraduate students with no prior exposure to writing phenomenology could access such a deeply complex process? Deep learning and transformative phenomenology are accessible to practically anyone willing to test its methods. Difficulties encountered during dynamic personal developmental phases of life were faced with courage and were reported on with probing sobriety. Out of the cohort of forty, we sample eleven. How did undergraduate students from across Europe tackle phenomenology? Did they understand it creates dialectical relationships?

Participant Contributions

The most promising students gravitated around themes of Deathworlds-to-Lifeworlds, unexpected effects of Collaboration Among Strangers, and Schützian typifications. Their writing proved personally transformative. The students have been given psuedonyms to protect their identities.

1) Helen – Trauma

Helen experienced transformation of apperception when she discovered how her mind created a trauma out of her hernia operation. She says, "I realized that my mind turned this event into a trauma because it was unexpected, it threatened my life, I was not in control, overwhelmed because I was a child." It is striking that, at such an early age, she recognized an internal cognitive action, her awareness of her perception acting as an agent to *create* the trauma. For many patients, trauma is simply the unreflected experience of suffering from injury and is typically labeled as such by attending physicians and medical staff. Once this terminology is adopted the label becomes part of the patient's narrative.

In this protocol, the experience of change as a result of a loss of control promised much. Thought processes were altered while simultaneously being monitored by the one experiencing them, apperception, proved remarkable and needed fuller exploration. The effect of engaging in a phenomenological protocol brought Helen's awareness of how her mind interacted with her injured body. It indicates transformation. If Helen deepens this meditation, her personal transformation might take steps in the direction of even greater self-awareness.

2) Bettina – Fear

> I learned the true definition of fear and how I felt when I was really scared. I described it. Then, I wished I had not had this event; as I wrote I was changing my memory. . . . I can say that observing my own thoughts brought about a conclusion and I now have a third eye.
>
> (Bettina, protocol, 2019)

There's a bit of a leap in the writer's text that requires the reader to fill in the chasm. How her memories changed with the writing is instructive, common even. How is a change in perception achieved with the simple act of writing about a memory? She doesn't say. Then, to jump from "observing my own thoughts," to "I now have a third eye," sounds plausible, but leaves the reader scratching his head. How is observing one's own thoughts (*apperception*) connected to experiencing a "third eye"? Whatever her explanation, discovering the activity of a third eye, or pineal gland, is an elementary yet transformative step in one's structure of mind.

Bettina uncovers the spark of "true" experience. Did writing truly *change* the memory or only *reveal* it in greater detail? She doesn't say. Even so, what memory one typically recalls is sourced from stocks of knowledge shaped in the natural attitude. In this exercise, she applied the phenomenological attitude to the memory, and, surprisingly, its underlying richness became evident. Perhaps this is the change referred to.

Contrasting a "true definition of fear," a kind of Deathworld, with whatever sort of fear had been felt prior is also rich with possibilities, especially if explored in the realm of imaginative variations.

3) Michael – Volunteering

In this example, Michael is keenly aware of how he is compensated for giving away his time, care and effort. He contrasts voluntary effort and its effects on his character, with today's common measure of a person, the accumulation of money. Volunteering may be an authentic expression of one's Lifeworld. Conversely, one may value selling one's time and labor for money as characteristic of a Deathworld, the reduction of human value to a mere currency:

> I realized that the sacrifices I made were worth it. They returned as much to me as I gave to them. They developed me as a human being. I became a more patient, devoted person. I can say that my sense of responsibility improved. Volunteering is not just action without money. It can be seen in every action carried out with sincere feelings. The reason why volunteering is called "action without money" is that the [dominant] measure of interest in today's world is money.
>
> Islam obliges us to give one-third of our earnings to people who do not have financial means. This is called *zakat*. According to my observations, my family is helping people not only because of religion but also because my family wants to help people voluntarily.
>
> (Michael, protocol, 2019)

In this protocol, Michael reframes his thoughts about "sacrifice," which implies something is given but nothing returned. He realigns with inner rewards that correspond to societal rewards for voluntary giving. The student contrasts effort for monetary compensation against effort freely given, and for that reason has the simultaneous effect of building up both society and one's character.

In short, Michael, through his experiences of volunteering his time and treasure, *transcends* cultural pressures, typifications conspiring to shape his attitude about his economic relationship to his community and himself. He chooses, at times, not to be paid in currency for his effort. Although he doesn't say it, he is also denying the corollary, that of withholding one's effort until there is a promise of payment.

When every act is potentially voluntary, he discovers, every act carries within it its own reward. This transformed view of action centers the locus of control squarely within.

4) Kathryn – Divorce

> [Father] was smiling but looking nervous, and then he told us that he asked his girlfriend to marry him. I was so shocked, my brother too. We didn't say anything. We never expected that; he was with this girl for a year when he asked her. My whole world fell apart. It took us weeks to 'accept' it, but we didn't have a choice anyway because the wedding was planned for August that same year.
>
> Dad left the house the first of September. He came back with some mover to take all his stuff two weeks later. This day is one of the first days I remember . . . It was a sad and weird moment. One of the saddest moments of my life.
>
> At that time, marriage was not considered as a link between two people but as the alliance of two families. For example, when two people were getting married, the marriage was arranged most often by the head of each family.
>
> Writing about my most poignant memory made me realize that my ideal family was totally and definitely over.
>
> The whole society gives its opinion about divorce. Society makes laws about what we can or cannot do, regarding if you are a man or a woman. All of our decisions are judged, and we are not as free as we think we are. (Kathryn, protocol, 2019)

In this protocol, Kathryn depicts an intensely personal physical social/emotional shockwave rushing through her and her brother resulting from the breakup of her family. She equates divorce with profound disruption leaving a deep fissure in society. For her, both marriage and society were, until then, stable and predictable.

Now, with her father leaving for another woman, everything is thrown into doubt, even the mores of society and the laws of the land. As if that isn't bad enough, she feels hemmed in by society's self-imposed rules and pervasive judgment. But that, too, may find its days numbered. Every line in this passage is ripe with possibilities for deeper phenomenological investigation.

5) Alex – Love and Death

> Someone I loved died. I couldn't accept that I couldn't talk to Grandpa anymore. Fear is a problem of uncertainty, triggered by the perception of a threat, disturbing and negative. Fear can create strong signals of response, when we're in emergencies for instance, if we are caught in a fire, or are being attacked. It can also take effect when you're faced with non-dangerous events, like exams, public speaking, a new job, a date, or even a party. It's a natural response to a threat that can be either perceived or real. For me, it's fear of death.
> I can say that my fears help me remember how much I care about the people I love. In some cases, it made my life difficult. Some deaths had a lasting effect on me. It made me think deeply about my actions or decisions. Since I was thinking of the worst scenario, I started to give up some of the things that I wanted to do. (Alex, protocol, 2019)

In this instance, Alex identifies fear as a paralyzing experience. His view of fear is based in a threat. The threat is his mortality. At the same time, it is his love for others that balances out the threat. By the end of his meditation Alex has acquiesced. He gave up activities he planned to do. Setting aside what one desires is a first step to accepting defeat. The writer has not yet taken the protocol through all its steps. What remains is deeper examination of his fear in order to overcome both through his own reasoning capacity.

6) Paul – Bribery

> The bribery demands were very horrible and scary for me. But that was last drop when he said, 'What is your duty? Are you student or worker?" His sharp words made me feel like I had been beaten by 10 people and I felt the ground slip under my feet. My heart beat faster and I felt something heavy in my stomach like I swallowed ten kilos of metal.
> Even now when somebody wants to convince me about something I pretend that I trust, but in reality I do not. That accident and accidents like that left in me a very deep wound which would last really long. The main thing that I learned is to just be straight about your target and do not be afraid of the risk.
> I realize, this is almost the end, but I am feeling something different in myself. I wrote something about myself in my protocols, that I lost my trust in people, and I will never get it back again. Now, because of sharing and collaboration, I feel that people who helped me in this class not only helped me with their advice but also with renewing my trust in people. (Paul, protocol, 2019)

In this protocol, we are left to imagine the circumstances under which Paul was involved in a bribery transaction with an authority figure. His naïve, untested trust in others was clearly shattered by it. Following that, the class on Collaboration Among Strangers and the sharing of poignant experiences allowed for an important breakthrough. It created an opening where he could begin to trust others again.

7) Emma – Meaningless Rules

> OCD.
> I did not feel time move faster or slower.
> My sense of space in that time was sort of cramped, stiff and tight.
> I did not tell my experience to friends or someone else, even for very close friend, I could not because I was afraid of being isolated from them, should I tell them my "story."
> – Stressful for me;
> – Felt self-disgust;
> – I made many "meaningless" rules in my own life and, even though I knew better, it did not have any meaning. I could not stop obeying.
> Many people around me said, "you are strange," in reference to the thinking I had.
> After knowing it:
> My loneliness disappeared because I knew there were so many people who have the same symptoms as me and they are suffering just the same as I do. At the same time, I knew there were treatments for the disease. That means, there is a chance that I could change the condition I had and be better.
> I felt: I see the light; relief, not lonely. (Emma, protocol, 2019)

In this unique protocol, Emma struggles to describe her inner mental experience of obsessive-compulsive disorder (OCD). She relates how alien she appeared to others but recognized that she is not alone in coping with her malady. Sensing that there is a "community" of others who also suffer in this particular way, brought her some comfort and a willingness to improve.

Rather than simply giving up in defeat to a Deathworld of OCD, she was allowed an opening to a new Lifeworld, even if it had to be of others suffering the same way. An opening to belong to a group and no longer experience alienation from others had a powerful effect.

8) Zoe – Coping with Depression

> I thought that I was crazy because my feelings were opposites, but my friends had the same feelings. So, I supposed that everyone in the same situation could have the same feelings or similar feelings. My friends and I shared the same illusion and fear of facing the new year and we were happy to overcome school together. But we didn't want this school period to end, because we were finally in our comfort zone.

> In my first protocol, I didn't tell others that during my father's fight with cancer I was diagnosed with depression. So, for me, it was so difficult to be happy at this moment, but I found I could cope and, if I could, everyone could. You have to win the battle in your mind, you have to spend the day thinking positive things. (Zoe, protocol, 2019)

In this protocol, Zoe relates profoundly painful experiences of a severe medical and emotional nature. But she overcomes the challenges of pain and illness – even the life-threatening bout with cancer by her father – by recognizing the deeper battle was in her mind, a mind over which she had control. The Deathworlds of cancer and depression were transmuted into a Lifeworld, a springboard she used as she overcame her setbacks.

9) Sakura – Loneliness

Phenomenon: Loneliness

> I'm going to write about my visits to a nursing home to see my boyfriend's grandfather. Upon entering, there was a hallway where several elderly people were sitting in wheelchairs. They could not move.
> In this phenomenon, I consider that the most important element in life is people. Attending my first protocol, if I had not seen these elderly people and had entered without seeing anyone, nothing would have made me feel lonely. And this means that even though I have no relationship with them, the feeling appeared.
> The problem with this feeling is that it ends in isolation. By loneliness, we understand the prolonged, unpleasant, involuntary feeling of not being significantly or closely related to someone. This feeling of loneliness is not produced inexorably by social isolation (for lack of links with others). It may appear because of the loss of a loved one, the removal of someone or some images as well.
> Thanks to the systems of relevance, I have learned that loneliness has been shown in the lives of all people in one way or another. Therefore, it is important to try to overcome this feeling and to see that it does not last long in our lives because it can trigger harder phenomena such as isolation. (Sakura, protocol, 2019)

In Sakura's protocol, she is introduced to a Deathworld of nearly meaningless human existence in a nursing home. Even though she was among strangers, she shows here a heightened sensitivity to her natural human links to others, registered in her ability and desire to relate to others. She contrasts her liberty and vitality as a young woman with that of elderly patients whose liberties have been radically curtailed and whose vitality is being eroded daily by the aging process.

10) Sara – Musical Identity

> I think my most poignant experience is in my relationship to music. When the music starts, I include all the other players in the space. But, if I remember well, I did not quite include the audience in the space.
>
> Then the adult asked me again if I wanted to sing. I think I didn't really look at her. I felt really tense and felt stuck in place and scared, and I said 'no' again.
>
> The funny fact is that even though I stopped playing over the last three years because of my university occupation, when someone asks me to present myself, I still consider myself to be a musician. It is something that just never leaves me.
>
> So, when I heard this contemporary music, I supposed I felt really frustrated because I was looking for certain kinds of chords (from my country or others) that were actually not present in the song.
>
> In this way, he can feel really himself as being different. So maybe music is also a way for him to assert his identity. Mainstream music doesn't represent his values; it follows the crowd. It is expected music, most of it doesn't have complex writing that makes you think. The music he listens to meets different values; it needs curiosity to find them. The composer tries something new, so he takes a risk by experimenting with a new style.
>
> (Sara, protocol, 2019)

Sara expresses how deeply connected she is with making music, how it is an essential part of her self-image, how moved she is by music, and how different forms of music represent different values, from the mainstream crowd-following type to music that captivates the listener and pushes him beyond the physical pleasures of music, causing the listener think.

The study of music leads to a reassessment of the values guiding one's life. It is more than understanding the biography of the composer, more than placing pieces in the pantheon of musical repertoire. Studying music is a study of physical emotion. How it is that by sounding a simple note, being struck by an ineffable quality in a human voice, or a captivating rich chord possess the power to reach inside and affect one so? These thoughts enrich one's Lifeworld, potentially transforming body and mind since, after all, music is physical before it is emotional.

11) Li – Anxiety, Disorder and Panic

> One time [my father] went to the hospital for a health check. The doctor told him there was a little arrhythmia with his heart. After that, he called me and he asked me, "is arrhythmia a problem?" He was so anxious about that, I told him "it happened to you probably because of stress. Don't worry."
>
> While writing, I felt every moment just as I remembered them. It was especially hard to write the first and second protocol. When I started to write about my first panic attack, I tried to remember how it was. I remembered all the chest pain, the fast heartbeat, being anxious, and just remembering makes me anxious again.
>
> (Li, protocol, 2019)

Conclusion: Many Cultures, One Humankind

Many of the students participating in the Collaboration Among Strangers project thought that they could find friends only within their language group. But as they gradually shared themselves and as they began to open up to others it became clear that they could be friends with people from different countries, because those "different cultures" were not so different after all.

It is only natural for a person to want to bond with others; it is a human instinct. We all seek love, understanding, and mutual respect. We all have our dreams and our demons. We all are afraid of something. What we are afraid of may be different, but the emotional experience is much the same. Perhaps feeling the same things makes us sense how vulnerable to others we are, and they to us.

If we open up to other people, we may not only see and bond with them, we may also receive insight, a startling new glimpse of ourselves. We all share, at bottom, the same essential humanity, somehow. And that is the curious beauty of diversity. We are so different, uniquely interesting, and somehow, we are more alike than different. Feeling that our students came to understand and appreciate that made us happy and proud of the great work they did. Maybe the experience really is remarkable after all.

References

Fleming, Ted (2002): "Habermas on civil society, Lifeworld and system: Unearthing the social in transformation theory". Retrieved from http://www.tcrecord.org/Content.asp?ContentID=10877, visited on January 29, 2010.

Haddad, David (2008): "Intentionality in Action: Teaching Artists Phenomenology". In: Rehorick, David/Bentz, Valerie (Eds.): *Transformative Phenomenology: Changing Ourselves, Lifeworlds and Professional Practice*. Boston: Lexington Press, pp. 193–207.

Husserl, Edmund (1936): *The Crisis of European Sciences and Transcendental Phenomenology*. Evanston: Northwestern University Press.

Moustakas, Clark (1994): *Phenomenological Research Methods*. Thousand Oaks: Sage Publications.

Rehorick, David A./Bentz, Valerie Malhotra (Eds.) (2008): *Transformative Phenomenology*. Lanham: Lexington Books.

Rehorick, David A./Bentz, Valerie Malhotra (Eds.) (2017): *Expressions of Phenomenological Research: Consciousness and Lifeworld Studies*. Santa Barbara: Fielding University Press.

Schütz, Alfred/Luckmann, Thomas (1973): *The Structures of the Life-World, Volume 1*. Evanston: Northwestern University Press.

van Manen, Max (1997): *Researching lived experience: Human science for an action sensitive pedagogy*. London: Althouse Press.

van Manen, Max (2014): *Phenomenology of Practice*. New York: Taylor & Francis.

Part II: **Experiences of Lifeworlds and Deathworlds**

> Perhaps it will even become manifest that the total phenomenological attitude and the epoché belonging to it are destined in essence to effect, at first, a complete personal transformation, comparable in the beginning to a religious conversion, which then, however, over and above this, bears within itself the significance of the greatest existential transformation which is assigned as a task to mankind as such.
>
> – Edmund Husserl, *The Crisis of the European Sciences and Transcendental Phenomenology*, 1936.

David Haddad and James Marlatt
Chapter 8
Restoring Lifeworlds Through Phenomenological Writing, Reflection and Collaboration

Abstract: Doctoral students from the University of the Virgin Islands participated in the "From Strangers to Collaborators" research project, using phenomenological protocol writing. Triggering a unique approach, they were instructed to identify and develop a "most poignant experience" to guide their meditation. A sampling of five writings is presented. Key elements highlighted in the writing include how strangers may become collaborators, the Qualities of Transformative Phenomenologists, Deathworld themes emerging from the protocols, and indications of personal transformation that occurred as a direct result of engaging in phenomenological writing.

Keywords: Transformative Phenomenology, Deathworlds, protocols

Introduction

Doctoral students from three universities located in the United States, Poland, and the Virgin Islands came together in virtual environments in an encounter with Transformative Phenomenology.[1] They were given several resources to use to acquaint themselves with the fundamentals and processes of writing phenomenology. Central to their efforts was the course objective of writing phenomenological protocols. The first of eight protocols involved selecting a memory, a most poignant phenomenon, on which to write a rich description of lived experience.[2]

The purpose of choosing a poignant phenomenon over a pleasurable or aesthetic phenomenon stems from the difference in their nature. Poignancy supplies

---

[1] Students participated in the multi-national and multi-institutional "From Strangers to Collaborators" participatory action research project. See Chapter 1 in this volume, and *Transformative Phenomenology: Changing ourselves, lifeworlds, and professional practice* (Rehorick/Bentz 2008).
[2] The protocol sequence was developed by Valerie Bentz while teaching phenomenology to doctoral students at Fielding Graduate University. See *Expressions of phenomenological research: Consciousness and lifeworld studies* (Rehorick/Bentz 2017).

https://doi.org/10.1515/9783110691818-008

depth and durability of conscious determinations, the judgments that surrounded the event, experience, or relationship.

The reasoning behind this choice is not unlike Robert Kegan's (1994) direction that his Subject-Object interviewees focus on a conflict (Lahey et al. 1983). The internal structure of conflict acts as a lens resolving in finer detail one's mental, emotional, and social distinctions. Kegan's work was not phenomenological; rather, it delved into areas of human development using object relations, measuring and revealing which level of mental complexity interviewees had obtained and by which they made sense of their experiences.

Nevertheless, the principle tracks well from one field to another. By asking our participants to mark the beginning of their protocol writing with a poignant experience, often such a memory will reproduce a keen residual sense of sadness. Natural paths of remembrance often prompt one to search out some way to reorganize years of emotional and social fallout from a most poignant experience, a reexamination that may eventually transmute it into something meaningful.

Mustering a poignant experience as a starting point, students were exposed to three theoretical lanes to guide them as they wrote rich descriptions, casting and re-casting their interpretations. The lanes were formed from the foundational work of Edmund Husserl (Husserl 1913/1931), the father of phenomenology, Alfred Schütz (Schütz/Luckmann 1973/1989), theoretician of the real-world implementation of structures of the Lifeworld, and Kenneth Burke's Dramatist Pentad (Burke 1945).

Our question in this chapter is, at what level can it be claimed that writing phenomenology, that is, following assiduously the steps of the phenomenological protocols, leads to personal transformation? Judging from samples below taken from doctoral students in the Virgin Islands transformation, as a thorough and dramatic change, begins almost immediately. Figure 1 below gives a sense of the work required to accomplish phenomenological writing.

It is difficult for newcomers to phenomenological writing to imagine that it is little more than another in a string of essay assignments, as in, "How I Spent My Summer Vacation." But the very first plunge into writing phenomenologically skips past the taken-for-granted approach to writing, demanding something deeper. Writers quickly realize they must come to terms with phenomenology and its nomenclature. This means spending considerable time gaining a solid understanding of what at first appears to be words bearing obvious meanings. Words like "Lifeworld" sound almost poetic. But phenomenology has a distinct definition of what it is and how to use it correctly. A common word like "bracket" appears to require no further explication. But the effort it takes to grasp its use in phenomenology is as challenging as doing it. Doing it means setting aside preconceptions (which first requires knowing what

Chapter 8 Restoring Lifeworlds Through Phenomenological Writing — 137

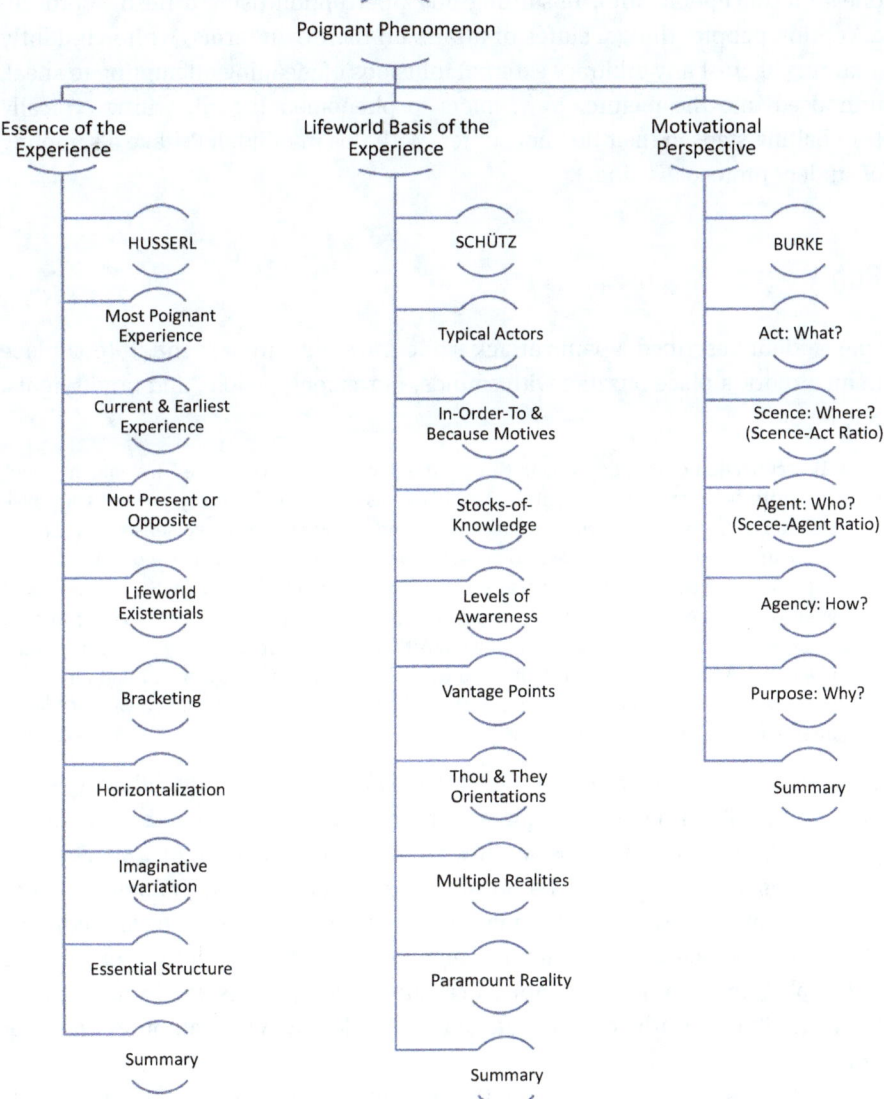

Figure 1: Techniques for the Exploration of Poignant Phenomenon through Writing Phenomenology.
Copyright (2019) by Valerie Bentz and James Marlatt, Reproduced with Permission, Original Artwork.

one's preconceptions are), re-starting one's perception using a fresh approach, accepting people, things, states of affairs on their own terms, while vigilantly guarding against any arbitrary external infusions of meaning attempting to sneak unnoticed into the picture. Newcomers to phenomenological writing typically take halting steps in their first encounter. With this in mind, let's take a sampling of student protocol writing.

Panic

One student described a panic attack while traveling with a friend. It took place in an airport, a place buzzing with sounds, movement, people, and bright lights. She reports:

> My recollection of that day was nothing but a lived experience where I was moving back and forth between two different worlds. It was as if I were physically present yet physically absent. I was . . . struggling to understand, struggling to make sense of what was happening to me. . . . It seemed to me as if I was suffering from a stroke or a blackout. I felt disconnected from the physical self and the environment. . . . I was worried about what or how my friend or others would react, [questioning] if ever I was going to fully grasp and express well what was going on. Although I did not sense any pain in my body, it was terrifying. . . . I was disconnected from the human body. It is as if I had an out-of-body experience. I could see me going through the ordeal, but not being aware of how to intervene in the flesh. This was terrifying for me. (protocol, 2019)

This poignant experience etched itself deeply in her psyche. By following steps of the protocol writing, she attempts to understand and describe the experience just as it happened but keeps well away from scientific accounts. Medical science has much to say about the physical, emotional, and psychological experience of panic. Resisting the temptation to borrow descriptions from medicine, she resolutely focuses her protocol exercise on her first-person lived experience of the phenomenon. Her description captures the rapid descent from a normal Lifeworld into a Deathworld, a state of mind and body where all order taken for granted seems obliterated.

At the end of her recounting of the sudden onset of panic and the years that followed the episode, she is able to round out the experience with some careful reflections. "My phenomena of panic and disconnect not only manifested in my Lifeworld but, more importantly, it has immensely transformed me and allowed me to search for ways to better connect, strengthening bonds and relationships with friends, especially my family."

Death of a Father

The experience of grief, bereavement, and loss is recounted by a student. Her episode occurred years earlier as she transitioned to adulthood:

> The earliest memory of my phenomenon was at the age of twenty. Grief confronted me when I was a junior in college. The phone rang. I went happily to the phone to embrace a happy conversation and eager to answer the person on the other end of the call. There was silence when I answered the phone and my happy self was trying to grasp who the person was and what they were trying to convey. I learned my father was hurt. At that moment, my world seemed to have been captured into a bubble, I appeared to be floating in space watching everything pass me by. I never imagined I would hear that my father was gunned down. I immediately froze. I became speechless, numb, and lost. I began to imagine this was a dream, a nightmare. (protocol, 2019)

The trauma of the news paralyzed her and her family. As she describes, "My dad passed, leaving us in silence, grief, feeling hurt, feeling lost, angry, disbelieving; the full gamut of grief encapsulated and gripped me and my family. We all were sad and lost. We were heartbroken!"

Moving to the horizontalizing stage of the protocol writing, she reports, "We can never exhaust completely our experience of things no matter how many times we consider them. A new horizon arises each time one recedes." A striking image and mental device she invented during horizontalization (Moustakas 1994) was the notion of shrapnel. She relates:

> Shrapnel is a good image for me to grasp tightly. Shrapnel is inside me as grief. I must let the pain of it ease on its own timetable. I have been schooled in a full course of grief. The pain is a reminder of my love and my memories of my former life, but it is also a way of keeping my dad close to me in my heart as I move forward. (protocol, 2019)

As she completed the protocol writing, her emphasis turns to the power of meaning-making, a central theme in phenomenology:

> My experience of grief in my Lifeworld has brought me to a place of peace and safety with my loss and separation from my lost love object, which is my father. I have hope and my human behavior is not of one who has no hope. (protocol, 2019)

In this instance, a profoundly traumatic personal experience, one never to be repeated, has been re-activated, then filtered through phenomenological writing. Trailing a long history of involuntary memories, she squarely acknowledges the abiding emotional scars that persist, yet brings us, finally, to a high endpoint: hope.

Failure

This student's early years were missing the social prompts to pursue the development of her innate talent, to master newly learned skills, to exhibit fidelity to obligation and duty, to take pride from the satisfaction of work well done, to meet personal challenges and overcome them through sustained accomplishment. Yet our doctoral student from the Virgin Islands tells her story as just that. Even though failure was the hallmark and social surround of her youth, she instinctively rejected it as unacceptable, abnormal. But not without strenuous determination.

Showing her spirit of defiance at the very outset of her protocol writing she declares, "failure is a great teacher." Then she freely admits the seeds of power to transmute negative experience were not planted in her childhood garden. She recounts:

> I remember thinking to myself, how I had very few role models throughout my secondary education. There were some educators who saw value in my constant failures and encouraged me to 'fail toward success.' But few placed their hands on my shoulders and assisted me with being my brilliant self. The education system was probably the first place where I felt like a true failure. (protocol, 2019)

She describes her secret rumination, "I was convinced due to the actions, words and thinking of others that failure must be connected to my lot in life." Her social roots are in a Deathworld of human failure, the ubiquitous loss and denial of one's innate ability to create a good life.

Compounding the false narrative of failure, her own mother seemed to betray her by holding her back one year to repeat the second grade. The message was unavoidable. "This was a jail sentence as far as I was concerned. How could she be so cruel and heartless? I *passed* the second grade and she was failing me! I carried this stain of embarrassment and failure throughout my life."

Nevertheless, following the phenomenological protocol sequence, with emphasis on imaginative variations (Husserl 1913/1931; Moustakas 1994), in particular, an effusion of new perspectives on an old memory came to light:

> Instead of my mother's plan, we could have worked with my teacher on ways to support my reading. My teacher could have played a more significant role by offering strategies to strengthen my reading during the year. To complement the instruction I received in school, a tutor could have been assigned to me. My teacher could have created an in-class book club for my classmates and me where we could have read books that interested us. Conversely, my mother could have mirrored the same activity for our family. Using the time to support my sisters and me rather than singling me out. Participating in reading circles held at our local library could have been another option, offering more opportunities to intersect with reading in a fun and nonjudgmental environment. In my opinion, any one or all of the suggestions listed above could have been used in this scenario. (protocol, 2019)

Is there room for Transformative Phenomenology at the adult stage of life through recalling painful formative childhood experiences even long after one has crossed fully into adulthood? The student reflects, "Since failure is a lived experience and everyone will be met with some form of failing, why not embrace it as a phenomenal life experience?" It is this balanced realization, made possible after she had bracketed "failure," met failure on its own terms, that finally transmuted the paralysis of "failure" into opportunity.

Healing

Skeptical of healing, the student, recalling the poignant experience of her grandmother's death, states her resistance:

> I wasn't too convinced in the power of healing at that time, nor counseling either. I always thought I was strong enough to deal with issues on my own. However, when grief and depression started affecting my life and daily functioning, my parents insisted on counseling. I hesitantly attended the first three sessions not opening up, not exploring my feelings. One day I was feeling especially down and my counselor suggested that I use a journal and write down what was bothering me. (protocol, 2019)

Her first brush with journaling opened the floodgates:

> That black and white writing pad changed my life! I jotted down my innermost thoughts and later discussed them with her. It became the highlight of my week to attend the sessions because, not only I was opening up, I was feeling better. This greatly influenced my faith in healing and the counseling process. (protocol, 2019)

Sometime thereafter, her mother passed away. Just one month after her mother died, she felt pressed by the question once more of what healing is, of how one must come to terms with reality, to "transition into a healthier mindset."

Following the protocol writing stages, now seen as a deeper guided process than journaling, the student began to bracket (van Manen 1990) specific elements of her grief. Through the bracketing effort, she was able to turn them into potent positive prompts:

> Healing is not a phenomenon that is readily accepted or understood. I was skeptical about the healing process and had to completely abandon my own thoughts and biases [through bracketing] (mainly needing scientific proof) and trust the steps. With faith and open mindedness, I came to peel away the layers of my grief and overcome them. Additionally, as a healer, I practiced having confidence in my skill to heal others. I have faith in my educational background as well as my experiences that I am a competent healer in my field. Acceptance was the most difficult layer to conquer! I can finally say that my mom is deceased to others. Up until this time, I was unable to outwardly write, speak or

> even think that my mom was no longer alive. I was stuck on the denial stage for over a year. Through healing, I am able to understand and accept her passing. (protocol, 2019)

In the end, following weeks of phenomenological writing, she clearly states:

> Schütz and Luckmann (1973/1989) posit that stocks of knowledge are related to situations and experiences. Stocks of knowledge help us define and master situations. In my case, my experience with grief and death as well as my training in the subjects helped me to reflect on and transition from my state of denial. I finally admitted that I was not in a healthy state of mind and needed to take steps and seek help. Additionally, my experiences working with others with similar experiences helped me to identify and correct in myself my abnormal reaction. (protocol, 2019)

Her admissions of transformative change support the theory that even initial exposure and early practice in writing phenomenology can have a profound impact. It is not viewed by practitioners as a single occurrence; rather, phenomenological writers view it as an ongoing process, performing afresh the protocol writing cycle and, with each turn, deepening the writer's awareness and mastery, discernment, and understanding, enriching the full meaning of an underlying state of affairs.

The Qualities of Transformative Phenomenologists

Signposts of proper phenomenological engagement were presented as a list of Qualities of Transformative Phenomenologists (Rehorick/Bentz 2017). This list was distributed to all students in this project. The signs are:
- adopting phenomenology as a way of being
- embracing embodied consciousness
- writing rich descriptions and collaboratively interpreting meaning
- embracing authenticity and wonderment
- adding to theory, method and the understanding of phenomena
- awareness of Lifeworlds as constructed through patterns of communication
- immersing in the work of our founders and colleagues
- working from the "Epoche" – looking beyond the taken-for-granted
- finding the "whatness" of experience
- transcending the everyday reality of lived experience

The many writings offered up by our doctoral students clearly evinced all of the qualities. For brevity, let's touch on a few: embracing embodied consciousness, authenticity and wonderment, and finding the "whatness" of experience.

Requesting that students focus on writing about poignant experiences opened fissures revealing reservoirs of deep feelings. Many reports were of a traumatic nature, as in the death of a loved one, a panic attack, or the overwhelming experience of a first love. Naturally, the bodily experience of extreme occurrences is entwined with the mental/social experience to the point that, in more than one instance, it is impossible to fairly disentangle which is producing the dominant influence.

In the case of the death of one's father, the environment seemed suddenly shut off. Her experience was that of being captured in a bubble. Being encapsulated bodily is a suffocating experience. She further described the alien sensation of paralysis. She couldn't move, couldn't speak, was locked in indecision as to what to do next. When trauma of the mind, especially when goaded by the shocking sudden death of one's most significant other, one's father, takes over, the body simply goes limp. The recognition that one's body won't take action on its own and requires an exceptional intentional effort even to raise one's hand is awkward, alien, numbing, frightening.

We heard an authentic voice describe the experience of being hit by a car at age four, how natural affectionate love of a family intermingled with the clinical expertise of medical professionals, a powerful generative brew that immersed the child for nearly a year following the incident. We heard authentic voices describe the terror of enduring hurricanes as they were left clutching to life while treacherous storms ravaged their island home.

Speaking with an authentic voice opens a path that leads one deeper, to the issue of "whatness," meaning, *what* really is rooted underneath the surface perception of the experience? At this point, the work became most challenging. For example, getting to the whatness, what is the root, the essence meant by one student who described the exhilarating experience of his first love? He couldn't immediately identify the essence of it. He says so early on:

> My initial feel for the assignment was just the mere idea of explaining the sequence of events that I thought was deemed appropriate to describe this euphoric state. That perception was incorrect. In fact, the assignment comprised a transformational journey that not only highlighted my lack of knowledge of what I felt at the time, but the miscues I encountered due to my novice actions. With reflective work such as protocol writing one is forced not only to question regular events but also to create a stage of heightened awareness that applies to other facets of life, not just the subject, the phenomenon under study. (protocol, 2019)

That is a voice of authenticity, a voice speaking of the whatness of life. When you read several pages of his protocol uninterrupted it makes your stomach feel queasy. Just like your own first love did. That is the voice of authenticity, of whatness, of wonderment.

Collaborating with Strangers

We asked our students to reflect on the impact of being a "stranger" while engaging in collaboration through "writing phenomenology." We asked them to reflect upon the impact of sharing a phenomenon of deep personal significance with others. What was it like to enter into "we-relationships" (Wagner 1970) as they shared their protocols with their fellow learners? Anxiety, vulnerability, discovery, intimacy, openness, empathy, and embracing diversity were some themes that emerged, pointing to the essence of what it is to collaborate. Some of these themes are encompassed in the following statements by our students.

From the What to the How

One student described how being fully aware of the meaning-making potential of collaboration can lead to revelations about the hidden nature of a phenomenon, akin to the phenomenological reduction espoused by Husserl.[3] "The act of being conscious of collaboration . . . provides a way to make meaning of the 'what' we are doing and gives insight into the 'how.' In this respect, we are consciously collaborating; which I believe is powerful."

Collaboration

Another writer comments on the emergence of a sense of community: "As we continue to share our phenomenological writing and give each other feedback . . . layers of 'stranger-ness' continue to peel away." While another makes a deep somatic connection through the sharing of poignant expressions with others:

> Collaborating with strangers were also moments of deep intimacy when the only thing I could do was to live the deep empathy for what I read while feeling and embracing the other, knowing that I had either touched an unknown expression of the other's humanness or I deeply touched myself through the eyes, hands, movements, and heart of the other.
> (protocol, 2019)

Two participants commented that "collaborating with strangers has improved as I worked to get to know classmates on a deeper level through their work" and that

---

[3] Husserl's phenomenological reduction spans from "noema" (that to which we orient ourself) to "noesis" (the interpretative act directed to an intentional object) – through asking "what is the nature of the phenomenon?" to asking, "how is the phenomenon experienced?" (Moustakas 1994).

"collaborating with others is to embrace the possibility to reach new horizons and to build things that I could never build alone." Sharing poignant experiences through phenomenological writing can offer a breakthrough to further exploration:

> What I find most interesting is what experiences my colleagues choose to share. Everyone seems to have distinct poignant experiences, so much so that the experiences seem to drive both their scholarly work and careers . . . sharing my experiences with strangers did not come across as tough, but rather redundant . . . writing phenomenology turned the broken record off . . . in sharing my lived experiences . . . I discovered that I have so much more to discover and talk about, than what I planned. Sharing these experiences with others has been a platform for discovery. (protocol, 2019)

Many of our students affirmed that they developed a deeper understanding of their phenomena, through the sharing of protocols, and the collaborative interpretation of meaning.

Anxiety

Students who come to Transformative Phenomenology for the first time often experience the push-pull of engaging with a new way of seeing and meaning-making[4] that is summed up in the following contribution:

> The initial experience of collaborating with strangers is riddled with anxiety and excitement. You are given the option of revealing your true self or presenting a façade to maintain your privacy. At some point, in phenomenological studies, you have to decide whether you want a genuine experience of learning and growing through sharing or if you want to make a minimal contribution in order to move forward. For some, it is easy to share their truths, but for others, it might be more difficult. I find it much easier to share truths with strangers rather than those who are closest to me. I think this is because there is no vested relationship with a stranger in which I am fearful of being judged. However, I will admit, I do not bare my soul, but will allow for information sharing at the appropriate time. (protocol, 2019)

For this student, the anxiety was reduced when social-distance from fellow student-strangers created a space where she did not feel judged for "speaking" her "truth."[5]

---

[4] "[Students] experienced the push-pull and feelings of hopelessness-dismay while trying to make sense of what phenomenological thinking is all about, how they could apply it to their own lives and projects, and what kept bringing them back to try again and again." (Rehorick/Bentz 2008, p.23)

[5] The sociologist Georg Simmel observed that the stranger "often receives the most surprising openness – confidences which sometimes have the character of a confessional and which would be carefully withheld from a more closely related person". *The Sociology of Georg Simmel* (Wolff 1950).

Vulnerability

There was a certain sense of vulnerability shared by students who willingly divulged their deeply personal protocols with other students. The following two writers succinctly summarized the perceived "opportunity and threats" involved in sharing, yet recognized value in their mutual vulnerability, through writing phenomenology, as a basis for entering into we-relationships:

> Being vulnerable is something that I have always struggled with, and this course is making me address a weakness. The fear of being judged, misunderstood, and/or rejected always runs through my mind. Thoughts of coming across the wrong way and having to defend myself because I jumped to conclusions, haunts me . . . reading the experiences of others, allows me to feel like I know them through their experiences. Starting this course, I was very unsure of how this would work out but seeing, hearing, and exploring their words have helped also to encourage me and forced me to think beyond myself.
>
> As I approach collaborating with strangers, there is both an opportunity and a threat. The opportunity is the potential to make new connections that enrich my life. Perhaps this person will teach me something about myself, or the world, that I don't know. Maybe I can add value to their life . . . I also think that the nature of phenomenological writing causes us to open up in a way that we don't typically do with strangers, thus expediting the vulnerability and connection process. (protocol, 2019)

It took courage and trust to overcome any reticence to share with strangers. But, for those who did, the reward, new ways of seeing and meaning making, was often well worth the effort.

Diversity

And finally, students recognized that learning together benefited from the feedback from engagement with others from different far-flung worlds who bring different vantages: "Overall, collaborating with strangers has been useful in that when you collaborate outside of the usual network, you are blessed with diverse feedback." Another stated:

> Alternate perspectives are another benefit of collaborating with strangers, as most of my colleagues are from different parts of the country, as well as lead lives much different from my own. Diversity among strangers can be so rich and valuable in the learning environment, but I think even more so when it applies to research studies of phenomena or any topic for that matter. (protocol, 2019)

These students affirmed the value of non-judgmental feedback from strangers.

Signs of Transformation

One of the surest signs of transformation is "surprise." When a phenomenological writer hits upon an astonishing discovery that was completely unforeseen, but welcome, freeing, empowering it fills one with a quiet satisfied sense of inner personal accomplishment. That's one way to describe the recurrent transformation phenomenologists undergo. It is the well from which they draw sustenance. We found early, promising signs of this in student writings.

Young lives are rarely set on parallel tracks, though that fact may be difficult for the young at heart to appreciate or accept. As divergent trajectories of life take hold, there are absences that cannot be wished away:

> I distinctly remembered sitting on the curbside at UVI, thinking to myself, "Absence does not make your heart grow fonder, it sends your mind into a quandary. Being alone with my thoughts of love, without any reciprocation was hard-hitting. Grief is the price we pay for love. My first semester at UVI made me realize how vital it is to separate what is real from what I feel. In this instant a level of growth and understanding was achieved through this impending hardship. (protocol, 2019)

His acceptance that the once heroic zenith of love would succumb to all that is merely mundane posed a transformation. Most might refuse it. Seeing that his most prized reality had taken an irrevocable turn and he had to follow is perhaps the most challenging transformation anyone can willingly endure.

A second instance of transformation is demonstrated in our student's recounting of a young life filled with a narrative of failure. Her private Deathworld gave way to an adult life of realism and balance, celebrating new possibilities through an honest appraisal of how failure always has in it the seeds of hidden success, if one will only press on and use a circumspect approach to resolving life's challenging issues.

The transformation in her story begins at the headwaters of enforced mediocrity finally giving way to a world of creative opportunity. In this case, transformation may be thought of as an about-face in attitude. By making the 180-degree turn, she gained the power of interpretation, powers of meaning-making that turned on its head the accepted wisdom of leading a life of defeat.

For her, transformation was akin to shedding an old skin only to find new life waiting beneath. Her transformation wasn't necessarily a radical change in her nature, only the radical change in which aspect of her nature she chose to live out of.

Summary

The many students around the world who participated in the Strangers to Collaborators project had never been exposed to phenomenology before, as far as we know. That means that their motivation to engage with it arose largely out of a common sense of duty to do well in a traditional classroom setting.

Our students took on the challenge of phenomenological writing not knowing what it was or where it would lead. Some read the source material, but not all. For those who did, the point of the class took on some theoretical boundaries, a framework in which to explore. For those who chose not to immerse themselves in the readings, the writing came with a bit more difficulty. And it wasn't the phenomenological side of it that proved most challenging. Their first challenge was trusting that they were in a safe learning environment where strangers could be relied upon to read and comment on each other's work without judgment, without violating their mates' vulnerabilities openly exposed by the learning process, and without making anyone feel foolish or guilty.

And they did it. They stepped over the line. When they did, when they wrote, shared, commented, and repeated the process, they found the barriers between them falling. They found they had more in common than they first guessed. Shocked by this New World approach, collaborative learning was not an easy adjustment. But the real payoff came when so many found that this new methodology, phenomenological writing, really had teeth. It was potent to aid in making sense of life's challenges. It led to deeper perceptions of life than had previously been accessible. In the end, it was freeing, empowering, and transformative.

References

Burke, Kenneth (1945): *A Grammar of Motives*. Berkeley: University of California Press.
Husserl, Edmund (1931): *Ideas I: General Introduction to Pure Phenomenology*. New York: MacMillan Company. (Original work published in 1913)
Kegan, Robert (1994): *In Over Our Heads: The Mental Demands of Modern Life*. Cambridge: Harvard University Press.
Lahey, Lisa/Souvaine, Emily/Kegan, Robert/Goodman, Robert/Felix, Sally (1983): *The Subject-Object Interview: Its Administration and Interpretation*. Cambridge: Subject-Object Research Group.
Moustakas, Clark (1994): *Phenomenological Research Methods*. Thousand Oaks: Sage Publications.
Rehorick, David A./Bentz, Valerie (Eds.) (2008): *Transformative Phenomenology: Changing Ourselves, Lifeworlds, and Professional Practice*. Lanham: Lexington Books.

Rehorick, David A./Bentz, Valerie (Eds.) (2017): *Expressions of Phenomenological Research: Consciousness and Lifeworld Studies*. Santa Barbara: Fielding University Press.
Schütz, Alfred/Luckmann, Thomas (1989): *The Structures of the Life-World Vols. I, II*. Evanston: Northwestern University Press. (Original work published in 1973)
Wolff, Kurt H. (1950): *The Sociology of Georg Simmel*. New York: The Free Press.
van Manen, Max (1990): *Researching Lived Experience*. London: State University of New York.
Wagner, Helmut (Ed.) (1970): *Alfred Schütz: On Phenomenology and Social Relations*. Chicago: University of Chicago Press.

Carol Estrada
Chapter 9
Be-*ing* with Dying: A Personal Experience with the Death of a Young Person

Abstract: This chapter is an exploration of be-*ing* with my son as he was dying of cancer at the age of 22. I used a process of self-reflection facilitated by writing phenomenological protocols. The sample of these writings articulates an exploration of just what it means to be-*ing* with dying. I look at my own experience as data. Taken together as a whole, phenomenology writing protocols are tools that assist us in taking a deep dive into our own experience.

Keywords: being with, dying, Deathworld, Lifeworld, phenomenology, self-reflection

Introduction

As a species we are experiential beings. Every day, every moment that we live brings with it an experience. We pay no attention to most of these experiences and moments. Instead, we end up taking them for granted until they begin to wane or disappear. It is common to find ourselves not living in the moment, but to push through life to get to future moments when we assume we will have time to live in the present. And so it was with me until my son's diagnosis with cancer at the age of 19. He died at age 22.

Arriving at My Experience of Be-*ing with* Dying

When my youngest son was diagnosed with cancer (Hodgkin's Disease). He, like most young adults, was full of vim and vigor. He was a university student, living on his own, supporting himself, feeling as though he was at the beginning of adult life. He thought of himself as invincible in more ways than one, and it truly seemed that way for a while. He started chemotherapy and easily went into remission. But when cancer returned 18 months later, it was resistant to several high-dose chemotherapy regimens, indicating that the disease was likely to take a turn towards an end-of-life trajectory. He wasn't ready! We weren't ready! What was *I* going to do if he died? How was *I* going to lead him on a path he was unprepared to traverse? How would *I* choose to *be-with* (Estrada 2016, p. 32) him? These questions and others occupied every waking moment – and perhaps, in my dreams as well. Intuitively, I knew I needed to up my game, increase my awareness, and endeavor to be present in the moment. This was true if *I* was to be of any help to my boy. I took it upon myself to ease his pain of loss and create a gentle path (if there can be one) from the land of the living (Lifeworld) to the land of the dying and dead (Deathworld).

Introduction to Phenomenology

A few years after JC (my son) had left us, I was introduced to the field of phenomenology. Little did I know that it would have such an impact on my life. I related well to phenomenological writing protocols as developed by van Manen (1990) based on the philosophical explorations and writings of Edmund Husserl and Alfred Schütz. In this chapter, I present how I navigated that very uncertain time when my son was traversing from Lifeworld to Deathworld.

Writing About My Lived-Experience

Following are the phenomenological writing *protocols* (descriptions of lived-experience) I used to get up close and personal with my experience of *being-with* dying. I engaged in these self-reflections six years after my son died. I approached these writings with the viewpoint that my *lived-experience* is readily available and easily accessible to me. I endeavored to explore elements that I might have taken for granted or had overlooked. In so doing, it was possible to uncover or to notice aspects of the experience that were not necessarily at the forefront of the experience – some were, and some were not. From a researcher's perspective, it is desirable to look at the experience as data itself. From there, it is entirely possible to see if my experience is the experience of others, just as it is equally possible that another's experience is my experience . . . or it may be different. Nonetheless, our experiences can be bound together by the nature of human experience itself as we strive to "get closer to the things themselves" (Husserl as cited in Wertz et al. 2011, p. 252).

Etymology

I started this process of writing by delving into the keywords of the phenomenon I wanted to explore – be-*ing* with dying. The experience of be-*ing* with is the basis of this self-reflection though the structure of phenomenological writings. Factually, be-*ing* with dying is my own lived-experience with my son. The suffix -*ing* is emphasized because it denotes either a continuing through time or continuing over a time period. As a family, we had a period of time in which to continue to hope that death would not come or at least it could be staved off for some time. During this continuation period, we also had time to adjust to the fact that death was on the horizon. This emphasis lent importance, to my actions and non-actions. I was consumed with the idea that I needed to proactively be present for my son. When not be-*ing* with him in the physical present my thoughts and learnings concentrated on the future. In this way, I could anticipate what might be needed or desired and not caught off-guard by new physical conditions or phases that he was entering.

My subjective lived-experience was in sharp contrast to the lived-experience of a dear friend who lost her young adult son a few weeks prior to my son's death. Her experience was one in which her son was alive and well one minute and gone (from her) in another – the tragic result of a combination of prescription medication and an over-the-counter drug. For her, there was no be-*ing* with dying. A continuing of time or through time did not exist for her. Time was compressed. There were no saying good-byes; no preparation. The juxtaposition of these two very different lived-experiences created a heightened awareness within me of what be-*ing* with dying meant and how I wanted to be with my son. Her experience made me keenly aware that nothing should be taken for granted during whatever remaining time there was to be. It was a tangible reminder to treasure every moment and to make every moment count. It also provided a reminder of how we should be with each other every day – no need to wait till death is knocking at the door.

Earliest Experience of the Phenomenon

Reflection on the earliest encounter of be-*ing with* dying took the form of a premonition. It occurred after the consulting doctor (prompted by my son's relapse) left us alone in the stark and sterile hospital examination room to ponder the poor prognosis she had delivered:

> I wanted to tell him that we would fight this, that no matter how hard it seemed now, no consequence the discouraging odds, that we'd find a way to make his body strong,

resilient, and invincible again. But what dared to sneak in and obscure those thoughts was the question "What if? What if my son dies?" I endeavored to push that thought away, but that was like trying not to think of the pink elephant in the room. The thought remained with me as I stood there holding him tight. It tugged at my sleeve, like a little child begging for attention. I had no choice; refused it for another day and another time.

(C. Estrada, protocol, 2019)

Most Poignant Experience of Be-*ing with* Dying

Exploration of the most poignant moment of be-*ing* with dying began by delving into the etymology of the word "poignant." True to its Latin root of *pungere,* poignancy elicits an emotion of a pricking or piercing nature. This, I definitely experienced! I wrote:

> The totality of my identity (body and soul) was pierced as I rumbled down the road in my son's Jeep to go grocery shopping. The Jeep–symbolic of his young adulthood identity–together they were invincible and indestructible, rugged, big and tough, cool and hip. Only now, in this time there was a sad, new reality (Figure 1).
>
> The day started out like every other day when I went out to do errands. But it was not like every other day! I hopped into the red Jeep and drove the mile or so to the store. As the Jeep bumped and bounced along the pot-holed road, it hit me . . . 'it' overwhelmed me . . . 'it' smacked me in the face . . . Ouch! . . . 'It' stung!
>
> My boy would never ride in or drive his beloved Jeep again. Could he even muscle his way into it by pulling himself up? I wondered if he could have even walked out the door of the apartment to the car parked so close by. I knew he couldn't. And with that, the world changed.
>
> Big, salty tears began to cascade down my cheeks. I was inconsolable. It was here–the time was here! Ouch! I was stung again! There would be no more fun – no more fun in the way that he liked to have fun. No more would he flash that big smile from the Jeep as he whipped out of the drive. No more would he give the Jeep sign of brotherhood to a passing driver in another Jeep. Oh, such carefree times–times of aliveness and breath, of drinking in the sun and basking in its warmth!
>
> There was no use holding back my tears. I didn't care that strangers might see me and stare. I was entitled. The life of my guy, with all his hopes and dreams was slipping away–from him, from me, from all of us. I couldn't stop it. I couldn't press pause and rewind–it would have been the same story anyway–all I could do was cherish every moment and *be with* him–present in the moment–in whatever way he needed at that moment in time.

(C. Estrada, protocol, 2019)

Figure 1: Beloved Jeep.
Photo by author, Carol Estrada.

The Opposite Of: What Be-*ing* with Dying Is Not

The writing protocol of "what it is not" was one of the most difficult writings to tackle. My first attempt at describing what the phenomenon be-*ing* with dying was not focused on birth/birthing/being born. I explored the beginning of life as the opposite of the end of life – dying and death. The *process* embodied what death is not; or what the objective of death is – the cessation of life. However, it eventually struck me that dichotomy created by looking at living and what it means to be alive (as opposed to birth and death) better captured a fuller picture of what be-*ing* with dying is not; in other words, the juxtapositions of Lifeworlds and Deathworlds:

> Be-*ing with* living – so full of life, energy, doingness. I see that big smile and the gleam in his eyes. I smile to myself. He's all grown up. He dashes into the house and out again. I want to keep him here to enjoy his presence, but I dare not. This is his time. He's finding out who he is, enjoying himself with friends, being young, growing up, making his life. I can hardly believe he is 6 feet tall. My "baby" has become a grown man. I can see him in my mind's eye, rolling his eyes at me if he heard me say that! He is full of life and boundless optimism. I let it go. No need to cling; other moments are in the offing. Life is before him and I can hardly wait for him to share it with me again.   (C. Estrada, protocol, 2019)

Much can easily be taken for granted as be-*ing* with living was reflected upon and examined. Without attention that is mindful of the present, I found it commonplace for me to rush around, to not be in the moment resulting in precious moments slipping by unnoticed.

In contrast, when one is be-*ing* with dying, every moment is treasured, noticed, appreciated; a perspective from which the living could benefit. In be-*ing* with dying time elongates and moments meld into one another. In this elongated time there exists a *quality* of time (Bergson 1910/2015, p.110) as opposed to a *quantity* of time – moments to treasure and hold close.

The Essence or Essential Structure of Be-*ing with* Dying

Phenomenology from a Husserlian perspective is the study of essences – the unified vision that makes a phenomenon or an experience what it is (Moustakas 1994, p.46). Therefore, when engaging in phenomenological writing concerning the essence, we want to consider the intrinsic components of that which is being studied or, in the case here, being reflected upon. However, attempts at using prose as the genre of expression failed to adequately capture for me the *essential nature* (essence) of my lived-experience. It was a struggle until the creativity of an acrostic poem format provided a way to reveal the purity of the act and actions of be-*ing* with dying:

> **Be-*ing with* Dying**
>
> **B**eing present
> **E**ver aware
> **I**nsisting on nothing
> **N**ot resisting
> **G**iving into all that is sentient
>
> **W**illingness to be with what is
> **I**nviting flows
> **T**ime has history, presence, and future
> **H**olding love close without restriction
>
> **D**eepening of surrender
> **Y**es! To all
> **I**ndelible imprints upon our souls
> **N**o grasping at attachment
> **G**ratitude

The Lifeworld

Max van Manen (1990, pp.1–34) asserts that the Lifeworld is the exploration ground for human science research. In it, we find different experiences and points of reference that separate one particular Lifeworld (as a reflection of lived-experience) from another. However, there are certain existentials that are common among all Lifeworlds – lived-space, lived-body or embodiment, lived-time, and lived-relationships as defined and described by van Manen (1990, pp.101–106). Additionally, as roles change (even as frequently as throughout the day) so do our realities change – at varying times we are a parent to our children, a child (even as adults) to our parents, a teacher, a student, and a business owner or an employee.

As I began to write about the *Lifeworld of Be-ing with Dying*, an alternative reality came into sharp focus as well: the reality of life soon to come to an end. This reality would exist in opposition to the taken for granted reality of continuing into old age. These realities were fundamentally different, not simply different aspects of the same world. When curative treatment was stopped, my son's taken for granted reality of continuing into old age began to fade. His new paramount reality was a *Lifeworld in Transition*. Pattison (1977, pp. 44–45) refers to this period as the living-dying interval. We were surrounded by transitions – transitions of space, time, embodiment, and relationships. It was as if one reality abruptly ended and "Presto!" we were dumped into a new one. In the reality of continuing to old age, he was looking towards the future, planning his life (even if day by day), enjoying his friends, and cultivating relationships. However, once hospice care began there was a new reality created by the crisis of the knowledge of inevitable death (Pattison 1977, pp. 222–225). It was a liminal state of betweenness – a reality of transition, often seeming like he had one foot in the Lifeworld and one into the Deathworld. This led to my awareness of multiple worlds and their relationship to one another and made me realize that I would have to navigate them.

The Multiple Realities of Be-*ing with* Dying

Even for me, on a day-to-day basis, there was the "reality of livingness" with my other young adult children as we gathered together in Florida. This contrasted with the very different "reality of be-*ing with*" my dying son, who often floated seamlessly from the land of living into the land of active dying – one minute he was here with us, the next off somewhere else in the time and space of a Lifeworld to which the rest of us were not privy.

The Lived-Space Aspect of the Lifeworld

As I observed and became aware of these different worlds, several facets of space itself were revealed to me. These facets are always present, but without the opportunity to reflect on them, some would have gone unnoticed and their significance overlooked.

Physical Space

My son had his own space in Florida. The small, student apartment was his in every sense of the word. He had made it a real home. The lease was in his name. He paid the bills from the funds he received from Disability Services. He maintained control of that space throughout his illness. He was the ruler of his kingdom. He exerted a tangible control over his environment. He called the shots. It truly was his place.

Personal Space

> At times there were up to ten of us in that small, cramped apartment. Each of the boys had their own room. "Ahhh!" the luxury they enjoyed! The rest of us shared – one daughter on the couch, another on the floor; other family members on inflatable mattresses; me on a series of lined-up beanbags – each of us carved out our own little territories.
> (C. Estrada, protocol, 2019)

Interior Space

> A pot of simmering chicken soup on the stove warmed and nourished our bodies from the inside out, as did mountains of potato tacos replete with shredded cabbage and spicy salsa atop. There's nothing better for the soul than perceptible and visceral taste and enjoyment of comfort food whatever it might be. As incredible as it might seem, JC ate 37 potato tacos in one day . . . and this was just three weeks before he died! He needed that comfort on so many different levels – physically, emotionally, spiritually.
> (C. Estrada, protocol, 2019)

Emotional Space

As one might imagine, emotions tended to run high and fragile as the end of my son's time with us grew near. It was hard to watch him stoically suffer through fevers that went off the chart. We stood by helpless as he hastened toward the end, our hearts breaking in two. Our petty foibles irritated each other as we dealt with the impending loss, each in our own way. From time to time, emotional silence was broken and yet in every arena, an oppressive silence enveloped our family. We all were suffering. We hoped he didn't notice. Not a chance! (C. Estrada, protocol, 2019)

The Lived-Body Aspect of the Lifeworld

Phenomenology provided the vocabulary and the framework in which to place the experience of, what up till then, I had described as "communal naptime." Like the action of the mother of a newborn baby who sleeps when her baby sleeps, as a family, we all slept when my son slept so that we would all be ready for whatever activity, desire, or road bump might be in store upon waking.

Lived Body

Tiredness washed over us producing a heavy, almost drug-like induced state. It seemed to emanate from my son; oozing from him as he was overwhelmed by his own body (the cancer spreading) and his own mental fatigue. The mental fatigue brought about by a combination of the medications he was taking, his fears and anxiety of the unknown-ness of death, as well as the extreme sadness and frustration of having to face his mortality at such an early stage in life. My heart was constantly breaking. I gave in to the heaviness of sleep and let the lids of my eyes shut out the world. I knew this was happening to others too. This "overwhelming" consumed all present; we could not fight it. We were re-enacting on a daily basis the slumber scene from *Sleeping Beauty*. We were the visceral manifestation of his physical, mental, and spiritual worlds.

The Lived-Time Aspect of the Lifeworld

I was traveling across the country every three weeks to be with my son whenever he checked into the hospital for a subsequent round of chemotherapy. I'd stay a week or 10 days, then fly home. But it was in the heat of August, a short three days after returning home from one of those Florida trips that he called. He said, "Mom I need you."

Lived Time

That was all it took. I didn't miss a beat! Time was marching on and it wasn't going to march on without me. My boy needed me. He had asked. I couldn't get time to move fast enough. There was so much to do. I wanted to be on that plane right that same day, but that was unrealistic. "Get me out of here," my body was screaming! Despite my impatience, time flew as I completed necessary tasks in preparation to be with my son. I even slept fast! It seemed the faster I worked the more I got done, but there was always more to do. True enough, now I was putting my life on hold. He could not do the same. Time didn't slow till three days later when I stepped off the plane. For the first time, I welcomed the heat and humidity of summer in Florida. The weather itself beckoned all to slow down, to take one's time. That's just what we needed–more time together; more time to cherish.

The Lived-We (Relationship) Aspect of the Lifeworld

Differences between our family and JC's friends rose occasionally to the surface. Those times boasted of conflict and disagreement and always needed kid-glove handling and management. This was one of the most difficult areas I had to deal with while be-*ing* with my son. On the other hand, there were moments of sheer bliss, when all of us came together, to act together, to be as one, and to bask in the beauty of relationships.

Lived Other (Discord)

The room spun. I was standing in the middle of it, near the foot of the bed. My son had died a short time earlier and yet I knew he (the spiritual being) was in the room with me. Tears were streaming down my face. I shook. I knew what needed to happen. I needed to hold it together, to be gentle, and to not scare him away. I sensed that he was upset (he never did like disagreement), but there had just been one. I was certain that I had to hold my position so as not to cave into the demands of others. This was my family, my boy, and I knew these were my last minutes together with him. In the moment, I'm feeling crazed! I don't care! I turned to where I sense him to be (location) and I make a verbal promise to him that I will make this right. He just needed to give me a moment . . . please.

I think to myself. Everyone knew; I had told everyone myself. I knew I had said that caring for our newly dead was a family thing. It was private, special, a time for delicate intimacy, a time for closure, a time to say "Good-bye." It was part of the ritual that had gone on for decades, maybe hundreds of years in my family – a connection of past and present. I was going to honor it, to honor him. I simply needed a moment to rein in the chaos and explain it all over again to those that had not understood or who had not chosen to hear what was to be.

Lived Other (Bliss)

My dying son, strung out on morphine and dealing with a raging fever, conspired with one of his sisters to bake a cake for my birthday. He designed a "Dream Cake" – some blur between his favorite and mine. It came complete with a set of instructions penned by his shaky, but clear intentioned hand and presented with a handmade candle at 3:00 am. It was one of those moments when time goes on forever and the air fills with the bliss of love, relationship, and connection (Figure 2).

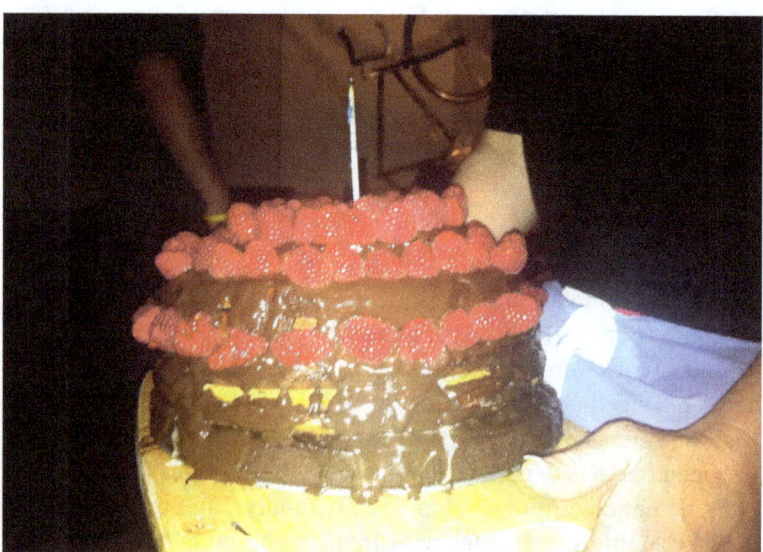

Figure 2: Dream Cake.
Photo by author, Carol Estrada.

Conclusion

Phenomenological writing brings to the forefront our personal knowledge; knowledge derived from our own lived experiences; and knowledge that can serve as "data." It involves the effort to articulate all of the details of our everyday life (van Manen 1984, p. 36). These details comprise the fabric of the lived-experience. Bentz and Shapiro (1998, pp. 96–99) point out that taking a phenomenological approach is desirable when one wants to learn and understand a given phenomenon. This can be for self or used to understand the lived-experiences of others. It forces us by its very nature to increase our awareness and become astute observers of the experience.

I found meaning through the self-reflection process using the various writing protocols as set forth by van Manen (1984, pp. 36–69). This has proved to be an enlightening and meaningful first step to in-depth exploration of be-*ing* with dying and other experiences that surround dying and death. The exercise of writing on the introspection of be-*ing* with dying has flushed out and raised awareness of biases, perspectives, and lived-experiences that I bring to this particular research area. The process has delineated precisely where I *am* in relation to the phenomenon of be-*ing* with dying. This has paved the way so that now I may more readily see and understand where others *are* without imposing my subjective experience on them.

Phenomenological protocol writing is a solo exercise. If, as researchers, we write *our* lived-experience, we are better prepared to know what it is that we are asking of our research participants. Together we can create an understanding of the human experience – of its depths, its reaches, and its boundaries. Starting with each of us individually, our experiences become a co-created social construct that can lead us to an existential view of increased knowledge and understandings of our world.

References

Bentz, Valerie Malhotra/Shapiro, Jeremy J. (1998): *Mindful Inquiry in Social Research*. Thousand Oaks: SAGE Publications.
Bergson, Henri (2015): *Time and Free Will: An Essay on the Immediate Data of Consciousness* (F. L. Pogson, Trans.). Mansfield: Martino Publishing. (Original work published in 1910)
Estrada, Carol (2016): *Telling the Story of Saying Good-bye: A Mother's Last Journey with Her Son* (unpublished Master's thesis). Pacific Oaks College, Pasadena.
Moustakas, Clark (1994): *Phenomenological Research Methods*. Thousand Oaks: SAGE Publications.

Pattison, E. Mansell (1977): *The Experience of Dying*. Englewood Cliffs: Prentice-Hall.
van Manen, Max (1984): "Practicing Phenomenological Writing". In: *Phenomenology + Pedagogy* 2. No. 1, pp. 36–69.
van Manen, Max (1990): *Researching Lived Experience: Human Science for an Action Sensitive Pedagogy*. Albany: State University of New York Press.
Wertz, Frederick/Charmaz, Kathy/McMullen, Linda/Josselson, Ruthellen/Anderson, Rosemarie/McSpadden, Emalinda (2011): *Five Ways of Doing Qualitative Analysis: Phenomenological Psychology, Grounded Theory, Discourse Analysis, Narrative Research, and Intuitive Inquiry*. New York: Guilford Press.

Tetyana Azarova
Chapter 10
Inspiration in Times of Personal Challenge: A Mindful Inquiry

Abstract: This phenomenologically based mindful inquiry looked at inspiration from a different lens as an embodied psycho-spiritual phenomenon that has an intrinsic relationship to an individual, including his Lifeworld, existential struggles, and personal development. Prior phenomenological research reported participants feeling inspired while in a situation of depression, personal challenge, or hardship. Inspiration may transform oppressed and fragmented Deathworlds into Lifeworlds where people could feel fully alive. This research looks at the meaning of inspiration in persons' lives by engaging nine individuals to reflect on their experiences of inspiration in a period of personal challenge and struggle. Individual stories of challenge and inspiration revealed eight themes: (a) paradigm; (b) tension or congruence gap; (c) challenge, radical opening, or "boiling point"; (d) "mirror" and connection; (e) expanded (embodied) awareness; (f) "the moment of truth"; (g) liberation, empowerment, and shift; and (h) integration. Inspiration plays an important role in human life as a cyclical process supporting personal development and consciousness evolution. Inspiration provides temporary relief from existential struggles, thus supporting personal well-being.

Keywords: inspiration, Lifeworld, phenomenology, spirituality, mindful inquiry

Introduction

Human inspiration is a phenomenon that has an intimate relationship with the individual Lifeworld and life itself. The word *inspiration* has the same etymological roots as "spirituality" and "spirit," linking these concepts to breath, air, or the physical act of inhaling. Inspiration as a breathing process literally supports life on the physiological plane. Similarly, it appears to support life on the psycho-spiritual plane. Phenomenological studies show that inspiration often emerges in the state of "dispiritedness" or struggle, tension, crisis, and problem. The opposite or absence of inspiration in one's life is commonly described as depression, anxiety, obsession, frustration, or "pulling back from life" (Hart 2000, p. 41), while inspiration seems to bring the energy to go forward (Azarova 2019; Hart 1993, 1998, 2000; Karakas 2010; Rourke 1983).

Inspiration is a potent human phenomenon conveying a sense of aliveness and well-being. American society and the global community currently struggle with rising incidents of mental illnesses, including depression and suicide. These can be seen as signs of profound dispiritedness and loss of life's meaning in Lifeworlds that in the past decades have turned into oppressed, fragmented, and commodified technological *Deathworlds*. Since inspiration is a life-affirming phenomenon, there is hope that a deeper understanding of individual inspiration can help to address this struggle and heal our fragmented Lifeworlds (Azarova 2019; Bentz et al. 2018; Hart 1993, 1998, 2000; Kessler 2012; Kleiman/Beaver 2013; Substance Abuse and Mental Health Services Administration 2017; Thrash/Elliot 2004; Thrash et al. 2010; World Health Organization 2018).

There has been confusion about what inspiration is because of its momentous and elusive nature, and because it appears intertwined with other phenomena, such as creativity, intuition, insight, illumination, revelation, ecstasy, and motivation. Among other factors contributing to this confusion are the reduction of inspiration experience to instances of remarkable revelations and creative insights, or its attribution to only extraordinary and creative people, such as artists, poets, scientists, and prophets (Assagioli 2007; Azarova 2019; Clark 2000; Hart 1993, 1998).

For many years scholarly discussion of inspiration lacked the recognition that human inspiration is connected to a Lifeworld of a particular individual and that this phenomenon does not exist without a person. Instead, inspiration was narrowly viewed as something random, externally triggered, momentary, and independent of an individual. The theories of inspiration in the literature often regarded inspiration as an external influence, gift, or blessing of some deity, where the inspired person was a passive recipient of this blessing, or as an extraordinary work of the mind of a genius. The dominant view traditionally has been that an individual's role is passive in the inspiration process (Azarova 2019; Clark 2000; Shiota et al. 2017; Thrash/Elliot 2004).

In this chapter, I present a different lens of looking at individual inspiration through its relationship to a particular individual and his Lifeworld. By examining the lived experience of inspiration through the prism of the Lifeworld of nine individuals, their struggles, and developmental tasks I found evidence that inspiration is not a random moment but a cyclical process that supports personal development and the evolution of human consciousness (Azarova 2019). Next, I will share the results of my phenomenologically-grounded mindful inquiry into the deeper meaning of an inspiration experience in a period of personal challenge based on the rich stories of eight individuals I interviewed for a dissertation study and my own lived experience.

Inspiration as a Transpersonal Phenomenon

As a starting point in my inquiry, I had to recognize not only the mental aspect of human inspiration, which was often the focus of mainstream research, but also consider embodied and spiritual dimensions of this phenomenon. I used Mindful Inquiry – a meta-framework that combines four approaches to knowing: phenomenology, Buddhism, hermeneutics, and critical social science (Bentz/Shapiro 1998). Considering inspiration as a transpersonal event I explored the intersection of three conceptual domains: inspiration, spirituality, and person. Closer examination of the conceptualizations of spirituality and its relationship to a person allowed me to see inspiration as a mechanism or process that helps to open up a person to a spiritual experience and shift the human being toward his true self (also known as the soul, authentic self, higher self), and *Spirit* (Assagioli 2007; Azarova 2019; Hart 1993, 1998, 2000).

The word Spirit is often used to describe a vital principle or life force that gives life to all physical organisms. Assagioli (2007) called the Spirit a "Supreme Reality" that defies concrete definitions because of the human mind's limitations to comprehend the fullness of this phenomenon. It is hard to define spirituality and Spirit; however, many cultures and traditions share common ideas and meanings to describe it. The word "Spirit" can be used interchangeably with the words "consciousness," "God," "Self," "life-force," "divine energy," "Qi," "Holy Spirit," "Tao," "prana," and others (Fry 2003; Karakas 2010; Wilber et al. 2008).

One of the basic definitions of spirituality is the feeling of connectedness with self, others, and the universe. The essence of spirituality seems to be reflected in two words: transcendence and interconnectedness. It can also be viewed as the fusion of positive emotions (love, hope, joy, forgiveness, compassion, faith, awe, and gratitude) that connects human beings with each other and with what they experience as "God." Most spiritual and religious traditions agree that Spirit, regardless of the name used, means goodness, truth, beauty, and love. However, humanity seems to be trapped in a constant spiritual struggle, feeling alienated and isolated from Spirit. Within many spiritual traditions, there is a notion that most people cannot connect with Spirit because they live in separation, duality, or an illusory state (Case/Gosling 2010; Mitroff/Denton 1999; Vaillant 2008; Wilber et al. 2008).

Individual Lifeworld and the Dominant Paradigm

During my inquiry into the deeper meaning of an inspiration experience in a period of personal challenge, I employed Lifeworld analysis to gain an understanding of participants' Lifeworld as the contextual background for challenging life experience and for inspirational moments. The concept "Lifeworld," developed by Edmund Husserl and Alfred Schütz, and a similar concept *being-in-the-world*, developed by Martin Heidegger, refer to the idea that humans exist in the world that is given to them before making any abstraction, theorizing, or rationalizing about it. This position of "being thrown" into the world means that an individual's existence, understanding, and action are biographically, socioeconomically and historically determined by the concrete characteristics of his world and life situations (Alvesson/Sköldberg 2000; Heidegger 1953/2010; Rehorick/Bentz 2008; Schütz 1970; Schütz/Luckmann 1973).

In his Lifeworld, an individual orients himself and directs his interests pragmatically using a "system of relevances" and "stock of knowledge at hand." In the core of the individual system of relevances is a governing *social paradigm* (system of values and beliefs), and personal value system. The need to be included, or at least tolerated, by social groups requires the individual to accept the group's values, rules, and meaning schemas or adjust one's values and meaning structures to the dictates of the group. All nine participants of my study were influenced by a *materialistic paradigm*, and it affected their values and shaped their experience of personal challenge and inspiration (Heidegger 1953/2010; Schütz 1944; Schütz 1970).

A materialistic paradigm is a specific set of values, beliefs, and rules that created the foundation and script of development for the current capitalist socioeconomic system and it is interconnected with conformist and achievement levels of human consciousness evolution. This paradigm influenced Western culture for several hundred years and was gradually adopted in other parts of the world. It has penetrated many aspects of human life, including science, politics, economics, education, family, relationships, and other areas, becoming a dominant worldview (Capra 1996; Capra/Luisi 2015; Four Arrows 2016; Laloux 2014; Macy/Brown 2014; Scharmer 2009; Wade 1996; Wallerstein 2007).

Prominent scholars and systems thinkers have for several decades been raising awareness of the global community about the multi-level crisis fueled by the materialistic paradigm. Otto Scharmer (2009) described this crisis as a deep split happening on three levels: economic, cultural-spiritual, and ecological. This crisis has also manifested in the individual being divided from self, others, and the universe, which ultimately appears in rising trends of addiction, mental illness, anxiety, depression, and suicides (Capra 1996; Four Arrows

2016; Macy/Brown 2014; Maté 2010, 2011; Meadows et al. 2006; Scharmer 2009; Scharmer/Kaufer 2013; Wilber 2000).

In my study most participants reported accepting the values of a materialistic paradigm as taken-for-granted in early adulthood and following on autopilot for a long time. This included being fixated on material achievements such as work, education, and pursuing an expected life path that is accepted as good and successful by the society in which they lived. Some participants later realized that this was *inauthentic* living, which created problems and tensions in their lives. For one participant, this inauthenticity appeared in society's obsession with maintaining a "face" or appearance of success and achievement in all aspects of life. Another participant compared this to wearing a mask in daily life. This resonates with Carl Rogers' (1961/1995) description of how society forces an individual to become a "façade," disconnecting from his true self. The focus on external symbols of power, success, and authority, and the need to show off a perfect image, creates a fundamental split in a person's psyche. This then manifests as denial or distrust of one's own subjective truth and authority.

Living in this materialistic paradigm could be quite lonely, stressful, and unbearable. The outcome of this often manifests in numbing the pain in addictive behaviors and drug abuse, as defense mechanisms against stresses of daily life. Indeed, even in my study, seven out of nine participants admitted becoming workaholics as a way of coping with the demands of the paradigm. One shared about her struggle with alcohol, and another mentioned trying drugs as a coping mechanism. One was severely traumatized by the paradigm through compulsory participation in a war. Several participants of this study used the metaphor of living in a cage or prison to describe their past life from the current position of a transformed individual (Fromm 1941/1994; Maté 2010, 2011; Palmer 2000, 2004).

The analysis of the dynamic between social versus individual paradigm and values highlights the deeply embedded and unavoidable tension of an individual living in the world – the tension between being thrown into the world and the inner call to find one's way, to rise to one's maximum potential. Martin Heidegger posits that ordinary individuals' way of living is being thrown into the world and falling prey to the dictatorship of "the *they*." It pushes an individual into a mode of inauthenticity and dependency. It is a mode of living focused on averageness, where the everyday Being (or *Dasein*) of being-in-the-world prescribes what to do and how to do it, and there is no room for anything original. This inauthentic mode of Being "dissolves one's own Dasein completely into the kind of being of 'the others'" (Heidegger 1953/2010, p. 123). In contrast, the ultimate dimensions of Being (Dasein) cannot be locked into the limits of any imposed paradigm.

This dictatorship of the *they* and the pressure of the external paradigm is vivid in the stories of participants in my study. For many, early in life, these people yielded to the demands of others in order to be accepted and socialized in the world. These participants adhered to their values, aspirations, and ideals of their development to the average accepted standards of the *they* in order to earn a living and have a successful career. This practice, as Heidegger observes, disconnects an individual from his authentic self. This is a problem encountered by most participants in my study, whose many moments of personal challenge and inspiration were themed around the discovery of the true self, authentic self, and connecting with one's core values.

Inspired Lifeworld Versus Uninspired Lifeworld

One of the ways to gain a deeper understanding of individual Lifeworld is to examine its structure from four existential angles: relationality, corporeality, spatiality, and temporality (van Manen 1990; Wertz 2005). In this study I looked at the structure of an individual everyday Lifeworld when it is completely uninspiring, or when it turns into a Deathworld, to see how inspiration transforms it.

Relationality

This dimension describes the relationship between lived self and other, including aspects of connectedness, communication, and community. Based on participants' stories, when the everyday Lifeworld lacks inspiration, deep problems in the area of relationality can emerge in the form of disconnection, or fragmentation, from the inner self as well as a lack of genuine connection with others. Relationships with others are often established on the principles of competing, dominance, and inauthentic behavior. The uninspiring Lifeworld is full of power struggle, emotional imbalance, and reactive ego. People are frequently playing roles and wearing masks. They struggle to be open, genuine, vulnerable, and imperfect. Uninspiring relations are emotionally grounded in fear, resentment, anger, judgment, shaming, and so on. This promotes further disconnection and blocks understanding and acceptance. In contrast, inspiration seems to heal these problems, bringing in connection, a sense of acceptance, love, appreciation, openness, authenticity, and integration. Inspiration at its core is about the most important relationship – connection with one's inner truth and congruence.

Corporeality

This dimension of the Lifeworld examines how the body is experienced and engaged in the world. A Lifeworld that lacks inspiration often shows a disconnection from the body, mistreatment of the body, and high psycho-somatic stress. It is also accompanied by a higher emotional imbalance. Somatic sensations used by participants to describe lack of inspiration were exhaustion, depression, feeling choked, suffocating, feeling an energetic hole in the chest, being drained, stressed, feeling dead, and lacking vitality. An unhealthy relationship with one's body appeared in addictive behaviors such as workaholism, and alcohol and substance abuse. In contrast, inspiration filled the body with energy, uplifted, and created a sense of well-being. It brought a sense of brilliance, peace, harmony, lightness, empowerment, and healing. Many participants discovered that inspiration was felt in their bodies: in the chest area, solar plexus, throat, cheeks, arms, and so on. Several participants described their distinct somatic patterns of inspiration.

Spatiality

This lens allows seeing how space is experienced in a Lifeworld. Participants in my study described the spatiality of an uninspiring Lifeworld as feeling caged, trapped, or imprisoned; being stuck or boxed; running in circles or having no path forward. Lack of inspiration was also connected to feeling unsafe or being invaded in a private space. On the other side, inspiration brought a sense of liberation, freedom, relief, or feeling boundless. Inspiration knocked down barriers and removed blocks. The moment of inspiration could be experienced as entering a different reality, opening a portal into another reality, transcendence, or being "on cloud nine." This effect of inspiration is aligned with the Schützian idea of "multiple realities" and transcendence of the everyday Lifeworld (Barber 2017; Schütz 1945; Schütz/Luckmann 1973).

Temporality

This angle of the Lifeworld allows a look at the individual experience of time in relation to the phenomenon of inspiration. In a Lifeworld lacking inspiration, time can be experienced as slow, dragging, stretching, and unbearable. In contrast, during an inspired state time may lose its sense, stops being a dimension of existence, it transcends. Inspiration may turn off a sense of time, replacing it with a continuous joyful flow state or "timeless" and powerful sense of now. During inspiration, time may also be perceived as a magic moment or as "a spell." In other words, inspiration allows what Schütz and Luckmann (1973) referred to as "transcendence of world time" through alteration of consciousness (p. 46).

In summary, there is a clear distinction when applying four existential lenses to uninspiring versus inspiring Lifeworlds. An uninspiring Lifeworld is an experience of "stuckness," inauthenticity, decay, and fear while an inspiring Lifeworld is one of liberation, authenticity, vitality, and joy.

Eight Phenomenological Themes

As a result of the phenomenological and hermeneutic analysis of lived experiences, a cyclical eight-theme pattern of individual challenge and inspiration emerged, which I named the Cycle of Expansion and Renewal. The steps of this pattern include (1) paradigm; (2) tension or congruence gap; (3) challenge, radical opening, or "boiling point"; (4) "mirror" and connection; (5) expanded [embodied] awareness; (6) "the moment of truth"; (7) liberation, empowerment, and shift; and (8) integration.

Theme 1: Paradigm

All participants in my study described that they engaged situations of personal challenges or struggles guided by a certain set of personal values and beliefs. Often, they talked about values that they adopted from parents, society, organizations, professional circles, and friends. Many of them spoke of taking this imposed paradigm for granted, assuming that it was the correct map of life to be followed as "my own." Some resonant phrases that they used to describe this were living on "autopilot," being on "default setting," being "stuck in a model," or behaving according to "computerized meta-program." The rules and models were deeply ingrained in participants' memories during childhood and early adulthood and it often took years to develop some awareness of stuckness. When they were young adults, participants rarely thought of rejecting imposed relevances.

This resonates with what Schütz (1944, 1945) called "thinking as usual" or adopting an attitude of taking-for-granted, that he described as a natural human predisposition to take the world and everything in this world for granted until the appearance of a shock or counterproof. Schütz (1944) spoke of this attitude:

> Any member born or reared within the group accepts the ready-made standardized scheme of the cultural pattern handed down to him by ancestors, teachers, and authorities as an unquestioned and unquestionable guide in all the situations which normally occur within social group. (p. 501)

One study participant shared this typical example of living within a certain paradigm:

> I was on default setting for most of my life. I adopted values that were handed down to me from my parents, particularly my mother . . . . I still think they were not negative values. But they were more materialistic values. They were more values around making sure that I was more financially self-sufficient, making sure that I could provide for myself – this sort of values . . . . But when I began to feel particularly empty, like: "Ok. So, I have achieved financial sufficiency! Now what?" That's when I had to re-evaluate my values, because that was my first time, when I actually thought about my own values instead of just adopting somebody else's.

Theme 2: Tension, Congruence Gap

All participants talked about a certain tension that was in the background of a challenging personal situation. Sometimes there were multiple tensions, problems, or threats of various kinds and to varying degrees. While living with a certain paradigm or a set of beliefs for a while, participants commented about at some point developing awareness of the tension, gap, or emptiness. Sometimes they could tolerate this tension for years. In other situations, tension could be strong, unbearable, or potentially threatening to the person's well-being, and this required quicker resolutions. In many instances, the specific situation of personal challenge or struggle that participants picked for discussion was already a culmination or sudden "last strike" in the previous tensions that led to this situation.

A participant developed tension in response to her stressful, high demand, and achievement-oriented career. This was masked by dependence on alcohol as a stress-coping mechanism and a social networking ritual:

> I was drinking daily and it was affecting my psychological and physical health, affecting my performance . . . . I was struggling to go to work, perform at work and this is connected with the struggles of trying to create something, build a practice . . . . And it was a way of coping with the high stress of my job for years! The alcohol masked issues that I had with the materialistic aspects of [my life]. So, it allowed me to ignore that it was ultimately quite an empty way of living.

Theme 3: Challenge, Radical Opening, "Boiling Point"

Participants presented many examples of a sudden personal challenge that was a result of uncontrollable events, such as becoming sick, losing a job, civil unrest in the country, being drafted to war, or the loss of loved ones. They also shared examples of challenges that erupted suddenly from previously accumulated tensions, such as relationship issues, marriage problems, feeling stifled or stressed in a workplace, dealing with old traumas and health problems, and others. These events often served as final strikes or reaching the "boiling point," opening participants' awareness of those previously suppressed and hidden issues or tensions. This theme represents a "shock," which Schütz (1945) considered necessary for an individual to interrupt his attitude of taking-for-granted. The resonant phrases that participants used to describe these situations were "falling off a cliff," "shock," "suffocation," "choking," "glitch of the system," and others. These often were the moments when the old tensions, the internal incongruence, or constraints of the current paradigm had to be faced openly and could no longer be avoided.

One participant described the relationship challenges which created an openness to a new awareness about the situation, and the accompanying inspiration to change the old patterns. This participant used the poignant phrase "boiling point," which captured the essence of the struggle:

> I was stuck in the anger, disappointment, resentment, and feel that . . . it gets to a boiling point, where I get afraid, and then I catch myself: "What are you doing?" And if I am lucky, I remind myself to calm down, and stay open. It gets to a boiling point, when you cannot take it anymore, and then you think in a split second "What are you doing?" And you have a tiny window of space, where you are open to actually hear what you need to hear.

Theme 4: "Mirror," Connection

This is one of the turning points in the personal struggle and inspiration dynamics mentioned in the participants' stories. Something appeared at a certain point that acted as a trigger of inspirational resonance or a mirror that allowed the person to see her situation of struggle in a new light. This trigger often provided a more transparent view of reality and brought up fears and insecurities that one needed to face openly and honestly. It touched on some deep pain points, spotlighted suppressed and ignored personal values, or showed the person denied and stifled dimensions of self. This is a point where participants commented on taking an honest look at self or a situation. Some of the resonant phrases, describing this mirror effect, are "I saw myself in him," "he provided a sounding board," "it was symmetry."

Here is an example of such a "mirror" shared by one participant about recurring moments of inspiration and insights that aided his growth and career-related objectives:

> That was the book *The Seven Habits of Highly Effective People*. And the one thing was, what I was focused on, was the circle of influence: Impact, focus on what you can influence, don't bother with other things. And I think at the time I was so involved in watching politics on TV and just one thing after another and realizing that: Well, I'm not going to be able to change that. And that was just impacting or influencing my day to day [life]. And then I realized that if I just focus on what I can do, and impact what I can impact, that my life will be different. And that was 180-degree shift!

Theme 5: Expanded [Embodied] Awareness

Prior phenomenological studies expressed that inspiration experience manifests as a change in Being and knowing (Hart 1993, 1998; Rourke 1983). The phenomenological accounts shared in this study confirmed that the shift in Being and knowing was indeed present in those experiences. Since participants described the experience in vastly different words, I chose *expanded awareness* to represent a collective expression of this shift. Describing such experiences was not an easy task. Because of the remarkable and unusual nature of such moments, participants sometimes lacked words and relied on metaphors to convey the depth of experience.

In many cases expanded awareness was expressed through felt sense – something that manifested somatically and emotionally. A similar observation was made in a prior study by Patricia Rourke (1983). Some participants described this shift through distinct somatic sensations in different parts of the body. Participants used the following resonant words to describe these sensations: tingling, energy burst, electrical pulse, blinding flash, chills, goosebumps, hot-cold swings, and chakra alignment, to name a few.

One participant described his feelings of expanded awareness as reaching a different level of consciousness and plane of reality during separate inspirational moments:

> Elation or just being on a different plane in terms of consciousness, higher sense of energy, maybe some brilliance . . . . When I say brilliance, I mean, like inside out. Wow! It's like light! I don't know if it's light, brilliance, whatever you want to call it. Those are the things that you can . . . they're almost tangible! You can almost feel that!

Theme 6: "The Moment of Truth"

In the moment of inspiration, after being opened to honestly consider a problem, or situation, or hidden dimensions of self, participants referred to facing "the moment of truth." This appeared in the words "truth," "true self," "core," "congruence," "authentic," "confidence," "affirmation," "certainty," and others.

To illustrate, one participant, describing her relationship struggle with her daughter, recognized this truth in the moment of inspiration:

> In that moment I was recognizing the truth in what she said! Seeing her and hearing her reflect back . . . not reflect, but catch me, point to me, tap on me, added that extra-dimension of challenge that made that moment just flip! I am saying to her: "Do this, do this, do that!!!" [with strict loud voice] . . . . And she is just a kid! And that really struck: "What are you doing?" It was the truth. It was the truth of it!

A different person described the moment of truth during his inspiration experience:

> That was stunning to me! I've never experienced anything before that or since then. That was that, I don't know, kind of mystical. It was true, it seemed true to me, seemed right to me. It was really a moment for me: shock, a little bit of amazement, a little bit of certainly not being believable; on the other hand, it had created some level of healing for me.

Theme 7: Liberation, Empowerment, Shift

Participants shared that the moment of truth during an inspirational episode often brought a feeling of freedom, relief, empowerment, and liberation. Sometimes this sense of relief was expressed with tears and a sense of cleansing. Sometimes it was pure exhilaration and joy. On a cognitive level, it was described as opening a new door, seeing new possibilities, change in priorities or values, or a complete paradigm shift.

For instance, one participant shared about the shift in her values that she started feeling after her poignant inspirational experience in the Grand Canyon. This shift has some signals about a possible deeper paradigmatic shift in the future (when the values of conforming, performing, and achievement lose their priority):

> I can feel [my value focus], feel that [it is] shifting. Yeah. I can see the change in myself. I would not say it's a total shift. I mean, work is still important to me and also perform well, but some things I think I do not pursue it as, or I do not perceive it as important as before – like the promotions, or even money, title – this kind of things. I don't think [that] I am really obsessed, or I was not obsessed, but I considered [it] very important before, but now it's not that important. The degree changed! I do think the connection with nature played a role in it. Yeah.

Another participant described her inspiration moment related to courage to stop drinking alcohol as a "life-changing moment" and "born-again day." She shared an enormous sense of relief, lightness, freedom, and empowerment coming from that event:

> It felt like relief. . . . Even, as I'm talking to you now, I can remember. It felt like I gave up! So, it felt like, something big in my heart lifted up, and then it felt like just the relief washing over me . . . like from my head down to my toes, just: "Whoosh!!" So, surrender! First of all, the surrender and being lifted, like [becoming] lighter, and then the washing off, like: "It's okay, it's going to be all right."

Theme 8: Integration

Participants in my study mentioned that discoveries and learnings coming from the episodes of struggle and inspiration required some kind of integration into the daily life and reality of the individual. In some cases, participants reported experiencing multiple inspirational episodes before a serious paradigm shift and integration of new learnings. Intensity and depth of integration varied between episodes of challenge and inspiration, and among participants' stories. Intensity and depth also depended on the degree of success in overcoming personal barriers, fears, and other blocks noted in previous steps of the whole pattern.

To give an example, one participant shared what steps she took to integrate her inspiring life-changing decision to stop drinking alcohol:

> I knew at that moment: "This is it, this is it! You are stopping for good, and you'll never drink again!" It was dead certain! And then, from then on it became a question of how I was going to do it! Not whether I was going to do it! And it was: Just to put in place all the resources that I needed. . . . [Doctor] did a blood test for me. She gave me a reference to a counselor. I rang my family members. I got support through online forums. I wrote up a plan and it was just . . . I never had a doubt after that I was somehow going to quit and quit forever! And that moment of . . . would I call it inspiration? I guess so! It was so clear: There was no more denying it and there was no more like bargaining or anything.

Summary

This study proposed a new lens for viewing an individual inspirational phenomenon through its relationship to a particular individual and her Lifeworld. Looking at phenomenological accounts of personal challenge and inspiration, this study confirmed that the experience of inspiration is aligned with personal values and meaning structures. It also provided evidence that individual inspiration can be considered not as a random moment but as a cyclical process that supports personal development and evolution of human consciousness.

Even though people often look at inspiration as an isolated episode, this is only one simplified frame of reference. If one considers its connection to the human Lifeworld, he may become aware of deeper symbolic layers of meaning of individual inspiration as a complex and intelligently conceived process. This study uncovered an eight-theme pattern of the Cycle of Expansion and Renewal that appeared in many episodes of individual challenge and inspiration. Inspiration facilitates connection and alignment between a person and her true self (also known as the soul, authentic self, higher self, etc.), and Spirit (notwithstanding name differences in spiritual literature).

Inspiration plays an important role in human life as a paradigm shift facilitator. This study presented clear evidence that, as human beings, we go through rounds of shifts in our values, belief systems, and operating paradigms. These shifts can be rapid, though often they are slow and take time to unfold. Individual lived experience accounts described how throughout their lives people repeatedly get stuck in particular belief systems and models. They often have difficulty transcending the limitations and freeing themselves from the constraint of these beliefs. Individual inspiration acts as a natural mechanism that helps individuals to transcend the limits of their operating paradigms and fixed frames. It supports personal growth within and between different paradigms.

References

Alvesson, Mats/Sköldberg, Kaj (2000): *Reflexive Methodology: New Vistas for Qualitative Research*. London: Sage.
Assagioli, Roberto (2007): *Transpersonal Development: The Dimension Beyond Psychology* (Rev. ed.). Forres, Scotland: Smiling Wisdom.
Azarova, Tetyana (2019): *A Mindful Inquiry into the Meaning of Individual Inspiration in a Period of Personal Challenge* (Doctoral dissertation). Available from ProQuest Dissertations and Theses database, UMI No. 13885807.
Barber, Michael (2017): *Religion and humor as Emancipating Provinces of Meaning*. Cham: Springer.
Bentz, Valerie M./Shapiro, Jeremy J. (1998): *Mindful inquiry in Social Research*. Thousand Oaks: Sage.
Bentz, Valerie M./Rehorick, David/Marlatt, James/Nishii, Ayumi/Estrada, Carol (2018): "Transformative Phenomenology as an Antidote to Technological Deathworlds". In: *Schützian Research* 10, pp. 189–220.
Capra, Fritjof (1996): *The Web of Life: A New Scientific Understanding of Living Systems*. New York: Anchor Books.

Capra, Fritjof/Luisi, Pier Luigi (2015): *The Systems View of Life: A Unifying Vision* (1st South Asia ed.). Delhi: Cambridge University Press.

Case, Peter/Gosling, Jonathan (2010): "The Spiritual Organization: Critical Reflections on the Instrumentality of Workplace Spirituality". In: *Journal of Management, Spirituality and Religion* 7. No. 4, pp. 257–282. DOI:10.1080/14766086.2010.524727

Clark, Timothy (2000): *The Theory of Inspiration: Composition as a Crisis of Subjectivity in Romantic and Post-romantic Writing.* Manchester: Manchester University Press.

Four Arrows (Jacobs, Don) (2016): *Point of Departure: Returning to our More Authentic Worldview for Education and Survival.* Charlotte: Information Age.

Frankl, Viktor E. (1978): *The Unheard Cry for Meaning: Psychotherapy and Humanism.* New York: Simon and Schuster.

Frankl, Viktor E. (1988): *The Will to Meaning: Foundations and Applications of Logotherapy.* New York: Meridian. (Original work published 1969)

Fromm, Erich (1994): *Escape from Freedom.* New York: First Owl Books. (Original work published 1941)

Fry, Louis W. (2003): "Toward a Theory of Spiritual Leadership". In: *The Leadership Quarterly* 14. No. 6, pp. 693–727. DOI:10.1016/j.leaqua.2003.09.001

Hart, Tobin R. (1993): *Inspiration: An Exploration of the Experience and its Role in Healthy Functioning* (Doctoral dissertation). Available from ProQuest Dissertations and Theses database. UMI No. 9316659.

Hart, Tobin R. (1998): "Inspiration: Exploring the Experience and its Meaning". In: *Journal of Humanistic Psychology* 38. No. 3, pp. 7–35.

Hart, Tobin R. (2000): "Inspiration as Transpersonal Knowing". In: Hart, Tobin R./Nelson, Peter L./Puhakka, Kaisa (Eds.): *Transpersonal Knowing: Exploring the Horizon of Consciousness.* Albany, NY: SUNY Press, pp. 31–53.

Heidegger, Martin (2010): *Being and time* (J. Stambaugh, Trans.). Dennis J. Schmidt (Ed). Albany: SUNY Press. (Original work published 1953)

Karakas, Fahri (2010): "Spirituality and Performance in Organizations: A Literature Review". In: *Journal of Business Ethics* 94. No. 1, pp. 89–106. DOI:10.1007/s10551-009-0251-5

Kessler, Ronald C. (2012): "The Costs of Depression". In: *Psychiatric Clinics* 35. No. 1, pp. 1–14.

Kleiman, Evan M./Beaver, Jenna K. (2013): "A Meaningful Life is Worth Living: Meaning in Life as a Suicide Resiliency Factor". In: *Psychiatry Research* 210. No. 3, pp. 934–939.

Laloux, Frederic (2014): *Reinventing Organizations: A Guide to Creating Organizations Inspired by the Next Stage in Human Consciousness.* Brussels: Nelson Parker.

Macy, Joanna/Brown, Molly Young (2014): *Coming Back to Life.* Gabriola Island: New Society.

Maté, Gabor (2010): *In the Realm of Hungry Ghosts: Close Encounters with Addiction.* Berkeley: North Atlantic Books.

Maté, Gabor (2011): *When the Body Says No: The Cost of Hidden Stress.* Hoboken: John Wiley and Sons.

Meadows, Donella/Randers, Jorgen/Meadows, Dennis (2006): *The Limits to Growth: The 30-year Update.* London: Earthscan.

Mitroff, Ian I./Denton, Elizabeth A. (1999): "A Study of Spirituality in the Workplace". In: *MIT Sloan Management Review* 40. No. 4, p. 83.

Oxford English Dictionary (n.d.): "Inspiration". Online edition. Retrieved from http://www.oed.com.fgul.idm.oclc.org/oed2/00118182;jsessionid=CBDA2A91A009A2222276EF771BAC41DE, visited on October 8, 2020.

Palmer, Parker J. (2000): *Let your Life Speak: Listening for the Voice of Vocation*. San Francisco: Jossey-Bass.
Palmer, Parker J. (2004): *A Hidden Wholeness: The Journey Toward an Undivided Life*. San Francisco: Jossey-Bass.
Rehorick, David A./Bentz, Valerie M. (Eds.) (2008). *Transformative Phenomenology: Changing Ourselves, Lifeworlds, and Professional Practice*. Lanham: Lexington Books.
Rogers, Carl R. (1995): *On becoming a person: A Therapist's View of Psychology*. New York, NY: Houghton Mifflin. (Original work published 1961)
Rourke, Patricia (1983): *The Experience of Being Inspired* (Doctoral dissertation). Available from ProQuest Dissertations and Theses database. UMI No. 8416189.
Scharmer, C. Otto (2009): *Theory U: Learning from the Future as it Emerges*. San Francisco: Berrett-Koehler.
Scharmer, C. Otto/Kaufer, Katrin (2013): *Leading from the Emerging Future: From Ego-system to Eco-system Economies*. San Francisco: Berrett-Koehler.
Schütz, Alfred (1944): "The Stranger: An Essay in Social Psychology". In: *American Journal of Sociology* 49. No. 6, pp. 499–507.
Schütz, Alfred (1945): "On Multiple Realities". In: *Philosophy and Phenomenological Research* 5. No. 4, pp. 533–576.
Schütz, Alfred (1970): *Reflections on the Problem of Relevance*. Richard M. Zaner (Ed.). New Haven: Yale University Press.
Schütz, Alfred/Luckmann, Thomas (1973): *The Structures of the Life-world*. Evanston: Northwestern University Press.
Shiota, Michelle N./Thrash, Todd M./Danvers, Alexander/Dombrowski, John T. (2017): "Transcending the Self: Awe, Elevation, and Inspiration". In: Tugade, Michele M./Shiota, Michelle N./Kirby, Leslie D. (Eds.): *Handbook of Positive Emotions*. New York: The Guilford Press, pp. 362–377.
Substance Abuse and Mental Health Services Administration (2017): *Key Substance Use and Mental Health Indicators in the United States: Results from the 2016 National Survey on Drug Use and Health* (HHS Publication No. SMA 17-5044, NSDUH Series H-52). Rockville: Center for Behavioral Health Statistics and Quality, Substance Abuse and Mental Health Services Administration. Retrieved from https://store.samhsa.gov/product/Key-Substance-Use-and-Mental-Health-Indicators-in-the-United-States-/SMA17-5044, visited on July 24, 2018.
Thrash, Todd M./Elliot, Andrew J. (2004): "Inspiration: Core Characteristics, Component Processes, Antecedents, and Function". In: *Journal of Personality and Social Psychology* 87. No. 6, pp. 957–973. DOI:10.1037/0022-3514.87.6.957
Thrash, Todd M./Elliot, Andrew J./Maruskin, Laura A./Cassidy, Scott E. (2010): "Inspiration and the Promotion of Well-being: Tests of Causality and Mediation". In: *Journal of Personality and Social Psychology* 98. No. 3, pp. 488–506. DOI:10.1037/a0017906
Vaillant, George (2008): *Spiritual Evolution: A Scientific Defense of Faith*. New York: Broadway Books.
van Manen, Max (1990): *Researching Lived Experience: Human Science for an Action Sensitive Pedagogy*. Albany: SUNY Press.
Wade, Jenny (1996): *Changes of Mind: A holonomic Theory of the Evolution of Consciousness*. Albany: SUNY Press.
Wallerstein, Immanuel M. (2007): *World-systems Analysis: An introduction*. Durham: Duke University Press.

Wertz, Frederick J. (2005): "Phenomenological Research Methods for Counseling Psychology".
   In: *Journal of Counseling Psychology* 52 No. 2, p. 167.
Wilber, Ken (2000): *Integral Psychology: Consciousness, Spirit, Psychology, Therapy.* Boston: Shambhala.
Wilber, Ken/Patten, Terry/Leonard, Adam/Morelli, Marco (2008): *Integral Life Practice: A 21st-Century Blueprint for Physical Health, Emotional Balance, Mental Clarity, and Spiritual Awakening.* Boston: Shambhala.
World Health Organization (2018): "Depression: Key Facts". Retrieved from http://www.who.int/en/news-room/fact-sheets/detail/depression, visited on July 24, 2018.

Lorraine Crockford
Chapter 11
The Deathworld of First Responders: Being a Stranger to Oneself

Abstract: The study of trauma incident response is a topic of relevance for research as the world faces the unforeseeable in the Covid-19 pandemic. First responders and those on the front lines attempt to navigate both the Lifeworld and the Deathworld of occupational exposure to trauma. The chapter presented is one based on a Schützian Lifeworld study (Crockford 2019) of six first responders excavating a deeper understanding to the phenomena of unprocessed, unaddressed trauma exposure; a factor that correlates to first responders' high rates of completed suicides, which are 10 times that of the general public (Heyman et al. 2018). The chapter considers the concept of the "The Stranger" (Schütz 1976, p. 91–105) in relation to first responders who purposely run toward trauma and dominate that realm; the affects from trauma exposure internalize as habituated patterns, a means for coping through the many and unsurmountable experiences they endure. Through managing chaotic situations, an emerging theme of coping in the aftermath of trauma exposure was to hold a sense of culpability and self-doubt. Emotional repression emerged as a way to cope in a Lifeworld where they are never off duty. This chapter draws on the first responder experience, in particular, to convey how the Lifeworld and Deathworld is negotiated in a type of hypervigilance and a splitting off of the emotional self for survival.

Keywords: Alfred Schütz, Lifeworld, lived experience, Deathworld, first responder trauma exposure

This chapter is based on a Lifeworld study of six first responders' experience of trauma including two police officers, two firefighters, a flight nurse, and an emergency medical technician (Crockford 2019). Alfred Schütz' (1962) Lifeworld ontology is a phenomenological approach that offers researchers a scaffolding from which to explore the intersubjective experience of trauma. The premise of the chapter is to show how traumatic experience leads first responders to become a stranger to themselves and others. The findings of the study showed that ultimately first responders become a stranger to themselves due to unprocessed, unhealed trauma derived from their attempts to help others and the repression of those experiences. Unprocessed, unaddressed trauma is significant to why first responders' rate of completed suicide is 10 times that of the general public (Heyman et al. 2018) and final act of estrangement by way of death. Trauma is at the intersection of the duality of first responders' lives, as they attempt to navigate both the Lifeworld and Deathworld.

Researchers of phenomenology who specifically explore Lifeworld ontology propose that "intersubjectivity is required to study relational experience" (Wagner 1983, p. 117). Intersubjectivity not only relies on direct encounters between individuals; it is also "linked to cognitive perceptions and emotions" (Wagner 1983, p. 109). The three regions of *self*, *other*, and *object* co-occur in reciprocity to one another. While intersubjective awareness requires a conscious acknowledgment of one's *self* and one's Lifeworld, trauma necessarily shuts off the ability to think and emotionally process the experience fully.

First responders enter the lives of people to help them. In an essay called "the Stranger," (1976) Schütz referred to the actor in one's social world who sees oneself at the center and whose intention is to be a dominant player in that world: the actor "organizes the world around oneself perceiving oneself at the center as a field of domination and is therefore especially interested in that segment which is within . . . [the actor's] actual or potential reach" (pp. 92–93). First responders see themselves as potential rescuers of those in their orbit. The people who first responders meet in this realm make a deep impression on them, especially in circumstances in which the first responders are not able to save them. In such circumstances, they, like one first responder in the study named Sully, are haunted by the image, for example, of holding a man in the middle of a freeway, while putting himself in danger as he comforted the man, telling him, "I'm a police officer, I'm here for you. Everything is going to be okay," even while the man is engaged in agonal breathing, which is breathing that occurs prior to one's death, when dying is the result of a violent traumatic incident. The police office, Sully, held the man and thought, "Do I save the baby [having seen an empty infant's car seat], save myself, or save this man in my arms?" which was impossible because the man was dying from his injuries. Sully would discover there was no baby, but at the time, it symbolized his dilemma, and when Sully reflected on his thoughts during these moments he described in vivid detail, he included the description of "a golf ball bouncing down the freeway in slow motion," adding, "Um, so I felt really, really helpless there."

Kirk is haunted in the memory of a colleague, a fellow officer and in not recognizing him in a moment of death; in coming across his body Kirk expressed that he felt "terrible" that he did not recognize him: "So, we rolled him over, and I asked Jack; I'm all, 'Who is it?' So he tells me, I'm like . . . I felt horrible. I'm like, 'I know this guy.' You know what I mean . . . . I've known him."

The first responders in the study expressed an unforgettable lingering in the memory of experiences in the death of another.

For Lucky, trying to rescue a female inmate is reflected in her dreams, "I would wake up thinking, did this really happen? I would replay it over in my head, you know, and not consciously, subconsciously. Like I would all of a sudden wake up going, 'Why am I thinking about this?'"

Sasha described, "I tend to magnetize chaos towards me. I have multiple people who call me and tell me that I'm addicted to chaos. I felt like I was a shit magnet for *ped's* and it was back to back, a lot of pediatric calls that were really bad. Really bad . . . within a very short period of time."

For Jill, "I felt like I had left my body, and I remember looking down on myself and seeing an aerial view, and it was like every detail, every person, every face, every doorway, every building just became crystal, crystal clear. I was looking for the gunman. For John, I caught a glimpse of it. I caught a glimpse of a person hanging and, goddammit, you know, I was like, 'Ugh.'"

The Role of Action

It is important to try to gain a nuanced understanding of why the situation that Sully related was so traumatic for him and other first responders. Action was a key component in Schütz' ontology and may be a key component to understanding Sully's traumatic experience. In Schützian ontology, "in order to" is the underlying motivation to action. According to Schütz, human beings are born into a historical culture that forms the strata of experience that underlie individual motivations to engage in specific action (Wagner 1970 p. 163). First responders' actions and interpretations are made possible by an antecedent stock of acquired knowledge from experience, whereby experiences shape how one might respond to future experiences in their Lifeworld. These contexts of meanings underlie the "in order to" motives first responders have in choosing an occupation that entails responding in action to help or save others. In the Lifeworld of first responders, the underlying motivations to rescue people from traumatic situations are influenced by their family of origin and early life experiences.

The three female first responders in the study spoke of histories of complex developmental trauma, in which they became conditioned early on to try to grapple with events beyond their control. Complex trauma is defined as a multiple and chronic traumatic experience that is prolonged in one's early development (van der Kolk et al. 2005). The early complex trauma experiences of the three female first responders, which involved witnessing domestic violence, neglect in an alcoholic home, and both physical and sexual abuse, initiated in them a desire to rescue others and a yearning to belong to a group. In all of these experiences, the women described a feeling of helplessness due to complex trauma in childhood (Herman 1992). These experiences can be thought of as stocks of knowledge that take shape our development.

In witness to domestic violence, one can imagine a child with a deep desire to rescue her parents from a situation in which they were hurting each other. For one of the women, neglect created a desire to belong to a group that cared for her. While the men in the study did not talk about complex trauma as part of their upbringing during the interview, one first responder did mention post-study being abandoned by his mother. The other two talked about being influenced by their families of origin, in which helping others was a multigenerational family value. These two also served in the military. Providing service to others became a personal meaningful action due to cultural familial value patterns.

All of the six first responders in the study derived meaning from providing a sense of safety and security to their communities. Understanding the importance of performing these personally meaningful actions illuminates why entering situations that were so undermining to their ability to be successful were traumatic.

Being A Hero and Being Helpless Creates Doubt

In executing the action to save lives, first responders are plunged into traumatic events that are outside of their control. At times, the situation is often so traumatic for them that it increases their sense of disorientation and doubt that they often cannot make sense of within the insensible. When articulating being in the midst of a traumatic incident, the participants described experiencing something like a shock that transported them instantaneously from one *tension in consciousness* to another. Schütz referred to a range of states in conscious and unconscious experiences (Schütz/Luckmann 1989), the *wide awake, awake,* and *half awake* (Schütz/Luckmann 1989). If individuals are wide awake, only the task at hand exists (Schütz/Luckmann 1989, p. 121) are attended to. In Schützian ontology, the consciousness of being wide-awake implies a shock or problem has initiated a capacity to question one's own reality; Schütz and Luckmann (1989) defined "half-awake" (p. 121) as a state of relative unconsciousness. In the study, first responders, the conditioned terror of performing in traumatic situations ignite states of pre-trauma awake to wide awake to half-awake or *asleep,* which constituted states associated with the after-effects of trauma. The state of asleep was *embodied trauma,* in which one participant, in particular, John, described waking up with an uncontrollable physical reaction to trauma:

> Then it was that night that I woke up. I thought I had the flu. I didn't know. I thought I was gonna throw up. I thought I was gonna poop my pants. I thought I had like . . . . I think, "I've gotta go home." I went out to the out-bay. It was like almost midnight. I just sat there, and I did some tapping and some breathing, and finally I was able to go, "Oh, my God. That's the effects of what I just saw." And I left it at that. I meditated for a bit, and I went back to bed.

John related that his somatic reaction was "the traumatic incident:

> That incident . . . woke me up out of my sleep. There was something that I saw, that I had tasted, that I had smelt, that . . . . I mean, I was like I woke up, and I was like, "I'm not even having a nightmare." I don't know, so that's how I woke up . . . . The vision isn't there, the traumatic incident that I've been having I've thought of. They're not clear like a picture, per se.

For those first responders, wide awake was a realm in which nothing else existed except what was in front of them at the moment, which they were a part of. As Bollas (2018) stated, "We dissociate from a lived experience when we find it shocking; indeed, dissociation is itself a form of shock" (p. 39). When participants described the traumatic incident state of being wide-awake, their descriptions denoted that they were vividly present, acutely aware of cognitive thoughts and imagery, as well as somatic sensory stimuli. This is in keeping with neurological and psychological research in which altered states of consciousness shift into the survival response whereby time appears to slow down, and the sense of temporality is distorted. In slow motion, the natural neurophysiological brain's protective survival response ensues and the sense of temporality is distorted, particularly in Sully's experience. This theme has relevance within the course of action and the emerging tension in consciousness as the participants were exposed to the phenomena of death: death's intersubjective presence and deaths non-presence:

> The vast province in which the tension of consciousness moves is bounded on the one side by the carelessness of accustomed and usual experiences and on the other by the clear attentiveness of actions as problematic situations. When he [or she] goes outside this province, a person is transported into exceptional states that are almost with exception of brief duration and can take him [or her] to the edge of sudden change into complete unconscious. (Schütz/Luckmann 1973, p. 121)

Due to these tensions in consciousness, which includes temporal distortions, such as Sully's recounting "a golf ball is bouncing down the freeway in slow motion," one starts to question their own sense of reality. In these moments, responders express feeling particularly helpless in terms of functioning within their role of responding responsibly. When the man died in Sully's arms, Sully was haunted by not being able to do something to prevent his death. Sully was filled with a sense of culpability, thinking he had not been prepared well enough. Even after firefighters on the scene told him there was nothing anyone could have done to save the man's life, Sully continued to believe he could have, if he'd had a first aid kit. Sully now even carries a first aid kit wherever he goes. In this response, there appears to be a devaluation of oneself in one's role. There's a sense of devaluing the self if the first responder cannot carry out his or her responsibilities in a way the actor deems is successful. First responders are heroes to the extent to which they believe they can do the impossible in impossible situations. However, being overly responsible for another person's life in uncontrollable circumstances may give them an unrealistic idea of what they can do.

Hero is what the society often projects onto first responders, and firefighters especially. Jill remarked that the hero reference was not correct because she took her job with such intention and responsibility, that being a hero was unreachable. Although the participants never described their roles in this idealized way, they nevertheless thought of themselves as responsible for the lives of those they were there to rescue. Richardson and James (2017) also found that while firefighters believe they are helpers, there are times that they cannot help and that "feelings of helplessness" (p. 320) threaten the identity of a firefighter. In addition, a qualitative study on nurses within ambulance services in Sweden, Jonsson and Segesten (2002) discovered that first responders described an intense association with the victim and at the same time expressed "helplessness" or "powerlessness" (p. 147) as they could not do more for them than their duty expected of them. Elmqvist et al. (2009) found that first responders experienced a distanced closeness to the injured person. In their study of firefighters, Hall et al. (2007) noted that occupational identities were crafted by the expectations of society and that in particular firefighters themselves tended to be "highly masculinized" (p. 314) within the organizational system. For example, the authors surmised that the firefighter identity tended to portray the firefighter in an objectified idealized way. In one of the important themes of the study (Crockford 2019), the sense of themselves as a hero was a way to convey the expectations they had of performing their duty well, which was to protect and to rescue lives.

Stranger to Oneself, One's Family and One's Colleagues

The aftereffects of trauma for first responders of this study included a lack of feeling prepared and self-culpability. Sully was unable to integrate the idea that he could not have saved the man. Sully's processing in repressing the emotional effect of the trauma, the feeling of helplessness, blame and doubt, is what disconnects Sully from his emotional experience of himself, and toward others. Therefore, first responders' attempts to embody the "ideal type" as hero collides with its counterpart, helplessness, in the natural attitude, and for Sully in creating an emotion of culpability while being haunted by the traumatic experience. In Schütz' Lifeworld framework, the natural attitude (1962) is defined in relation to a tension of doubt that evolves between our natural inclinations and the desire to adhere to societal or organizational constructs. "It is the world of physical, including my body" (p. 549). With this explanation, one may stand in the intersection of tension between the conscious self and the construct of both the Lifeworld and Deathworld that elicit the subjective experience of terror and doubt. Doubt emerges as a result of the conflict in tensions between what one wants to do, and what one is required to do, such as perform while "tested by self or others" (p. 549).

In the after-effects of trauma, first responders as actors continue to adhere to the repression of emotion, which splits off the actor [first responder] from self, which is then banished to a realm of existence that is isolated from his or her emotional processes. This splitting off of the self that experienced the trauma is what lies beneath the realm of disconnect from the self and from a full human existence connecting via an emotional language that cannot always be executed or expressed. In addition, this process may underlie the action that some first responders take to complete suicide in order to extinguish the pain of the self.

Without processing the emotions underlying the traumatic experience, first responders in this study appeared to lose touch with themselves, which affected their relationships with significant others and colleagues. Participants were not aware of this; they only recognized that physiologically, they were never off. However, as one participant, Jill, noted, the people the first responders live with are usually the first to recognize that something is not right. For example, Sully's wife complained of the way he embodied the trauma when he was home. The anxiety from unprocessed trauma turned into an obsession about time and being prepared, and he carried this aspect of his life into every domain. His wife

Chapter 11 The Deathworld of First Responders: Being a Stranger to Oneself — 187

said he was always worried about being prepared at home. He explained his wife found this aspect of him difficult:

> She's like, you, you make me neurotic when you're asking about when do we leave, when do we have to be there? What time, you know, what about traffic, what about this, you know, all these kinds of things. And so I've been trying to like [tell him], "Chill out a little bit about those kinds of, those kinds of things," right.

Kirk's wife sensed there was something terribly wrong after Kirk responded to a call involving the death of a fellow police officer that he knew. She insisted that he attend therapy.

This idea of taking the unprocessed exposure to trauma home and having it affect one's relationships may also be linked to the idea that first responders did not recognize time on the job not responding to a call as being meaningful. In the study, both John and Sully found it difficult to even talk about time on the job not responding to a call. John had difficulty even with the question. John could not qualitatively characterize his time on the job not responding to a call.

The first responders described being in a state of continual hyper-alertness. As soon as they arrive on the job, they begin preparing for a call both cognitively and somatically. While on the job, they are in a state of awake, preparing for the unknown. For example, John described his chest tightening; Lucky imagined putting on a suit of armor emotionally to toughen herself up. Jill said she believed that no part of her shift would belong to her in any way. Kirk described this awake state in a physical way: arriving in the parking lot sweating. In talking about not responding to a call, John said, "Basically, I was getting ready to go back into work, but I was never really off."

In Schütz' ontology, conscious realms of being within the Lifeworld, reflect a particular meaning distinct to the individual's natural attitude in sensing experience. Part of the purpose of exploring the first responders' Lifeworld was to discover the meaning first responders ascribed to time at home, the time responding to a call, and time not responding to call when on the job. However, in the study, the first responders did not view their home life and time on the job not responding to a call as distinctly different from their time responding to a call. Participants took the trauma home with them and embodied the experience over time to the extent to which somatically and cognitively they were never off duty. Lucky stated, "I don't turn it off very well. That's the problem." Kirk stated, "It's hard for us to do . . . that's really hard for us to do." For Sasha, she lost her sense of time. On the one hand, she felt she needed the support of others, and on the other, she felt she needed to isolate herself. John said that he was in a constant loop whether he was on or off the job. He was either revving up, "amping up," or trying to "decompress." and Jill said, "What happened was that when I would get home, I was still on duty. I was still . . . on."

It appears that first responders push forward no matter the circumstances, and when at home they are still persevering to keep everyone safe in a mode of responding. These findings are in keeping with those of Jonsson and Segesten (2002), who identified a theme from the narratives of first responders called, *Impossible to leave the meaninglessness behind*. In the theme, the ambulance workers described how they could not "shake off" the traumatic events, especially due to intrusive memories.

Not only do first responders become estranged from oneself and one's family, out of their preservation they slowly become unable to recognize themselves through the eyes of colleagues who have alienated themselves and therefore may not be able to recognize the experience of the trauma survivor. Intersubjective awareness requires the ability to recognize one's *self* and others in one's Lifeworld, whereas unprocessed trauma can interrupt this capacity. The organizational culture was also filled with trauma survivors, and these organizations did not appear to be able to create an environment in which emotional responses to trauma were acceptable. John's remark epitomized a type of culture that purposefully devalued discussions of emotional responses to trauma:

> You know, you still don't pour anything out, it's a macho thing, it's an ego thing. You don't want to show weakness in front of your coworkers. You don't want to show any emotion because we're all the same, we all think the same, we should all be . . . . "Hey, let's get over this [traumatic experience] and get on with it." It's the culture. It's a very sick culture. It really is. There are some good people out there but it's pretty sick.

Trauma involves a splitting off of emotions in order to not have to experience extreme overwhelm and to minimize the power of emotional content through repression; in the Lifeworld of first responders, emotions were not viewed as being something of value to be understood and navigated; they had to be ignored and dismissed because they were perceived to be getting in the way of first responders being able to do their job. The cultural belief seemed to be that emotional reactions are not appropriate for someone in the emergency profession (Kopel/Friedman 1997). Fay et al. (2018) stated that the distressed emergency responder may project a facade of competence while harboring a feeling of insecurity and shame. In the study, Jill told a story about feeling like a stranger amongst her colleagues. She said she went into the kitchen to make a pot of coffee while her crew was sitting around the table watching. She emptied the pot that was there and made the coffee. She turned around and said, "Hey guys, I just made a fresh pot of coffee," and one of her crew who had watched her all the while said, "that was a fresh pot of coffee that you threw out." As silence ensued,

Jill described having an eerie feeling of being disconnected from her crew. It struck her to the core in that she no longer felt safe with her crew. The phenomena of distancing pertain to cultural patterns of separatism, disconnection, dissonance, and feeling as Jill did, like a stranger within an organization where all workers are exposed to trauma incidents.

When Untreated, Traumatic Experiences Lead to Transformation of Identity

In the study, participants described themselves as being "jaded" and "always on." Whereby ingesting the trauma through exposure leads to a state of being hyperalert, and the expectation that bad things will continually occur. John described this as paranoia: "God. Sometimes I think I'm like paranoid or something, or I'm very aware of things, of my surroundings. I tend to be brief and to the point, a bit short." Jill described it as, "I just always assume that there's gonna be a bomber" when she enters a crowd. Kirk described the same experience as never having his back to the door in public places. Kirk also stated he constantly seized up people. The placing of others before themselves in the course of duty over the years entails a consistent minimization and isolation of the self over time. Participants talked about becoming not only more isolated but more "cynical" and "hardened" over time. By conditioning themselves to ignore their emotional responses, they lose the perspective of others and their Lifeworld. As Kirk said, "I look at people and I sit in judgment of people." Participants are expecting threatening people to be everywhere. Some lose their ability to understand the perspective of the other in everyday life and the ability to connect due to years of disconnect, emotional repression, and hyperfunctioning.

Conclusion

Alfred Schütz contributed a theoretical framework that has rarely been applied pragmatically, to real-life situations. Belvedere (2013) stated, "Schütz does not propose a science of facts in this realm of appearance but a science of essences in search of the mind" (p. 73). Schütz' aim in this regard was to consider the subjective as well as the intersubjective, leaving an opening for other researchers an approach to Lifeworld inquiry within specific applications to social science. The study, which used his framework to understand more deeply the

Lifeworld of first responders, has provided a lens into just how compromising the experience of occupational trauma is to their day-day-reality and their relationships. In fact, according to Schütz, the world of work is the core reality of the Lifeworld (C. Belevedere, personal communication, May 2, 2019). This aspect of first responders' Lifeworld and Deathworld is accentuated because of the lack of distinction between their work world and other spheres that surround the life of the first responder.

The impetus to rescue others in traumatic situations is often thwarted by the inability to do so because of the nature of these tumultuous situations. Not being able to feel successful in doing one's job when lives are at stake links to the phenomena of helplessness. In this study, the core trauma appeared to be this sense of repeatedly being in a helpless mode over multiple traumatic incidents in face-to-face contact with death, which results in a typified experience where the phenomena of unpreparedness, uncertainty, and often a realm of disbelief exist. When coupled with complex trauma of childhood these experiences carry a certain familiarity in habituated patterns predetermined to repress memories and emotions. When the affect from trauma exposure is not processed, first responders become isolated from others. Jill expressed that first responders don't ask for help they kill themselves instead. It is challenging to hold a sense of meaningfulness when the self is intentionally abandoned. The distant closeness within the intersubjective nature between life and death is ingested through the experience in a role void of emotional language until one's natural attitude and occupational identity are adversely affected. It might be challenging to have a sense of meaningfulness in life where a void intersects the emotional connection to the self and others. The ultimate price first responder's pay is through the devaluation of emotion that acts to repress the overwhelm of traumatic exposure. When repression of excruciating painful emotion is no longer an option, the ultimate solution is too often seen in the rate of completed suicide, a final solution in death estranged to life.

References

Bollas, Christopher (2018): *Meaning and Melancholia: Life in the Age of Bewilderment.* Milton Park, New York: Routledge.
Belvedere, Carlos (2013): "What is Schützian Phenomenology?". In: *Schützian Research* 5. No. 2013, No. 65–80.
Crockford, Lorraine (2019): *A Life World Inquiry into First Responders' Experience of Trauma While in the Course of Duty* (Doctoral dissertation, Fielding Graduate University).

Elmqvist, Carina/ Brunt, David /Fridlund, Bengt/Ekebergh, Margaretha (2010): "*Being* First on the Scene of an Accident - Experiences of 'Doing' Prehospital Emergency Care". *Scandinavian Journal a/Caring Sciences*, 2–1(2), 266–273. doi:10.1 I l l/j.1471-6712.2009.00716.x

Fay, Joel/Kamena, Mark. D./Benner, Al/Buscho, Ann/Nagle, David (2018): "Emergency Responder Exhaustion syndrome (ERES): A Perspective on Stress, Coping and Treatment in the Emergency Responder Milieu". Retrieved from https://www.scribd.com/document/21992797/Emergency-Responder-Exhaustion-Syndrome-5-1-06, visited on October 12, 2020.

Hall, Alex/Hockey, Jenny/Robinson, Victoria (2007): "Occupational Cultures and the Embodiment of Masculinity: Hairdressing, Estate agency and Firefighting". In: *Gender, Work, & Organization* 14, pp. 534–551. DOI:10.1111/j.1468-0432.2007.00370.x

Herman, Judith (1992): *Trauma and Recovery*. New York: Basic Books.

Heyman, Miriam/Dill, Jeff/Douglas, Robert (2018): *The Ruderman White Paper on Mental Health and Suicide of First Responders* [White paper]. Retrieved from https://issuu.com/rudermanfoundation/docs/first_responder_white_paper_final_ac270d530f8bfb, visited on October 12, 2020.

Jonsson, Anders/Segesten, Kerstin (2002): "The Meaning of Traumatic Events as Described by Nurses in Ambulance Service". In: *Accident and Emergency Nursing* 11. No. 3, pp. 141–152.

Kopel, Heidi/Friedman, Merle (1997): "Posttraumatic Symptoms in South African Police Exposed to Violence". In: *Journal of Traumatic Stress* 10. No. 2, pp. 307, 318.

Richardson, Brian. K./James, Eric. P. (2017): "The Role of Occupational Identity in Negotiating Traumatic Experiences: The Case of a Rural Fire Department". In: *Journal of Applied Communication Research* 45. No. 3, pp. 313–332. DOI:10.1080/00909882.2017.1320573

Schütz, Alfred (1962): *Collected papers I: The Problem of Social Reality* (M. A. Natason, Trans.). The Hague: Martinus Nijhoff.

Schütz, Alfred/Luckmann, Thomas (1973): *The Structures of the Life-world*. Vol. 1. Evanston: Northwestern University Press.

Schütz, Alfred (1976): "The Stranger". In: *Collected papers II*. New York: Springer, Dordrecht, pp. 91–105.

Schütz, Alfred/Luckmann, Thomas (1989): *The Structures of the Life-world* (R. M. Zaner & D. J. Parent, Trans.). Vol. 2. Evanston: Northwestern University Press.

van der Kolk, Bessel A./Roth, Susan/Pelcovitz, David/Sunday, Suzanne/Spinazzola, Joseph (2005): "Disorders of Extreme Stress: The Empirical Foundation of a Complex Adaptation to Trauma". In: *Journal of Traumatic Stress* 18. No. 5, pp. 389–399.

Wagner, Helmut R. (Ed.) (1970): *Alfred Schütz: On Phenomenology and Social Relations*. Chicago: University of Chicago Press.

Wagner, Helmu. R. (1983): *Phenomenology of Consciousness and Sociology of the Lifeworld*. Edmonton: University of Alberta Press.

Part III: **Lifeworlds and Deathworlds in We-Relationships**

I know more of the other and he knows more of me than either of us knows of his own stream of consciousness.

– Alfred Schütz, *Collected Papers Vol. 1*, 1961

Whitney P. Strohmayr and David R. Jones
Chapter 12
Grief and Unraveling in Romantic We-Relationships

Abstract: Two collaborators in the Deathworld to Lifeworlds research project explored the intersection between their respective phenomena: *unraveling* and *grief*. If life and love provide the opportunity to bind together intricate strands from one's stocks of knowledge, typifications, and Lifeworlds to form a coherent tapestry of meaning, what experiences face the individual suddenly unraveling from the loss of that love and sense of meaning? Whitney explored the phenomenon of unraveling from a toxic relationship. David explored the grief that ensued from the sudden withdrawal of a romantic partner. Descriptions of unraveling and grief appear separately before a description of the authors' collaborative meaning-making that occurred when they negotiated the significance their phenomena assumed in light of each other. In grief, where does unraveling locate? Does unraveling happen to the individual with the loss of the object of love? Does the individual unravel from grief, or does grief cause an individual to unravel? We conclude that grief results from and catalyzes unraveling. Moreover, we discovered ironies: that grief and unraveling often work as rivel forces and our collaborative work represented raveling and unraveling as we attempted to discover the whatness of unraveling and grief.

Keywords: grief, raveling, unraveling, we-relationship, Lifeworld

Grief and Unraveling in the Lifeworld of We-Relationships

Throughout life, individuals gain and lose. We develop friends and distance ourselves from family members. We shed childhood friendships and reconnect with siblings. We fall in love – so deeply in love. We relish our love. We celebrate and commemorate and idealize our love. We lose our love.

We lose our love for various reasons. We sometimes lose love all at once. A sudden decision culminates after years of abuse. An opportunity arises. An act we cannot forgive. Or we lose our love without any explanation. We answer a call. The person across from us begins, "We need to talk . . ." The rest of life follows. Just like with human capacity, we gain, and we lose. The following passages consider the gaining and losing that follows the end of romantic relationships, as individuals *unravel* and *grieve* in the life that follows such an end.

The following passages accomplish more than considering two phenomena: two authors bring their understandings of disparate notions. We – these two authors in question – bring together seemingly disparate notions and epitomize and perform some of the very concepts we discuss below. All at once we describe these concepts and embody them, collaborating to create new understanding.

We did not know each other before being a part of the "From Strangers to Collaborators" research project using phenomenological protocol writing to clarify something of importance. Jones was participating in the University of the Virgin Islands cohort and Strohmayr the Fielding Graduate University cohort. The phenomenon of raveling and unraveling developed by Strohmayr appealed to Jones and so began the collaboration.

We-Relationships, Romantic Partnerships, and the Lifeworld

Before we launch into an exploration of raveling and grief, it serves to establish some quintessential points about the relationships that invite us to ravel or provoke grief. For not every relationship – even those that appear most enduring or constituent in our day-to-day activities – elicits either or both of these phenomena. Here we recall the notion of we-relationships – those dyads in which either individual shares consciousness and perceptions of shared experiences (Wagner 1983, p. 88).

We-relationships stand apart from relationships that occur because of incidentally occupying shared space, observing a similar feat, or interacting habitually in the performance of daily functions. We-relationships name those interrelations that share consciousness, wherein partners relate through an ongoing reorientation to each other (Wagner 1983). Schütz (1951) and Malhotra (1981) noted that we-relationships occur across all types of relationships, exemplifying, for example, how we-relationships build within groups of musicians. We, however, focused on romantic relationships through our collaboration. And while elements of other types of we-relationships may peek through the following discussion, our interest primarily culminated in appreciating our respective phenomena through romantic we-relationships experienced in our lives.

More generally, we identified the we-relationship as requisite for the emergence of either phenomenon. That is, in our discussion, both raveling and grief occur as a function of the we-relationship. Raveling displays the acceptance of an invitation to participate in a we-relationship. Inversely, the presence of grief from love lost assumes that a we-relationship existed.

The stage wherein actors ravel in we-relationships and into romantic unions carries the title Lifeworld. The stage – the Lifeworld – also includes grieving as a natural occurrence in the world of everyday life (Wagner 1983, p. 109). This Lifeworld represents the subjective experience – albeit a subjective experience displayed obviously – of the world that endures as others participate with or contend against us.

Unraveling

The word *ravel* means "to untangle, disentangle, unwind;" it also means "to entangle, become tangled or confused". The word contradicts itself but is "reconciled by its roots in weaving and sewing: as threads become unwoven, they get tangled". The prefix *un-* means not: therefore, *unravel* translates to not tangled or confused (Online Etymology Dictionary n.d.).

The key element that makes up the phenomenon of unraveling includes taking apart or untangling the parts that comprise the whole. Before unraveling begins, one must assume that the parts wrap together tightly. Perhaps last year's Christmas tree lights provide an illustration. In a rush to end the holiday season, the lights wrap tightly into a heaping mess, shoved into a box, and shelved to wait for next year. Perhaps the tangled mess of lights somehow represents confusion, hurried carelessness, inattention, or the thoughtless "throwing together of something" as a means to an end. Raveling, then, may represent unintentional wrapping together of parts – a surprise of sorts forms the whole. The raveled heap includes more than the parts one cautiously and systematically included. Hence the surprise at the end that so much more comprises the whole. Unraveling requires the separation of the parts from the whole back to parts. All the parts, stuck together in disdain or nestled together in comfort, break from the whole – unwind and come apart. The parts appear and the whole disappears in the phenomenon of unraveling. I find opposites present – raveling occurred before unraveling takes place – tight and loose, wind and unwind, tangle and untangle, together and apart, ravel and unravel, always the opposite.

The experience of unraveling must include action: the separation of the parts from the whole. If unraveling contains action, then it must also include change. Transformation happens when the whole unwinds into parts. As transformation occurs, space emerges during unraveling as the whole opens up, unwinds, and pulls apart to reveal the parts. A catalyzing event precedes the process of unraveling. Someone opens the old box of Christmas tree lights and pulls the lights apart – a relationship ends, or we lose a loved one.

Unraveling in the Lifeworld of We-Relationships

Schütz described face-to-face interactions as "paramount situations" (Wagner 1983, p. 91). Within the context of intimate, romantic relationships, face-to-face interactions fuel the we-relationship. Gestures, facial expressions, social gaze, and bodily contact provide opportunities to unravel from tension, fears, or insecurities. The inner dynamics unravel from the sense of self, transcending the self's stream of consciousness to enter the we-relationship.

When each individual completely unravels from the past into the present moment, awareness turns to the other. The only relevance at that moment is the other (beloved). In this capacity, the vantage point changes from the self to the other. As each unravels from old insecurities or hurt – unravels before the beloved – a new vantage point emerges, one focused on the beloved and laden with potential. Intrinsic relevance arises and turns the individual away from protecting the self toward unraveling into vulnerability, trust, and security.

Surrendered and unraveled from the past, volitional relevance (Wagner 1983) surfaces. The individual turns attention to the beloved simply because she wishes to do so. Each becomes wide awake in the presence of the other, wholly raveled together, and both unraveled from the past. The new moment – when both appear before each other unraveled, although wide awake to the moment – may also feel like a daydream, an unreality, or perhaps simply a new reality.

A romantic relationship signifies its reality, often separated from worlds of families and worlds of work. Both individuals in the we-relationship experience their subjective reality. As such, "all realities are equally real" and the paramount reality exists in "the sphere of everyday life in all its aspects" (Wagner 1983, p. 180).

The individuals might unravel from the veil to find a "specific experiencing [of] one's self" that incorporates the new reality representing "the total self" (Wagner 1983, p. 181). The individuals in the romantic relationship may experience a "specific time-perspective" (Wagner 1983, p. 181) in the reality of daily life, depending on one's level of consciousness at a point in time. Outer time may cease to exist when one gives full attention to the other, the beloved.

Entering the We-Relationship

One may arrive in the relationship raveled – wound tightly – in insecurities, memories, and previous hurts. I envision the collection of the past as emotional walls. Imagining another variation, the threads of the past ravel to form a thick cloth one might wear as a veil, protecting the individual from the future hurts. The veil casts a shadow making a connection to the beloved (other) impossible. Regardless, the individual, or both individuals, may enter the relationship raveled, in some capacity, in all the emotional wounds of past relationships, childhood memories, past failures, and hurts.

Yet, entering a we-relationship with a beloved requires unraveling from all the yesterdays, unraveling from the hurts that create a separateness that prevents the individual from connecting with another. The separateness may include fears, doubts, worries, insecurities – the shadow, or veil, that prevents the lovers from truly knowing the other. The separateness prevents the individual from becoming the other's beloved. In the Lifeworld of intimate, romantic relationships, the two must unravel from the shadow selves to overcome the separateness. Once unraveled from the shadow – once the threads of the veil unravel – the lovers can ravel together to form a union, a beautiful Lifeworld.

Unraveling from a Romantic We-Relationship: Whitney's Story

We spent the preceding years raveling together. The beginning of the relationship felt magical. We wove together the parts of our lives, stitched together all the different aspects of daily existence into one cloth. I dreamt of the beautiful Lifeworld we would create together. My mind envisioned a perfect version of him that fulfilled my fantasies – a doting partner, best friend, soul mate. Every brush of his hand against mine set the butterflies in my stomach free. Each day that went by we each folded another piece of ourselves into the relationship, each raveled another thread. Sometimes the whole day was spent wrapped up in each other without a care or thought of the outside world. I often wondered if the outside world continued its existence.

For a while, I shifted to an alternate state of reality – one that included only us in it. We spent hours that stretched into days, sharing words, ideas, dreams, hurts, gazes, embraces – we raveled together. Those hours made time into an illusion – a cosmic joke that must have made the Gods roar with laughter when they watched us mortals rush about from this to that. We laughed then, too. Nothing mattered but sharing presence.

We continued raveling together, each day folding in pieces of the past. My past became our past as we added moments, experiences, shared hopes and dreams. In the beginning, we each carefully chose the threads we wanted to weave, we brought the best threads we could find to the relationship. I brought my golden thread – my ability to love unconditionally and unapologetically. He brought a vulnerability from a lifetime of past hurts, like silk I wanted to stroke against my face. All those threads represented the parts that comprise the whole. All the parts raveled together to form something new – to form us – raveling into the "we" in the Lifeworld of the we-relationship.

After a while, he stopped bringing the best threads, the best parts to the relationship. The start of our beautiful tapestry showed signs of snags and messy loops here and there. Our raveling together started to look more like the product of a broken sewing machine – all the threads wrapped around a heap of cloth with a broken needle holding the heap together. As the days went by, our raveling together turned into an ugly, tangled mess.

I no longer felt woven together into a neat braid, a beautiful Lifeworld. Instead, his threads strangled me. In the blink of an eye, the weight of him bound, gagged, and suffocated me. His threads wrapped around me so tightly, cutting off my circulation and turning my limbs blue. I tried to move, tried to free myself from the tangled mess, but that only seemed to make things worse. My struggle wound the threads tighter and tighter. Every day brought a new part, a new thread to ravel. The new parts no longer filled with hopes and dreams, instead power, control, jealously and greed. I desperately gasped for air as my Lifeworld spiraled into a Deathworld.

Darkness set in. Too many parts to see past, too many parts covering my eyes. I could no longer tell which threads belonged to him and which belonged to me. All the threads raveled around me until I no longer recognized myself. I could no longer see past the tangled mask I wove and hid behind. The threads of inauthenticity turned into ugly thick burlap. I was soaked in sweat from the heat of his fury under the burlap. I reeked of decay – stale air, dead skin, deflated spirit. Before I knew it, I lay helpless at the center of a jumble, completely raveled in a mess and unsure how I got there.

Those few words cut the threads that bound us together. They severed the ties that brought our lives together. In that instant, the ever-expanding tangled mess paused ever so slightly, like the top of the breath before an exhale, before furiously unraveling us and all that I had become. I fumbled around trying to orient myself, but I couldn't see through the dark and the wind blew so hard around me that I couldn't hear my thoughts. I was caught in the spin of the tornado's wall, caught in the death roll that spun me as the threads wildly unraveled. I frantically flailed about looking for something to hold onto, but my fingers could find nothing to grasp. Panic coursed through my body and confusion thorough my mind as the storm seized me in its grip.

I flailed about as our threads unraveled, but I started to breathe again. As each of his threads detached from mine, I breathed deeper and the blood returned to my limbs. After the last thread stretched and snapped, I felt alone and uncertain, deflated and defeated, but I was free. The freedom felt fresh. I welcomed the quiet that filled the space. I laid on the floor in a disheveled heap wondering what to do next. My eyes were open, but the space was still dark. I realized the mask I raveled still covered my face. It covered my heart, too. I needed to figure out how to take off the mask, unravel the messy threads I wove around myself.

Grief and Unraveling: Davey's Story

Considering grief in contrast to joy, the latter word can be defined as a feeling, expressing, or causing great pleasure and happiness. The derivative "joyful" conveys a fullness that spills into expressions of pleasure and happiness. By contrast, "grief" suggests a sense of external weight that pushes down while "joyful" suggests a fullness that buoys. Grief disrupts expression and accompanies a sense of emptiness while joy fills up a person. A joyful person sings, greets others, and talks a great deal. A person who experienced significant loss, however, would be pathological if they demonstrated such behaviors. A person experiencing grief might remain quiet and avoid others and express a limited range of topics or only in certain ways.

When Grief Was Absent

I have this memory – a perfect moment in the history of us – and it comes back to me all the time. She sits on the rug, wedged between the sofa and the ottoman. The living room and the adjoined dining area surround us, the white tiles, computer desk, laptops, and books all silent and insignificant. She faces me.

Morning light and the sounds of the fountain filter into us like a looping soundtrack. She talks to me for hours. Or minutes. I don't know and we took the clock down last night, so I don't even know if time still exists. She talks to me. She makes me talk back. She wonders what I think. She wants to hear me speak –

one of her infinite ways of loving me. She watches me the entire time. She pours her ideas into me and talks about mine. Her love covers me like a soft blanket thrown up above my head, floated down, folded over me, settled into my curves and edges.

She must look away if only for a second. I look away because she fills me so full with what she says. What did she even say? And the way she attends to me with her gaze. I can't imagine that she feels comfortable sitting that way, with her toes crammed into the crevice of the sofa. I feel the cushions soft against me. I un-cross and re-cross my legs. My toes dig into the shag fibers of the rug. The morning air breezes against my shirtless torso.

I look away from her, out at the gray light coming through the sliding glass door. I watch a gecko run across the screened porch. I study the rhythm of the palm trees and the poise of the orchids. I look away from her partly because the brightening sky outside casts her face in deeper shadow and the contrast wearies my eyes. I look away from her mostly because I brim so full that this moment might spill through my eyes and down my cheeks.

She talks and I talk. Everything about the way she speaks and listens shows me that this conversation means everything to her. Then why don't I remember what we said? We filled that space with inspired and brilliant ideas that might have revolutionized the world. But I only remember the sound of the fountain outside. I remember everything about the look of her.

I want to stretch that moment – our Lifeworld – into infinity. The moment already resides in infinity. I don't know. But it comes back to me and seems always the same way. And always with her eyes fixed to mine. Nothing else of consequence but the connection I feel to her in that moment, our raveling more tightly.

Grief Essentially

Grief pertains to loss. But what I didn't realize in the midst of grief – caught in the throes of all its milling about, topsy-turvy – is that the loss I thought mattered was not the loss that made me grieve. That statement does not intend to diminish a loss. No. The parent who lost a child lost something miraculous and the person who lost a spouse after decades of learning to love that person and appreciate the depth of love they received – that person lost something immense. And the person who lost the love of his life when she walked away – he lost something utterly spectacular, too.

But the people that we lost are lost only to us. The people who left only shed a particular form that they inhabited. Maybe the person transfigured into a beam of light and now courses the length of the universe or maybe the person woke up with wings and a harp to stand in a chorus of angels and welcome the next arrivals. Or maybe the rest of the world has her. Maybe. Lucky world. The hapless fellow that I am.

When we say we grieve we mean that we lost someone. But the person is not lost. Except to me. To me the person is gone. Then what I mean to say is I have lost. In fact, I am lost. I wander lost within a Deathworld of ancient emotions and memories and what has been. I lost my sense of why I go through life. When I lost her – when I lost everything – I lost all the parts of me that I had once so suddenly discovered because she reflected back things I had not known. She showed me new parts of myself, parts that had waited all winter long for some bit of sunshine to crack through the snow and invite their purple faces to open onto the world.

Conclusion: Raveling Grief and Unraveling

Grief and unraveling accompany the closing of a we-relationship as described in the preceding passages. We discovered this – the overlap in our phenomenological writings – and the ways that our encounters with our phenomena touched on related contexts. The realization demarcated the moment each of us began to unravel from our tightly wound understandings and create a new one. What an irony: that in exploring how we each understood our own and the other's phenomenon, we unraveled from previous conceptions and into a new, shared one.

In the Lifeworld, we move in and out of we-relationships, raveling, and unraveling. Do the words grief and unraveling describe the same phenomenon? Neither of us thought so. After all, and as mentioned above, unraveling from a relationship sometimes connotates positive feelings: liberation, rejuvenation, and appreciation. Does one cause the other? When grief and unraveling co-occur, does grief cause one to unravel? Does unraveling cause grief? Or what? We each used the ending of an intimate, romantic relationship to depict our phenomenon, an observation that suggests a connection. How do the phenomena connect?

We contend that grief both results from and catalyzes unraveling. This explanation satisfies us, the authors. Unraveling seems inevitable when people lose another. However, grief may not follow. Perhaps grief occurs for another reason or at least only when additional criteria accompany the loss.

But perhaps this: perhaps we owe ourselves the privilege of grieving every time we lose. Maybe we owe ourselves grief even if anger and pain occupied our last, most salient condition in the relationship. Perhaps, without grief, heartache and anguish haunt us. Years later, we find traces of the relationship – joy, and pain – still raveled around unexpected sensations, moments, or artifacts. Perhaps those relationships have not closed completely. Inversely, grief fails to complete without unraveling. Loss fails to complete without grief and unraveling. We arrive at a moment, a proverbial space of choosing ways through the yellow: Life- or Deathworld. Which way will we turn? A grieving person may move habitually as if the world still contains the lost other. The grieving-but-raveled person prepares meals, sets the table, coordinates reservations for two but only one person attends. Love notes litter the kitchen counter because no one comes to claim them anymore. He remains raveled; his grief fails to mature into a sufficient expression.

Only as we allow ourselves to unravel and grieve can we do either fully. To the earlier questions – Does grief cause one to unravel? Does unraveling cause grief? We, the authors suggest yes. Yes, grief may propel our unraveling, soften the threads so they begin to separate. Yes, unraveling may incubate our grief into a mature, healing expression. And neither one – grief nor unraveling – can work without the other. The loss of another imposes a (sometimes sudden) unraveling. The extent to which we unravel depends on whether we allow ourselves to grieve. Grieving allows us to unravel further, more completely. In the way that grief and unraveling complement and propel each other, they work as raveled forces.

But unraveling, remember, represents only the half. As in all our life, we continue to gain and lose. The process of unraveling pertains to the thing or person that we lose. And grief derives from and contributes to such unraveling. While grief and unraveling epitomize less-than-desirable states, we do well to realize that unraveling and grieving perform the necessary process of opening us up to the other half – the process of raveling to something, someone new.

References

Malhotra, Valerie (1981): "The Social Accomplishment of Music in a Symphony Orchestra: A Phenomenological Analysis". In: *Qualitative Sociology* 4. No. 2, pp. 102–125.
Online Etymology Dictionary (n.d.): "Ravel". Retrieved from https://www.etymonline.com/word/ravel#etymonline_v_3410, visited October 11, 2020.
Online Etymology Dictionary (n.d.): "Unravel". Retrieved from https://www.etymonline.com/search?q=unravelling, visited October 11, 2020.
Schütz, Alfred (1951): "Making Music Together: A Study in Social Relationship". In: *Social Research* 18. No. 1, pp. 76–97.
Wagner, Helmut (1983): *Phenomenology of Consciousness and Sociology of the Life-world: An Introductory Study*. Edmonton: University of Alberta Press.

Lori Davidson, Jennifer Decker, and Dagmara Tarasiuk
Chapter 13
Overcoming Deathworlds of Addiction, Self-Injury, and Stress

Abstract: Pressure and power have two sides; both of them have positive and negative aspects. They can motivate and oppress us. Pressure can be our power and power can be our pressure. This relationship is especially noticeable within the Deathworldly provinces of meaning of addiction, self-injury, and stress. This chapter presents a collaboration of three student researchers who explore the Lifeworldly affirming activities of weightlifting, personal training, and yoga in relation to obtaining power to overcome Deathworlds, as well as reducing Lifeworld pressures. We discuss the somatic connection between pressure and power in order to reveal how it is possible to communicate body knowledge through exercise. Additionally, the pressure of middle-aged women who endanger themselves in exercise to obtain a younger body-image, and consequently a perceived power is explored. We conclude that by obtaining this power and relieving the Lifeworld pressures, an individual will move through a transformation. Along with examining this topic, we also discuss our self-observations of transformation, which occurred through the phenomenological process to deeply understand our phenomena.

Keywords: addiction, stress, exercise, yoga, phenomenology

Introduction

The following chapter is the result of a collaboration between three women who participated as doctoral students in the "From Strangers to Collaborators" international research project. Though many kilometers apart (USA and Poland), we discovered a personal connection through our exploration of the phenomenon of pressure and power in the context of overcoming Deathworlds of addiction, self-injury, and stress. Through our collaboration we found that our Deathworlds

---

Note: Part of the article written by Mrs. Tarasiuk was carried out as part of the research project: NCN, Opus 15, project number 2018/29 / B / HS6 / 00513, Experiencing corporeality and gestures in the social world of hatha yoga. Meanings and knowledge transfer in body practice.

https://doi.org/10.1515/9783110691818-013

shared a common denominator – they are associated with the worlds of physical activity.

At the root of each of these activities – weightlifting, personal training, and yoga – each of the researchers found pressure. It turned out that pressure can be a positive motivator to undertake healthy physical activity, which helps overcome the Deathworld of addiction and stress. On the other hand, the pressure of having a young and firm body can also lead to an unhealthy addiction to physical activity and push towards the Deathworld of self-injury.

There is also an element of power in these activities. The power from weightlifting helps in the fight against addiction. The power of exercise found in yoga helps to overcome the stress associated with the realities of work. Women compromising their well-being for the sake of body image have a dangerous sense of perceived power during personal training sessions.

Our descriptions of lived experience (*protocols*) were written from a Schützian (1970) perspective. We explored the essential elements of power and pressure and described the actors and multiple realities experienced in the Lifeworld and Deathworld. The protocols were written from the vantage of our personal lived experience and, in some instances, we recognized "that we know more than we can tell" (van Manen 2015, p. 113).

Lori's Vantage Points

After entering recovery, I memorized a prayer that I recite every night. The prayer is known in many circles, but to me, it is known as the addicts' prayer, "God, grant me the serenity to accept the things I cannot change, the courage to change the things I can, and the wisdom to know the difference." Acceptance, courage, and change are vital elements of this prayer and connect closely with the phenomena of power. In order to remain in recovery, I first needed to accept that I am powerless over my addiction, and then, through finding personal power, I find the courage to change my behavior. The question is, how does one find their power? In my case, power was brought to me through the experience of weightlifting.

I propose that strength training may prevent relapse for those in recovery from addiction. The power one gains from strength training may transform itself into personal power for the addicted person, which allows for somatic growth, thus decreasing the desire for the former Deathworld of addiction.

Jennifer's Vantage Points

As an observer of the phenomenon of middle-aged women who endanger themselves exercising for body image, I have identified three common biographical determinants: their life stage (age), their socio-economic status, and their gender. These three aspects of the phenomenon play a role in how the actors move through past, present, and future, and how time influences the manifestation of endangerment.

In their mid-forties to early sixties, the women experiencing this phenomenon adopt a specific cultural-historic perspective. Attitudes regarding gender and physical activity have evolved over the decades. Some middle-aged women may be new to exercise thereby affecting how they participate in it.

Each of the women I am discussing in this phenomenon are wealthy. Personal training is one of the many commodities available to these women. Their wealth allows them to pursue optimal health and age-concealing measures. Because of their relationship to me, as a personal trainer, I can glean insight into their Lifeworlds.

Women have a unique experience of aging as compared to male counterparts. King (2004) stated that far more than the male body, the female body is subjected to the "gaze" of the other. Aging women may feel increasing pressure to conform to body image standards because their bodies are constantly scrutinized by society (Chonody/Teater 2016). Therefore, gender plays a critical role in how one experiences aging.

Dagmara's Vantage Points

My experience is that of being under enormous time pressure. This is a very uncomfortable position, which not only causes stress but blocks creativity, killing the joy of work. In this sense, it is a kind of Deathworld. I will describe how pressure impacts the Lifeworld of a doctoral student entering the social scientific community, where the feeling of pressure to make it – to succeed in academia – is present. Yoga became a means to re-enliven this Deathworldly experience. I look at how yoga helped in fighting both external and internal pressure. I understand yoga not as a sport, not as a challenge, not as a competition, but as an opportunity to stop, to look inside yourself, and an opportunity to look closely at ourselves under pressure.

Personal Power through Weightlifting: Fighting the Deathworld of Addiction

> Power is everywhere' and 'comes from everywhere' so in this sense is neither an agency nor a structure.
> – Michel Foucault in *The Will to Knowledge,* 1998, p. 63.

There is no easy road out of the Deathworld of addiction. The fractured self, seeking the path, must first find the road to recovery, which is often hidden by addiction. When one is ready, the path will appear, and then it is up to the self to remain on it each and every time they come to a fork in the road. For the self to remain in recovery one must admit their powerlessness, as well as embrace their power.

Weightlifting provides both a feeling of powerlessness and powerfulness. Powerlessness when one is unable to achieve the desired lift and powerfulness when one does, especially when the action proves to be a personal best. In my case, the movement known as the barbell deadlift brought power into my life, which continues to transform as well as provide motivation. The deadlift was not universally known until the early 1900s but can be traced back to the early 1700s. The movement is basic, almost primal, and instinctive as one lifts a dead weight from the earth. I correlate the deadlift with addiction in that the power of the drug, once lifted, similar to pressure, yields the feeling of powerfulness. Below is a lived experience description of the power achieved through weightlifting.

The Deadlift

> Every weight training session takes me to another level, sometimes it is negative because I did not achieve the goal, but more often it is positive because I did. My mirror image changes daily, but one thing remains: the feeling of power. The power of making healthy choices, the power of feeling power through lifting weight, and the power of knowing that no one or thing can take the achievement from you. It is yours to own, to control, as long as your mind and body will allow you to do it.
>
> "It's time to learn to go heavier," he says. I love deadlifting, as it is one of the most powerful lifts. There is something about picking up a heavy weight and holding it, just standing with it in your hands, and looking at yourself in the mirror. I agree with him and we head for the garage. It's cold, so we turn the heater on, it's evening, so the single long, fluorescent bulb is flickering to the side of us. The mini lamp is also on, which emits a soft glow, displaying our shadows on the walls. It smells like oil or gas, because of the parked cars behind us, but I quickly forget about the smell once I rub my hands with chalk. The bar is set up on the platform on wooden risers instead of the platform itself. He turns on the music, which is loud (the group Disturbed, Down with the Sickness) and intoxicating,

as I begin to enter the "zone." I step in front of the bar and try not to look at the weight. "I don't want to know," I think to myself, "I just want to pull it." I breathe in and tighten my weight belt, I bend over and grab the bar, it's cold, and the knurl digs into my skin. I look up and lock eyes with myself in the cracked mirror. It's not pretty because I'm split in half, but this is weightlifting, it's not intended to be pretty. The music gets louder and the shadows dance faster on the walls as I begin to pull the weight from the risers. There are no other thoughts, just to pull, just to rise, just to stand and the bar slides up my legs, and I'm squeezing, I'm tight, I lean back and I'm standing. I pause, my eyes, still on me, I see me and I see power and I see accomplishment. I slowly begin my descent with the bar and release it once the weights touch the wooden risers. My heart is racing, as I pop off my belt and inspect my hands for evidence of the accomplishment. Euphoria races through me, as I begin to think about the next goal. (L. Davidson, self-observation, 2019)

An actor entering recovery needs to know it will be hard, the hardest thing they have ever done in their life because it never ends – you practice it every day. You have to practice effective time management and find ways to manage stress levels. I recommend adopting a physically healthy lifestyle because once you are capable of this the mind and spirit will follow. I cannot say there was someone who saved my life, but I can say there is something, a phenomenon, that keeps me in recovery and that is the power achieved through weightlifting.

Whether or not an actor in recovery chooses to remain anonymous in another reality is their choice. However, finding a healthy balance between the realities is often a struggle, without sharing their history, and tends to be an area of extreme pressure, which then leads to relapse.

The following protocol provides typifications of the actors in recovery based on Schütz (1973):

Newcomer: The newcomer is fresh out of rehab or jail and is looking to connect with likeminded folks to maintain sobriety. This person is both excited and scared as they are struggling to find their sober self. They will be searching for a sponsor, preferably an Old Timer, with 10 plus years of sobriety, and of the same gender, because this is what their counselor or probation officer told them they need to do. This person will be a chain smoker and, depending on their drug of choice, will have a hankering for coffee or candy.

Old Timer: This person is well known throughout many meeting rooms and has 10 or more years sober. They feel strong in their recovery, and have fully embraced the reality of recovery, though they are wise enough to know that the rooms are part of what helps them maintain their sobriety so they "keep coming back." They will be the first to reach out to the Newcomer, as well as put the Relapser in her place. When the Old Timer shares stories in the meeting rooms, she will reflect on hope, inspiration, and gratitude. The Old Timer no longer smokes and has adopted a healthier lifestyle. The Old Timer is likely someone's sponsor and/or is head of the chapter which oversees the meetings.

Relapser: This person is stuck between the reality of recovery and Deathworld of addiction. She struggles with maintaining sobriety due to person, places or things and may have not yet fully detoxed from her drug of choice. This person has not yet hit a "rock bottom." This person may have a sponsor but does not follow the sponsor's advice. This person has been unable to break her link to the seductive Deathworld of addiction, despite being told many times there is only sobriety, incarceration or death. She attends meetings in the hope that she will find "something" more powerful than the addiction Deathworld.

Maintainer: Like the Old Timer, this person has fully embraced recovery and all the gifts it offers. She only attends meetings as needed but has managed to remain sober by discovering other coping mechanisms to replace prior behaviors. The Maintainer has rules, which she adheres to in order to maintain her sobriety. Fear is what drives her to remain sober as she knows a relapse at this point would mean death. The Maintainer is also driven by a great sense of power and achievement. (L. Davidson, protocol, 2019)

Movement Between Realities

For the Relapser, the pressure of balancing the realities is a common theme, and they will often lose power. The Newcomer has not yet totally experienced all the realities but is aware of their existence. The Old Timer and the Maintainer have become experts in balancing work, family, recovery, hobbies, goals, etc. The Old Timer is typically satisfied with this balance, however, the Maintainer focuses and pushes towards new goals, as she has a strong sense of personal power and accomplishment.

Motives

The motives of each actor will change over time and as they maintain sobriety (have power), or not (lose power). In the addiction Deathworld, motives are extremely selfish and this behavior does not necessarily diminish once one has detoxed. Typical motives for entering the world of recovery are legal and health. The prime motive is referred to as one's "rock bottom." Fear is a motive worth exploring, fear of jail or death. As with the addiction Deathworld, there is typically a "rock bottom" that one may experience in achieving power through weightlifting. However, this bottom is not as significant or profound as in the addiction Deathworld. There are many motives for remaining in the world of recovery; some mention health, family, self-esteem, achievement, finances and power.

Below is a segment from a writing protocol discussing power and my archetype:

One of the first things an actor entering the recovery world will hear is, "you must surrender to a POWER greater than yourself." What is this power? It is different for all of us. Could it be this supernatural being that Schütz and Bentz describe or it could be based on faith? For this actor . . . in case you haven't figured it out by now . . . wait, I will let you guess which actor I am, but in my case, it is both, a supernatural being who I have faith in to have my back. She looks like the Phoenix and I see her when I lift weights, I see her when life gets hard, but I also see her when life is good. I even try to look like her, perhaps this is another area worthy of further exploration. (L. Davidson, protocol, 2019)

Schütz (1973) references work from William James and Kierkegaard when addressing the sub-universe and transitions from paramount to non-paramount realities. Specifically, Schütz references the *leap*, as Kierkegaard called it. The shock of the leap is experienced when our consciousness is forced to change its attention. I think this shock occurs at several pivotal moments in the realities of addiction, recovery, and weight training. Below is a protocol addressing this paramount reality:

Addicted Reality > Recovery Reality > Weight Training Reality

Addicted Reality (fantasy, powerless):
- difference in time and spatiality
- noema (that to which we orient ourself)
- concept of self and others
- meanings and motives

Recovery Reality (socially acceptable Reality, powerful):
- all of the above, as influenced by what is labeled as socially correct behavior
- world of work, the world of family
- time is short

Weight Training or Reality of Power (all other worlds are incorporated into or influenced by this world):
- behavior based on what feels good or right
- world of work and family satisfied if there is a healthy balance between these and the world of self
- time is long (even when it might be short) and manageable if you are focused

The shock is specifically experienced from the addicted world to the recovery world or one could see it as the powerless world to the powerful world. As the senses begin to live again, this is both good and bad, overwhelmingly powerful in many aspects as the consciousness moves from the goal of intoxication to the pressure of the maintenance of sobriety. (L. Davidson, protocol, 2019)

The Pressure Phenomenon

Thanks to discovering the phenomenon of pressure, reflecting on its examples, and analyzing my life in its context, I noticed that living under pressure is my normal way of functioning. As if this phenomenon was necessary for me for effective living.

Pressure motivates me to act. However, this motivation (*in order to* motivation [Schütz 2008]) is a negative motivation. I'm doing something in order to not to think about the negative consequences of inaction. This motivation is forced by fear. Motivation forces me to work, but in the short term. Eventually, pressure overwhelms passion, enthusiasm, and joy of performed activities.

Thanks to the pressure, I will sit down and start writing a fragment of the text, but this weight will be with me all the time. The greater the pressure, the greater the compulsion, the greater the resistance. Under pressure, I try to do my job, but the same pressure prevents me from continuing. The constant tension I feel under pressure takes away my natural motivation, so the pressure is a motivation killer in the long run. The very word "pressure" evokes unpleasant associations. Even if it pushes you to act, any coercion ultimately always resists.

Constant exertion of internal pressure keeps individuals in check of a planned, forced, but known and safe life. It allows automatic operation according to a previously developed scheme. Living outside pressure requires the ability to get out of this pattern, requires flexibility and trust in your intuition. Getting out of pressure begins when the motivation "I need" and "I should" turns into "I want" when the in order to theme is a natural motive, not a compulsion.

Looking at my own pressure, it is easy to see that in most cases, my internal pressure has arisen because of external influences. The pressure of the environment is usually the expectations of others as to what we are to be like and how to live. Expectations become pressure and coercion. Social pressure imposing the need for a healthy and slim figure forces me to play sports. Pressure related to the need to maintain social balance can lead to seeking peace through yoga. But isn't that another kind of pressure? Is yoga not the result of pressure to find harmony? Is finding balance not just another goal, right after the perfect figure, set by a vibrating society?

I think we can even talk about the pressure of being under pressure. Consumer society, the society of excess, promotes a busy lifestyle full of pressure, especially the pressure of time in which individuals constantly strive for something and advance. Any attempts to stop this race and escape from pressure are a sign of weakness and inability to adapt to the rest.

The following fragment of my protocol was written during participation in the project in which I focused on the phenomenon of pressure and its dual nature:

Pressure for me has double face – good and bad. Pressure can be motivating and suffocating. It can give us some adrenalin but also can drive us to be overburdened. I don't like this feeling, but I think that my life will be worse without it. I know that I am a lazy person and maybe without pressure, I couldn't achieve anything that makes me happy, maybe without pressure I won't feel fulfilled. Originally, I view my phenomenon only in a bad way, but now I think that I was unfair or simply I wasn't aware.

Now I notice more and more good aspects of pressure. I think that without pressure we can't really feel pleasure, we feel it too facilely. In the world of repletion, and the excessiveness of potential we feel pressure to make a decision. And we have to make it. Pressure eases this task for us. Maybe it is violence but maybe it is "wise" violence. Without pressure maybe I will not take part in this class. I felt some safe pressure in that I want to take part in it because it can be important for me. It can help me to develop myself. A pressure force to focus on, to activate life. But pressure also limits me and invites me to release, to get out from under the pressure, to make a break, feel lightness, feel freedom. And finally, I asked myself – do I want it? I don't know. If I want to be an aware person maybe I should see pressure off. But I think that without this feeling my life wouldn't complete. That freedom can't exist without pressure. Peace, calm, can't exist without stress, pressure. That lightness also can be unbearable and can make pressure.

For me, pressure is something more. It's something important, something that provides harmony though it is associated mainly with disorder. It's like power, which can support people but which can also destroy them. It can provide a chance for growth, collaboration, and advancement. With pressure, I feel that I can live. Maybe without pressure, my life will pass through my fingers unnoticed. But pressure can also lead to the risk of bad rivalry, and inequality. It motivates me, but it can also break me. That's why I should be aware of my pressure and try to control it. (D. Tarasiuk, protocol, 2019)

Pressure in the Reality of Higher Education

The higher education system in Poland promotes individuality and competitiveness. The functioning of students and employees in the points system generates a continuous race in terms of publication and number of appearances at conferences. The so-called "pointosis" translates into the quality of the resulting texts and papers, which are produced en masse. Therefore, the scientific life of a doctoral student is accompanied by constant frustration and pressure related to the need to gather research data and develop subsequent articles at an ever-faster rate.

On the other hand, although I feel the pressure of individual development, the opposite is also expected – interdisciplinarity and scientific cooperation. Because "the relativity and selectivity of our experiences force us to constant dialogue" (Waldenfels 1989, p.254), researchers who are serious about their scientific careers are even obliged to cooperate, especially internationally. To participate in it, they face the problem of understanding, sometimes interculturally. Coming from different realities, they must not only jump out of the world in which they live in their free time into the world of research but also jump into the open model of learning, suspending the individual work style. Therefore, scientific cooperation seems to be a particularly difficult kind of cooperation, due to the researchers themselves, who participate in a project at the same time as they are developing their scientific careers. So, with the inevitable more or less important differences in individual motivation, the common goal, or the in order to motive, is very important. While the divergence of the "because" motive may hinder or even prevent the cooperation process, but not waste the potential, the lack of a common goal means a lack of cooperation.

In scientific cooperation, the pressure of hierarchy may also be a problem. When a professor by virtue of his title gives himself the role of an expert in a research group, he may underestimate knowledge outside his narrative and not create conditions for dialogue and full cooperation. In an extreme case, cooperation may be limited to gathering the material together and taking further steps in the research process by the expert alone, without taking into account the voice of others, which cancels the cooperation. Its guarantee is an open dialogue and exchange of thoughts, and the assumption that a truly great teacher always learns from his students (Schütz 2008, p. 129).

However, redefining relationships from hierarchical to partner, in which each expert discusses even-handedly with others, can be difficult due to the general fear of conducting constructive disputes in scientific circles (Zielińska 2013, p. 177). Disputes should be understood as a creative exchange of views, which consists of adding and including data that were not previously considered in their argumentation. In scientific cooperation, it is not enough to reach peaceful compromises or averages, which are accepted by the general public but are not represented by the majority of participants.

A phenomenological attitude, especially the practice of *epoché*, seems to be inspirational and helpful in conducting a good and effective dialogue, which is the basis of all scientific cooperation. By analyzing Schütz's recommendations regarding the understanding of the Other, we receive general advice on efficient and fruitful dialogue. So how can we cooperate in practice? First of all, Schütz notes that direct contact is the most effective form of communication: "It [range of the expression field] may reach the maximum level when there is not only a unity of time but also space between the partners, i.e. in a situation which by sociologists is called a face-to-face relationship" (Schütz 2008, p. 29). Since at the beginning it was established that scientific cooperation is based on dialogue, and the dialogue is best carried out live, it can be assumed that scientific discussion during a direct meeting will be more effective than calling via Skype or exchanging emails.

But not only distance can be an obstacle to mutual understanding. Clinging to one's assumptions, lack of readiness to accept the unknown, can cause an inability to leave the circle of established habits and close oneself to the suggestions of co-researchers. Moreover, "the most common attitude is to impose on others our perception of things, and even to stubbornly direct conversation to our own experience. This is a testimony to the exuberant narcissism that encloses us" (Depraz 2010, p. 14). Participating in the process of agreement, it is worth adopting the opposite attitude, the phenomenological epoché, which requires constant questioning of one's own assumptions and asking oneself and others questions, which will allow seeing the problem from many perspectives. Epoché consists of:

> Radical "refraining" (Enthaltung) from what is observed . . . . In this way a space is created without any judgment or, at least, a space where the passing of hasty judgments is delayed or stopped. The typical of observer lack of prejudices further strengthens the withdrawal by introducing a kind of blockade to our natural tendency to judge, i.e. to take objects in the mode of "it goes without saying," to a mode of acting without asking yourself. (Depraz 2010, p. 32)

Epoché allows to be more open to the comments of others, not make initial assumptions, and thus improve communication. It enables, at least partially, the suspension of emotions, suspension of one's reasons (or even ego), and one's assumptions in order to be more open to the Other and his perspectives. Practical application of epoché is an exercise of active listening and interchangeability of points of view, it is not putting yourself at the center of the social world: "Everyone who becomes a social researcher must make a mental operation in order to put in the center of the world not oneself, but someone else, namely the observed person" (Schütz 2008, p. 125).

By participating in the From Strangers to Collaborators project, which was to be based on openness, cooperation, and mutual inspiration, I understood that I was not ready for this mode of work yet. Because I needed pressure to produce individual achievements and I always worked under constant time pressure, it turned out that I cannot work (or cooperate) in an atmosphere deprived of "motivation" which, until now, was pressure for me. This was probably because I didn't know how to motivate myself otherwise. The pressure was the only known motivation for me. I was afraid that if I gave up my life under pressure, I would stop caring about anything. I would lose my motivation to act. In fact, I clung to my pressure not realizing (for a long time) how serious the consequences could be. Being under pressure in both academic and private life, I was afraid to change something, but at the same time, I was asking myself how others can function in their worlds and move forward without the weight of pressure. Where should I look for another motivation tool (although pressure is a force tool)? How can I find a willingness to not act under pressure? Finally, where should I look for an environment without pressure?

Yoga Practice

The answer may be yoga practice. Initially, I expected progress in yoga. My everyday habits transformed through the experience of yoga. I imagine how I stand on my hands, how my body becomes athletic. But coming regularly to classes, I began to understand that a mat is a place where I do not think about what is ahead of me, I do not think about progress and instead allow myself to be in the present. The reality of yoga is about being in the here and now, there is no specific goal in it, there is no expectation so there is no pressure. This short time in which I leave the world of pressure is salutary for me.

I cut myself off, tangibly, physically. I cut myself off from the rush of many thoughts at once, from everyday challenges and tasks. Everyday life involves a compulsion to constantly think, analyze, plan and set strategies. The pressure of multitasking, the pressure of many thoughts from many worlds at the same time.

Yoga is time off. A moment just for myself. I am among the people whom I only say hello to, but I who I have no relationship with. They are neutral, so they do not have dependencies, challenges, tasks or responsibilities. There are only a mat and a teacher who gives further "orders." Yes, during practice I want to receive orders. I follow her voice and my body carries out her instructions. For an hour and a half, it is not me who manages myself.

But I do not feel like I am under the pressure of the teacher's orders. Conversely, my teacher, my master, releases the pressure of making decisions from me. When I started my adventure with yoga, I was completely unaware of my body. I felt that the teacher knew my body better than me! She knew my options better. I willingly submitted to her corrections. Thanks to the teacher, I learn to listen to my body, understand the work of muscles, their arrangement. My teacher also teaches me that yoga is an activity that is not about rapid progress and that you should patiently and systematically teach how to listen to yourself and your body. In yoga, you are not under anybody's pressure and you cannot put pressure on your own body, otherwise, you will get injured.

Living without pressure requires self-confidence and intuition. It requires trust that you are the person who knows best what is good for you. In order to be able to start such cooperation with yourself, it is good to start by understanding your body. Yoga helps in this. Yoga releases you from pressure, which makes you feel that you have to be better and the best. Yoga is not a competition. It's not a race against others or a race against yourself. Yoga is development, self-improvement, but not at all costs, and at its own pace, not imposed from the outside. The yoga teacher does not behave like a motivational trainer. Instead of a kind of pressure like: "do it, you can do it," the yoga master will say "do it if you can."

In contrast to somatic practices which are oriented toward the performer (such as diet, bodybuilding, personal training) and which are often motivated by the desire to satisfy others (Shusterman 2016, p. 46) by submitting to social pressure associated with an attractive appearance and a healthy lifestyle, yoga turns us to ourselves. It is not oriented at improving the external appearance, but at improving the internal experience, at sharpening self-awareness.

When performing asanas, I focus on the pleasure arising from the activity itself. It is easier to allow yourself to follow this approach during the practice of yoga than, for example, watching the series unproductively, because we are constantly accompanied by the thought that I am doing something for my body and soul. I do not think that I am wasting valuable time, on the contrary, it is for me a kind of investment in internal peace and harmony. And most importantly, I do it for myself and not for others. I do not want to satisfy others, I do not want to adapt or give in to social, external pressure; I want to focus on myself during practice and derive satisfaction from this.

The Pressure to Conform: Women who Risk Injury and Death to Maintain Body Image Standards

There are elements of both perceived power (changing one's body through exercise) and pressure (patriarchal body-image ideals) present in the phenomenon of middle-aged American women who endanger themselves exercising. It is possible to view this phenomenon through multiple lenses in my Lifeworld. I define *exercise endangerment* as when an individual places themselves in risky exercise situations in pursuit of an ideal body image. With this definition in mind, the phenomenon is not exclusive to middle-aged women. However, the phenomenon of middle-aged women who take exercise risks is nuanced in two main ways: 1) women are vulnerable to ageist attitudes coupled with patriarchal ideals of feminine beauty, and 2) their perception towards exercise may be influenced by gender stereotypes. These two points give exercise potentially a very different meaning to middle-aged women and in turn, may be embodied in contrasting ways. For these reasons, I have focused on women as opposed to both men and women.

I have worked with hundreds of middle-aged women during my personal training career. A handful of these women appear to endanger themselves exercising to enhance their body image. This is evidenced when one pursues an exercise that is far too advanced for them or exercises too hard, placing themselves in a position of risk of injury. Each of the women I am discussing share similarities regarding race, social class, and habitation. As white, upper-class, central Pennsylvanian, middle-aged women, they share similar moral codes and Lifeworlds. I recognize that because of my experience with the women I have trained, my interpretation of the phenomenon may present itself in unique ways. Although there is variation in attitudes amongst middle-aged women, for the scope of this text, my discussion will be based on the women I have trained rather than a generalization of the entire population of middle-aged American women.

Experiencing their Lifeworlds

Cosmetic surgery, fast and flashy cars, lavish purses, and expensive jewelry appear to give these women their sense of value. In a society that idealizes youth and beauty, middle-aged women may feel pressure to compete with younger versions of themselves to be noticed. Moreover, women who do not conform to these standards may "experience her body as ugly and alien" (Levesque-Lopman 1988). Due to the societal attitude that young and beautiful women are valued more than others, some women are inclined to take extreme measures to conform (Dolezal 2015).

American women are expected to adhere to contemporary beauty standards (Ponterotto 2016). King (2004) asserted that many well-documented fashion trends practiced by women are not only time consuming and expensive, they are also potentially damaging, such as corsets, cosmetics, waxing, cosmetic surgery, and high heels. Therefore, the pressure to conform to mainstream American body image standards can be resource consuming and damaging to physical and psychological health.

Dolezal (2015) discusses the notion of the "seen" body which is with what other people form conscious impressions of us. She argues that being "seen" by others is one way in which we experience what she calls *body shame*. Cosmetic surgery, extreme exercise, dieting, and high fashion all exemplify how women may go to great lengths to circumvent shame. Dolezal's idea of body shame is a profound force in human experience and is resultant of the body itself. We, humans, experience an embodied shame that not only intrudes on our psychological space but affects our bodies and how we experience them. From this standpoint, middle-aged women who endanger themselves through exercising may be attempting to mediate how society, one that idealizes youth and beauty, views them, and consequently their aging body. These women may feel like they have power through exercise, cosmetic surgery, and extreme dieting, in that they are able to change their bodies.

Actors in their Lifeworlds

Identified as typical actors (Schütz/Luckmann 1973) in this Lifeworld are 1) Mrs. Hardcore, who is driven by autonomy and power, is an over-achiever, and epitomizes strength, 2) Mrs. Insecure, who has low self-esteem, is self-conscious and often feels unworthy, 3) Mrs. Attention Grabber, who is flashy, bold, and extravagant and, 4) Mrs. Material Girl, who places importance on riches, material things, and is very worldly.

The actors I have identified have seemingly contradictory elements. For example, Mrs. Hardcore epitomizes strength, whereas Mrs. Insecure has low self-esteem. However, each one of them is motivated by having an ideal body image. Mrs. Insecures' low self-esteem is a product of being an aging woman in a patriarchal society. Consequently, Mrs. Hardcores' desire for power may be compensatory because of the pressure the aging woman feels to have an ideal body image. The aging woman amid a patriarchal society may feel she must position herself to try to look and be younger in order to be seen as meaningful thereby participating in risky exercise, and other potentially harmful body corrective measures, such as dieting and cosmetic surgery, for an improved body image.

Seeking attention with lavish clothes, jewelry, fast and expensive cars is a way one may attempt to compensate for being ignored in a society that places unequal, undue value on young, attractive women. Furthermore, Mrs. Hardcore utilizes her agency in ways that she feels is giving her power, such as changing her body by exercising to extremes, dieting, and cosmetic surgery.

Typifications

My typifications and stocks of knowledge all contribute to how I view the other (women), placing myself at the heart of the inquiry. Therefore, second-order constructs are important in the discussion of this phenomenon as it is me, the phenomenologist, that is interpreting the women's Lifeworlds. I cannot ignore that my personality and my work with these women, as their trainer, are intricately involved in my discussion of this phenomenon. Furthermore, my influence on them may play a role in how they are actors in my Lifeworld and vice versa. As I take an intense approach to fitness (I train my body very hard) I understand that my attitudes about exercise may influence how my clients feel about it. However, although I train hard, I also recognize, and stress to my clients, the importance of a balanced lifestyle which includes self-care.

This protocol reflects a lack of self-care and is the epitome of the phenomenon of middle-aged women who endanger themselves exercising for body image:

> I just finished training five people in the morning hours before 9:30 am when Paige and I were scheduled to train. It was a beautiful spring morning: a little chill and a little warmth in the air. The fragrance of fresh flowers wafted about my fitness studio as I needed to leave the door open to regulate the temperature. This day I was feeling dreamy and aloof; spring does that to me, yet I regained composure as Paige walked through the door.
>
> I noticed she was moving in a way that made me think something was wrong with her knees. I confronted her, and she sheepishly confessed that her knees had been tender for a while! I told Paige that we should focus on more gentler, appropriate exercises until her pain subsided. However, she didn't want to take my advice. She continued by jumping up and down on a box. That was a sure way to blow out her knees for good! I felt so angry that she would not listen to me because I could predict how this would go. She would hurt herself and not be able to be as active, and she was at the age that it might be hard to regain her excellent physical shape.
>
> Another issue is that she could walk away and associate the injury with her training here with me at my studio! A responsible, educated trainer would never allow clients to move in a way that they know is risky. Her defiance infuriated me. Not because she didn't listen to me as much as she was placing herself in a position of undue risk.
>
> At the end of our session, Paige and I began to "debrief" (like I usually do with my clients) by discussing how the workout felt and taking the time to talk about whatever she wanted. This time was different. She started telling me that I should ask for expensive bags from men, not jewelry. I don't ask for anything. I don't live in that world where material things become the objects of pursuit and having expensive purses and jewelry gives me value. All that she said this day befuddled me. I felt sad for her. It seemed as if her life was full of expensive things yet very empty. However, listening to her confirmed that I don't need those things to be happy and the flowers began to smell stronger to me, I could hear the birds chirping, the weather was warming. As she walked out of that door that day I knew in my gut that I would never see her again. Instead of feeling upset, I went right back to feeling dreamy. (J. Decker, protocol, 2019)

These women's desire for a younger body image may compel them to take exercise risks and seem to outweigh their perception of the negative consequences associated with those risks. The motivations can be examined from an embodied perspective, in that women's experience of their bodies relative to the social world and their multiple realities are profound and a part of meaning-making. Additionally, as Dolezal (2015) argues, women's fear of shame is a powerful driving force that is capable of causing these women to jeopardize health and safety for an ideal body. Middle-aged women who endanger themselves in exercise may feel a sense of personal power by changing their bodies. Further, it appears that as some women age, they feel that jewelry and expensive things may compensate for their aging bodies, giving them the attention they had in their youth.

Imposed Relevances

Women are profoundly impacted by how people critique their bodies. Higher status jobs and higher earning potential are given to women who wear cosmetics, thereby indicating that women who are perceived as more attractive have better social standing (Mileva et al. 2016). Socially imposed *relevances* (Schütz/Luckmann 1973) are possible factors that drive some women to risk health and welfare while exercising or through other potentially risky body corrective measures, such as extreme dieting and cosmetic surgery. Schütz and Luckman (1973) argue that the actions of other people "place themes before the individual to which he must turn himself" (p. 190). Therefore, because a woman who is perceived as younger and more attractive will have more social possibilities, it is reasonable to assume that many women would desire to remain young and attractive.

The pressure to conform to contemporary body-image standards becomes a socially imposed relevance for these women. Their shift to maintain equilibrium between the pressure of body-image, the social implications of such, and the perceived power of obtaining an ideal body-image. However, this pursuit is futile. The perceived power is not real power because power comes from autonomy or the ability to do. It does not come from catering to an intellectually ignorant society – in the sense that in this society the way the body appears becomes more important than how it functions, and the somatic aspects that make us intelligent and compassionate beings. Furthermore, in this phenomenon, the effort put into exercise is the result of subservience to a patriarchal society rather than an act of autonomy and personal power.

Between Lifeworlds and Deathworlds

The women I am writing about all experience pressure to conceal their aging body in a patriarchal society. In pushing themselves during exercise, they feel a sense of personal power. It appears as if, to them, the risk of injury outweighs the consequences of abstaining from the exercise. This mentality is echoed by Dolezal (2015) when she states that "physical pain or discomfort is preferable to shame," which, in her example, includes the prospect of disfigurement and even death as a possibility of ambitious cosmetic surgery.

A complementary perspective is that these women become addicted to exercise. Spano (2001), taking an intrapsychic stance, conducted a study in which 210 research participants completed: the Trait Anxiety Scale of the State-Trait Anxiety Inventory, the Obsessive-Compulsive Personality Scale, the Narcissistic Personality Inventory, the Commitment to Exercise Scale, and the Frequency of Physical Activity Form. A simultaneous linear multiple regression analysis demonstrated that anxiety and obsessive-compulsive traits were correlated to exercise commitment. Spano (2001) found that given some individuals view their physical appearance as their societal worth, these individuals may be inclined to incorporate maladaptive behaviors, such as excessive exercise, which can lead to injury and social problems.

The notion of *compulsive exercise*, "characterized by a craving for physical training, resulting in uncontrollable excessive exercise behavior with harmful consequences, such as injuries and impaired social relations" has been recognized since the 1970s (Lichtenstein et al. 2017, p. 1). From a physiognomic perspective, body-image becomes a significant reason an individual can become addicted to exercise (Lichtenstein et al. 2017) due to the idea that what people see broadly impacts one's social standing and quality of life.

Jee asserts that exercise addiction is similar to other addictions (2016, p.68). I argue that the act of risk, as well as various addictions, contributes to an individual's Deathworld. The actor falls further into despair the more they try to conform to unrealistic, fleeting notions of what it means to have social value. It is this attitude that contributes to the idea of a Deathworld (Bentz et al. 2018) in that the actions of the actors are driven by social forces that are damaging, which are not a product of love and caring intentions. Moving from a healthy Lifeworld of balance and self-respect to endangering themselves in exercise for body-image, is an example of how these women migrate toward Deathworlds.

Connecting Worlds

Our society is filled with pressure and power. For some, these elements may lead to a Deathworld, and for others, it may be the beginning of a Lifeworld. The pressure that addicts feel to remain substance-free can mean the literal difference between life and death. Some populations may feel pressure to conform to society's standards even if it means risking health and well-being. The societal pressure related to the image and presence of our body in the intersubjective world of other bodies is associated with various types of pressures, which may be dangerous to health and well-being in its goals, ultimately leading to bodily harm or death.

Society does not typically view addiction as a disease. A common misconception is that addiction is a moral weakness, or powerlessness, by those who lack education on the topic, or perhaps by those who have deep scars from an addicted loved one. It is true that in the addict's Deathworld, we are weakened due to the power and pressure of the addiction, but I have learned, through the physical transformation through recovery, we find power in the pressure that is both physical and mental.

In the case of middle-aged women, they are not the only population that may risk health and welfare to achieve the ideal body image. This group of women experiences body changes that have a profound impact on their social relevance. The pressure that they feel to conform to body image standards may have a unique impact on their actions. A transformation of thought, one in which they put their well-being first, would allow these women to move from a Deathworld to a Lifeworld. Although they may have a perceived power from exercising to extremes, it is a fallacy because their actions are a product of others' desires. However, the power and pressure, whether internal or external, which may be experienced through exercise can give all of these populations strength and an improved body-image, outside of societal norms, to not only break stigmas but to live in good health.

Sometimes compliance with standards does not result from social pressure, but from the pressure of a specific reality. The scientific world is filled with pressure, both external and internal, which scientists impose on themselves. Focusing on their own careers, functioning in a world of pressure focused on achievements, they forget about the benefits of cooperation. Paradoxically, entering the world of yoga, which directs the gaze on oneself, allows you to notice more around you and to stay open to others. Yoga relieves us of the pressure to be the best in comparison to others and allows us to be the best on our own.

In all of these examples, we notice the enormous power of pressure which forces people to improve their body, mind, or both. On the other hand, in society, there is pressure on power, again both power of mind and power of the body. Pressure seems to have more oppressive consequences, just as power is more motivating. By connecting deeply to our inner selves through physical activity we can transform and turn this negative pressure into a power that moves us from Deathworlds to Lifeworlds. Otherwise, without deep contact, our inner strength will come only from external pressure. This pressure condemns us to remain in our Deathworlds and interferes with our internal transformation, leaving only the transformation of the body for consolation.

References

Bentz, Valorie Malhotra, David Rehorick, James Marlatt, Ayumi Nishii, & Carol Estrada. (2018). Transformative Phenomenology as an Antidote to Technological Deathworlds. Schutzian Research, Vol. 10. 189–220. DOI: 10.5840/schutz20181011.

Chonody, Jill & Barbara Teater. (2016). Why Do I Dread Looking Old?: A Test of Social Identity Theory, Terror Management Theory, and the Double Standard of Aging. *Journal of Women & Aging*, Vol. 28. 112–126. DOI: 10.1080/08952841.2014.950533.

Depraz, Natalie. (2010). *Zrozumieć fenomenologię. Konkretna praktyka*. Warszawa: Oficyna Naukowa.

Dolezal, Luna. (2015). *The Body and Shame: Phenomenology, Feminism, and The Socially Shaped Body*. Lanham, MD: Lexington Books.

Foucault, Michel (1998): *The Will to Knowledge*. London: Penguin.

Jee, Yong Seok. (2016). Exercise Addiction and Rehabilitation. *Journal of Exercise Rehabilitation*, Vol. 12. 67. DOI:10.12965%2Fjer.1632604.302.

King, Angela. (2004). The Prisoner of Gender: Foucault and the Disciplining of the Female Body. *Journal of International Women's Studies*, Vol. 5. pp. 29–39.

Levesque-Lopman, Louise. (1988). *Claiming Reality: Phenomenology and Women's Experience*. Rowman & Littlefield: Totowa, NJ.

Litchtenstein-Vidne, Limor/OkonSinger, Hadas / Cohen, Noga / Todder, Doron / Aue, Tatjana/ Nemets, Boris / Henik, Avishai (2017): "Attentional Bias in Clinical Depression and Anxiety: The Impact of Emotional and Non-emotional Distracting Information". In: Biological Psychology 122, pp. 4–12.

Mileva, Victoria, Alex Jones, Richard Russell, & Anthony Little. (2016). Sex Differences in the Perceived Dominance and Prestige of Women with and Without Cosmetics. *Perception*, Vol. 45. 1166-1183.

Ponterotto, Diane. (2016). Resisting the Male Gaze: Feminist Responses to the "Normatization" of the Female Body in Western Culture. *Journal of International Women's Studies*, Vol. 17. pp. 133–151.

Schutz, Alfred. (1970). *On Phenomenology and Social Relations*. Chicago, IL: The University of Chicago Press.

Schutz, Alfred, & Thomas Luckmann. (1973). The Structures of the Life-World Vol. 1. Evanston, IL: Northwestern University Press.

Schutz, Alfred. (2008). *O wielości światów*. Kraków: Zakład Wydawniczy, NOMOS.

Shusterman, Richard. (2016). *Świadomość ciała. Dociekania z zakresu somaestetyki*. Kraków: Universitas.

Spano, Linda (2001): "The Relationship Between Exercise and Anxiety, Obsessive Compulsiveness, and Narcissism". In: *Personality and Individual Differences* 30. No. 1, pp. 87–93.

Van Manen, Max. (2016). *Researching Lived Experience*. New York, NY: Routledge.

Waldenfels, Bernhard. (1989). *Rozumienie i porozumienie. Filozofia społeczna Alfreda Schütza*. Fenomenologia i socjologia. Warszawa: Państwowe Wydawnictwo Naukowe.

Zielińska, Ewa. (2013). *Design Thinking. Model Pracy Badawczej w obliczu dzikich Problemów Nauk Społecznych*. Stan Rzeczy, Vol. 1. pp. 168–185.

Michelle Elias and Darlene Cockayne
Chapter 14
Military Wife and Mother: Lifeworlds and Deathworlds Surrounding Military Life

Abstract: Darlene (wife of a United States veteran) and Michelle (mother of a United States soldier) shared their experiences of military culture as participants in a research project focused on collaboration between strangers. Using the process of phenomenological writing, these two women explore their worlds to gain an understanding of their current Lifeworlds. Darlene's world is infused with her husband's Deathworld through his depression and suicidal ideations. Michelle's world becomes consumed by her son's deployment to the war zone of Afghanistan. Through numerous digital/video conference calls, their lives began to change and transcend the difficulties faced. Understanding and a return to an acceptable Lifeworld (infused with Deathworld) have been the outcomes of this collaboration.

 The purpose of this writing is to explore two phenomena: the lived experiences of two members of the military community and the collaboration between these two "strangers." Both women belong to military families; one as a spouse and one as a mom. Darlene searches inward when faced with her husband's depression, suicide attempt, and health issues. Her husband was an E-5 in the U.S. Army, he has been a veteran for over 15 years and he still struggles with life in the civilian world. Darlene continues to wrestle with his Deathworld that permeates her everyday Lifeworld. Michelle's phenomenon is of a mom whose son, Carl, joins the Army at 25. Carl is, at the time of this writing, an active duty medic. Michelle explores the changes that occurred when she incorporated the military into her schema of being Mom. The addition of "a soldier" to the "mom" identity brought a *Blind Fear* into her experiences as a mom.

Keywords: Lifeworld, Deathworld, military families, warrior, depression, suicide, collaboration, phenomenological writing

Phenomenology and Phenomenological Writing

Phenomenological research has its roots in the works of Edmund Husserl. Phenomenology involves the study of the Lifeworld and brings real understanding by "actually doing it." Studying through phenomenology, learning what people

https://doi.org/10.1515/9783110691818-014

go through in life, is not an attempt to solve a problem or create a theory but a means to understand. One becomes aware of that which has been taken for granted by giving attention to lived experiences (van Manen 2016).

Phenomenological writing involved reflecting on rich descriptions of lived experience. The reflection involved a systematic exploration to find meaning in the experience. When successful, this form of writing has the power to draw the reader into the story. The reader becomes an active participant and searches for significance through their own experiences. Along with the writer, they are transformed; touched, shaken, or moved by the story (van Manen 2016, p. 120).

Michelle and Darlene became acquainted through writing and sharing phenomenological protocols about their experiences of being the mother of a soldier and the wife of a soldier – through participation in a Fielding Graduate University writing phenomenology course, and involvement in the "From Strangers to Collaborators" research project.

Who is the Stranger? And Who is Not?

"Don't talk to strangers." This is what parents tell their children. But who is the "stranger"? Alfred Schütz (1944) defines the *stranger* as "an individual of our times and civilization who tries to be permanently accepted or at least tolerated by the group which he approaches" (p. 499). Strangers find themselves in a situation that requires them to interpret the cultural pattern of a social group they approach and to orient themselves within it (Schütz 1944). In other words, in order to no longer be a stranger in a social group, the individual needs to figure out the rules.

The Warriors and the Families

The warriors, the military personnel, make up the core of the military culture. They are the center from which their families are connected. The warriors maintain a bond that even the families cannot understand or break unless they themselves are military personnel. This bond can create distance and difficulty in connecting with families. To better understand this concept, one must understand military culture.

Culture is the sum of the ways of life in a particular society. Military culture is based on a unique tradition; mission, structure, and leadership. There are unwritten rules, perspectives, and operating procedures that are followed in every detail. The attitudes, values, and ideals were set forth generations ago by individuals never met. However, they are influenced by the civil culture. Anthropologist Frank Boas (1911), gives the best definition of the military Lifeworld idea. He states the military culture is comprised of the mental and physical reactions that characterize the social group and the individual. It also includes the result of the activities and the individual's role within the group. Culture affects the relationship to the natural environment, the self, and others. Military culture is best summarized as the way of life for the people.

Although the military experience for all warriors varies depending on their branch of service (Marine Corps, Navy, Army, Air Force, or Coast Guard), their rank, their job (MOS–Military Occupational Specialty), and the period in which they serve, there are many things they have in common that can unite the warriors into a common culture. Sacrifice is at the very top of the list, along with discipline, holding self to higher standards, teamwork, being part of something greater, belonging, loyalty, brotherhood, never giving up, suppression or denial, dark humor, sarcasm, concerns about seeking care, and moral injury.

Warriors sign their name on that dotted line to give away a piece of their individuality to become a part of something bigger than themselves. This centers uniformity: dressing the same, speaking the same, thinking the same, behaving the same. Despite giving up certain privileges, working as a team, and being able to rely on your "brothers" inspires a sense of pride, belonging, loyalty, and brotherhood (Burek 2018). Therefore, most service members feel a sense of comfort and connection with other service members, even if they have never met or served together before.

In the civilian world, an individual's beliefs and values can be vague and may change over time. In the military, values are spelled out and taught from the very beginning. Of course, each branch holds its own core values. However, despite some differences in verbiage, honor, courage, duty, and service above self are common among all. These traits and ethics exemplify holding oneself to a higher standard and will remain with the warrior over the course of their lifetime (Burek 2018).

How does this explain the overwhelming camaraderie of the warriors with each other that excludes the outside world? In the military, warriors become extremely close to the soldiers around them. They are battle-tested, they bleed together, drink together, fight together, sleep, and eat together. It is no surprise that under those circumstances, the warriors bond so tightly and develop an extremely close support network. Soldiers are told from the beginning that feelings and emotions involving anything not related to the mission are meant to be put in the background, including family and home life. The problem with that thinking arises when the warrior goes home. They hold onto that mindset of "it takes misery and conflict to build a tangible relationship with other people and let them into your life" (personal communication). Another common thought of the warrior is that the people at home cannot possibly understand the language that the warrior is used to speaking with his "brothers" in the military. Speaking flippantly about death and dying is not morbid to them, but a way to cope. Some warriors feel that if they open up and use the sarcasm that they are used to at home or in civilian life, people will not understand, and things could be misunderstood. Instead of opening to the civilian world or even to their families, warriors tend to go into lockdown mode and push everyone far away. All parties involved (the warriors, families, and friends) are left feeling lost and disconnected, searching for some sort of support network to survive.

The United States military is a complicated set of relationships where individuals are both strangers and non-strangers simultaneously. The warrior lives in a dichotomy of movement and rest; of going and returning. There is an *insideness*, and *outsideness*, in relationship to their home. Insideness, or home, is identified as a place of comfort and safety. Outsideness brings a sense of difference, separation, and alienation from the place, home, and the individuals in that place. There is a sense of strangeness, discomfort, and unreality. There is movement, and rest, in the deployment cycle. The movement of deployment has taken the warrior away from home to a war zone. The experience often changes the warrior. When they return to rest, there is a tension between the insideness and outsideness (Seamon 2018). Military personnel, throughout enlistment, come home from deployment, or combat, to homes they no longer recognize. Is this because the home environment has changed, or the individual has changed due to the deployment experiences? Returning personnel need to re-establish old intimacies, we-relationships, and re-align with the social norms in order to no longer be strangers (Schütz 1945). However, in some sense, military personnel continue to be strangers since they maintain certain common characteristics and share with others; but not all is shared. There is both closeness and distance.

For the families of the warriors, we are looking for that camaraderie that our loved ones who are serving or have served feel. We want to share our fears, concerns, values, and support just the same. Just as military personnel have a culture that connects them, there is a separate circle that bonds families of the warriors into a type of social structure or military family.

Visualizing three concentric circles, military personnel occupy the center of the circle, with dependent families sitting in the next circle out. This would consist of the spouses and children, those that move from duty station to duty station. The outermost circle consists of the extended family. This is everyone else: parents of the warrior, siblings, and others that are considered close family (Figure 1).

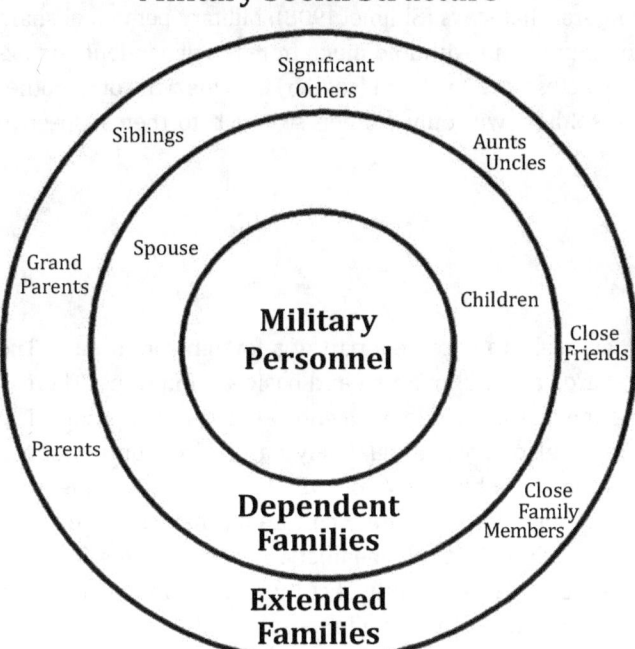

Figure 1: Military social structure.
Copyright (2020) by Michelle Elias and Darlene Cockayne, Used with Permission, Original Artwork.

The family, those who have never served in the military, do not have the perspective of the military personnel. They do not have the same experiences: Basic Training, Military Occupational Specialty (MOS) training, deployment, combat, etc. This creates a divide; a form of "strangerness." Similarly, military personnel do not have the same experiences as those in the "outer circles." The families deal with the fears of combat without knowing the actual combat. This can be an extreme fear where the imagination takes over. The families restructure themselves during times of deployment, becoming more independent. These differing experiences and limited sharing of them creates a distance in relationships while maintaining a level of intimacy. The families and the personnel have a "stranger" relationship to military culture. However, the families have a kinship among themselves similar to the comradery the personnel hold for each other.

As difficult as it may be to imagine, the family (dependent and extended) would be considered strangers to the military personnel that occupy the center circle in the military culture diagram. Even though they are family, a community, there is a cultural distance that separates the families from the brotherhood of warriors. They are a wanderer that stays (Simmel 1908). Military personnel share some aspects of their community but withhold much from the dependent and extended family members. As close as a husband (soldier) is to his wife, or a mother to her son (soldier), the soldiers will only confide so much to their respective families.

Non-Strangers

The stranger, the outsider, seeks to become a part of a foreign community. The community consists of shared cultural patterns and basic assumptions. There is a shared linguistic component; shared idioms, technical terms, and jargon. The members of the community also share a "relatively natural conception of the world" which is not questioned. (Schütz 1944, p. 502). At one point in time, Darlene and Michelle were strangers to the military culture but have since become members of the culture through their family members. However, under Schütz's criteria of membership in the same community of culture, they are not strangers to each other even though they have never met in person.

The military family kinship, their membership in the Military Social Structure, brought an instant connection between two women. Throughout their collaboration, conversations occurred that would not happen with others. Others don't always understand. They may empathize, but often (as was expressed by a colleague) the families' contributions and sacrifice are overlooked (personal communication). Darlene and Michelle understand what is difficult to articulate. This understanding simplifies communication, rather than adding to the stress. The fear, stress, and concerns are not revisited with each conversation; they don't have to be explained. They fall into norms, the language, and the "matter of course" thinking (Simmel 1908) instinctively because we belong to the same social/cultural construct of military families.

Darlene and Michelle met through their studies at Fielding Graduate University but they both graduated from the same program at Adler University: Master of Arts in Psychology with a specialization in military psychology. The deeper connection is, however, the commonality of their membership in the military culture; Darlene as a dependent and Michelle as extended family.

Lifeworld

Bentz and Shapiro (1998) describe the Lifeworld as:

> The lived experience of human beings and other living creatures as formed into more or less coherent grounds for their existence. This consists of the whole system of interactions with others and objects in an environment that is fused with meaning and language (for human actors) and that sustains the life of all creatures from birth through death. It is the fundamental ground of all experience for human beings. (Bentz/Shapiro 1998, p. 171)

A Lifeworld exists when beings coexist within their environment. It is experienced by living in conjunction with the environment without causing damage to that environment. The individual's Lifeworld is the taken-for-granted world. There is a grounding in place and community. The habits of place transform place into a lived place or Lifeworld (Seamon 2018). The morning routines (brushing of teeth, face washing, and brushing hair), over time, turn the bathroom into a Lifeworld of place. That same place, when coupled with a fearful and dark situation, can be transformed into a Deathworld. A world that can be filled with anxiety.

Deathworld

The Lifeworld is better understood through a discussion of the Deathworld. The simple explanation of a Deathworld is that it is the opposite of Lifeworld. Deathworlds occur when the beings within the environment do damage to the environment or other beings within that environment.

Deathworlds can be experienced in many ways. They can be experienced within an individual when beings lose their way or lose sight of their personal needs. They may appear to be Lifeworlds, with one fighting to "save" another; however, it cannot be if the individual is dying inside. Another may be to inadvertently cause damage due to a preoccupation with personal thoughts. These thoughts can get in the way of the individual being responsible towards others that also occupy that same environment.

Darlene's husband was in the Army since he was a teenager. He thought he would die in the Army, and he was ok with that. He has said many times that he made peace with dying for his country. But he didn't; he didn't stay in the Army, and he didn't die in the Army. He has been a veteran for many years and able to live in the civilian world. He has held down a great job, owns a home, and has a family. But he is not here, he is still in the Army. He suffers everyday with depression, anxiety, suicidal thoughts, and near attempts. One thing he has mentioned over and over is the missed brotherhood of the military life, even with his family around and (non-military) friends to talk to. He says, "the act of feeling lonely is not necessarily being alone."

Michelle's son, Carl, is a combat medic. He has had multiple tours in Afghanistan during Operation Enduring Freedom (OEF). OEF began when the United States President, George W. Bush, declared war in Afghanistan. After the attacks of 9/11, the Taliban refused to turn over Osama bin Laden, the al Qaeda leader that orchestrated the attacks (Al Jazeera 2017). This led to the 16-year war into which Carl was deployed.

Carl doesn't talk about his experiences with Michelle. Stories have been told to other family members, also veterans, which have gotten back to her. He's kept soldiers alive for extended periods only to have them bleed out when air-lifted and evacuated. He's also kept others alive when the evacuation helicopter had been shot up. When Carl came home after the first deployment, he requested no honorary escort and a quiet leave. He expressed anxiety about people on the streets. "I'm used to not knowing if a person on the streets is a suicide bomber or not" was his reasoning. Death was a common experience; a peaceful death was not common.

War is inherently destructive and produces a Deathworld whether it is a civil war within its own country or between multiple countries.

Darlene's Story

The first time I felt an overwhelming sense in my soul of what being alone truly meant came a few years ago when the man I chose to marry, the father of our children, attempted suicide. When I think about it, I can still feel everything I felt that day. I can see that moment playing out so vividly in my mind's eye. The smell of staleness and hopelessness in the bedroom was overpowering. The empty bottles of pills lying on the floor next to his side of the bed. That bottle stood out so vividly, it looked almost comical in the sense that it seemed giant-sized, something you would see made for a comedy skit, or in the theatre. The coldness of his skin was of someone who had been holding ice for a long time and yet it seemed natural. His eyes were glassy and black like coal.

This was not my first experience with depression and suicide; it began eleven years ago when my husband started to show signs of the battle with depression that he was hiding. Up until we met, the phenomenon of fear associated with leaving military life for civilian life, and the struggle it can be for veterans and their families to overcome, was new to me. Of course, being a student of psychology and human development, I had attended numerous college courses that focused on depression, so I was not naïve about it, or at least that is what I thought. When it is on paper, in a book, or at a lecture the thought that goes through your mind is: "I understand," "I will be able to help others," "I will see the signs before anything happens." But in that moment when it is happening to you, all those thoughts are gone. It doesn't matter what courses I have taken, what I should be doing, or what I should know. All I knew was that "I don't understand what is happening," "I can't do anything to help," and "I didn't see the signs."

What Fear Really Feels Like

My husband was a Sergeant in the United States Army. He served as a Combat Medic (91 Bravo), and Infantry (11 Bravo). We had known each other for many years before we married and even a few before we dated. At the beginning of our courtship, things were great. One day, about a year into our dating, he didn't show up to my house – which was strange, to say the least. I called him, no answer. Texted, waited . . . waited . . . waited . . . waited for over an hour and still no reply to either the phone call or the text. At this point, I was beginning to get concerned. I felt it in my stomach like a mother would feel when her child is sick or in danger. It was a strange feeling. I just knew something was not right. It wasn't one of those, "oh no the relationship is over" feelings. It was different. It was deeper. So, I went over to his house, used the key, and went inside. Immediately it was cold. Not cold as you would say temperature, but cold in the sense that the atmosphere was lifeless and stale. I didn't feel I was in danger, but I felt fear. The hairs on my arms were standing up, I could feel the sense of doom, but I didn't know why. There was just something black in the air. It was different. It felt like time had stopped and yet the Earth was moving so fast I could hardly walk a straight line. I called out his name, and the only thing that called back was the sound of silence. As I searched the house, it looked like it had been abandoned for years. It smelled of what aloneness must smell like; I could almost taste the stale, coldness in my mouth. When I finally got to the bathroom, I stood at the door and it felt like it was moving away from me. When I finally was able to move, I reached up to turn the handle and it was like it was made of ice. I thought it would crumble it beneath my hand. I looked down at the door handle and it was like I had forgotten how to turn the knob. The door finally opened and there he was, curled up in the bathtub – fully clothed, no water – just lying in a ball in the tub . . . motionless.

I didn't know what was going on, he was breathing – he was alive, but not really. The air was heavy, so heavy. Time stopped. I don't know how I managed to walk to the edge of the tub, I don't remember doing that, I don't remember sitting down but I did. I still don't know how long I sat on the floor next to the tub just waiting, waiting for him to move, acknowledge me, return to wherever he was, anything.

While he lay curled up in a ball in the bathtub, so many questions flooded my brain, questions that I knew I would not have the answers to. Who is this man that I have always viewed as strong and fearless? How did I not see this part of him? What do I do now? Where do we go from here? I didn't know the words to say. I just felt unsure of everything that I thought I knew about who we both were.

Re-occurrences

Unfortunately, this was not to be a one-time thing. Rather it became a part of who we were. After the first time his depression showed up in our lives, it would be months at a time before a bout of depression came back. Once the moment was over, everything seemed to go back to what it was. Happy family, laughter, and a positive future. But, every time the "blackness" was in my home, I would feel fear and a deep sense of failure and aloneness. In the beginning, those feelings would fade after the attack. The more the depression appeared, the longer my fear of the future and my failure at being his wife would stay around.

In 2016, my husband suffered a heart attack and had to have six bypasses. When the surgery was over, the doctor came to me and said that my husband's history of depression could be exacerbated by heart surgery. The doctor was correct; not a month after he came home and was trying to get back to a "normal," healthy life, the darkness came with such a strong force it took my breath away. It felt like someone had punched me in the stomach.

Life goes on, never knowing what the day will bring. The depression keeps getting more and more frequent, lasting longer and longer at times. Our life together as husband and wife is suffering. My desire to be his wife is drifting away. The smell of his aftershave, which used to be one of my favorite scents, is now repulsive and I loathe when it lingers in the bathroom after he leaves. The one thought that wakes me in my sleep is, "I can't do this anymore, I don't want to do this anymore."

What About Me?

That first moment of being utterly alone I had when he tried to commit suicide begins to creep back in on me. I should be able to help him; I should be able to help myself. I have been studying and devoting my whole academic career to this topic. I, of all people, should be prepared to face this, even if I must do it alone.

For years I have been focusing on finding veterans groups and organizations that my husband might join to help him have other veterans who can meet the social-emotional needs that I believe he has been yearning to satisfy since he left the military. That military culture and his Lifeworld, while there, was what he was so accustomed to. He had to leave it all behind and is still looking for some way to rebuild another Lifeworld out here in the civilian population. All the while, I was neglecting to give the same to myself. I was forgetting that I too needed to find that collaboration with someone sharing my Lifeworld ideals and values so that I could begin to heal in my own way. Things became clearer when I met with a fellow military family survivor.

While working towards my Ph.D. in human development at Fielding Graduate University, I signed up for a course (called *Knowledge Areas* or *KAs*) titled Writing Phenomenology. In this course, I had the pleasure of getting to know another doctoral student and military family survivor. She and I immediately developed a connection that was not the same as with other classmates I had met. Michelle and I are from military families. We share a special community that *civilian* (non-military) family individuals do not live. Michelle has been someone that, although a physical stranger, I can collaborate with in a way that allows me to be authentic and drop my mask of stoicism. I can talk about my home life and the fear that I have involving the depression my husband deals with. Sometimes the unspeakable must be voiced. Words are not meant to solve the problem, because, in my case, they cannot. They are meant to be understood (van Manen 2016). I can talk to her and not be judged and misunderstood. She has become a part of my Lifeworld that I need to learn to accept – and better yet, she has let me own and accept my Deathworld in a way that I never thought I could.

Michelle's Story

Being a Mom

As a parent of an Army medic, I have experienced a myriad of emotions over my son's career. In his few years, I have been proud, scared, fearful, overwhelmed, and tearful (just to name a few), sometimes all at the same time! Being a mom is tough, but nobody ever said the job was easy.

As with many moms, remembering the day I became a mom brings back those mixed emotions. Holding that little person for the first time brought the realization that this person was completely dependent on me to provide food, shelter, and warmth. This was a new job; it filled me with apprehension, joy, and even a level of fear. Most of all, there was love. That love brought a deep understanding that I would do anything to provide, protect, and keep that little person safe as long as I drew breath. When the second child was born, those feelings didn't change. If anything, they were stronger since now there were two of those dependent little people.

Being *Mom* is an ever-evolving role, dependent on the children's ages. Gradually, over 20 or so years, children grow more responsible and less dependent on Mom. Mom becomes a more supportive role over those same years, even though the feelings of love and the desire to protect don't diminish. Being supportive when a child is deployed to a war zone is in direct conflict with that desire to protect. Another dimension, conflict and fear, becomes an aspect of "being Mom" when the "of a soldier" is added.

Being Mom of a Soldier: Blind Fear

When my son enlisted in the Army, nothing really changed. The pride was still there. I may not have understood why he enlisted but I could respect his decision. But then came the first deployment cycle. This world was new to me and I wanted to know everything. I asked questions; lots of questions. Some were answered, others weren't. Those unanswered questions brought fear. Fear of the danger he would be subjected to in Afghanistan, a war zone with no end in sight. Fear of being powerless over what he would encounter. Fear that all he would experience would change him. Fear that I'd never see my son alive again. Fear of the unknown. Fear took over the quiet moments that were not occupied by anything more than the most routine activities or thoughts. That fear was often so overwhelming that I didn't attend to the situation at hand. This came to a head one day prior to Christmas 2009. Driving the local freeway near a large shopping mall, traffic got heavy rather quickly. Without even knowing what happened, I heard a loud crash. The sound of the crash was sudden, unexpected, and loud – louder than almost anything I've ever heard before. I had plowed into a car in front of me. The car was a tan Ford Taurus; not a big car, but not a compact car either. A young boy was in the back seat of that car. The trunk had accordioned into and taken over a portion of the back seat. I never even saw that car! It felt as if I wasn't driving; Blind Fear was driving instead. Thankfully, the young boy in that back seat was not injured.

After colliding with that car, I knew something had to change. This fear was not going to go away, so I needed to learn how to incorporate it into my identity as a mom. I needed to compartmentalize this new aspect of my Mom identity. It was going to be a very dangerous year for my son and me if I failed. The veil of stoicism began to emerge. Blind Fear had to be removed from my everyday life; it could not be attended to every day. Blind Fear could only be attended to when I was in a safe environment; one that would not put me or others in physical danger. Keeping my thoughts occupied was my first attempt at living with that fear. Learning all I could, eliminating as much of the unknown as possible, became almost second nature. I gravitated towards everything military, even earning a master's degree in military psychology.

Deployment

My son's first deployment was my first real experience of being a military mom. Better stated, it was my first experience of being a Mom of a Soldier, or as we often say – MOS. Yes, it's a play on words. My son's Military Occupational Specialty (MOS), his job, has been as a medic. My MOS, is being Mom, nothing more – and with all the title entails. When my son first called to tell me about his deployment, it was just a regular phone call. He simply called to tell me that the training cycle for deployment was beginning but he didn't know when and wouldn't know, until just before he was to leave, when he would be going. The conversation was short with minimal information about training. This was the beginning of one of the toughest months of my life so far. He would be deployed out of Germany, and I wouldn't see him before he left.

As I look back, the timeline is a blur. What I remember are the feelings in moments and the overall emotions. My boss at the time would reassure me that the Army and soldiers always take care of their medics. The medics were so vital to the operation. This would often ease my concerns. Whenever I'd worry, get anxious, feel that nausea in my stomach, and almost shake with fear, I'd remember his words. I'd repeat, "They always take care of the medics." When Carl (my son) first enlisted, I found a group on Ravelry (a knitting and crocheting social media site) called Moms of Soldiers (MOS). The play on words caught my eye. This small group of moms would become my lifeline. We shared the excitement and pride in our children and the love of needlecraft. We bonded over those children and those knitting patterns that required concentration.

In July 2010, things changed. Carl called to say he was deploying earlier than planned. He was requested by Command because another medic was killed in action. So much for some semblance of safety. As I attended the funeral (he was a local man), my heart sank for his mother. I never want to be in that position. The tears flowed silently down my cheeks; the altar appeared so far away. The Catholic church, full of mourners showing respect, had an honor guard at the back and outside protecting the family from would-be protesters. I wanted to shrink away; my son was still safe, hers was being taken away in a box.

The day came when Carl finally left for Afghanistan. He called to say he'd see me soon and told me he loved me. Hanging up, the weight of my body took over, tears began to fill my eyes and my throat began to close. It was time, I could break down for a few minutes. I gave myself permission. Sitting on the sofa, my comfy, cozy home felt so empty, like nothing could ever fill it again. I don't know how long I cried, maybe hours, maybe minutes. Time stood still for me in those first few moments. Luckily, I had my MOS support! They were there, helping me stay sane.

Learning to Live with the Fear

In my Ravelry MOS (Mothers of Soldiers) group, we had a few sayings that needed no explanation: "I'll keep the flashlight lit for you," "I have the pillow," "I have the extra batteries." I even had a "keeper of the news." It is difficult to explain these to others. The keeper of the flashlight was there to help when it became too dark in the soul. That darkness could become all-consuming for me. These times felt like nothing else mattered, the emptiness in the darkness could be overwhelming. The women were all holding flashlights with their care and compassion, so the darkness didn't overtake the whole world. The pillow was there for those days when I'd want to just crawl in a ball and sleep the day away, or days when I felt no one understood what I was going through. It was a symbol of comfort, a place to just cuddle up and step away from the world for a while. Insensitive comments by so-called friends were common. The anger would well up like a roaring lion! Knowing that these women understood, didn't criticize, and were there to listen when I'd vent, calmed that roar.

The roller-coaster ride continued. Some days I would stay occupied with work or knitting. Other days I would sink into my cave, dark and cold. I couldn't move. It was too much to even shower. Finally, Christmas came. Carl had let us know that he'd try to call. But December 25 came and went – no call. Fear. The next day, somewhere in the early evening, my computer rang. Carl was on the other end of the Skype call. Technology made it possible to video chat with him, to see him! Just like a new mom, after the first hellos, it was "show me your fingers and toes!" Well, he wouldn't show me his toes, but he did assure me that all appendages were intact. The tension in my shoulders relaxed. Fear subsided. Seeing him was so reassuring – much better than just hearing him over the phone.

Within days, Carl sent word that he was coming home! The anxiety got more intense. "Please don't let anything happen to him," I begged the Universe. He got home, to Germany, just after the New Year. He was skiing in the Swiss Alps the next day. The relief of getting off that roller coaster lifted my spirits and I remember not being able to stop smiling. He came home to Southern California at the end of January – in time for his birthday! Meeting him and his wife at the airport was a different kind of anxiety; that butterflies in the stomach, lighter than air kind of anxiety. Driving to the airport, I got lost and was behind schedule. As I was getting off the freeway, about the same time Carl's flight was to arrive, I saw an airplane fly over. There was my boy, just overhead! Almost there!

Waiting for him to come down the stairs, I couldn't keep still. I remember bouncing and switching feet. I told everyone who would listen that I was there to meet my son returning from Afghanistan. When he finally got down those stairs, others thanked him for his service. I couldn't let go when we hugged . . . but of course, I had to. Relief and pride welled up again! All was right with the world! At least for now.

Collaboration: Transformation from Deathworld to Lifeworld

The immediate connection between Darlene and Michelle made collaboration a "double-edged sword." Phone conversations and computer conferencing through Zoom took on a life of their own. Sometimes very little work got done. It was in these conversations that the transformation of both women took place. Darlene was able to drop the stoic persona and Michelle was able to speak from the heart. In Darlene's words, "that connection helps me to breathe again."

Sharing narratives brought a "fresh set of eyes" that allowed for some distance from the writing itself. These writings helped with further reflection, leading each to find more meaning in both hers and the other's writing (van Manen 2016). Each was so close to their phenomenon that learning from them was difficult. Stepping away and seeing it from the other's perspective was transformative. The discussion brought innermost feelings to the surface which meant they were no longer secretive. This alone has started to change Deathworlds into Lifeworlds. The feelings of isolation began to thaw. There was someone else that could help put words to the feeling even when one couldn't do it. The two became "comrades in arms" through a shared understanding of the fear, and other shared feelings. Sharing these feelings with their loved one was not an option. Expressing fear for their safety could cause the warrior to be thinking of that fear instead of the "mission at hand." This creates an unsafe situation in a combat zone. The soldiers' minds must be free from the worries of home to be the most effective and safe (personal communication). They have been able to share what cannot be shared with loved ones for fear of their safety. If those innermost fears are shared, then warriors would be thinking of that instead of the "mission at hand" which would create an unsafe situation in a combat zone not only for them but their fellow warriors. With the understanding that of not being "in this alone," came a sense of confidence. This came gradually over the months and was not even identified until one of the last conversations.

As of this writing, Darlene walks between her Lifeworld and her Deathworld. She tries to keep a Lifeworld in focus for herself and her daughters while walking through the Deathworld that her husband occupies. Darlene is comfortable sharing her experiences with Michelle, who also feels the heaviness of her Deathworld. Their conversations lighten their shared load for both of them.

Conclusion

Through the phenomenological writing process, Darlene and Michelle gained a deeper understanding of their worlds. Their explorations brought understanding to the military culture with its shared language and emotions of fear. Their membership in the Military Social Structure brings a degree of companionship that is not matched in the civilian world. The shared language which would need to be explained to outsiders does not need explanation. Under Schütz's criteria, this shared culture does not qualify them as strangers. The Lifeworlds they live through the military culture transcends the physical "strangerness." Their "instant" connectivity, while not expected, was not surprising. Given our instantaneous connection, we recognize that this phenomenon of instant connectivity has not been explored by social scientists. This was a new discovery for us, which should be further developed through research.

The logistics of long-distance collaboration was challenging. Time differences and life circumstances contributed to the challenges. However, when they have been able to connect, the conversations helped Darlene begin to come to terms with her Deathworld. She has, partially, accepted what has been forced upon her by her husband's attempts at suicide. Michelle has learned to compartmentalize the fear that has blinded her in the past. The Lifeworld has to be transformed to include stoicism in order to survive.

References

Al Jazeera (2017): "Timeline: U.S. intervention in Afghanistan 2001 to 2007". Retrieved from https://www.aljazeera.com/news/2017/08/2001-2017-intervention-afghanistan-170822035036797.html, visited on October 8, 2020.
Bentz, Valerie M/Shapiro, Jeremy J. (1998): *Mindful Inquiry in Social Research*. Thousand Oaks: Sage Publications, Inc., p. 171.
Boas, Frank (1911): *The Mind of Primitive Man*. New York, Boston, Chicago, San Francisco: The MacMillan Company.
Burek, Gregory (2018): "Military Culture: Working with Veterans". In: *The American Journal of Psychiatry Residents' Journal* 13. No. 9, pp. 3–5.
Schütz, Alfred (1944): "The Stranger: An Essay in Social Psychology". In: *American Journal of Sociology* 49. No. 6, pp. 499–507.
Schütz, Alfred (1945): "The Homecomer". In: *American Journal of Sociology* 50. No. 5, pp. 369–376.
Seamon, David (2018): *Life Takes Place: Phenomenology, Lifeworlds, and Place Making*. New York, Milton, England: Routledge.
Simmel, Georg (1908): "The Stranger (R. Mosse, Trans.)". Retrieved from https://thebaffler.com/ancestors/stranger, visited on August 24, 2019.
van Manen, Max (2016): *Researching Lived Experience*. New York: Routledge.

Barton Buechner, Ann Ritter, and Rik Spann
Chapter 15
Embracing Endless Liminality: Improvisation and the "Practical Mystic"

Abstract: The "From Strangers to Collaborators" project connected three international scholar-leaders who may have never otherwise had an opportunity to meet. Through writing and sharing phenomenological protocols we discovered a common experience of liminality in our own lives and in the social spaces in which we live and work. The authors explored several metaphors, including nautical navigation, somatic and mindfulness practices, dance improvisation, and jazz. We imagined these as useful for enabling communication among a universe of relative strangers. We acknowledged the common experience of permanent liminality, as represented by military veterans and families, international students, and professionals and their families required to transfer workplaces as part of an evolving career path. We found a way from liminality to practical mysticism. Our social worlds and lived realities are constantly being created and re-shaped. As practical mystics, we may promote a shared and precious global humanity.

Keywords: liminality, practical mysticism, somatics, jazz improvisation, social construction

Introduction

The authors of this chapter discovered through reflecting together on our experiences in the "From Strangers to Collaborators" project, that liminal space is unfamiliar and filled with the unknown. Yet it need not be only a place of loneliness and discomfort, of rootlessness, a zombie-like half-life of not belonging anywhere, but it also can be a place of possibility and readiness, a place to step out from, a place of "yes/and," reflecting an integration of multiple realities and potential unity. One way to describe this phenomenon is captured in the term "no-where" to "now-here."[1] The first iteration describes an apparent lack of grounding or context, where the second is reminiscent of the admonition of

---

[1] This phrase stems from a local motorsports event in Lodz, Poland titled "the race from nowhere to nowhere" observed by co-author Buechner during the From Strangers to Collaborators

https://doi.org/10.1515/9783110691818-015

the late Baba Ram Dass to, "be here now" (1971). The duality of this statement speaks to openness to the emergent and unexpected that we have experienced individually and together, as illustrated further in this chapter.

Liminality and Communitas as Transformative Space

The concept of *the liminal, or threshold or in-between space*, was first defined and applied within the anthropology of religion as part of an initiatory state or process and therefore seen as temporary (Turner 1978, 1987; van Gennep 1909). In his early work, Turner examined ritualized rites of passage within societies, often where individuals formally left behind childhood and assumed the rights and responsibilities accorded to adult members of their tribes or sects. These represented clearly marked, if only symbolic, Deathworlds after which the individuals were welcomed into new Lifeworlds that were intended to be permanent and sustainable, or new ways of being carried out in "dynamics of (social) activity" (Turner 2012, p. 220). Turner's career-long study of "modern *communitas* movements," including those within contemporary Christianity, caused him to question his original definition of a liminal state as associated only with ritual, initiation, or rites of passage, and as therefore being temporary. He noted that *communitas* movements, "try to create a style of life that is permanently contained within liminality" (La Shure 2005), otherwise described as a sort of being 'in' the world but not necessarily 'of' the world that surrounds you. Career paths and choices such as military service, foreign diplomacy, journalistic and corporate postings, and even the paths taken by refugees, turn into a series of moves. This requires a constant reframing of identity and meaning-making within different social worlds.

The capacity to create shared insights in communitas following shared experiences of liminality can also lead to a transformative shift in worldview and consciousness at the collective level (Buechner et al. 2020). The impact of such collective realizations may further expand persons' ability to better navigate states resembling permanent liminality and may also bring new insights to others who have not shared these experiences directly. The chapter's co-authors explore mutual interests on the topic of liminality in the sections that follow:
- Ritter: the impact of somatic mindfulness practices on awareness of, and ability to skillfully navigate liminal spaces

---

project. Co-Author Spann pointed out the two possible interpretations in our discussions when writing this article.

- Spann: the process of improvisation in the co-construction of meaning using a jazz metaphor
- Buechner: Storytelling and the reconstruction of meaning after war and trauma.

Ritter's Experience: Natural Observer of Liminal Lifestyles

Co-author Ann Ritter grew up in a community where a large portion of the economy was fueled by three major military installations, each of which was reliant on the other two. As a result, both of her parents had long and stable civil service careers with the U.S. government. But it also meant Ritter stayed put while watching young friends and playmates come and go quickly each school year – sometimes even during the school year. She learned early on not to become overly attached to a friend who might not be around come the following September, even as she happily went on playdates, ate the different and sometimes exotic foods that the families of those children had learned to cook while living outside of the United States, and spent time looking up and learning about the place names where families had lived before postings in her hometown.

Just as she turned 11, Ritter, an only child, lost both her father and grandmother within four months. She spent the naturally awkward period of puberty and middle school also grieving in a *Deathworld* of lost childhood and strong parental mentoring, coupled with prolonged isolation brought on by the necessary distraction and busy-ness of her now single working mother. She entered high school painfully shy, a condition in which she often ran into former childhood friends whose families were re-posted nearby. How Ritter envied the facility with which those returned military dependent children made friends and successfully integrated themselves into sports teams and other activities, their self-assurance, and capacity for navigating social situations with an ease that took her years to develop. Although the same age, she and former close friends now had seemingly nothing in common.

It was as a Fielding student that Ritter began to understand the pain that might have been included in so many moves and the necessary expenditure of energy when starting over again and again in new places. Running into one former classmate as an adult, Ritter related her perspective and received validation for a metaphor she had developed for those military children: developing an innate ability to "transplant" or successfully "re-pot" oneself. Conversely, the childhood playmate told Ritter that she and her peers were always fascinated by locals like herself, whose family had been in more or less the same community for more than 200 years.

Ritter came to Fielding Graduate University and later to this project by virtue of one of several burning questions that fueled her doctoral work: why did her business communication students at Georgia State University (GSU) who were not native speakers of English get nervous and "lose their English" in the middle of graded public speaking assignments and team presentations? Beyond why, how could she, as an instructor and coach, better understand the reasons for this, and help the students overcome this critical stumbling block to their professional development?

GSU is among the top 20 colleges and universities in the United States for the size of the international student population. Within this natural laboratory of "relative strangers," Ritter soon discovered that she was living into a coordinating management of meaning (CMM), in which each speech act taking place is shaped by context (Pearce 2007, p. 142), even though she did not have sufficient words for it at that time. It was not until she came to the CMM Institute learning exchanges that she was able to clarify for her students the layers of identity formation that take place in conversations – even public speaking events – and to recognize the socially constructed nature of the worlds in which they lived, studied and worked daily. Ritter's time at Fielding also introduced her to Valerie Bentz, and the rich vocabulary of embodiment to be found in the concentration on phenomenology, somatics, and communicative leadership (SPCL) that Dr. Bentz had developed.

At GSU, Ritter followed a hunch and gave a set of somatic exercises to a small group of her business students. The set contained short yoga and meditation protocols and simple breath work (Shannahoff-Khalsa 2006) that the students should practice several times a week. Before a single semester had passed, Ritter discovered that each of the students to whom she gave the protocols had shifted his or her consciousness and awareness to the extent that the student was able to verbally articulate the underlying cause of their discomfort, and name whatever layer of identity and meaning was causing stress in the presentation setting (Ritter 2015). Once that layer was explored, the discomfort and symptoms of nervousness disappeared. Allowing the students their own individual, somatic experiences drastically shortcut the time it might have taken for them to overcome their struggles in presenting and public speaking by other means.

When entering the shared space of the From Strangers to Collaborators project, Ritter appreciated that the sessions were conducted with attention to embodiment, as many of them started with yogic breathing, meditation, or other shared somatic activities. All co-authors of this piece share the view that such practices helped us to recognize our common humanity, and that embodied awareness is an important antecedent to opening ourselves to a deeper and more mindful way of connecting, of rejoicing in the liminal.

Spann's Story: Navigating Liminality

Rik Spann, half a generation younger than co-authors Buechner and Ritter, spent his early life following a model of unity and developing a consciousness much more like those of many third-culture kids. For those forty and below, relocation and career travel have become the accepted norm in a global economy. In the first six years of Rik's life, his father was captain of his own small commercial ship, and home was wherever the ship traveled, with brief periods spent living in land-based homes in various ports within The Netherlands and Germany. Rik's experiences were foundational to his becoming an artist and jazz musician, and to his accepting liminality as a norm, as he explains here:

> When I could barely stand on my own feet, I was standing next to my father while he was holding his hands on the steering wheel of his ship. Much later I would learn where the word 'cybernetics' comes from: from the Greek word kybernes, or steersman of a ship. Yes, you have some 'control', when steering a ship, but only in a very subtle, dynamic relationship with waves, wind and whatever emerges from whatever happens. I liked to stand next to him. It felt like home.
>
> I remember the first six years of my life as a fluid blend of tons of river and mixed up periods of brick houses in Germany and Holland. My first experience of something called "mess." No chronology at all. Jam structures, the Kairos way. Home was inside. But liminality (the permanent kind) was already built-in. I liked it.
>
> I guess I always had to rely on my "home" in my mind. I thought, for a very long time, that I was isolated. Outside of the real world out there. Linear logic, causality and such. So I tried to learn that language. And I got closer and closer.
>
> Then, in my twenties, I discovered jazz. What's this? It's like jamming with waves, wind and whatever emerges from whatever happens. This is certainly not certainty. Curiosity on default. The art of not knowing. Riddles and riffing. Lost souls finally found in the waves of the groove. An invitation to jam. Home is where the welcome is.
>
> And again I was standing next to my father. His hands on the steering wheel. When I look at the clock, the measurements next to the wheel, I think I'm in control. Sweet illusion. When I look at my father, calmly watching the bends of the river coming in from the distance, firmly shaking his hands in micro gestures that respond to the tiniest movements of this giant boat creating its way through the waves, I know I'm not in control. Sweet reality. Permanent liminality. A home that trembles around the edges and stays with me through all my stumblings.
>
> My father is not a Jazz man. He doesn't like the music. It makes him nervous. But he whistles when he goes to work. It makes him happy. Next to him: the captain's son. And I take a deep breath. The river answers. Theme and variation. Call and response. Frame and freedom. Kybernes. Jazz. Even the clouds jam along.   (self-observation)

This story reveals a level of comfort with liminality, suggesting that it may well be an increasingly prevalent phenomenon of modern reality.

Those born later in the 20th Century, as well as individuals born into the 21st, are more likely – as was Spann – to be differently acculturated, or exposed to a liminal existence from early life. This has implications for the way we educate young people to make meaning in an increasingly complex and fluctuating social context, as envisioned by the "Cosmopolis 2045" project and "Cosmokidz" initiatives, respectively (Jensen n.d.). It also suggests different ways to conceptualize mental health, as an aspect of communication and social connection.

Buechner's Experience: Liminality and the Making (and Breaking) of Moral Code

Bart Buechner has spent a lifetime collecting phenomenological moments that illustrate the unity of self as developed from the military service of his father and grandfather. As he describes it, neither man talked much about his military experiences, but the impact of this period was very much evident in the way they both were in the world. Later, after both of them had passed on, Bart went on to attend the U.S. Naval Academy, where (counter to established norms) he majored in English Literature, played in the Academy Jazz Band, and wrote a satirical column in the otherwise-conservative LOG Magazine. He went on to achieve the rank of Captain in the U.S. Navy, and then worked for nearly 20 years in a close-knit community of veterans in Northern California. In this role, he met and befriended many veterans of World War I, like his grandfather, and World War II, like his father. From his time spent in presence of his own veteran ancestors, (the Captain's Father and Grandfather), he gleaned a deeper, yet not verbally expressed, understanding of some unique, yet universal, aspects of wartime service from these combat veterans. From their stories describing what he later came to see as liminal aspects of their lives, he learned to differentiate between the effects that combat and military service have on the human psyche, particularly the distinction between forms of combat stress and moral injury (Buechner et al. 2018). This was not due to anything that was contained or conveyed in any of his Father's stories or their conversations, but more as a way of being that was grounded in liminal experiences, outside of normal time and space. The following illustration describes this non-verbal, yet profound, connection:

> I remember my father, much like his own father who served in World War I, as a kind and quiet man, who would drop what he was doing at any time to help others. He seldom showed emotion, and did not talk much about his wartime experiences, nor what he might be feeling about things going on with the family or work, but at the same time, he was deeply sentimental. Not usually given to anger, he reserved this emotion for any situation in which he perceived that the powerful were taking advantage of the weaker.

His favorite thing to do was to get up early in the morning and go out on the lake in a small boat, either rowing or using an antiquated outboard motor to find just the right place in a channel where he had a sense the fish might be lurking amongst the weeds. Very often, he would take me, or maybe both my younger brother and I, along with him, as long as we were willing to be quiet and patient, as he was. It was there, with the sun just breaking the horizon and the early morning mist arising from the lake, that he seemed most comfortable. Although he seldom spoke much at such times, it felt that this was where we made our deepest connection, although I could not at the time verbalize this.

It was only later that I came to understand that many veterans of his era struggled in other ways with their wartime experiences, and I became interested in learning more about this phenomenon. While living and working at a veterans' home, I spent a great deal of quite time with veterans of World War I, World War II, Korea, and Vietnam. Sometimes they spoke, and sometimes they did not, but either way, the unexpressed, yet deeply felt, emotional impact was present in our interactions.

As I learned more about posttraumatic stress disorder (PTSD), and the ways that it was being categorized, diagnosed and treated, I had a felt sense that we were missing something important, and that this was only part of a much larger story. Later, while doing my own dissertation research with veterans of Iraq and Afghanistan, I found the construct of PTSD as it had been applied in veterans' mental health services to be even less applicable to what they had actually gone through, and only vaguely connected with the meaning they were making from their experiences. Digging deeper into the phenomenological roots of veterans' stories and experiences, it became clearer that what was actually being described in these otherwise unheard, untold, and untellable stories was something different. Something that was better described as a form of moral injury, or the breaking of the moral grounding of what is right and true and proper. This realization helped me not only understand my Father's anger at injustice, and his ever-present willingness to consider and help others; it also created a deep insight into the ineffable effects of spending time amidst the Deathworlds that accompany war, and how that knowledge can point towards the most life-giving and positive aspects of our own potential for being in the world.

(personal account)

As in the case of Rik's experiences with his Father, Bart's story offers a glimpse into forces that could not be described in words, at play in a state of liminality afloat on the water and away from the world of social rules and reason. In that space, navigating the forces of the river current or the memories of war, there was an exchange of meaning outside of language, space and time. Later, when Bart participated in the "Becoming Mature" replicative study with Valerie Bentz at Fielding Graduate University, the influence of some of these childhood forces became clearer and more present. Unlike the childhood "ghosts and spirits" reported by most of the women in the original study (Bentz 1989) the ghosts were not a result of direct experiences of trauma, and the spirits spoke in ways that only became apparent after the fact. The replicative study (Bentz 2014) brought out some stories that later acquired meaning. For example, Bart's mother once told him he was named after a character in a 1950's TV show, Dr. Barton Crane.

Only later, after earning his Doctorate in Human Development at Fielding, did he realize that both he and his namesake were "Doctors of Psychosomatic Medicine."[2] This apparent coincidence and Bart's involvement in trauma research and mental health advocacy for veterans were emergent, rather than intentional, phenomena. Like Rik's father, Bart's dad was no musician, but in unseen ways, the experiences he shared with him moved Bart towards the arts–music, poetry and literature in search of deeper meaning, possibly connected in some mysterious way to wartime experience that he could not otherwise describe. These are the modalities that societies have traditionally turned to in a search to describe the ineffable.

Liminality in the World – Emergence from a Century of Change

We move next to an integrative discussion of ways that the lived experiences of the authors intersect various theoretical and practical perspectives on liminality and its influence on the human experience. Because the original definition of liminality included highly prescribed and limiting behaviors and rituals with intended goals and outcomes, the idea of ongoing, permanent liminality must also be bounded by conscious form and ritual as a way of creating a container or way of living one's life from day to day, and of looking at the world – a concept of viewing "home" as within oneself, wherever that self might be.

A pioneering study of third-culture kids – mid-20th-Century children of diplomats, military personnel, and foreign missionaries – offered the first documented evidence of the long-term effects of a permanently liminal lifestyle – both positive and negative (Pollack/van Reken 2017), which has continued to be tracked across the decades since. The authors of those early studies have made careers of updating and enriching the literature of the same populations over time. Until recently, these effects were not directly linked to the concept of liminality. But the experience of moving among and between worlds, *and* finding a unified consciousness within oneself was clearly being explored in literary works that have grown more numerous with time. One such exploration is in *The Far Pavillions* (Kaye 1979).

---

[2] The City Hospital series aired on CBS from 1951–1953, with Melville Ruick playing the role of Dr. Barton Crane.

This "both/and" approach to navigating complexity and liminality is explored further using modalities and metaphors of mindfulness practices and contemplation, musical and dance improvisation, and healing from trauma.

Somatic Mindfulness: Conscious Navigation of Liminal States and Deathworlds

Although not a jazz musician like Buechner or Spann, Ritter did have an early performance background in live theater, storytelling, and dance that left her familiar with the value and benefits of many forms of improvisation and comfortable with the idea of collaborative riffing.[3] Although she had stopped dancing when graduate business school and career took up too much of her time, Ritter found that embodiment was deeply connected to her learning style, and her health and wellbeing. In many ways, she was experiencing this as another sort of personal *Deathworld* – a negative impact, or absence, even though she was by all other measures outwardly successful. Of necessity, Ritter replaced the time spent dancing with a yoga and meditation practice that has served her for more than 30 years. During a still later *Deathworld* period – major health challenges that pointed to a necessary career change and refocus of energy in her early 40s, Ritter would find her way back to embodied learning through a postmodern dance form, contact improvisation (Pallant 2006), where sessions are "jams."

In *contact improvisation* (CI), the body is the instrument and the individual is responsible for his or her own safety and body use, or performance, while also being dependent on a dance partner or partners who enable the form to come into being. Shared weight, balance, physical listening, a state of readiness, creative tension – these and other aspects are at the core of CI.

---

[3] Buechner, Spann, and co-author Ann Ritter were together for the first time at a Coordinated Management of Meaning (CMM) Institute Learning Exchange outside of Munich, Germany, in fall 2015. Rik and Bart, both jazz-influenced musicians, were invited by a mutual friend to be co-presenters of an improvisation-themed workshop. Although they had never met before, they unpacked their guitars and, at different times during the conference, improvised for several hours without rehearsal or musical scores. The extended "performance" included a finale, where Ann was an audience participant, as a way to musically summarize the essence of the conference interactions in a closing ceremony. What Ann remembers is that the music seemed to provide a special kind of resonant closure to the event and that when everything was concluded, many participants seemed reluctant to leave and go back out into their respective worlds.

The richness of the CI form's possibilities draws Ritter back to the form occasionally. During two additional but separate periods of major external changes – her son leaving home for college, and a major illness and move away from home for her young adult daughter – several months of attending CI jams has helped Ann reorient herself within her body and adapt to a new way of being through *training perception*.

The Phenomenology and Embodiment of the Lifeworld

Just as somatic practices focus our awareness on the embodied nature of our awareness – in essence slowing the mind down to reveal otherwise unexamined inferences and unconscious responses to sensory triggers – so does phenomenological contemplation increase our capacity for mindfulness, or mindful awareness (Bentz/Giorgino 2016). At its core, phenomenology, as a study of consciousness, directs our attention back to the nuance and essence of what constitutes lived experience. Hermeneutic exercises, focusing our attention on certain referential and contextual aspects while setting aside or bracketing others, is one way of capturing such lived experience. Yet another way is unbracketed, or heuristic, phenomenology – the immersive, lived experience in action (Moustakas 1990). Our social worlds are also created and sustained in processes of communication, the dynamic and constitutive nature of which is described in various social constructionist theories including the Coordinated Management of Meaning (CMM) (Pearce 2007). The heuristics, or interpretive models, of CMM, can help to illuminate the impact that communication itself, as a process, or pattern of engagement, contributes to perceptions of reality, and how these perceptions may come to be embodied in the intersubjective space. CMM, as a practical theory, can also help uncover new possibilities, including finding common ground (Wasserman/Fisher-Yoshida 2019, p. 63).

Cosmopolitan Communication and the Bridging of Differences

Pearce (1989) described how forms of communication used in social systems may develop progressively over four levels of complexity in engagement with others. This development begins with *monocultural communication*, where everyone is viewed and treated as having the same social reality; followed by *ethnocentric communication*, where we recognize otherness but treat those we view as "other" as being lesser or inferior; then *modernistic communication*, where everyone is viewed as distinct and different; and finally *cosmopolitan communication*, which considers and values both individual differences and societal unity. Cosmopolitan communication transcends many of the barriers inherent in monocultural, ethnocentric, and modernistic forms of communication by recognizing that everyone is both similar *and* different, enlarging the social sphere. In this view, differences are taken into account, not ignored or discounted (Matoba 2013). Cosmopolitan social interactions are enacted through communicative forces of *coordination* and *coherence* as well as a third force or quality critical to bridging differences and navigating liminality: Mystery. We designate *Mystery* with a capital M, which represents emergent properties that are neither pre-programmed by culture nor externally imposed by systems or structures (Buechner et al. 2018). The quality of Mystery or emergence is extremely important in collaborating with strangers, as described earlier through the jazz metaphor of improvisation. By opening ourselves to "strangeness" in a way that does not make it a quality of the "other" but rather a shared and liminal quality of being, we may also be opening a channel that allows something new to emerge, as in Heidegger's *clearing*.[4] In such a channel, or space, unanticipated and unplanned things, like shared meaning between relative strangers, increased self-knowledge, or spontaneous musical compositions, can come into existence and find the proper form. One way to express and enact this type of emergent space is to communicate in such a way that *Mystery* is our primary objective, or the highest level of context, for what we are making together (Pearce 2011). This implicates ways of being together that are inherently creative or open to experimentation.

On reflection, we have found that these dynamics of cosmopolitan communication and social construction resonate strongly and directly support several of the "ten qualities of phenomenologists" (Marlatt/Bentz 2019) observed to be at work in the From Strangers to Collaborators project. The writing of *protocols* (rich descriptions of lived experience) can be viewed as an act of *coordination* that allows relative strangers to work together outside of a commonly-shared culture. By sharing these and reflecting together, they were able to develop *coherence* among the group, enhanced by heuristics that revealed both Lifeworld and Deathworld patterns in their stories. In some cases, something unexpected (Mystery) emerged among them, embodying the quality of "embracing authenticity

---

[4] Martin Heidegger referred to the clearing as a space of "un-concealment" in which we have access to what we are not, as well as what we are. It is a space where "new beings may emerge." (n.d.)

and wonderment" (Marlatt/Bentz 2019, p. 8). It is this quality that may be essential to navigating permanent liminality.

The (Mature) Self and Mystery

The foregoing discussion of opening self to Mystery raises the question of the integrity of self and identity in the presence of liminality. If we are to meaningfully connect with others in liminal space and communicate in the cosmopolitan sense, then we need a *Self* (denoted by a "Big S") that resonates with the transcendent potential of Big "M" Mystery – yet grounds us in a state of being which is at home amidst liminality. Ann Ulanoff describes this as a sense of center, similar to finding a home within ourselves:

> Our desire to align ourselves with transcendence affects the whole body. It is like a plant: in living true to our nature we also make oxygen for everyone to breathe. Desiring the center in ourselves, which is in the center of all selves and all things, we unclog an artery, making passage from and to the center easier for everyone, and others' efforts make it more accessible to us. Together we build up the spiritual atmosphere. In chaos theory, the "butterfly effect" means a butterfly lifting its wing can change the course of the whole cosmos. Similarly, one or two of us, desiring to be planted in the center can open the way to it and it to us for all of us. The Self exists in us as a predisposition to be oriented around a center. It is the archetype of the center, a primordial image similar to images that have fascinated disparate societies throughout history.   (Eisendrath/Dawson 1997, p. 198)

This insight, when applied to the model of Cosmopolitan Communication, is particularly useful in interpreting our place amidst the co-constructive dynamics of engaging with others amidst liminal space. Such a Self is not dependent upon culture or system for meaning and integrity and can connect with other Selves around centers as they emerge. Yet, at the same time, a centered community generates potentially transformative energy, much like the condition of *communitas* envisioned by Turner (Buechner et al. 2020). The kind of Self that has the capacity to be open to the forces of Mystery (and other Selves) while remaining centered is very much in line with what Bentz describes as a "mature personality" or "person incarnate," possessing qualities of "artistic creativity, philosophical reflection, and authentic love" (Bentz 1989, p. 16). Bentz further defines this state of maturity as something of a "gift" not being "fixed or fixated" but rather engaged "in a living dialogue with his (/her) own immaturity . . . and . . . some measure of disorder" that is wonderful, particularly because it cannot be "predicted, controlled or constructed" (Bentz 1989, p. 16–17).

Having established the notion of the Self as a form of mature personality which is capable of engaging with emergence and the presence of *Mystery*, we will later consider how such a Self may operate as a *practical mystic*, walking between the worlds of visible and unseen forces and, at times, making useful connections. Cultural and artistic representations of successful liminal existence remain important, and they are becoming more common and widespread, just as they need to continually operate from a defined liminal place is likewise growing. In the following section, narratives from the co-authors' own lives, their work, and their teaching touch on the liminal as they have come to know it.

The Jazz Metaphor of Collaboration Among Strangers: Jamming into an Unfinished Symphony

A musician walking onto a symphony stage in the presence of a conductor will expect to be compelled towards certain responses and ways of being, might have a more closed, rigid attitude than one would find in an intimate night club. The latter scenario and its attendant environment invite a player to pro-actively engage with ("riff on") whatever emerges, without paying close attention to a pre-programmed outcome. Such emergence requires mutual trust, as well as a cultivated skill to recognize and engage in musical patterns. When a player riffs on another player, there is nothing to be proven. It's all about probing the emergent, and in the process, deliberately setting aside any prior notion of a plan. Every setup by one musician serves as a scaffold to enable the collective exploration of the potentialities by other members of the group. As such, every gesture that emerges is fresh. Every response is new. Structure emerges and keeps its fluidity.

Many traditional organizations operate from a perspective similar to the symphony, which then requires members to follow pre-scripted forms of enactment and forecloses many other possible outcomes. This form of "closing the mind" is something that – from a reductionist perspective – is often assumed to be necessary as a way of maintaining standardization, predictability, and order. For many purposes, this may be correct. However, our focus in our exploration of the dynamics of collaboration among strangers focused on the enactive potential of creating something like a permanent liminal space, free of many restrictions and in which spontaneous collaboration could emerge.

In framing the issue this way, we challenge the notion that it would take a pro-active step to collaborate with strangers. Instead, we see the invitation as the removal of an artificially imposed barrier to what otherwise might be happening spontaneously. When the strange-ness in strangers is perceived as something integral to life and living *together* in true community, we can engage collaboratively in enacting Mystery together, also described as "hold(ing) (an open) space for many possible interpretations, especially those of others who are different from oneself in some way," (Jensen n.d., p. 3).

On Engaging the Lifeworld as a Practical Mystic

Every one of us is a mystic deep in our hearts, or so says Beatrice Bruteau in her preface to *The Mystic Heart* (Teasdale 2001). Bruteau goes on to discuss the challenge of raising consciousness to an explicit level, a level that reveals the knowledge that we are not mutually alienated from one another and that each of us is sufficient "as is." The practice of acquiring this knowledge is how we can become mystics in experience as well as potentiality.

Bruteau's view parallels the type of practical mysticism espoused as necessary by Evelyn Underhill's work more than 100 years ago as she witnessed events leading to the outbreak of World War I. Recently reissued, her work (2002, 2010) resonates with the type of global thinking and accountability of self that is not just desirable but critical – economically, socially and politically – as we move forward through the 21st Century. Both authors echo many of the concepts, features, and implications of the cosmopolitan communication model (Pearce 2007), developed out of the author and scholar's coordinated management of meaning (CMM).

Pearce's hierarchy of meaning, cosmopolitan communication, and other models of social construction through conscious language and behavioral choices help show that identity is multi-layered and complex and that the layers are fluid rather than static. As a practical theory of social construction, these heuristic models of the CMM offer working insights to help individuals perceive – and often change – patterns of communication as they unfold. Similarly, a liminal identity or practical mysticism – a capacity for being with whatever is emerging at any given moment – opens up ways of being that teach authenticity, and the ability to recognize what is being made in (and through) a complex dance between what Pearce called "episodes, selves, and relationships" (Pearce 2007, pp. 101–102). Pearce further describes the emergent properties associated with these entities as patterns of communication, forms of consciousness, and relational minds (2007, p. 102). Heightened awareness of these emergent properties, in turn, allows the practical mystic to determine the appropriate facet of oneself to privilege in any given situation in order to enact a higher-level reality. Achieving such flexibility and intentional complexity of identity may also improve resilience – the ability to bounce back from adversity – and what many yogis call operating from a neutral mind (Khalsa 2007).

Consistent with Bruteau's holistic vision, unity is here for all of us right now. Although technology and the current scope of social media are potentially isolating and divisive, at the same time, they also can be unifying. We can allow the sheer volume of information and the forces of division to polarize our thinking, or we can just as well harness these forces for social justice and global parity. Such technology allows relative strangers to work together in real-time, to co-create, to bear witness, and to improvise in the presence of liminality. This is primarily the phenomenon that our co-authors of this chapter have attempted to explore, embrace and describe.

Mysticism, Mystery, and History

For some further context on practical mysticism, it may be helpful to further consider the connections between the work of G. H. Mead (1934) and Evelyn Underhill. When Underhill first began addressing mysticism, World War I was brewing in Europe. A new introduction to her republished work (2010) rightly concludes that the past 100 years of both global upheaval and global interconnectedness indicate the necessity for mystical traditions to strongly re-emerge and makes some suggestions as to how and where they might.

As did Mead, Underhill grounded much of her exploration of mysticism in the West from the early lectures given by William James. But as she refined and continued to publish, Underhill's views on mysticism began to shift. Rather than agreeing with James's conclusions about the features, or markers, of mysticism being fixed in place, Underhill (2002) concluded that the life of a mystic unfolded in stages – awakening, purgation (including transcendence of the ego), illumination and a dark night of the soul as her first four stages, followed by the last, permanent stage: a unitive life. In a similar vein, Mead stated that the common problem of the "artist, philosopher and critic" was to face "the relation between permanence and change" (Mead 1934, p. 322).

Eventually, Underhill refined her work again so that rather than five stages, there were three forms, which in turn resemble the three yogic stages of development – discipline (commitment to practice), attention (to shifts in consciousness and the necessary effect of those shifts on the Lifeworld, including Heidegger's concept of the clearing where we connect with universal consciousness (Chai 2014) and eventual mastery (unity, or a unitive life).

If World War I was the beginning of a period of world-wide awakening, as Underhill (2010) suggests, the rest of the 20th Century gave us plenty of chaotic and attention-getting material to help move our planet along its mystical path. Not one but two world wars and many other serious military conflicts around the globe, the birth, and popularity of jazz music, the movement of yoga and meditation to the Western Hemisphere from India – these are only some of the indicators of a world-wide shift in consciousness that was nearly 100 years in the making. This global awakening – or the opportunity for awakening – would have completed during the latter half of the 20th Century, followed by the breakdown of old social orders and systems (*purgation*), out of which may arise both illumination *and* a societal dark night of the soul. In light of this duality, we must collectively realize that each of us is responsible for ourselves *and* that how we choose to behave will affect others – a kind of butterfly effect Applying this logic, we can postulate that the simultaneous existence of Lifeworlds and Deathworlds may be an inevitable consequence of what we may recognize as *post-truth* social worlds (Buechner et al. 2018). In the current political situation, leaders and their corporate sponsored media spread polarized narratives one day and contradict them the next, thereby further confusing an already traumatized and unsuspecting public. This realization not only gives us important choices, but requires us to – more than ever before – acquire the capacity to be comfortable with, and skillfully navigate, the liminal spaces in between, where the existence of multiple realities and the principle of "both and" (Pearce 2007, 41–42) is a fixed part of the landscape.

Conclusion

As we acknowledged from the beginning, the prospects of collaborating with strangers, and doing so in an ongoing liminal state, can be a bit unsettling. Because Turner's original definition of liminality included highly prescribed and limiting behaviors and rituals with intended goals and outcomes, the idea of ongoing, permanent liminality must also be bounded by conscious form and ritual as a way of creating a container or way of living one's life from day to day. To help ground this type of liminality in some familiar metaphors, we presented some concepts from jazz improvisation, dance, yoga, and other somatic practices to offer practical models for engagement. These practices offer a way of looking at the world that encompasses a concept of viewing "home" as within oneself, wherever that (Big "S") Self might be.

Training and awareness to raise personal consciousness and some kind of daily somatic practice or activity are vital to creating such an internally focused sense of the mature self as grounded or "home" while not being rigidly fixed. Although not an exclusive list, examples are mindfulness or vipassana meditation, along with some system of hatha yoga, or a comprehensive yoga system that also emphasizes a meditative component (kundalini yoga and meditation, for example, which includes movement, and both chanted meditations and stillness).

The more the body is activated first through a somatic practice, the more likely the mind is to be stilled and ready to access information being brought forth in any situation through cellular memory. The continued repetition of a somatic practice will create and strengthen neural pathways that sustain such bodily informed and conscious behaviors. The result will be an individual who is "at home," who acts authentically and appropriately from within themselves. The more consistent the practice of self as home, the more masterful an individual will become at feeling like a whole, integrated human being, regardless of where he or she is in the world.

The notion of a "practical mystic" as one who can remain grounded in liminal space while at the same time observing the world around them, takes on great significance when we consider the simultaneous existence of Lifeworlds and Deathworlds as equally real but opposing potential realities. The ability to discern (and change) these patterns, like the capacity to make one's self a home, is something that can be further developed by practices that can, over time, be transformative. These include phenomenological writing (Bentz/Rehorick 2008), critical reflection, and looking directly at (not through) patterns of communication (Pearce 2007) to discern the socially constructed nature of the emerging realities in which we find ourselves enmeshed.

Acting as a practical mystic in this context begins with cultivating a new way of seeing and being in the world and takes the necessary next steps by serving to interpret and translate what is seen into a viable or actionable Lifeworld context. The skills are available for anyone to learn.

References

Bentz, Valerie (1989) *Becoming Mature: Childhood Ghosts and Spirits in Adult Life*. New York, NY: DeGruyter.
Bentz, Valerie (2014): "Becoming Mature Thirty Years Later: A Replicative Study." Annual Conference, Society for Phenomenology and the Human Sciences, New Orleans.
Bentz, Valerie & Giorgino, Vincenzo (Eds.) (2016). *Contemplative Social Research: Caring for Self, Being, and Lifeworld*. Santa Barbara, CA: Fielding Graduate University Press.
Buechner, Barton, Van Middendorp, Sergej & Spann, Rik. (2018). Moral Injury on the Front Lines of Truth: Encounters with Liminal Experience and the Transformation of Meaning. *Journal of Schutzian Research* 10 (2018) 51-84. Open Source publication. Retrieved from https://www.zetabooks.com/docs/Barton-BUECHNER-Sergej-von-MIDDENDORP-Rik-

SPANN_Moral-Injury-on-the-Front-Lines-of-Truth_Encounters-with-Liminal-Experience-and-the-Transformation-of-Meaning.pdf., visited on October 11, 2020.

Buechner, Barton, Dirkx, John, Konvisser, Zeiva, Myers, Deedee, & Peleg-Baker, Tzofnat (2020) From Liminality to Communitas: The Collective Dimensions of Transformative Learning. *Journal of Transformative Education* Vol. 18 No.2, pp. 87–113.

Chai, David (2014). Nothingness and the Clearing: Heidegger, Daoism and the Quest for Primal Clarity. *The Review of Metaphysics* Vol. 67 No.3.

Dass, Ram (1971) Be Here Now. San Anselmo, CA. Hanuman Foundation.

Eisendrath, Polly and Dawson, Terrence (1997) *The Cambridge Companion to Jung*. New York, NY: Cambridge University Press.

Heidegger, Martin (n.d.): Stanford University article. Retrieved from https://web.stanford.edu/dept/archaeology/cgi-bin/archaeolog/?p=69, visited on October 11, 2020.

Jensen, Arthur (n.d.) A Cosmopolitan Future: Enacting Mystery and Cosmopolitan Communication to Meet the 21st Century Head-on. CMM Institute (In Press).

Kaye, Mary Margaret (1979). *The Far Pavilions*. New York: Bantam.

Khalsa, Hari Singh (2007). The Aquarian Teacher (fourth ed.). Espanola, NM: Kundalini Research Institute.

La Shure, Charles (2005). *Liminality: The Space In Between*. Retrieved from http://www.liminality.org/about/whatisliminality/, visited on October 11, 2020.

Marlatt, James/ Bentz,Valerie (2019): "Transformative Phenomenology: Collaboration among Strangers Based on Writing Phenomenological Protocols". Annual Conference, Society for Phenomenology and Human Sciences (SPHS), Pittsburgh.

Matoba, Kazuma (2013). Global Integral Competence for Cosmopolitan Communication. *CMM Learning Exchange*, CMM Institute, Oracle, AZ.

Mead, George Herbert (1934). *Mind Self and Society from the Standpoint of a Social Behaviorist*. Chicago: University of Chicago Press

Morrison, Van (1970) Into the Mystic. On *Moondance* (record) New York, NY: Warner Brothers Records

Moustakas, Clark (1990). Heuristic Research: Design, Methodology, and Applications. Sage Publications, Inc.

Pallant, Cheryl (2006). *Contact Improvisation: An Introduction to a Vitalizing Dance Form*. Jefferson, NC: McFarland & Company, Inc.

Pearce, W.Barnett (1989) *Communication and the Human Condition*. Carbondale, IL: Southern Illinois University Press.

Pearce, W. Barnett (2007). *Making Social Worlds: A Communication Perspective*. Malden, MA: Blackwell.

Pearce, W. Barnett (2011): "At Home in the Universe with Miracles and Horizons: Reflections on Personal and Social Evolution". In: Littlejohn, Stephen/McNamee, Sheila (Eds.): The Coordinated Management of Meaning: a Festschrift in Honor of W. Barnett Pearce. Malden: Fairleigh Dickinson University Press.

Pollock, David, Pollock, Michael, van Reken, Ruth (2017): *Third Culture Kids: Growing up Among Worlds* (third edition). Boston: Brealey.

Rehorick, David & Bentz, Valerie (2008). *Transformative Phenomenology: Changing Ourselves, Lifeworlds, and Professional Practice*. Plymouth, UK: Lexington Books.

Ritter, Ann (2015): "Permanent Liminality: Transcultural Hierarchy of Identity in Professional and Personal Life." Discovering Cosmopolitan Communication! Crossover Dialogue between Past and Future/Theory and Practice/West and East. Institute for Global Integral Competence, Munich.

Shannahoff-Khalsa, David (2006, October). A Perspective on the Emergence of Meditation Techniques for Medical Disorders. *Journal of Alternative and Complementary Medicine*, 12 (8),709–713.

Teasdale, Wayne (2001). *The Mystic Heart: Discovering a Universal Spirituality in the World's Religions*. Novato, CA: New World Library.

Turner, Edith (2012). *Communitas*: The Anthropology of Collective Joy. New York: Palgrave McMillan.

Turner, Victor (1978). *Image and Pilgrimage in Christian Culture: Anthropological Perspectives*. New York, NY: Columbia University Press.

Turner, Victor (1987). *Anthropology of Performance*. New York, NY: PAJ Publications.

Underhill, Evelyn (2002). *Mysticism: A Study in the Nature and Development of Spiritual Consciousness*. Mineola, NY: Dover Publications.

Underhill, Evelyn (2010): Practical Mysticism. Whitefish: Kessinger Publishing. (Original work published in 1915)

Van Gennep, Arnold (1909). *Les Rites de Passage*. Paris, France: Emile Nourry.

Wasserman, Ilene & Fisher-Yoshida, Beth (2017) *Communicating Possibilities: A Brief Introduction to the Coordinated Management of Meaning*. Chagrin Falls, OH: Taos Institute Publications.

Part IV: **Deathworlds and the Indigenous**

Life and Death
We understand who we are –
We know where we came from –
We accept and understand our destiny here on Mother Earth – We are spirit having a human experience.

– Dianne M. Longboat, Mohawk Nation

Debra Irene Opland
Chapter 16
Indigenous Worldview and the Vision of a Peace Educator

Abstract: Documenting my lifelong quest to achieve peace through self-understanding, I analyzed personal and professional lived experiences related to the divided-self phenomenon as the root cause of problems in society-at-large. Growing up Euro-American in peaceful post-WWII South Dakota, the Vietnam War shattered my idealism. I underwent a dysfunctional rite-of-passage, manifested as divided self-identity issues throughout adulthood. By age 50, my wounded spirit had yet to heal when I became an educator. For 20 years, teaching at-risk youth in poverty-stricken Indigenous communities on and off Western South Dakota reservations, I witnessed students exhibit the same split identity symptoms typical of most youth raised in cultural climates of fear, violence, and war. Evoking personal and existential reawakening, the protocols of transformative phenomenology pattern an ancient rite-of-passage to Enlightenment: On my *ičhimani wáȟwala* (Lakota for "journey to peace"), unique self-discoveries led to universal truths, adopting Indigenous worldview as a vision of peace – a way of belonging to humanity, being human, and becoming whole. Primal precepts are founded upon the oneness principle, exemplified in the Lakota concept, *mitákuye oyás'in*, translated as "all my relatives" or "we are all related" on the quest for understanding and peace. Acknowledging this ideal, peace can be achieved through self-understanding, as each fulfills their ultimate human need to help others – by making a contribution to community, collective knowledge, and the greater good. Seeking the restoration of Indigenous Lifeworlds, I share my story, hoping to empower all my relatives to do the same.

Keywords: Indigenous worldview, peace, transformative phenomenology, divided self-identity, self-understanding

My *Ičhimani Wáȟwala*, Journey to Peace

Much like the agrarian societies of our Indigenous ancestors, I grew up within a culture of peace – post-World War II, White, middle-class, rural USA. We were blessed by an idyllic upbringing, grounded in protestant Christian values brought by both sets of grandparents from the old countries of England, Wales, and Norway.

After wartime service, my folks returned home to Sioux Falls, South Dakota, with the sole purpose of raising a family. Dad and a church friend built our house by remodeling an old army barracks. Until Mom passed after 66 years of marriage, that home meant a warm, welcoming sanctuary – the smell of fresh-baked bread, games set up for weeks on the same Monopoly board, and songs sung with either Dad (self-taught at the piano) or Lawrence Welk on the record player. Family attendance was required at the table for all meals, as it was for nightly prayers and church, a central part of social activities.

Doors were rarely locked, neighbors became extended family, and every house on the block felt safe. We thrived without TV, computers, arguments, abuse, alcohol, or drugs. Faith, fortitude, laughter, and loving served as the best medicine for any ailment. My folks lived by the Golden Rule found in most spiritual beliefs worldwide.

In childhood, I perceived a world at peace. As an adolescent, new TV sets brought the reality of the Civil Rights Movement and the Vietnam War into our living rooms. Some family and friends returned in caskets, while others were spat upon for serving, whether draftee or enlistee. Most suffered from post-traumatic stress disorder (PTSD), as some died slowly from cancer-causing Agent Orange. Soldiers rarely talked of their experience, until years later, one described confrontation with non-combatants of any age, identified by communist ideology rather than uniforms. I watched loved ones leave with a whole soul, only to return with a fractured self-identity that reflected my own, mirror images of a deeply fragmented nation.

During the 1960s, presidents and peace leaders were assassinated, student protestors killed at Kent State, and Black babies burned in a Birmingham church. Those of us who questioned the establishment were further denied our rights to free speech and assembly. In a country cracked with controversy, my idealistic perceptions of childhood, citizenship, and Christianity became distorted by deception, an American dream corrupted by colonization and capitalism. Our country has yet to heal. My lifelong journey to become a peace hero reflects an enduring desire to return home to a time of trust, a place where my soul felt whole.

From Wallflower to Flower Child

A model student, I was a reserved, studious, innocent wallflower, fearful of breaking the rules or speaking out. Dictated by dress code, girls never wore pants, yet, in the age of miniskirts, we either knelt with hems touching the floor or went home to change. Education was highly regarded in our family, including the arts, in and out of school. With a fine voice, Father shared his love of music as I learned the piano, memorizing popular songs and hymns. Proud to be a housewife, mother exercised her interest in theatre by wholeheartedly supporting my involvement in it, including a production of *Viet Rock*. Although this war protest play was not well received in conservative South Dakota, we won national awards. The experience served as an introduction to a non-violent revolution and a rebel spirit lying latent inside my soul.

Too nervous for acting, I preferred behind-the-scenes roles: designing costumes, collecting props, and most of all, functioning as an assistant director to my favorite teacher. His liberal politics were tolerated by the school only out of respect for lifetime achievements in state and national arts education. Well-loved by students, his teaching style was so different from many others of the time, who were advocates of strict classroom management, with zero tolerance for diversity or those labeled as deviants.

My love of theatre evolved into a college major. Freshman year marked my first time living away from home yet, follow thespians became an electric, eccentric group of friends who declared independence from the sorority-faternity scene by becoming peace activists. Discussions led to the hypocrisy of war waged for peace, and we expressed admiration for pacifists like Einstein. By 1931, Einstein petitioned governments not to use his inventions for weaponry and war:

> Peace cannot be kept by force. It can only be achieved by understanding. You cannot subjugate a nation forcibly unless you wipe out every man, woman, and child. Unless you wish to use such drastic measures, you must find a way of settling your disputes without resort to arms. (1931/2009, p. 67)

Ever since this quote appeared on protest posters, I have asked: In a world so deeply divided, how can peace be achieved through understanding? Barely 18, I lacked the maturity to contemplate such issues, as life's changes led me to leave college my sophomore year, marry, and move to California. Until then, I had led a sheltered existence but grew up fast to become a peace-love hippie in this experimental culture of sex, drugs, and rock-n-roll. Although I was destined to spiritually remain a free-spirited flower child forevermore, my role of protestor ended with the war. I joined what Freire (1970) called a "culture of silence" – personal, social, and collective consciousness dominated by duality and ambiguity, inundated with fear and mistrust.

Divorced within three years, I returned to the Midwest to obtain a B.S. in photojournalism, complete graduate work in anthropology, and travel, before residing permanently in the Black Hills of South Dakota for 30 years. Another marriage brought four exceptional children into my life and a stable career in small business as co-owner of an art gallery. This false sense of security ended the morning of September 11, 2001, when the bombing of the New York World Trade Center was broadcast live on every network.

The events of 9/11 fueled fear and patriotism in many young hearts, including my stepson, who enlisted with childhood buddies. When one was killed in Iraq, it took me three days to reach my stepson by phone at boot camp, battling officers who insisted his military family would care for him. His screams will forever echo in my mind, as his generation asked me the same questions activists posed without answers fifty years ago.

Youth coming of age since 2001 have known nothing of peace. Children are massacred in classrooms, worshippers slaughtered in synagogues, as fearful rhetoric of political pundits encourages hatred and hostility evidenced everywhere – the media, movies, video games, business, sports, and most traumatically, schools.

East River Debra vs. West River Debbie

A useful metaphor for describing my own divided identity, the states of North and South Dakota are both split by the Missouri River, a natural barrier separating ecological habitats, subsistence patterns, and demographics. Why had they not created an East and West Dakota? The reasons become clear from the perspective of settler-colonialism, motivated by a "Manifest Destiny" (Greenberg 2018) creed of greed, gluttony, and glory. Each state demanded their fair share of natural resources on opposite sides of the river – primarily rich arable farming land east side compared to precious minerals and semi-arid ranchland out west – open range, gold, coal, and oil. With native tribes relocated to reservations, the majority of the present-day population resides in the eastern half, representing a greater control of state government, business, and industry. West-river ranchers exhibit an independent spirit, yet this Republican-red state reflects a sociopolitical atmosphere I define as "right-to-the-right-of-righteous."

Throughout adulthood, I experienced a disconnect between the internal idealism of "West River Debbie" and the external realism of "East River Debra." Although I could assume the roles of dutiful daughter, respectable businesswoman, and well-behaved mother, I believed my true self to be the innocent, idealistic child who became a peace-love hippie. Frequently ridiculed for being an optimist, too sensitive, and trusting every time my tender soul was hurt by the outside world, I nurtured that crazy rebel spirit deep inside. Balancing this divided identity often became unbearable, resulting in depression, anxiety, and addictions – mental illnesses regularly misunderstood in our narrow-minded society, and therefore, hidden.

While I had acquired considerable knowledge and matured professionally, I experienced little personal growth, self-understanding, satisfaction from helping others, or true peace. Subconsciously, my split soul searched for significance, surfacing in this deep-sleep dream: A dark indigo sky filled with stars that transformed into faces of Indigenous elders – wise, troubled ebony eyes silently pleading with me to come to help the people – before fading back into the black. For two months, I had four such visions but never one since. Later, Lakota friends told me stars represent sentient souls, sent to Earth with a purpose; once served, their spirits return to the heavens to become shining examples of lives well lived. At that time, I did not comprehend the full meaning of the prophecy, yet felt a subliminal message leading me on a quest to fulfill old goals.

Peace Educator Persona

Although my heart filled with pride for entering the honorable teaching profession, I soon discovered those who serve honorably are seldom honored for that service. Obtaining elementary teacher certification, I was highly qualified to teach in the make-believe learning environments idealized in methods classes, yet woefully unprepared for reality in today's diverse classrooms. Just as my peace-love hippie identity was ill-suited for today's rage-based reality, my peace educator persona was rejected by most authoritarian systems.

Education is heavily influenced by right-wing state politics, part of a national structure to inculcate the dominant worldview, based upon fear, violence, and war – standardization instituted through the No Child Left Behind Act (NCLB). In favor of academics, students lacked opportunities to develop social-emotional coping skills proven to be a prerequisite to school proficiency and productive citizenship (Goleman 2006). Teachers are inadequately trained in behavior management, yet oppositional, defiant students make up an ever-growing segment of student bodies nationwide, leading to the prevalence of bullying, suicide, and school shootings (Hall/Hall 2003). Socially alienated, the basic human needs of a growing number of at-risk students are not met by family or community – sustenance, security, shelter, and above all, love are not assured. This places a greater burden upon teachers to provide such necessities, even though teacher instructors and school administrators discouraged us from developing compassionate relationships with children and families. I was once terminated as a substitute for caring too much for a class of 2nd graders.

I experienced covert and overt discrimination against those of us who questioned authority to defend students. For five years, I was denied permanent employment in a competitive good-old-boy job market. Taking several short and long-term substitute positions, I found it increasingly difficult to confront behavior management issues and teacher-school politics. Horrified by hegemony and hypocrisy, my peace activist persona reappeared.

The personal mission to heal my divided soul became a professional one when, in 2002, I enrolled in the Educational Leadership Studies program at Fielding Graduate University,[1] a leading institution seeking social-ecological justice. Over-educated and under-experienced, I became a scholar, but not yet a practitioner. Reservations were always in need of highly qualified teachers, so I made the difficult decision to leave family, commuting each week to teach two-hundred miles from home – to enter a land so foreign to me, called the "Rez" in vernacular slang.

On the Reservation (The "Rez")

For Indigenous peoples, this country is not the sweet land of liberty it was for me during childhood. Living the American dream, I knew nothing of poverty or racism, nor do I remember seeing any "coloreds," especially Indians, except in Thanksgiving plays and movies – White folks face-painted brown portrayed screaming savages circling the wagons. I recall the head-dressed chief in front of souvenir shops when we took our beloved annual camping trips to the Black Hills, visiting Mt. Rushmore, a symbol of freedom and democracy.

Traveling 350 miles across a state filled with spacious skies and amber waves of grain, we were unaware that only a century before, the landscape had been covered with an estimated 30–60 million bison. Told to Mother by her grandmother, I heard a few homesteading stories from the 1880s, describing grasslands covered with rotting bison carcasses, their skulls piled 10-feet high for trophy photos. Bison provided sustenance for hundreds of Indigenous peoples for thousands of years. They had more than 200 uses for every part of that animal, yet Western settler-colonists only valued the coat for robes. My great-grandmother was appalled by the waste, without realizing the real reason for plunder and pillage.

---

[1] I left the program in 2005, reentered in 2006, left in 2009 and reentered in 2019. I will be Dr. Opland in 2021.

Following the Civil War, the U.S. government continued their Manifest Destiny mandate, declaring the Indian Wars to justify hostile takeovers of their lands for economic and political interests – the extermination of tribes was enforced by the rallying cry, "the only good Indian is a dead Indian." Thousands perished before the first shot was fired in the Indian wars, entire villages were wiped out from bedding infected with smallpox and other diseases, some purposefully. Natives had no immunity from blankets or bullets, yet total annihilation was not possible against the resilient spirit of these people. Therefore, settler-colonists resorted to cultural genocide, legislating assimilation and alienation policies and practices.

Allotment, land-grant, and homesteading laws were implemented not only to righteously transform these hunting/gathering cultures into agriculturists, Christians, and Western thinkers, but realistically, to dispossess them of their land, timber, minerals, and other natural resources (DeLoria, Jr. 1999). Provoked by the discovery of gold in the Black Hills in 1874 and the Battle of the Little Bighorn in 1876, the government embarked on resettlement plans. The First Nations that made up the *Seven Council Fires of the Ochéti Sakówin* – the nomadic horse cultures who once roamed all of America's northern Great Plains – were forcibly confined to seven reservations and two designated tribal areas in South Dakota, more than any other state. Three of these share borders with the poorest counties in the country. The people were systematically deprived of health and human services, and their lifestyle and livelihood destroyed when the bison were massacred to the point of endangerment. Only 5000 wild bison remain in the United States (Buffalo Field Campaign 2020).

Education was designed to inculcate the dominant, dehumanized warlike worldview of Euro-America, a mission-vision statement expressed as "kill the Indian, save the man." Youth were removed to boarding schools far from home and loved ones. Their clothes were burned, hair cut (considered sacrilege among natives), names changed, the language was forbidden, and customs scorned; they suffered malnourishment, neglect, and abuse – verbally, physically, socially, and sexually (DeLoria, Jr./Lytle 1983).

I have interviewed elder boarding-school graduates, one who showed scars on her hands, punished with a metal ruler for speaking Lakota. Another, born in 1937, had grown up peacefully according to the old Lakota ways, in a village along the banks of the Missouri River. When that waterway was dammed and their village flooded, her family was forcibly relocated from the west to east side of a massive lake, separated from relatives outside the waterline. We stood in the cemetery where her ancestors had been reburied without markers. At age 5, she was shipped off to boarding school, granted few trips home, nor could her parents afford to visit. At age 15, she was hurriedly getting ready for a dance, excited about seeing the boyfriend who became her husband. She checked out an iron to press her dress but broke the rules by allowing a friend to use it without checking it back out under another name. Without explanation, a nun used a broomstick to knock her teeth out. Since then, she seldom wore ill-fitting dentures, while few pictures show her smiling or the anger suppressed deep inside. In the wake of prolonged dehumanization, reservations have become Deathworlds, leaving future generations cursed by historical trauma, a carcinogen that has metastasized in the divided souls of the children I came to teach.

Rookie Year on the Rez

Accepting my new job two weeks before school started, I crossed the Badlands, first named by French fur traders to denote the stark landscape. For me, the unique scenic beauty prompted childhood memories of annual vacations camping in the Black Hills. Windows wide open, my curly head wafted in the warm wind, solitary yucca bloomed atop razor-edged escarpments, horses ran free of reins, and buffalo grazed, motionless as birds picked bugs from their backs. Cedar, sage, and sweetgrass provided aromatherapy, as pastel sunsets melted into sandstone of the same shades. What seemed so rightfully real and wondrous on my youthful trips now became a frightful reality check as I crossed from preserved parklands onto the reservation.

Often called third-world countries, reservations represent a blend of Lifeworlds and Deathworlds, far different from the fantasy lifestyles once promised by peace treaties and now glamourized on TV. An invisible demarcation line signifies a rapid depreciation of property values, ramshackle houses, fallow fields, rusted-out autos resting on blocks, feral dogs chewing garbage by roadsides, and bubble-nosed drunks stumbling along ditches. Looking past the decay, some homes are painted with lovely murals of medicine wheels and graffiti covers a church wall with one word: "RESPECT." Pastures bloom with wildflowers, colts suckle contentedly, the red tails of hawks radiate in sunlight, while farm boys shoot hoops into a bottomless bucket tied to a tree. On the streets of small towns, the sweet scent of fresh-baked fry bread intermingles with the odor of unwashed clothes, smelling like cat pee if worn too many days. The lilt of Lakota language and toothless grandma giggles contrast with the tweak talk of meth-heads, hiding their sunken cheeks and rotted grins behind hoodies. Youngsters with filthy faces, unkempt hair, and loaded diapers play alongside others adorned with squeaky-clean smiles, spotless jerseys, and new Nikes.

Most dramatically, the state's white majority becomes a minority. These colonized people had just cause to prejudge me for the lack of color in my skin, for suffering experienced at the will of racists, and opportunities granted freely to me but denied to them. At first, I experienced disgust, distrust, and hatred not always hidden, sometimes confronted by those who defined the worst problem with "my kind": too many had come to dictate quick fixes for their problems, only to leave matters worse.

With a shortage of teacher housing, for the first two weeks, I lived in my van. After moving down our motorhome, I endured another three months of microwave cooking with no restaurants nearby, wondering how to explain a lack of Internet to my online graduate school. Then, the RV steps broke and so did my ankle, though an ancient X-ray machine diagnosed it as merely sprained. I crawled in and out of my tin home, walking in a painful boot for a week before getting a better diagnosis and surgery to place pins in a broken bone. Impoverished communities have poor health services. Finally, an apartment was vacated by a young, stressed-out teacher quitting her first year early. My ankle healed and I escaped to a comfortable home, unlike many of my students.

Byproducts of boarding schools, modern systems wallow in underfunded dysfunction. Unable to meet state proficiency requirements, standardization now serves to perpetuate assimilation policies, providing hegemony in place of fair, equitable, high-quality education for all. My first classroom was covered with layers of dirt, desks piled high underneath, intermingled with books, supplies, and confidential records. With a high transition rate, I had 24–28 students at any given time, when a maximum of 15 is considered feasible for a single 5th-grade teacher without aides. Few schools could afford permanent paraprofessionals.

Told they were the worst class in school, my students came with an incredible amount of psychological baggage, taking every opportunity to test rookie teachers. Daily, I was subject to verbal abuse, scratched, or targeted with rocks or flying garbage cans. Others told me, "You're too nice, Ms. Debbie. We're used to yelling so we will listen." Avoiding specific identifiers, I illustrate the depth of the problems I faced during this first year:
- About once a month, we had both soft and hard school lockdowns – the former if only a threat of violence was made, and the latter, if a weapon was brandished.
- One Monday morning when standardized state tests were set to begin, five students entered the classroom late. A white-looking native boy had his backpack stolen on the bus, threatened with a beating if he told. A brother and sister were up all night in a hospital waiting room because their drunken father had broken their mother's leg. Another girl said her sister failed at a suicide attempt and was medevacked to a hospital 300 miles away. A different student showed pictures of her mother and the vodka they shared. When I questioned the test administrator about the possibility of skewed

results, she stood tall in a three-piece suit, insisting all students be tested. Her stiletto heels clacking on the titles a she patrolled the classroom.
- One of my brightest students said her mother and grandmother would often force her to smoke pot or leave her to babysit two younger siblings while they left for days to gamble. She had not spoken of this for months, fearing she would be separated from her sisters. When I asked police about prosecution, they told me I had to understand rez law: abandonment was not an issue if children are old enough to dial 911, and drug abuse was not a concern unless the substance was stronger than pot.
- Another time, a school administrator chased a student back into the classroom for committing the crime of trying to board the bus knowing he needed to attend after-school study hall. Steaming with uncontrollable anger, face raspberry red, the principal wrapped her hands around his neck in a chokehold, screaming, "You are not allowed to mouth off to my staff!" He had his back to me, but I could see his body stiffen with fear. I, too, still in a walking cast, froze with fright. Realizing others were watching, she let go and stormed out of the room. He collapsed at his desk crying. I comforted him as best I could, vowing to seek justice, yet powerless to do so. I accepted a counselor's advice to let it go, regretting that decision ever since.

Twenty Years of Rez Reality

The incidences summarized above only touch on four traumatic occurrences during my first year of teaching, compared to the hundreds I have experienced in 20 years working with at-risk students in poverty-stricken communities on and off the reservations of Western South Dakota.

After teaching in my first reservation school for two years, I deeply regretted the time spent away from my daughter and returned home for her senior year. I also realized I had gained much more through everyday praxis than the scholarship of dead White men, finding higher education far removed from reservation reality. In 2009, I withdrew from Fielding. My mother passed away in 2010, and by 2011, I divorced. Without my beautiful home in the Hills, I lost my sense of place and depression became a way of life.

Substituting for another two years, I was finally offered a position with a non-profit, servicing predominately Indigenous communities in Western South Dakota – connecting children with sponsors worldwide through a pen-pal exchange of letters. The organization had been in the area for 25 years when they suddenly chose to no longer service native communities. During their departure, they were disrespectful of communities and culture, leaving unresolved problems and bittersweet resentment among the people. It broke my heart to break ties with the people until they assured me they blamed the company, not me. I stayed in rez schools for another two years, as counselor and teacher. When my father passed in the Spring of 2018, I diagnosed myself with an acute case of PTSD – the pain of others commingled with my depression and anxiety. Overwhelmed by exhausting impotence, I felt powerless to effect change within these systems or my own life.

Systemic dysfunction is obvious, often expected, on the reservations, but the White world remains hidden under the façade of an idealized vision of prosperity, the illusion of safety and security. The Black Hills have always been a place of peaceful sanctuary for me, yet, this time I moved back to discover my own neighborhood was no longer quiet, middle-class suburbia. On Father's Day, a neighbor held his wife and child hostage at gunpoint, and then, made an unsuccessful attempt at suicide-by-cop; all afternoon we listened to him beg the SWAT team to kill him. Every day I hike the forest only to hear target practice, at times the sound of rapid-fire from an AR-15. Blocks surrounding a nearby elementary school are posted as drug-free zones, yet, I see sidewalks lined with meth needles, beer cans, liquor bottles, condoms, and vape pens. Each piece of litter represents the life of a child suffering from a dysfunctional rite-of-passage into adulthood. Whether on the rez or off, I have watched far too many children endure the same inescapable split-identity issues, alienated from self and society with no sense of belonging or being loved.

According to Brokenleg, in this materialistic, fast-paced culture, many children have broken circles, and the fault line usually starts with damaged relationships (Brokenleg 2019). Therefore, having no significant bonds to adults, youth chase counterfeit belonging through gangs, cults, and promiscuous relationships. Some are so alienated that they have abandoned the pursuit of human attachment altogether – guarded, lonely, and distrustful, they live in despair or strike out in rage. Finally, he added, families, schools, and youth organizations are being challenged to form new "tribes" for all of our children so there will be no more *psychological orphans*.

Unemployed and uncertain of the future, when I last drove back from Badlands to the Black Hills, I had plenty of time to let my thoughts tend to my sorrowful soul. Old memories mingled with a whole new perspective on the landscape as I realized I was no longer a stranger to the rez – this place was now more home to me than Euro-America. As both scholar and practitioner, I had gained the ability to look beyond the Deathworld façade of modern existence to find signs of life. Within my mind's eye, I gained strength remembering the resiliency of Indigenous peoples and hope in the lifelong relationships I developed. The ancient faces of my old dream renewed their plea for help as I repeated this question: How can peace be achieved through self-understanding?

Gabbard (2006) said individual schizophrenia is created under the dominance of a worldview that places humanity out of context with the universe. He urged decolonizing researchers to join hands with the colonized:

> For Americans of European descent, embracing such a project will require a unique process of healing . . . the wounds left by the sins of our fathers on the backs of Indigenous People across the planet, we must simultaneously heal our own wounded spirits. Left unhealed, as most recently witnessed in the invasion of Iraq, where the genocidal patterns of colonialism have resurfaced, those wounds condemn us to perpetuate those same sins generation after generation. (p. 223)

Divided-Self Phenomenon

In January 2019, I returned to Fielding, with a renewed purpose to achieve peace through self-understanding. Senge (1990) documented the difficulties involved with using the master's tools to rebuild the master's house. I was pleased to find a greater acceptance of multiple perspectives and alternative research methodologies.

Throughout my dissertation, I follow the protocols of transformative phenomenology to analyze personal and professional lived experiences that relate to the divided-self phenomenon first documented by Montessori during her studies of traumatized orphans in industrialized, post-World War II Italy (Montessori/Lane 1972). Her conclusions are based upon this premise: as education is dehumanized within cultural climates of fear, violence, and war, children develop divided self-identity crises that manifest in adulthood to become the root cause for most problems in society-at-large.

Several studies find that the phenomenon has increased dramatically within techno-scientific societies dominated by the Euro-American worldview. Colonialization and globalization of Western thought have contributed to the loss of linguistic and cultural diversity, intergenerational knowledge representing cultural alternatives to the Western way, and biodiversity in the degradation of natural systems, threatening all life on the planet (Bowers 2003). Capra stated: "Inner fragmentation mirrors our view of the world outside." The awareness of self as an isolated ego existing separately from society and the environment becomes the main reason for present-day problems worldwide (Capra 1975, p. 23). In too many communities and classrooms, souls split easily and often. Society suffers forever.

Through writing phenomenological protocols (rich descriptions of lived experience) in our "Collaboration with Strangers" project, I determined the essence of the divided-self phenomenon. World problems stem from a *crisis of consciousness* – the disconnect between the dominant warlike Western worldview and cultural constructs based upon Far Eastern mythology, the peaceable precepts of Indigenous wisdom.

I sought consensus within the collective conscience, following the second protocol to analyze the essential structure of the phenomenon and align the problem with purpose. Since education is the primary proponent of enculturation, Freire (1990) advocated decolonization and humanization effected locally with concurrent cultural climate change and educational reforms. I join a growing number of scholars who believe these goals can be accomplished through the restoration of Indigenous Lifeworlds. Harris and Morrison (2003) stated peace education researchers must first envision a culture of peace to create a new consciousness.

As I explicated assumptions grounded in the misconceptions of my Euro-American heritage, I completed the next protocol to experience epoché. Looking beyond the fear, violence, and war of my Euro-American heritage, I envisioned Indigenous worldview as the place of peace from whence we came, and to which we must return for future sustainability. Originally, the terms "human" and "humane" shared synonymous meaning. Primal perceptions of peace were founded upon the oneness principle – exemplified in the Lakota concept of *mitákuye oyás'in,* defined as, "we are all related in the quest for understanding and peace."

A final writing protocol documents the experience of moving from epoché to enlightenment. Giorgino and Bentz (2016) analyzed the phenomenology of consciousness as contemplative inquiry; upon reaching epoché, one is destined to not only undergo a personal transformation but generate an existential reawakening within society-at-large. My research was not only intended to raise consciousness personally and socially but incite a revolution collectively and peacefully.

Adopting Indigenous Worldview to Achieve Peace through Self-Understanding

Evaluating restorative justice practices of Indigenous peoples, McCaslin and Breton (2008) urged researchers to accept the challenges of decolonization by acknowledging the original Indigenous vision of community-based healing and transformation: To seek consensus about how to achieve peacemaking in any given situation, scholars must first acknowledge the oneness principle – mitákuye oyás'in – and second, be mindful not only of how we are all related but how we can relate to building relationships at peace with each and all:

> Moral and spiritual values are guidelines for how we can acknowledge our relatedness and be good relatives . . . People come together with a commitment to hearing the stories on all sides and working together to put things right to everyone's mutual satisfaction. (p. 528)

Unconditional Care of Each Becomes the Universal Cure for All

Harris and Morrison (2003) reiterated the principles of peace education research: Human beings must work together to transform human values – a process of understanding ourselves and our position in society. To comprehend the consciousness of self in relation to others, Bentz and Shapiro (1998) challenged researchers to not only focus on the accurate and deep interpretation of meaning but also, on the alleviation of suffering, with respect for the Lifeworlds of all involved. Mother Teresa (1997) said depression is a form of selfishness; by helping others, we heal our own souls. Likewise, generosity is highly valued among Indigenous peoples, for it takes the greatest amount of courage (Four Arrows 2016).

Throughout my teaching experiences, I encountered far too many instances where children lacked care, that human need to be loved and belong, without which we cannot gain understanding or esteem. I found major differences between students who had a caring adult in their lives and those who did not. Even those who did care, usually grandparents, felt helpless and hopeless as they watched their Lifeworlds disappear.

Martin and Martin (2012) discussed the work of Nouwen (1974), who focused on care as the basis and precondition of all cure. Like me, they discovered life as others experience it, and thus learned about the generosity of caring, putting the needs of another person ahead of our own comfort, and sometimes, our own rights. Therefore, caring is always associated with risk. Professionals may care, but we are taught to keep a professional distance or are simply overwhelmed – social workers with heavy caseloads or schoolteachers in overcrowded classrooms. Although it is impossible to measure the number of children we help, they suspected a few of them will be the ones who gave us the most grief. For sure, all of them will be the ones who knew we cared. They asked us to remember the stories that grow out of the risk of caring. My research evolved from those stories and the risks I took to care.

Sharing experiences with veteran teachers became much more valuable than methods classes. They taught me how to balance idealized standards, unjust regulations, cultural relativity, and rez reality. Having been there 30 years, one Lakota teacher had former students visit her on their way to college, to thank her for caring. When asked how she did it, she replied, "Once children cross the threshold of my classroom, I never let them go."

Frequently during my first year on the reservation, I heard the Lakota phrase mitákuye oyás'in used in greetings, prayer, ceremony, and sweat lodges. Eventually, I incorporated this philosophy into lesson planning – every morning, reminding students of both their dual citizenship and their universal inheritance. We not only said the "Pledge of Allegiance," but recited mitákuye oyás'in. Following the Indigenous way of council, we gathered in a circle to pass a feather as a *talking stick*, a symbol that combines respect and responsibility for native cultures (Zimmerman/Coyle 1996). Only the feather-holder may speak. Each student was asked to state, "I respect myself because . . ." Some responses were phenomenal: "I talked to my Dad in prison last night, first time in a year"; "I told my friend no when he offered me pot"; "When my sister talked of suicide, I told her how much I loved her"; "For the first time, a teacher defended me and I learned never to underestimate her."

Students grew to trust this White teacher, as did their families, elders, and other community members. I learned most from those who protected the old ways, either directly or from stories repeated by children. A matriarchal society, a Lakota grandmother is called *unci*, highly respected for leadership, their power silent but absolute. Many have become the chief caretakers of children among poverty-stricken, ethnically oppressed populations. Without pride or prejudice, they helped me incorporate cultural traditions and Indigenous wisdom into the curriculum and classroom. One day after school, an Unci came to give me a big hug, saying, "In Lakota *phiámayaye*, meaning 'thank you,' but to you I say *wophíla*!" She explained this word is not used very often, only to convey a deep appreciation for the care I was giving the children.

In my class, students are asked what they can give back to their community. One replied, "Hope and faith!" Another, "Respect and honor!" When asked, "who taught you that?" the first answered, "My grandmother!" The second, "My teacher!" Lakota people honor special teachers with star quilts. At graduation one year, an unci wrapped my first quilt around my shoulders and it now hangs in my living room as a symbol of my commitment. Later, cleaning up in an empty auditorium, I looked up to see two of my most difficult students, one who had contemplated suicide. Without a word, they shaped their hands in the form of a heart and pointed at me.

I came a stranger to the rez, but became a trusted teacher, collaborator, and ultimately, accepted as family, forever – a feeling of unconditional love that I had not known since childhood. Together, we discovered our human similarities far outnumbered cultural differences. Although we each had taken a unique path to get to this place, we found the universal truths inherent within the Indigenous worldview of our ancestors, mitákuye oyás'in, we are all related on the quest for understanding and peace. This wisdom of oneness is placed within every human heart at birth (Four Arrows, 2016).

Following an ancient rite-of-passage on my *ičhimani wáȟwala* (Lakota for "journey to peace"), I finally completed Dad's Sunday School lesson, discovering the Way, the Truth, and the Light – a peace that surpasses all understanding. I had gained *wolokokiciapi*, Lakota for "practicing a sense of peacefulness in all relationships." By relating my personal journey to become a peace hero, I can professionally empower others to do the same. Restoring Indigenous Lifeworlds through the education of our children becomes my contribution to the collective. Connecting past to present to create a sustainable future, we nurture whole souls for the benefit of the whole world. If you grow close to a Lakota, they adopt you as a *hunka* relative. In this way, I became their sister, aunt, and unci. One hunka friend, a fellow teacher, honored me by saying I now have an "Indian heart." I like to think I have a human heart. We all do.

References

Bentz, Valerie M./Shapiro, Jeremy J. (1998): *Mindful Inquiry in Social Research*. Thousand Oaks: Sage Publications, Inc.

Bowers, Chet (2003): "How an Eco-justice Pedagogy Contributes to the Revitalization of the Commons". Unpublished manuscript. Retrieved from http://education.utsa.edu/images/uploads/CA%20Bowers%20Relevance%20to%20curriculum.pdf, visited on October 27, 2020.

Brokenleg, Martin (2019): "Martin Brokenleg: Cultural Healing and Resilience". Retrieved from https://martinbrokenleg.com, visited on March 20, 2020.

Buffalo Field Campaign (2020): "How Many Wild Buffalo are There in the United States? Where are they?". Retrieved from https://buffalofieldcampaign.org/how-many-wild-buffalo-are-there-in-the-united-states-where-are-they, visited on October 18, 2020.

Capra, Fritjof (1975): *The Tao of Physics; An Exploration of the Parallels Between Modern Physics and Eastern Mysticism*. Boston: Shambala Publications, Inc.

Deloria, Jr., Vine/Lytle,Clifford (1983): *American Indians, American justice*. Austin: University of Texas Press.

Deloria, Jr., Vine (1999): *Spirit and Reason; The Vine Deloria, Jr., Reader*. Golden: Fulcrum Publishing.

Einstein, Albert (2009): *Einstein on Cosmic Religion with Other Opinions and Aphorisms.* Mineola: Dover Publications. (Original work published in 1931)
Four Arrows (Jacobs, Don) (2016): *Point of Departure: Returning to Our More Authentic Worldview for Education and Survival.* Charlotte: Information Age Publishing.
Freire, Paulo (1970): *Pedagogy of the Oppressed.* New York: The Continuum Publishing Company.
Freire, Paulo (1990): *Education for Critical Consciousness.* New York: The Continuum Publishing Company.
Gabbard, David (2006): "Before Predator Came: A Plea for Expanding First Nations Scholarship as European Shadow Work". In: Four Arrows (Jacobs, Don) (Ed.): *Unlearning the language of conquest: Scholars expose anti-Indianism in America.* Austin: University of Texas Press, pp. 219–231.
Giorgino, Vincenzo Mario Bruno/Bentz, Valerie (2016): "Introduction: Opportunities for Human Potential in the *Great Transition*: An Embodied Perspective at Work". In: Bentz, Valerie/Giorgino, Vincenzo Mario Bruno (Eds.): *Contemplative Social Research; Caring for Self, Being, and Lifeworld.* Santa Barbara: Fielding University Press, pp. 16–25.
Goleman, Daniel (2006): *Social Intelligence: The Revolutionary New Science of Human Relationships.* New York: Bantam Books.
Greenberg, Amy S. (2018): *Manifest Destiny and American Territorial Expansion* (2nd ed.). Boston, Buffalo: Bedford/St. Martin's, Macmillan Learning.
Hall, Philip S./Hall, Nancy D. (2003): *Educating Oppositional and Defiant Children.* Alexandria: Association for Supervision and Curriculum Development.
Harris, Ian/Morrison, Mary Lee (2003): *Peace Education.* Jefferson: McFarland & Company, Inc.
Martin, Lloyd & Martin, Anthea (2012): *Small Stories: Reflections on the Practice of Youth Development.* Lennox: Circle of Courage Publications.
McCaslin, Wanda/Breton, Denise (2008): "Justice as Healing: Going Outside the Colonizers' Cage". In: Denzin, Norman/Lincoln, Yvonna/Smith, Linda Tuhiwai (Eds.): *Handbook of critical and Indigenous methodologies.* Los Angeles: Sage Publications, pp. 511–529.
Montessori, Maria/Lane, Helen R. (1972): *Education and Peace.* Chicago: Regnery.
Mother Teresa (1997): *In the Heart of the World: Thoughts, Stories, & Prayers.* Becky Benenate (Ed.). Novato: New World Library.
Nouwen, Henri J. M. (1974): *Out of Solitude.* Notre Dame: Ave Maria Press.
Senge, Peter M. (1990): *The Fifth Discipline; The Art & Practice of the Learning Organization.* London: Random House.
Zimmerman, Jack/Coyle, Virginia (1996): *The Way of Council.* Ojai: Bramble Books.

Tsolmontuya Myagmarjav
Chapter 17
Colonization of the Lifeworld of Sheepherder Communities of Mongolia

Abstract: Mongolia is known for its steppe lands, traditional livestock-herding lifestyle, and a population of 3 million people. An estimated 25% to 40% of the population live as nomadic herders. It is central to culture and identity. Opencast mining causes degradation of natural pastures and permanently hinders the migration of animals between pastures. This is a serious threat to traditional pastoralism, which is of high importance not only from an economic point of view, but also cultural.

Keywords: Mongolian herders, dzud, migration, colonization

From Lifeworld to Deathworld

I was born and raised in the desert of Mongolia. Coming home always brings back memories of an unbelievably wonderful childhood. Spending the whole day outside, pasturing sheep and goats, or driving camel, we fulfilled our duties as livestock herders, even during the frozen wintertime in minus 40 °C temperatures. I remember how soft camel fur is, and the feeling of warm wool on my skin. Now, it's sometimes hard to believe a desert girl could live her dream, studying for a Ph.D. in economic-environmental science at the University of Łódź in Poland, a country so far away from the land of my birth – eight days by train, 24 hours by aircraft, and almost three weeks by car. It's unbelievable what I have now, what I am doing, and who I am, and that all of these things are connected to my childhood in the desert, to my dissertation research topic regarding *Land Rehabilitation After Mines* back home.

The world's most sparsely populated sovereign country, Mongolia is home to 3 million people, originally a rural nation of nomads, a horse culture of shepherds living in a desert climate on approximately 600,000 square miles of little arable land. Moving every season, the nomads of Mongolia have multiple pasturelands to allow for regrowth, making fields usable for many years, rather than overgrazing them until the ground is unable to support the herds. For the better part of the year, these nomadic households are individualistic, but during the warmer seasons, multiple households gather together at one pasture and spend the season with other households. Mongolian nomads live in traditional round tents known as a *ger* or *yurt*, made out of felt or animal skins to protect against the extreme winter weather, yet they can disassemble them to be carried by horses or other livestock when families travel to the next pasture.

For thousands of years, the Mongolian people sustained life in this manner. Then from 1929 to 1932, the Chinese Communist Party seized property from more than 800 religious and secular leaders, about 700 heads of households were killed or imprisoned, and 600 feudal estates (herds and fixed property) were confiscated. Expropriation was followed by collectivization – the organization of all land and industry to be owned and managed by the government. By 1931, more than one-third of the stock-raising households had been forcibly communized. The brutal collectivization of herdsmen was rapid, causing bloody uprisings. Once suppressed, the party then attacked the entire monastic class, nobility, nomads, and nationalists. They imposed high and indiscriminate taxes, confiscated private property, banned private industry, forced craft workers to join mutual-aid cooperatives, and nationalized foreign and domestic trade and transportation. Extremism instigated greater dependence on Soviet aid. Pastoral cattle and sheepherding societies were unprepared for residential life in the communes. Mongolia's economy rested entirely on animal husbandry, a nomadic lifestyle now destroyed, as was the national budget. The failure of communes, the hasty destruction of private trade, and inadequate Soviet supplies contributed to spreading famine. Thousands suffered from severe food shortages, which, together with the people's reaction to terror, had brought the nation to the verge of civil war. To squelch the uprisings, the government was forced to end its extremism.

My research trip back to my homeland in 2019 was stimulated by the phenomenology seminar in which I participated with Dr. Bentz that spring at the University of Łódź. Here is what I wrote at that time going back to my memories of childhood as part of the herder community:

> I came back to my childhood. As I was a little girl playing with my friends by sands or grass in natural. I remember there wasn't broken ecology. My toys were natural, not made of plastic or harsh for the environment. Because of the natural food without any concentration of pesticide or plastic packaging, people were rarely sick. My mom taught us to be kind to the animals around us and to nature. As a nomadic life-style citizen, nature was a resource of life, a resource of everything. We were so close to nature, understood each other, and talked in the same language.
>
> But in modern times we are losing this way of life more and more. Every day we are making more and more trash. Now it is common to see broken land and polluted water around the world. Buying a bottle of water or juice, nice looking cookies, packaged sweeties . . . there is no end to this list . . . But in the end, there is trash.
>
> (T. Myagmarjav, protocol, 2019)

Since de-collectivization, many pastoral herders are less nomadic, due to a lack of resources and the capacity to move, but they also need to secure their pastures so that other nomads or common thieves do not take their property (Myadar 2009). Consequently, fields are overgrazed, making them susceptible to *dzud*, the effects of summer droughts followed by harsh winters, that depletes the herds. Dzud is a Mongolian term for a severe winter in which a large amount of livestock dies, primarily due to starvation from being unable to graze, or, in other cases directly from the cold. There are various kinds of dzud, including white dzud, which is an extremely snowy winter in which livestock are unable to find nourishing foodstuff through the snow cover and starve.

As nomads lose their livelihoods off the land, underground in the country, the Earth has remained rich with deposits of other natural resources – primarily copper, gold, and coal – now coveted by outside political and economic interests. Recently, mining exploitation has increased, generating widespread concerns about damage to the environment, traditional agriculture, and the herder lifestyle of the Indigenous peoples. The nomads and mining companies are competing with each other for the same land and water resources. Mining practices have resulted in erosion, sinkholes, loss of biodiversity, and the contamination of soil, surface- and ground-water, polluted by the chemicals emitted from mining processes. The nomads need the land and water to sustain their herds and livelihoods, while the mining companies search for more land to expand their extraction sites, as well as large quantities of water to perform their operations. Mining exploitation is the main reason for overgrazing grassland. Almost 40% of the territory in Mongolia has been licensed for mining exploitation operations. Usually, pastoral herders move with the animals four to five times a year to conserve grasslands; now, they move only one to two times and the land is overgrazed. Since nomadic existence has always depended upon natural resources, Lifeworlds are quickly being destroyed through the miners' ecological devastation and subsequent dehumanization of community social infrastructure – the creation of Deathworlds.

Deprived of subsistence in their cultural homelands, herders are forced to migrate to the capital, Ulaanbaatar, a city of 1 million, one-third of the national inhabitants. As the sole researcher, I conducted my study during July and August of 2019, collecting pen-and-paper interviews with 145 migrant herder families. During the meetings, families said they had no choice, either move or die. Due to climate change and the ecological imbalance caused by mining, dzud had decimated livestock herds, making life no longer sustainable in this rural environment.

My research was anonymous and organized as a paper-based questionnaire study. I handed questionnaires out directly to herdsmen by the Pen-and-Paper

Personal Interview method. The respondents were 50% women and 50% men. Most of nomads (about 58%) were in the 40–49 age group (Figures 1 and 2).[1]

Figure 1: Mongolian nomads live around the capital, Ulaanbaatar, with their nomad lifestyle. Photo by author, Tsolmontuya Myagmarjav.

Almost all of the respondents have noticed changes in climate (99% of surveyed herders) and considered it to be the main cause of the worsening of the quality of their pastures (98% of respondents) (Figures 5 and 6).

The unrestrained movement of shepherds and their herds has become more and more difficult because of the development of open-pit mines. Additionally, mining is exhausting water resources which until now were the basis for the functioning of local communities, leading to the destruction of the traditional pastoral economy (Burchard-Dzubińska/Myagmarjav 2019).

In desert regions, heavy vehicles driving on unpaved roads raise huge amounts of dust. The dust adversely affects the health of herders and results in an increase in respiratory illnesses, such as bronchitis. Also, dust, noise, and

---

[1] The sample is not representative in that I simply gave a questionnaire to all I could reach.

Figure 2: Me interviewing nomads who migrated to the capital.
Photo by author, Tsolmontuya Myagmarjav.

water pollution directly harm the health of livestock. Due to emotional stress, animals are experiencing poor weight gain and low fat gain, which makes it less likely that they will survive the harsh South Gobi winter. The livestock grazing near the roads are dying off and, in some cases, are found with black lungs resulting from the inhalation of dust. The decrease in quantity and quality of livestock has an adverse economic impact on herders (Figure 3 and 4).

In the past two decades, Mongolia has experienced an enormous mining boom. The mining sector brings significant economic benefits to Mongolia, but their distribution is uneven. There are dozens of large-scale mines, with many more being planned. However, the country, and particularly the Gobi Desert, is more than a vast store of mineral deposits. It is also home to people, mostly herder's families, and to many plants and animals now endangered because of rapid environmental degradation.

The greatest challenge for Mongolians is to strive for ecological justice. As it was confirmed in research conducted in recent years, mostly by foreign civil society organizations, the lack of ecological justice is becoming a huge problem in this country with a young democracy. Particularly, it relates to the Indigenous

Figure 3: Sometimes I took my baby with me during the interview. My daughter is exploring the Mongolian nomad lifestyle.
Photo by author, Tsolmontuya Myagmarjav.

people living in the Oyu Tolgoi region, where one of the world's largest projects of extraction of copper and gold has been developed. Some communities don't have access to clean water, safe living conditions, and environmental protection. The degraded zones are called *sacrificed zones*. The nomads and mining companies are competing with each other for the same resources – land and water. The nomads need the land and the water to sustain their herds and livelihoods, while the mining companies search for more land to expand their extraction sites and need large quantities of water to perform mining operations. Too little attention is paid to the risk of resource nationalism in Mongolia, which is growing and is a serious concern. The environmental and social impact of resource extraction on natural pastures and herder's families has not only been underestimated. It seems it has been ignored by politicians in Ulaanbaatar. The destructive impact of mining is amplified by climate change.

My initial research results indicate the strength of the interdependency between the Mongolian herders and their herds; integrity that has been broken as local communities suffer from social, economic, and emotional hardship before

Figure 4: The Nomad's livestock look for grass around the capital.
Photo by author, Tsolmontuya Myagmarjav.

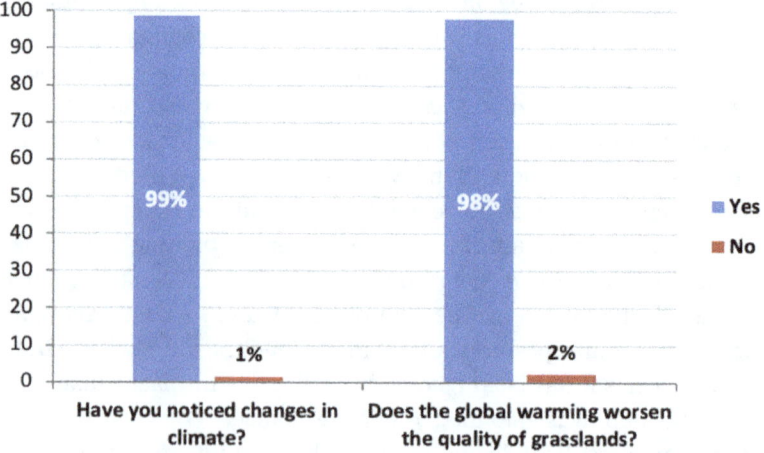

Figure 5: Climate change and the quality of grasslands.
Chart by author, Tsolmontuya Myagmarjav.

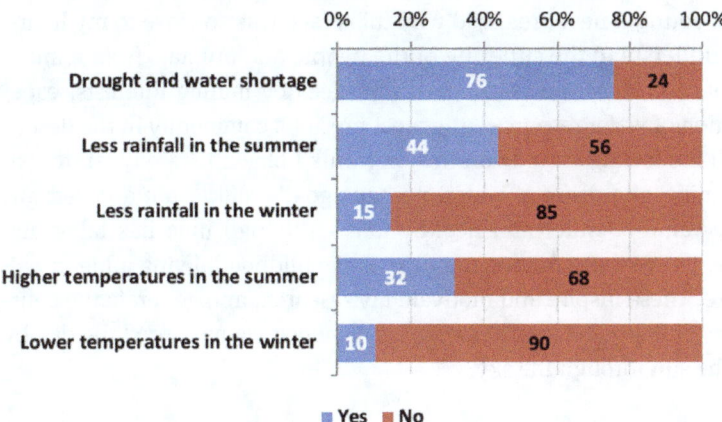

Figure 6: Consequences related to global warming noticed by Mongolian nomads. Chart by author, Tsolmontuya Myagmarjav.

they disintegrate. The nomads that I interviewed knew that I missed my homeland as much as they did. My heart broke as they described the devastation that initiated their migration. What was once the peaceful life of a sheepherder on the land of running streams and green plants, is now a subsistence on land overgrazed, covered with huge holes left by mines, with dried riverbeds, polluted water, and herds with black lung disease from mining dust, that also pose a health risk for humans. In the city, migrants face more problems. Without skills, work in the urban arena has been hard to find. With the intense increase in migrant moves, the urban infrastructure is deteriorating, and healthcare and educational facilities are overburdened. Although the majority of the migrants have chosen to keep their culture and traditions, some relocate from city apartments to the outskirts of the capital that allows space for their livestock. All of this has spurred resentment from longtime capital residents.

Herding was a way of life for one-third of all Mongolians, of symbolic importance to the whole country, but during the past few years, my desert home has become a Deathworld. Admittedly, the mining industry has played an important role in the economic growth of developing countries, but at a very high price, threatening the extinction of traditional Lifeworlds, and therefore, the existence of the nomadic pastoral cultures of my people. Where we played in the natural landscape of sand and grass is now contaminated with plastic and other trash, water has become polluted, and normally healthy people are contracting diseases. I see pieces of plastic wrapped around animals' necks, choking off their air, or pollution destroying the water supply for all living beings. More and more in modern times, we have lost respect for nature. Once damaged, it is hard to repair Earth.

When I was young, I never realized why this place was so close to my heart, or how much I understand the suffering of the people and animals from climate change, drought, and social and ecological injustices by mining interests, especially the depletion of water resources, the most precious commodity in the desert. I remember well the feeling of thirst on the long walk home after a day tending to the herds, dreaming of a drink of water, perhaps goat's milk. I am a desert girl who knows the value of water and healthy land. Although time has taken my childhood away, I have those fond memories of my childhood, living a life in balance with nature. These inspire and motivate my research, and generate the courage to restore my childhood desert home, to a time when we measured the day by the passing of the sun through the sky.

References

Burchard-Dzubińska, Małgorzata/Myagmarjav, Tsolmontuya (2019): "Traditional Pastoralism or Mining? Conflict of interest in access to Natural Pastures in Mongolia and the Problem of ecological and Environmental Justice". In: *Ekonomia I Środowiska* 4. No. 71, pp.56–68.

Myadar, Orhan (2009): "Nomads in a Fenced Land: Land Reform in Post-Socialist Mongolia". In: *Asian-Pacific Law & Policy Journal* 11. No. 1, pp.161–203.

Małgorzata Burchard-Dziubińska
Chapter 18
Deathworld Encroachments on the Amazon Rainforest

Abstract: Modern forms of exploitation of natural resources of Amazon have put an end to the traditional forms, so important for Indigenous tribes because of their material and cultural aspects. The first one responsible for the Indians' survival in a physical sense, the second responsible for the possibility to continue their own traditional lifestyle and preserve their spiritual and religious values. What is more, the predatory exploitation of the Amazon rainforest impedes its important function, which is protecting biodiversity, climate and the ecosystem at the global level. The chapter's focus is on looking for answers to two questions: "Is it possible to form a coalition of Indigenous peoples and defenders of the Amazon forest in order to fight for ecological justice perceived from a local and global perspective?"; and "Can such a coalition present a counterbalance to various legally and illegally operating entities focused on the ruthless exploitation of natural resources of the region, without paying attention to the costs borne directly by the Indigenous peoples and indirectly by the international community losing access to the public good of global significance?" It seems that ordinary human greed and short-term microeconomic goals continue to dominate over long-term benefits for the sake of all human beings.

Keywords: Indigenous people, Amazon, sustainable development, human rights

As a young girl, I greedily read books about distant lands, especially fascinated with descriptions of nature, wild animals, and mysterious cultural ways of the inhabitants. Once, in a book by Polish author Arkady Fiedler (Fiedler 1955, pp. 188–189), I came across a part that deeply touched me, concerning the development of various forms of oppression and violence in Amazonia during the 1930s, including slavery, which to some extent, has survived to this day. He said many people in all areas of the Amazon were professionally catching and selling Indians, often making use of, or inciting existing hatred between tribes. Fiedler wondered if the Peruvian government knew of these practices, yet assumed they turned a blind eye to it all. In addition, he said many civil servants were involved in the Indian slave trade, making it legally acceptable to kidnap children from tribes to be adopted by a *haciendado* or patron, and technically, made "part of the family" but forced to work for free and in the event of an escape, the "ungrateful son" was chased down by the authorities. If the patron wanted to give the child to someone else, he did so for a proper payment, although not called the sale price, it was received as reimbursement for the cost of raising the child and his education. Fiedler concluded, the buyer gained all the rights to the child from the patron and he could at any time sell the child again like an object or domesticated animal. Fiedler's description of slave trading among the Indigenous peoples of the Amazon has remained with me forever. Today, working as a scientist, I promote sustainable development, integrating social, natural, and economic issues. By sharing my work, I hope to make others aware of the social/ecological injustices done to these cultures, as the destruction of this unique Lifeworld and the Indigenous guardians of the Amazon carries drastic consequences for all of humanity.

Conducted between 2004 and 2018, my research included an analysis of literature, legal acts, statistical data, and interviews with the inhabitants of Brazil and Ecuador regarding the deteriorating situation in the Amazon region of South America. Modern exploitation of natural resources is not only destroying the ecological balance of the region, but also cultural/spiritual traditions so essential for Indigenous tribes who have inhabited Amazonia for thousands of years. Most important, predatory exploitation of the rainforest impedes its crucial function, protecting life worldwide – biodiversity, climate, and ecosystems. Human greed and short-term microeconomic goals continue to dominate over long-term benefits for all. The Amazon is now an area of struggle between the natural order of things and predatory modernity, between impending /coming Deathworlds and the survival of Lifeworlds. In this study, I focused on two questions. From a local and global perspective, is it possible to form a coalition of Indigenous peoples and defenders of the Amazon forest, to fight for socio/ecological justice? And, analyzing the costs borne directly by the Indigenous peoples and indirectly by the international community, can such a coalition present a counterbalance to various legally and illegally operating entities focused on the ruthless exploitation of natural resources in the region?

As the title suggests, the *border-between-two-worlds* outlines a theoretical demarcation line separating the ancient Lifeworld of the Indigenous peoples and the outside, represented by nation-states, and working through them, interest groups motivated by purely economic factors. Recently, a new group of stakeholders has emerged – the defenders of the Amazon – formed to recognize the rainforest's vital role in the sustainability of Earth's ecosystems. This region was first discovered for the Old World by the Spanish and Portuguese conquistadors in the 16th Century, but it wasn't until the 19th that the Amazon became the arena for a multi-faceted conflict of interest. Since then, the Indigenous inhabitants of the area have not only experienced the direct degradation of their environment through deforestation, but the indirect dehumanization of their political, economic, and socio-cultural structures, leading to the collapse of their communities. Nation-states and business interests do not show any concern for protecting the ecological integrity of rainforest infrastructure, endangering many species of plants and animals, including humanity and all life worldwide.

Like most Indigenous cultures, the Amazon people have sustained a symbiotic relationship with their rainforest for centuries before contact with European invaders. Reflecting an array of tribal, linguistic, and cultural diversity, this area of South America extends along the basin of the Amazon River for 2.7 million square miles; a tropical climate zone, the majority is rainforest jungle with some savannahs. Although their cultural makeup differs, Indigenous inhabitants developed knowledge and skills to sustain life in this extremely rich natural environment. Yet, the jungle can appear scary and hostile to outsiders. For European conquistadors, the forest caused a fear that influenced the way they treated the local population (less than human).

Whereas the Indigenous peoples utilized natural resources without endangering the sustainability of local ecosystems, nowadays, the Amazon rainforests are an arena of acute conflict, stemming from the greedy desire to exploit the region's riches – rubber, gold, oil, gas, wood, and land for arable agriculture (Barrionuevo 2008; Caffrey 2002). Contemporary stakeholders in the area are represented by three groups: (1) Indigenous peoples for whom the rainforest is home – about 400 ethnolinguistic groups inhabiting nine countries; (2) nation-states and investors representing big capital interested in intensive exploitation of natural resources; and (3) a new group, surfacing as a result of scientific research and recognition of the area's importance to the world, the international community for whom the protection of the rainforest is vital for survival and sustainability.

Realizing the different interests and intent of each stakeholder becomes important for shaping mutual relations between Indigenous peoples and the so-called national societies that formally exercise authority over the territory of each state. From the beginning, contact with Europeans had a deeply destructive influence on native populations. Diseases wiped out entire ethnic groups; the invaders' desire to get rich quickly prompted fear and hostility. With a technological advantage, Europeans introduced firearms, violence, slavery, and oppression, which also created disharmony between tribes. Most practices were often ignored by governments, and many survive to this day.

The first group of stakeholders, native Amazonians, do not believe they own the land, but that they belong to it, holding great economic and cultural importance because their livelihood depends upon hunting, fishing, and gathering.

These people declare the forest their pharmacy, market, university, factory, and warehouse for household appliances – hard for those who do not live here to understand (Garćia Hierro 2004). For Indigenous peoples, the use of land and its natural resources has always had two interrelated functions, material and cultural. The first one ensures survival, while the other offers the possibility of continuing their traditional lifestyle and preserving one's own spiritual and religious values (Krysińska-Kałużna 2012).

The second group of stakeholders consists of business representatives, often large international corporations, whose destructive march through Amazonia is indicative of an ever-new rush for resources. The first highly destructive activities related to the exploitation of rainforest riches took place in the middle of the 19th century, to acquire a rubber supply for the demands of industry, and a few decades later, of transportation. The growing fortunes of rubber barons during the boom years of 1897–1912 were accompanied by the increasing misery of the Indigenous populations and the clear-cutting of primeval forests for rubber tree plantations. That business collapsed as farm-bred trees were more susceptible to fungal disease, and rubber seeds were secretly being exported to Asia where competition grew. The Amazon gold rush began in the 1980s, initiating the building of overland roads, the hostile takeover of mineral-rich lands, and the massacre of Indigenous residents – a fight that frequently became brutal and bloody, leaving many issues unresolved today. Oil and natural gas are also coveted in the world economy. To seize land, companies conducted an illegal resettlement campaign of Indigenous peoples, clearing the way for settler-colonists to gain possession with mineral rights for free. Construction of roads and oil pipelines marked the beginning of accelerated deforestation. Creating Deathworld environments, large amounts of toxic waste from oil production poisoned the atmosphere, polluting the water and soil. Authorities moved the boundaries of national park preserves to displace Indigenous residents and militarized the region. Prostitution, alcoholism, venereal diseases, and violence began to spread. Considerable revenues from oil and production license fees were used by the government to build roads, subsidize cattle farms and plantations, and cause more large-scale degradation. Over the last decade, 30% of deforestation in Brazil has been performed by farmers seeking land for cultivation – including drug production and distribution influenced by the growth of the narcotics industry – for new plantations, airports, and infrastructure to support development (Rocha 1999; Capa NSC Total Política 2008).

The third stakeholder group recently formed as a result of scientific research and recognition of the area's importance to the world – the international community for whom the protection of the rainforest is vital for survival and sustainability. A reservoir of biodiversity, the wealth of Amazonia has not been fully researched or described as yet but has been recognized as a crucial element of the Earth's hydrological cycle, playing the key role in mitigating global warming by capturing and storing carbon dioxide produced during the burning of fossil fuels. An estimated 20% of the world's oxygen comes from the Amazon forests. Now human activities are negatively influencing the natural environment, depleting life-sustaining resources, degrading ecosystems, and impairing the planet's natural ability to absorb waste. Can the human impact on Earth's ecosystems be re-directed?

Perceiving the problem from different perspectives, the protection of the Amazon rainforests is of interest to various parties and is motivated by numerous factors. Indigenous peoples struggle to preserve their home, ways of knowing and learning that allowed a harmonious coexistence with nature and others. From the time of the conquest until the second half of the twentieth century, there were no effective institutional solutions to protect these people, their culture and the forest. In the 1970s, native peoples worldwide drew the attention of the United Nations (2007), leading to their *Declaration on the Rights of Indigenous Peoples*, a non-binding law that strengthens movements to respect of their territories, resources, and autonomy, requiring their consent for the implementation of investment projects. Progress enforcing the declaration remains slow, however, in the Amazon, the Belém Declaration (Krysińska-Kałużna 2012, p. 355–361) calls for: Official recognition by the governments of isolated Indigenous peoples, territories, and their right to live in isolation; assuming responsibility for their protection; immediate cessation or modification of all projects that may result in damage due to deforestation or colonization; acknowledging the supremacy and superiority of isolated Indigenous peoples by instituting national and international policies for the protection of biodiversity and the creation of natural protected areas. It's no surprise that hard-won international protection agreements do not give rise to the acceptance or practical implementation of such measures, especially those that require the instant cessation of destructive practices. Supporters of international cooperation face clear resistance from interest groups who seek short-term benefits without respecting the principles of sustainable development, ignoring international agreements regarding human rights and environmental issues.

Despite these limited efforts, the oppressive exploitation of the Amazon's natural resources and Indigenous peoples continues, with little attention paid to social, economic, and ecological consequences. Summarizing my study, I answer the two questions posed above. From a local and global perspective, it is possible to form a coalition of Indigenous peoples and defenders of the Amazon forest, to fight for ecological justice. Yet, analyzing the costs borne directly by the Indigenous peoples and indirectly by the all humanity, I cannot determine if a coalition between local communities and international community understanding the importance of Amazon forests, can present a counterbalance to various legally and illegally operating entities focused on the ruthless exploitation of natural resources in the region. What prevails is greed, striving for quick enrichment without paying attention to external social and ecological costs. A coalition is possible due to the convergence of interests among stakeholder groups, however, each of these groups perceives the problem of rainforest degradation from a different perspective. Indigenous peoples hope to protect their home and lifestyle. For the representatives of the international community, Amazonia is important for the whole of humanity, as a reservoir of biodiversity and an important factor stabilizing global climate and ecosystems. Outsiders who are involved in the protection of the Amazon region are usually willing to give Indigenous peoples these lands, so they can continue their traditional ways of life. However, this idea that could be attractive among nation-states to improve international relations, is demonstrably rejected as an attempt to interfere in internal affairs. Yet, for Indigenous groups wanting to remain isolated, a coalition with forest protectors presents no solution because of the preferred option – lack of contact. Only the outside world, the oppressors, can truly guarantee them the right to live in isolation by respecting their privacy. A moral dilemma arises from the need to assess whether refraining from interference in the affairs of these peoples is better than attempts to civilize them by force. Historically, Indigenous peoples – both those who established lasting contact with the outside world and those living in isolation – have no chance of survival in the event of a confrontation with big business circles going after profits.

In an assessment of the exploiters of wealth, the fulfilment of expectations of the Indigenous peoples and the defenders of the Amazon nature is not profitable. The interests of the Indigenous peoples and defenders of the Amazonia's nature, although different as to the reasons for taking protective measures, converge on the purpose. The rainforest and its ecosystem services perceived in this way, however, are not present in any market that would have priced them. The market valuation of wood, crops, gold, oil or gas originating from the Amazon does not take into account its absolutely unique natural values and significance they represent for the Indigenous cultures. Even if, using available techniques, we attempted to make such a valuation, the institutional solutions that apply here would not create any possibility to collect a fee for using and benefitting from the wealth the Amazon forest offers. A valuation of socio-cultural assets cannot be made in economic terms. The second group of stakeholders, the representatives of legal and illegal business interests alike, perceive of profit only in terms of money and ignore other forms of benefits. Although foreigners to the region, they have greater power over the other two stakeholder groups, limiting the possibility of collecting fees from them for reforestation and rehabilitation of the culture of Indigenous groups. The local communities experience the curse of the abundance of natural resources. The resource rent-seeking becomes a source of grievance not only because Indigenous peoples are excluded from the benefits of natural resource exploitation but because they lose their home and socio-cultural identity.

One of these foreigners to the region once remarked: "A man, walking into an Amazon forest, experiences only two pleasant days. The first, when he dazzles it with glamorous splendor and power, thinking he has just entered Paradise, and the last day, when he, half-insane, flees from the green hell back to civilization." It was like that in the past. Today, foreigners, strengthened with the achievements of technology, are boldly exploring new areas. Their presence can be seen from afar – thousands of fires started to clear the area from trees, paving the way for further exploitation. Today's Amazon world is described by Deathworlds: conflagration, exploitation, violence, social degradation. The Indigenous peoples of the Amazon have seen many outsiders come and go. Maybe it will happen again. The jungle has been and should remain, their home. They have been, and should always be, its guardians, not solely for self-subsistence, but for the good of all life on the planet.

References

Barrionuevo, Alexei (2008): "Whose Rain Forest Is This, Anyway?" NY Times, May 18, 2008. Retrieved from https://www.nytimes.com/2008/05/18/weekinreview/18barrionuevo.html, visited on July 15, 2019.

Caffrey, Paticia B. (2002): "An Independent Environmental and Social Assessment of the Camisea Gas Project". Retrieved from http://www.oxfamamerica.org/whatwedo/where_we_work/south_america/news_publications/pdfs/camisea_eng.pdf, visited on July 15, 2019.

Capa NSC Total Política (2008): "Todo Mundo Acha que Pode Meter dedo na Amazônia, diz Lula". Retrieved from www.nsctotal.com.br/noticias/todo-mundo-acha-que-pode-meter-dedo-na-amazonia-diz-lula, visited on April 5, 2018.

Fiedler, Arkady (1955): *The River of Singing Fish* (Ryby śpiewają w Ucayali [in Polish]). Warszawa: Państwowe Wydawnictwo Iskry.

García Hierro, Pedro (2004): "Territorios Indigenas: Tocando a las Puertas del Derecho". In: Surralés, Alexandre/García Hierro, Pedro (Eds.): *Tierra adentro. Territorio indigena y percepción del entorno*. Copenhagen: IWGIA, p. 277–306.

United Nations (2007): *Declaration on the Rights of Indigenous Peoples*, A/61/L.67. General Assembly resolution 61/295. Retrieved from https://www.un.org/esa/socdev/unpfii/documents/DRIPS_en.pdf, visited on October 11, 2020.

Krysińska-Kałużna, Magdalena (2012): Yamashta This One Who Almost Died (Yamashta czyli ten, Który Prawie Umarł [in Polish]). Oficyna Naukowa: Warszawa.

Rocha, Jan (1999): *Murder in the Rainforest. The Yanomami, the Gold Miners, and the Amazon*. London: Latin America Bureau.

Valerie C. Grossman
Chapter 19
Sustaining Lifeworlds in the Face of Famine, Water Shortages, and Malaria

Abstract: Phenomenological reflection prepared me to work with the Mizo people to prevent a historical cyclical famine known as Mautam. Further work through the network of connections facilitated the development of the nonprofit, Health Reach Canada, Inc. (HRC). One HRC project resulted in the provision of life-giving water access in Majuwa, Nepal, a leper village. This work led me to be in Tanzania at exactly the right place and moment to save my life, as I had suffered from undiagnosed malaria since the work in Mizoram. That experience not only changed my life but my Lifeworld context as Schütz presented it.

Keywords: Mautam, Mizoram, Tlawmngaihna, Lifeworld, phenomenological bracketing

Introduction

> The word Mizo means giving of self, or humility.
> – Tochhawng, personal communication to the author, January 15, 2020

How one brings the self to another culture, be that an organization, or country, can significantly impact how one works with others to attain desired collaborative inquiry outcomes. Collaborative inquiry is a process of working with others to understand issues and to mutually create positive outcomes. One may be thrown off balance by unintended events even though content preparation and expertise is skilled. Being open to local cultural clues and underpinnings allows collaboration and assistance to occur. Local knowledge is crucial and can lead to elegantly crafted positive results. No matter the subject matter or location, how one presents to a culture makes a difference to outcomes. The unprepared-for circumstance, when whatever is planned or addressed fails to materialize, is the subject of this discussion. My experience as I came to understand rat-induced famine in Mizoram brought this to light.

I share three narratives. The first is a collaborative inquiry research experience to prevent famine in Mizoram, India. The second is an experience helping a leper village in Nepal to access life-giving water. The third is my personal experience which began in India, March 2000 and finally ended positively in Tanzania, June 2007. All three address movement from the prospect and actuality of death to hope and an improved life.

Mautam

Introduction

Mautam is the Mizo word that describes a specific type of famine experienced in Mizoram, a state in North East India. "Mau" is Mizo for the type of bamboo which blooms only in Mizoram. "Tam" is Mizo meaning famine. The Mizo people use the word to describe both the phenomenon and the outcome. In the past, and even with the last Mautam, much suffering and some death occurred. This is the story of working with the Mizo people to help prevent Mautam.

Figure 1: Aizawl, Mizoram.
Photo by author, Valerie Grossman.

The Fielding MART (Mizoram Action Research Team)

I first entered Mizoram in 2000 as part of the Fielding Graduate University research team led by Dr. Valerie Bentz, Dr. Steve Figler, and Dr. Marie Farrell who went there at Mizoram Government request to assess the state's systems and to begin an Action Research Center. Dr. Laliana Mualchin, Bentz's friend and colleague, an esteemed Mizo leader and social activist living in California invited Bentz and the Fielding research group to Mizoram. Eighteen of us travelled to Mizoram and worked in small groups to assess all state systems including education, economic, agriculture, health, social, and government systems. We completed our work with a report and recommendations presented to the government. Due to unforeseen events, the Mizoram Action Research Center materialized but was unsustainable. As a result of the research, I became aware of Mautam, a life-threatening cyclical event (Figure 1).

The final Mizoram Action Research Team 2000 trip event was a celebration dinner and evening. Speeches of thanks and hope for future gains filled the talk. Then one Minister spoke. He noted the upcoming famine. I was taken aback that the State of Mizoram spent so much looking after us when they knew they faced a predicted famine. I wondered why that funding was not directed to famine prevention and preparation. I politely asked a few questions when the formalities concluded. The Minister's responses left me keenly aware I understood nothing. As a result, I queried if I might ask further questions at another time. Receiving the minister's positive response, I requested email contact information. That was how this project began.

Planning the Project

Over a period of two years I learned about the predicted sequence of bamboo blooming, rat outbreak and famine predicted to occur in 2007–2008. This became a four-year research project, including a strategic action plan and recommendations to prevent famine. It was followed by more research and a final outcome report following the 2007–2008 famine (which occurred as predicted). It included recommendations to prepare for the next *Melocana baccifera* bamboo blooming, rat outbreak, and famine predicted for 2057–2058.

Mizo elder narratives, strategies employed and the written report following the mitigated 2007–2008 famine are the only documented evidence of this cyclical event and its societal impact (Figure 2). A copy sits with the State of Mizoram Department of Agriculture to help guide them to prepare for the next event. Prior to 2007, mitigation strategies were not adhered to by 40% of the people (who did not believe the event would occur), therefore only 60% avoided famine. Next time, if the Mizo believe bamboo blooming and rat outbreak will occur, most if not all could avoid this negative outcome.

The State of Mizoram had an oral culture. Nothing was written. Mizo history and the story of recurring famine caused by a cyclical 48 to 50-year Melocana baccifera bamboo blooming and subsequent rat outbreak was only orally held. As the Mizo lifespan is 48 years on average and the previous outbreak occurred in 1959, there were few surviving healthy elders with memories of the last bamboo blooming and subsequent rat outbreak-induced famine. Younger Mizos heard stories, but most of the population did not believe what they heard. This fact made gaining entry to elders crucial.

Challenges to Self

Once in Mizoram, I met first with Chief Minister Zoramthanga. He assigned a Department of Agriculture person, James Lalsiamliana, to work with me. At my request, several Mizos who were part of the first systems research team formed a group.

I also invited John Bourne, a rodent specialist from Canada. We quickly learned strategies applied in Canada were not applicable in Mizoram. Those strategies would only exacerbate the Mizo rodent outbreak. In isolated conditions, applying rodenticide can be successful; however, in the conditions Mizoram faced, the technique would only enhance the rat population increases. Partial elimination rather than eradication opens space for exponential growth.

We worked collaboratively to learn what occurred in 1959 and prior. However, to really understand, I would require access to elders who had lived through the event. Though it seemed easy to accomplish, it became clear that gaining this access was an issue.

I learned things are done differently in Mizoram, and my conception of reality was not shared by Mizos. Outsiders are not welcome. They are seen as a threat. Historically, in relationship with India, this was the case and is still the case today, though less obviously so. This meant I required time to understand differently in order to gain a modicum of acceptance.

I realized I had to let go of preconceived ideas. The following experience clarified the crucial importance of suspending expectations concerning what I thought should occur.

Challenges of Alternative Realities

This particular week had been difficult. Meetings were cancelled. I was stuck in traffic jams. Nothing seemed to work. Needing a positive indicator, I hoped to be invited to church. Not being active in the Church separates one from the culture. Though the Mizos informed me they were animists until the arrival of missionaries in the 1890s, Christians currently comprise approximately 94% of the population. Mizo society is held together by the church, and Church membership means cultural acceptance.

A core Mizo Church rule is that no one must go without food or a roof over their head. Known as Tlawmngaihna, it is the cultural practice of selflessly looking after others coupled with the binding force of religion. Though the community is educated, there are few new jobs. This leads to feelings of worthlessness, substance abuse, and negative outcomes. Orphanages, homelessness, and substance abuse (though alcohol is illegal in the state) are increasingly common. In part due to this, the Church has become more important over time. Recognizing this importance, I had placed great significance on receiving an invitation to church. No invitation came.

Context in a culture is commensurate with what Schütz and Luckmann (1973) term the Lifeworld, or all that is meaningful in one's conscious acts. Understanding of our world is based in our stock of experience, the accumulation of learning to that point, which over time is internalized. Our stock of experience is transmitted socially, and this interaction between meaning and environment constitutes what Schütz termed the Lifeworld (Schütz/Luckmann 1973, pp. 8–11). I had no understanding of the Mizo Lifeworld. I needed to do nothing and wait.

I spent the weekend alone at Government House keenly aware I failed to understand the Lifeworld I entered. I wondered if I had said or done something to offend a group member. I decided to wait to see what would happen next, if anything. "The life-world . . . is the arena as well as what sets the limits of my and our reciprocal action . . . I must understand my life-world in order to be able to act in it" (Schütz/Luckmann 1973, p.6). I also decided to ask no questions. Either the inquiry would continue or not.

Following my solitary weekend, James, my Agriculture Department colleague, spent Monday with me looking at the countryside to help me understand how the people manage to successfully grow mixed crops, including dry rice, on the sides of steep mountains. This was important information as this cyclical famine occurs when entire crops are destroyed overnight, causing famine. Upon our return, I still had heard nothing from my Mizo colleagues. Again, I resolved to set aside expectations.

On Tuesday, the group met. We went about our work. We stopped for tea and chatted. Still, there was no mention regarding church or the previous weekend. The meeting concluded; as we walked out, I learned of a parent's illness and need to travel to the village making it impossible to invite me to church. This next Sunday, my Mizo colleagues informed me, we would go to church.

Not only was I invited to church, I was also given private information. Having learned a little regarding Mizo cultural norms, I realized I was becoming an inside-outsider (Grossman 2004).

An inside-outsider is a researcher or person who comes from the outside, but who is able to let go of prior cultural understandings to enter the world of those with whom the research is being done. This allows the researcher to move closer to a point of understanding what those with the issue experience (Grossman 2004, p.63). Cultural understandings, the internalized norms and values learned from one's society, often go unnoticed until one is in another culture, another

Figure 2: Valerie and Elders.
Photo by author, Valerie Grossman.

environment, another Lifeworld. The ability to discern the difference between my Lifeworld and the one entered was crucial; elements of social research do not always go as planned.

Had the information and the invitation not been forthcoming, the research may have ended. I was not yet enough of an inside-outsider to gain the needed access to elders and their knowledge of the 1959 event, but this turn of events gave me hope. My being there was with purpose. The month-long trip concluded. Though it took another year of email with group members and another month-long trip to finally be invited to meet and speak with revered elders, I had gained knowledge of the culture and some acceptance.

"Bracketing" Expectations

The foregoing story illustrates the importance of letting go of, or *bracketing*, one's expectations to allow a different understanding of others. It is only when one sets aside thought to examine feeling that different meaning can be constructed. "it is only after I 'bracket' the natural world and attend only to my conscious experiences . . . that I become aware of this process of constitution" (Schütz 1967, p. 37). Setting aside, or bracketing, previous understanding allows new understanding to develop. At these times "I no longer have before me a complete and constituted world but one which only now is being constituted and which is ever being constituted . . . an emerging world" (Schütz 1967, p. 36). I experienced this repeatedly.

Bracketing was crucial to collaborative inquiry success. Following initial discomfort, the sooner one moves to bracket or set aside expectations, the faster one can open space to understand in a new or differently constituted way. Failing to bracket expectations results in an inability to understand experiences. Not bracketing my expectations would have given my Mizo colleagues reason to end the inquiry.

The Mizos acted as usual in their typical way and their "life-world confronted me in their typical character" (Schütz/Luckmann 1973, p.7). Presentation of anything typical configured or seen as a norm is understood as a *typification* in Schützian terminology. I was unable to understand how the typifications I was presented constituted in Mizo stock of knowledge. Later, I understood I was outside the Mizo Lifeworld and societal meaning.

Taking notice of the difference between one's own norms and values versus those of another culture creates awareness and the opportunity to achieve a new understanding. To let go of, or bracket, preconceived understanding, one must become aware of that understanding.

According to Schütz, a "we-relationship," is a condition where "I can always (again and again) find confirmation that my experiences of the life-world are congruent with your experiences of it" (Schütz/Luckmann 1973, p. 85). Such understanding is necessary to apprehend difference and to bracket ones thinking and feeling to allow for increased understanding. To be aware of another's Lifeworld, apprehension of what is important to that person must be developed.

From outset of the inquiry, I was forced to become aware of the Mizo Lifeworld and culture difference. I came to learn what was important to me was not always a priority to those I came to work with. Other emergent events and responsibilities took precedence. It took time for me to not only understand Lifeworld difference but to be able to bracket my thinking and hopes. Retaining cultural norms and paradigms from one's own culture can not only get in the way of research inquiry but end it.

Mautam occurred as predicted in 2007 and 2008. With the goal of avoiding the suffering, starvation, and death seen in the 1958–1959 Mau bamboo blooming, rat outbreak, and famine, the Mizoram Government supported four years of famine prevention research. It appointed the Department of Agriculture, James Lalsiamliana, to work with me and a Mizo team. The aim was to oversee, educate, and assist the Mizo in instituting strategies to prevent the predicted 2007–2008 blooming and rat outbreak from resulting in famine.

A vision, strategies, and actions were developed. The vision was no starvation as a result of famine because rodents are under control meaning no outbreak populations, jhum (fields) are diversified and not paddy (rice) based, people are prepared and equipped, infrastructure is improved, and Government policy is flexible.

Several recommendations were made. Traditional pesticide methodology applied in the Mizo environment would have opened space for even larger populations than if no pesticides were used. Therefore, it was determined that fields should be left fallow just prior to blooming and all food stored safely. This would prevent rats from eating when forest supplies had been depleted, causing the rats to die off with minimal impact on human food sources.

As a result of the research, in 2005 BAFFACOS, the Government of Mizoram comprehensive Action Plan for Bamboo Flowering and Famine Combat Schemes was instituted by the Chief Minister. People were called together to prepare a comprehensive plan so the people would not suffer. The implementing and overseeing agency was the State Planning Board of Mizoram. However, planning and follow-through did not meet peoples' expectations. Several issues resulted in unsuccessful implementation.

Under James' leadership, The Department of Agriculture mobilized human resources from farmers and NGOs. Seminars, workshops, training, and awareness campaigns were held. However, contrary to our advice, the Government continued a traditional program of paying bounties for rat tails, which affected the population as pesticides would, opening space for exponential growth.

Additionally, monies allocated to Mizoram for famine prevention by the Central Indian Government were not used as intended. Originally allocated to five departments, funds for needed items such as safe food storage containers and large storage facilities (go-downs) was spread to 15 departments by the Government of Mizoram and used to buy other things. The Central government provided a large sum of money for debt relief measures and related agriculture activities for farmers and others which did not benefit intended recipients. Projects undertaken were not focused on farmers and villagers and did not help the people. Reports indicate poor planning and mismanagement of funds.

This inconsistent application resulted in inconsistent outcomes. Mizoram population in 2007 at Mautam was just under one million. 40% of the population, approximately 400,000, experienced their crops being eaten overnight, or their improperly stored food disappearing, and not having access to money or food. Many died. No exact numbers were ever publicly provided. 60%, approximately 600,000, avoided famine. They were those who did not plant because they believed Mautam would occur or were skeptical enough as the result of programs and information provided.

These inconsistencies are understood as general disbelief in the actuality of a famine. Mizos thought it was a myth. Only oral stories of Mautam were passed down.

As I undertook the famine prevention in Mizoram, I met others not connected to that work. Several became friends and then colleagues. I was approached for assistance including water provision, and orphan needs. I met people from Nepal who wanted help there and an American who wanted me to go to Tanzania. It took until 2005 to realize I could not help on the scale required without establishing a helping organization.[1] Health Reach Canada Inc., a 100% volunteer non-profit organization registered in Canada and the USA, was born. The organization resulted as an outcome of the research process. It continues to help create positive change with not one failure to date. The success is attributed to the philosophy and methodology employed as a direct outcome of the Mizoram collaborative inquiry.

---

[1] All expenses are covered by the Board of Directors; 100% of all donations go to help. For more information, please visit Health Reach Canada on Facebook or www.healthreachcanadainc.org, visited on October 12, 2020.

In 2009, while I was CEO of Health Reach Canada Inc., the Mizoram Government invited me back to Mizoram. I presented the Chief Minister with Elder Narratives and recommendations resulting from the research and from outcomes experienced through Mautam to help prevent the next predicted event in 2057–2058. The documents are housed at the Department of Agriculture in the hope they will be employed to prevent another famine.

The following narrative is one of many water-provision projects we undertook as the result of meeting different people while I worked in Mizoram to prevent famine. It is a story that begins with the meeting of a woman in Mizoram. Years later, I was contacted by this same woman asking for help to provide water at a desperate village in Nepal. The people there were barely surviving.

Majuwa

Introduction

Majuwa, Nepal is a leper village of approximately 1200 located close to Pokhara, the second-largest city in Nepal after Kathmandu. A family member must have leprosy to live there. Water was always an issue in Majuwa, but now it was extremely scarce.

I became connected to Majuwa through a Mizo government worker; Vuli Khiangte helped me navigate the Mizo government system to access people regarding Mautam, to make applications, and to meet those who could assist outside the research group itself.

Several times when at Vuli's office another woman came to work there on another computer. The woman's name was Vanthanpuii[2] or Vani. Following the initial introduction, no conversation occurred any time I saw this woman. We only nodded to acknowledge each other. As with Mautam prevention, I recognized it was not culturally appropriate to initiate conversation or to ask questions. Her reason for being there was not shared. I decided if I was to know this person it would occur at some point. I bracketed my curiosity.

Following the Mautam inquiry, the Mizo government requested provision of water purification training and bio-sand water filter training to Mizoram Public Health and Environment (PH&E) Department staff. Health Reach Canada Inc. partnered with the Center for Affordable Water and Sanitation Technology (CAWST) to provide the government with requested training.

---

2 Many Mizo have one name and are referred to by part of it.

A Problem

Approximately a year following our last face to face interaction I received an email from Vani, a Mizo woman who had married and raised a family in Nepal. She was in Majuwa. The people there were very poor. The biggest need was access to water. Could we help?

I learned Majuwa relied on the Government of Nepal for water. The only water access was located in a ditch just outside the village. Water to the only pipe was turned on three times a week. No one knew when the water would come on or for how long. There was no schedule.

Every day, children and elders stood by the water pipe waiting for water to come out of the pipe. Elders could do nothing to assist their families. Children did not go to school. The village was held captive by the water pipe (Figure 3).

Figure 3: Waiting for water.
Photo by author, Valerie Grossman.

Every family needed to decide how to use their water when it was collected. It would be used to drink and cook, seldom clean the house, wash bodies, or wash clothes. Many were sick with ailments other than leprosy. No one knew why. They just were. Many died.

There was one nurse, Danmit, in town. She spent her own money to buy dressings and disinfectant to dress the wounds leprosy caused. She had a small room apart from her house where she treated those with wounds. Her husband's mother had leprosy and that was the reason they lived in Majuwa.

Resolution

Approximately a year later I travelled to Nepal. I first went to Kathmandu where Vani met me. We stayed there for two days so I could acclimatize. Then we took a full day bus ride to Pokhara and then continued to Majuwa. The Sharmas provided accommodation in their home.

The next morning, I was woken early. Everyone was excited and waiting to meet me. I went with Vani and Suman Sharma to meet the villagers outside their homes. The new piping provided now went into each family's yard where there was a pipe with a tap. Villagers left a container under the pipe to catch the water each time the water was turned on.

I learned a lot about how the people lived. I also learned while part of the water issue was solved it was still an issue. People still had to wait for water. It didn't take long to understand the water storage need.

Once back at Sharma's house, Vani, Suman and I discussed what we saw and what we thought was still required. Suman took responsibility to locate and purchase one 1000 litre water storage tank for each house. Luckily, I had enough funding and I was there for five days, long enough to see the tanks delivered and to see some installed.

As scheduled, the tanks arrived. The entire village gathered in an open area where they were taken off the trucks. One by one, the women from each house came to collect their tank. The custom is the women do the hard labor. They are the ones who either carried or rolled their tanks to their homes. We saw tanks everywhere. Most already hooked up to the piping. Everyone greeted us with smiles and thanks.

Suman informed me village culture changed. I said I did not understand and requested he explain. Everything was different, he said. Elders and children no longer stood by the pipe waiting for water. Elders helped with chores and visited each other's homes. All the children went to school. Drinking water, cooking water, cleaning, and washing water was available. No choices needed making. Everyone was clean, fed, and much happier. Fewer people were sick and villagers would have access to water all the time (Figure 4).

Figure 4: Taking tank home.
Photo by author, Valerie Grossman.

Celebration

Later that day Suman came to say the village wanted to thank me at a meeting precisely scheduled at 7:00 am before my departure later the next morning. I said it was not important and I was sure villagers had much to do. He said it was important to the village and I must go.

The next morning a knock on my door reminded me it was time. I headed out to the village meeting spot. I was surprised as I was greeted by the entire village. Vani translated as villagers spoke and I was laden with flower leis they had made. The head of the village council spoke last to thank me and Health Reach Canada Inc. on behalf of the village. Finally, it was time for juice and cookies. This was a very big gesture as juice and cookies are very expensive. An act such as that is not done often or maybe ever in that village. I was overtaken with emotion at how the small changes we helped make possible changed Majuwa village life.

Chapter 19 Sustaining Lifeworlds — 309

Figure 5: Village women- Vani standing 2nd from right.
Photo by author, Valerie Grossman.

This collaborative inquiry not only worked but was sustained over time. It changed people's lives from barely surviving, to living without constant concern over water access. It was necessary that someone go there to understand what the villagers experienced every day. It required putting personal judgment aside, bracketing personal and cultural paradigms, to learn what they wanted and how they wanted it (Figure 5).

The village wanted water piping. They were invested in learning what to do and how, which made the project not only possible, but viable. Villagers wanted water piping and invested their time and physical labor to make it a sustainable reality. They wanted water access which inadvertently changed their reality and village culture.

Years prior, during, and following the Majuwa water piping and storage tank provision I experienced feeling unwell. The illness was like a flu that came and went. It seemed to occur most often when I overworked or became overtired. It occurred over and over from the time I first travelled to Mizoram. The medical community tested me in various ways over time and determined nothing was wrong. The following narrative shares my lengthy experience with malaria.

Malaria

Introduction

I went to Mizoram, NE India the first time in March 2000 to participate in the systems research recounted earlier. The first afternoon there, I stood outside the government guest house with several others enjoying the conversation and the air. The weather was relatively warm. I wore a three-quarter sleeve and noted getting bitten on my right forearm but thought nothing of it. I knew about mosquitos but was not consciously aware of what one bite could do. My reality was a Western one.

Aftermath

Three weeks later I felt fluish over the weekend and mostly rested. Monday, I felt better and carried on with the systems work I committed to.

I took antimalarials as prescribed prior to travel, through the time in Mizoram and following my return to Canada. I continued my busy life. I worked full time, studied, took care of my family, and watched over my elderly mother. I became ill when over-tired or over-worked. Still, I thought nothing of it. I dealt with what I thought was the flu over and over.

My husband was concerned each time I endured another episode, but I noted there was nothing I could do. Doctor visits, blood work, and even a brain scan showed no problems. The medical community said there was nothing wrong with me.

I got sick more often than previously and surmised it must be age-related. My husband disagreed. Seven years went by. I worked hard. When one commitment dropped off, I added another. I still got sick (Figure 6 and Figure 7).

Another Episode

In June 2007, I went back to Tanzania where Health Reach Canada Inc. rebuilt an orphanage, provided water access, supported Safe Motherhood Mobile Clinics, and looked to help a hospital feed its patients via the provision of water to hospital land. It was the year we were also asked to help support promising but destitute medical students who were being forced out of medical school at Hubert Kairuki Memorial University. They were unable to pay tuition and the university could not carry them. I arrived in Dar es Salaam on a Wednesday feeling very tired from what I thought was the 34 hours it took to get there. I rested Thursday and began planned activity Friday.

I was close to the family where I stayed each time I went to Tanzania. By 2007, they felt more like close relatives than hosts. Happy held down a significant job one rung down from the head at the Small Industry Development Organization. Her husband, Guard, was the Director at Mission Mikocheni Hospital, recently renamed Kairuki Hospital, the hospital with which Health Reach Canada Inc. worked. Their two children also became close and called me Auntie. I always went with gifts for everyone and still do.

Saturday is errand and shopping day in Tanzania. Happy wanted to buy sheets before going to buy food at the different markets. Markets are outdoor open areas where vendors bring goods. Traditional food shopping requires going from one market to another depending on the food wanted. Fruit and vegetable markets are different than a chicken or fish market. Red meat must be purchased from a butcher. Decisions regarding the route followed needed making before we left.

We stood in the kitchen chatting. Then Happy nonchalantly noted she had a headache, was achy, and felt a bit nauseated. She thought she had malaria. When she said that, I noted I felt the same, but it was not malaria. No matter how well I could understand others, malaria was not anything I could understand. Malaria was not in my cultural paradigm. I just travelled a long distance and experienced the effects of an 11-hour time change. Besides, I said I felt like that every time I travelled since 2000. Happy noted I could feel tired from travelling but the rest of it sounded like malaria. We would both go to the hospital after we did the shopping and we would both get tested. Even though I resisted and explained my symptoms away, Happy was adamant.

We went straight to the laboratory. The personnel there knew we were coming as Guard notified them in advance. They took us separately to the laboratory and drew blood.

Results

Tanzania practice is to test for malaria and have people wait for the half-hour it takes to get the results. Treatment begins right away.

It was a warm breezy day and very pleasant as we waited outside. I was sure I didn't have malaria. Happy thought she did. She's had it many times, so she was quite sure.

Half an hour later we returned inside and waited. Happy was called first. She went to her husband Guard's office. She had malaria just as she thought.

Next, it was my turn. I went to the office. I also had malaria. My malaria was worse than Happy's. I was shocked.

Sunday is a rest day, a church day, and a day to visit friends and relatives. We went to church. Then we rested.

Monday is a workday. Mama Kairuki, head of the Kairuki Health and Education Network, and the charging force behind the hospital and Hubert Kairuki Memorial University decided I must rest. Following lunch, she sent a car so we could go to the beach. We lay under the umbrellas and rested.

Figures 6, 7: Malaria.
Photos by author, Valerie Grossman.

A week later Happy and I went back to the hospital for retesting. It is usual practice to test following a round of malaria therapy to make sure it worked. Happy was clear; her malaria was gone. I was not so lucky; my malaria was worse.

Standing in Guard's office I could not believe what I heard. He told me my malaria was not good. I informed him I felt much better and whatever I had was gone. I thought he was joking. He told me to sit down and said it was not gone; it was just dormant for the moment. When I got overtired or stressed it would return. The more tired or stressed the worse it would be. It was entrenched in my system, as I had had it for some time.

Guard knew I experienced the same flu-like symptoms repeatedly since March 2000. I finally understood the severity of the situation; my paradigm changed. I was in the culture, part of the culture, not looking at it as closely as possible. I understood what Tanzanians live with. Malaria is part of the cultural reality. At that moment I was no longer *muzungo*, a foreigner, but part of the culture.

I had to make a choice. Did I want to try other pills, or did I want daily injections? I opted for injections. Injections meant I went to the hospital every day for five days just like the locals who had severe malaria. I was injected in the rear and told to go home to rest and instructed to drink at least three liters of water each day to help wash out the parasites. I intimately understood one aspect of Tanzanian culture and on that level, I was no longer an inside-outsider; I became an insider with a Schützian we-relation to all those who suffered the effects of malaria.

Outcomes

Happy and Guard worked, and the children were at school while I lay alone every day. Several days the power went out so that meant no electricity for light or to pump water for a shower and my computer could not be used. I could only rest and listen to music until the power on my phone died. The power usually came back the same time someone in the family arrived home.

Lying there that week I imagined dying. It was not a farfetched thought. I had malaria and I was on the second treatment in two weeks. Death was a possibility.

I cried when alone and thought about that very real possible outcome. I thought about not being able to tell my husband, children, and mother how much I loved them and how much they meant to me. How would they ever forgive me for travelling to the developing world? How would they get my body back? I didn't want to die. I was too young and had too much to do. I drank and drank and rested and rested and tried to think positively. I would beat this; I was strong.

A week later it was time to learn the outcome. I went back to the hospital yet again. I went straight to the laboratory for another blood test. Half an hour later, I went back into the hospital and sat in front of Guard's office. I trembled. My life sat in the outcome of this test. Guard's nurse ushered me into his office and closed the door on her way out. Though he offered me a seat, I could not sit down. "You are at zero. It is good news. You do not have malaria." I said, "Thank you. I'll let you get back to work. See you at home." I turned and left. My insides churned. I knew I needed to settle, but how?

If I was lucky, later I could call home and tell my family what happened. Since I did not want to worry them, I decided two weeks earlier not to inform them until it was all over. I was lucky on all fronts.

Two of four weeks in Tanzania were wasted taking medication and not doing what I travelled around the world to accomplish. Mama Kairuki and I got to work. We managed to make things happen and overall the trip was more highly successful than hoped. I was treated and recovered from seven years of malaria in addition to the work I went to address.

Conclusion

Once home I made an appointment with my family physician. I told her of my experience and how I was treated. I wanted it on my record.

She was devastated and wondered out loud how she missed it noting she did every possible test but the single one required. Canadian medical thinking regarding malaria, where cases are rare and always brought from elsewhere, was that taking an antimalarial always prevented or killed malaria parasites. There was no need for malaria testing following a round of antimalarials. The Canadian medical community, unlike the Tanzanian medical community, was not aware of virulent malaria parasites not killed off by antimalarials, not versed in malaria detection, and had little in the way of treatment. Even now in Canada, twenty years after the bite and thirteen after treatment, there is little more in the way of knowledge, detection, or treatment methods.

I count myself fortunate on several fronts. I went to Tanzania. I lived with a family who knew what to do. I opened my mouth at the right moment, and I was treated exactly as needed like an insider. That made it possible to live to tell this story.

Summary Conclusion

The foregoing three stories illustrate my experience addressing death possibilities and outcomes to help move them to life outcomes. Mizoram, India, famine prevention presented unexpectedly and provided serious opportunity to assist in preventing famine and death on a large scale. As described, strategies were successful to a point but were not one hundred percent successful due to people's disbelief in the event. The 2007–2008 famine prevention outcomes following Mautam and strategies for the next predicted bamboo cycle blooming and predicted famine were provided to the government of Mizoram Department of Agriculture to assist them to prevent a famine following the next Melocana baccifera blooming predicted in 2057–2058. There is a strong possibility that prevention strategies could be 100% effective if the entire population complies. Then no one will suffer the effects of famine. Majuwa, Nepal, water piping and storage became a fact as the result of a woman who literally hung around in Mizoram. The leper village barely survived with little water access. Many did expire, not only as the result of leprosy but due to water shortage. Piped water to all village homes and provision of water storage tanks provided water access. The outcome made it possible for the village to move from living at the edge of death to living without worry regarding when the water pipe would provide water. Reliable water provision made it possible for villagers to live their lives more fully. My malaria experience caused me to face prospective death as those we assisted did. It was as close in life as I have come to understanding others as they understand themselves. I understood deeply. That experience helped me understand the crucial nature of letting go of assumptions regarding any issue one is asked to help with. That is the underlying difference that makes collaborative inquiry what it is. It helped in a way no other process can. Dire death facing circumstances changed to life-giving situations.

References

Grossman, Valerie (2004): *Preventing Mautam: Participatory Action Research and Phenomenology at work to avoid rat induced famine in Mizoram, India*. Ann Arbor: ProQuest.
Schütz, Alfred (1967): *The Phenomenology of the Social World*. (G. Walsh/F. Lehnert, Trans.). Chicago: Northwestern University Press.
Schütz, Afred/Luckmann, Thomas (1973): *The Structures of the Life-World* (R.M. Zaner/ H.T. Engelhardt Jr., Trans.). Evanston: Northwestern University Press.

Part V: **Transformative Phenomenology Practice**

> I attempt to lead, not to instruct, and only to point out, to describe, what I see. I make no other claim than that of speaking according to my own best knowledge and conscience, first and foremost before myself but in the same manner also before others, as someone who has lived through the fate of a philosophical existence [Dasein] in all its seriousness.
>
> —Edmund Husserl in "The Crisis"

Valerie Malhotra Bentz, David Rehorick, James Marlatt,
Ayumi Nishii, and Carol Estrada

Chapter 20
Transformative Phenomenology as an Antidote to Technological Deathworlds

Abstract: The concept of Lifeworld as posited by Husserl and developed by Schutz reveals key aspects of human social life. What happens when organized forces of human control tear Lifeworlds apart? Gebser warned that without a transformation of consciousness humans would destroy their world. Habermas pointed out that humans were destroying Lifeworlds with little awareness of the consequences due to the predominance of rational/legal thinking, thus creating "Deathworlds." Transformative Phenomenology has become a community-of-practice that is an antidote to Deathworld-Making. Transformative phenomenology includes hermeneutics, somatics and leregogic practices and phenomenologists trained in this way exhibit ten qualities of being. We offer the Rising Sun project, a phenomenologically based social innovation, as a case example. The call to maintain and restore Lifeworlds is the call to oneness and peace. In the era of growing Deathworlds, we, phenomenologists, are urged to respond and contribute to this call.[1]

Keywords: consciousness, Lifeworlds, Deathworlds, somatics, transformative phenomenology

Part I: From Lifeworlds to Deathworlds

> The eternal, the infinite, the omnipresent, the omniscient is a principle, not a person. You, and I, and everyone are but embodiments of that principle, and the more of this infinite principle is embodied in a person, the greater is he (she) and all in the end will be the perfect embodiment of that and thus all will be one as they are now essentially. This is all there is of religion, and the practice is through this feeling of oneness that is love.
>
> (Vivekananda 2018)

"Whirling death machines need to be stopped . . . Stop funding these gigantic whirling death machines!" exclaimed Chelsea Manning (2018), American activist, whistleblower, and politician, speaking of the military, prison systems, and colonized communities in the U.S. and elsewhere. Following in Schutz' footsteps

---

[1] This chapter was first published in Schutzian Research 10, pp. 189–220.

https://doi.org/10.1515/9783110691818-020

but extending Lifeworld to include the other life forms, Bentz and Shapiro define Lifeworld as:

> The lived experiences of human beings and other living creatures as formed into more or less coherent grounds for their existence. This consists of the whole system of interactions with others and objects in an environment that is fused with meaning and language and that sustains the life of all creatures from birth through death. It is the fundamental ground of all experience for human beings. (Bentz/Shapiro 1998)

The late Husserl (1954/1970), in the *Crisis of the European Sciences and Transcendental Phenomenology*, posited the "Lifeworld as the fundamental ground for all human action" (p. 103F). Schutz had begun exploring this concept before he was aware of Husserl's work on Lifeworlds, which Schutz felt Husserl had left unfinished. The Lifeworld to Schutz was independent of all concepts in the social sciences, including "system" and "culture."

Schutz delineated the elements of "Lifeworlds," which mostly are taken for granted as humans pursue their tasks. Ironically, humans in pursuit of tasks have developed organizations that have led to the destruction of Lifeworlds along with the myriad of other creatures, both plants and animals. It would take a much longer treatment to encompass all the structures of the Lifeworld as detailed by Schutz in this paper. However, we will highlight just a few here, which seem most pertinent to our argument that post-modern society is Deathworld oriented.

Schutz' work highlights the unique position of each person in every Lifeworld to realize the importance of their position and to fully participate (Barber 2004). In this way Schutz implicitly calls upon us all to preserve and improve Lifeworlds upon which we depend (Barber 2005). Lifeworlds to varying degrees allow for and support emancipatory "provinces of meaning," (Barber 2014) such as the arts religion and humor (Barber 2017a). However, may not these activities, significant for mental and social well-being, also passively allow or even facilitate the continued expansion of Deathworlds, as in "fiddling while Rome burns?"

A taken for granted assumption of the Lifeworld is that humans are "free actors" living in the social world as "free beings" (Schutz cited in Wagner 1975). "The mind by its fantasizing acts creates in succession in inner time the various projects, dropping one in favor of the other and returning to, or more precisely, -re-creating, the first" (Schutz cited in Wagner 1975, p. 159). The actions of persons are carried out within a system of plans and projects of a higher order already existing. Schutz' Lifeworld includes "imposed relevances" which we are born into such as family, social class, physical condition, gender, and later job, economic, etc. constraints and conditions (Schutz cited in Wagner 1975, p. 321).

With the increased colonization of the Lifeworld (Habermas 1979) there is doubt as to who is making the choice or whether a person can be free. When one's mind is always activated via Internet, iPhone, text messages, or television, how free are such supposed choices? How developed is the higher-level processes of logic, or in Vedantic thinking, the I, behind the I, that may make choices?

A Google design ethicist blogs about ways in which the structure of events online lead one's decisions and thoughts (Harris 2016). Casacuberta (2016) analyzes the way the design of computer interfaces lead to a disembodied way of being. He presents an alternative to such "affordances" which would be designed to address the needs of humans as living beings instead of as mental machines. This relates to the developing field of neurophenomenology.

Along similar lines, the relevances, which are apparent to the actors in any Lifeworld are predetermined and skewed by the nature of the cultural milieu. Habermas (1989) outlines processes of the colonization of the Lifeworld, which give predominance to systems of oppression and domination – Deathworlds. This has been amplified further by Oliver (2004) and explored in *The Colonization of Psychic Space: A Psychoanalytic Social Theory of Oppression*. Technocratic thinking becomes an ideology that overcomes the practical interests of living beings in the interest of increased expansion of technical control and power according to Oliver. This power and control has come to supersede Lifeworlds, which constitute meaning for citizens and communities.

To Schutz, death was a phenomenon within the Lifeworld (Schutz 1975, pp. 173–174). One of the features of the Lifeworld is the "taken for granted" concept that the world will continue on as it is and our daily life will go on as before. Yet, humans face the fundamental anxiety that our lives will end and our capacities to continue actions and activities as in the past will diminish. Today humans are faced with a much greater anxiety – that of the death of all life on the planet. Over the ensuing decades since Schutz died, more than half of the species on earth face extinction by the end of the century due to the pursuit of greater control of the planet by technoeconomic forces (McKie 2017).

The concept of "World" underlies the concept of Lifeworld. As Donn Welton said, "The world in which we live and with which we are most familiar, day in and day out, is not the one projected by scientific thought" (1997, pp. 736–743). Various sciences took on segments of the world allowing them to produce material effects and gain greater control over the forces of nature. However, only in recent times have some scientists begun to look at the overall effects on the ecological system as a whole. Modern science "yields ever greater mastery over things of nature, which results in science losing any recognizable bond to the Lifeworld" (Welton 1997, p. 738).

With the decoupling of systems and Lifeworld (Habermas 1989, p. 153) the increasing destruction of living environments for humans and other creatures, the continued loss of species diversity, the planet is facing increased "Deathworlds" or social economic political systems which produce death and zones of death on the planet that can no longer support life.

Michael Welton (1995) wrote concerning the decimation of the roles of workers and citizens through the overcoming of Lifeworlds in favor of systems of control. Instead of workers and citizens the roles of "consumer" and "client" have been inflated. Students have become "customers" (note similarity to consumers) and citizens have increasingly become targets of "experts" who are trained to manage them through therapy, coaching, change management and "correctional" processes. Welton continues: "A commodified, utilitarian life-style increasingly prevails . . . and mass culture is replete with hedonistic siren-calls away from communicative rationality" (read: Lifeworld based upon authentic dialogue and deliberation; Welton 1995, p. 146). These processes move the system to fragmented Lifeworlds and fractured selves, instead of coming from a healthy Lifeworld of citizens engaged in the creation and sustaining of viable and joyful Lifeworlds:

> Society grows smarter, people get dumber . . . The consequences of the fragmented consciousness for persons are quite devastating. Our life compasses go awry and we do not know how to orient ourselves any longer, and it becomes more difficult to construct a coherent life narrative. (Welton 1995, p. 146)

A poignant example of the loss of self-orientation (as described above by Welton) was the outcry of a woman leader of an Indigenous North American group. At a conference in Surrey B.C., this woman, clearly of power and well respected in her community, burst into tears, saying, "I don't know who I am!" She, like countless others from Indigenous and repressed communities, feel the generational effects of the active repression and destruction of their historical Lifeworld including the lands, plants and animals upon which their livelihood rested. The continued protests of Indigenous people to save their remaining lands from the TransCanada Pipeline of oil sludge is an outstanding example of the oppression of economic/system powers over Lifeworlds.

Heeding Heidegger's despair, that humans cannot overcome the deadly force of technology (Heidegger 1966b), Kida pointed out that technology came about prior to human reason, and therefore humans through reason alone cannot change the trajectory towards self-annihilation that is clocked by the nuclear scientists of the world (2013). Commenting on the effects of the collapse of the Fukushima Daiichi nuclear reactor and following an earthquake, Kida said: "no one has even come up with a satisfactory means of dealing with the ever-increasing quantities of radioactive water. One has the impression that technology has broken free of human control . . ." (2013, pp. 8–9). He urges younger generations to think deeply about things before acting and to reject the continued push toward higher levels of so-called economic productivity. Additionally, Kida asks us to muse on the similar origins of technology and art, as well as their fundamental differences.

Expulsions and Deathworlds: The Brutality of Complex Systems

As the survival of life forms on earth is in question, humans must overcome the economic and technological forces leading to Deathworlds. Deathworlds are human worlds focused on destroying meaning, coherence, we-relationships, and intersubjectivity for humans and other life forms. Once totally destroyed these worlds become "dead zones" killing or expelling all life. In the current epoch, complex arrangements of legal, financial, technological, corporate and governmental structures have created powerful dynamics that create great wealth for some and expulsions for millions and the persistence of Deathworlds. Sassen in her monumental synthesis characterizes these processes as "expulsions" (Sassen 2014). Extreme mining practices, such as mountain top removal and hydraulic fracking, the creation of abstract financial instruments leading to massive home foreclosures, the usurpation of farmlands, the devastation of millions through wars are connected to the intentions and deliberate actions to increase capital for some. At the end of 2011 there were 42.5 million persons displaced by war and conflict (Sassen 2014, p. 56). Massive unemployment and incorrigible underemployment, millions of foreclosures, shrunken economies (for example 30% of the labor force in Greece lost homes, jobs, prospects overnight) and increased incarcerations in for-profit prisons are the results.

These forces lead also to increased dead zones or Deathworlds from the oceans to inland water sources to vast uninhabitable areas. Sassen calls for these areas to be recognized on maps, to be brought above ground. She asks: "What are the spaces of the expelled?" which, are invisible to the standard measures of modern states and economies. These spaces places should be conceptualized, as they are "many and growing." Making them alive as real spaces and places on our maps and awareness, including regular news reports on them, could become "the raw spaces for making new local economies, histories and modes of membership" (Sassen 2014, p. 222).

We should include also an analysis not only of dead zones and Deathworlds, but of "death-making zones." President Trump marketed billions in warheads and drones to Saudi Arabia, while providing support for fueling their planes as they bomb Yemen. Fragments of these bombs were found to be made by Raytheon a company located in Goleta, California, near the wealthy community of Santa Barbara and home of the Fielding Graduate University. DemocracyNow! reports:

> In news from Yemen, U.S.-backed Saudi forces have launched a new series of attacks on the port city of Hodeida, sparking fears of a humanitarian crisis. The charity Save the Children has warned disruption to supplies coming through Hodeida could 'cause starvation on an unprecedented scale.' The group warns 5 million children are at risk of famine. Meanwhile, CNN is reporting new evidence confirms U.S.-made bombs have been used in a series of attacks killing Yemeni civilians since the Saudi assault began in 2015.
>
> ("Yemen: New Evidence . . ." 2018)

Gebser's study of the evolution of human consciousness points to a way out by involving humans who look deeply at their own internal selves. The consciousness required for life to continue on earth is neither collectivistic, which submerges the individual self, nor egoistic, which espouses that individuals foster their individual gains for wealth and power:

> Weapons and nuclear fission are not the only realities to be dealt with; spiritual reality in its intensified form is also becoming effectual and real. This spiritual reality is without questions our only security that the threat of material destruction can be averted. Its realization alone seems able to guarantee man's continuing existence in the face of the powers of technology, rationality, and chaotic emotion. If our consciousness, that is, the individual person's awareness, vigilance, and clarity of vision, cannot master the new reality and make possible its realization, then the prophets of doom will have been correct. Other alternatives are an illusion; consequently, great demands are placed on us, and each one of us have been given a grave responsibility, not merely to survey but to actually traverse the path opening before us. (Gebser 1985)

Ray Kurzweil, the inventor of artificial intelligence, has predicted that the human world is becoming a vast "singularity" where humans will no longer have bodies. The contents of brains will be uploaded into a giant computer grid, which will maintain itself (Kurzweil 2006). This is the ultimate triumph of technology over life into one giant Deathworld. (There is a laboratory at Massachusetts Institute of Technology (MIT) devoted to creating the "Singularity.")

Habermas' Grounds for Truth-Seeking

How can persons get in touch with truth? Habermas points out that power distorts communication, which in turn fosters false communications (1979). Truthful communication must be *understandable* (speakers share norms and ways of speaking and writing so that they can accurately interpret meanings); *true* (assertions are cogent and recognizably affirmed in the actual world), *truthful* (speakers are sincere and able to examine their own ideological and experiential distortions); and have a sense of *rightness* (speakers follow valid moral norms) (Bentz/Shapiro 1998). Can one find any instances of public communication these days that exemplifies these characteristics? It is a premise of this paper that these conditions may only be realized when we develop and implement a means to create consciousness change. Such change becomes reality though processes like Transformative Phenomenology which allow for such communication to be developed, and which act as antidotes to Deathworlds.

In the following, we will explain what we call Transformative Phenomenology (Part II) and share a hermeneutic reflection on a public communication that was grounded in Transformative Phenomenology as a case example for a phenomenological antidote (Part III). We will also discuss community-of-practice as a vessel of collectively and socially enacted Transformative Phenomenology (Part IV), and end with our vision of a way forward (Epilogue).

Part II: Transformative Phenomenology as an Antidote for Our Times

> But if you look, the content of so-called modern education – very much oriented about material value. Not talking about inner value. So now, today the best educated people, emotionally – lot of problem! (H.H. The Dalai Lama 2018)

Transformative Phenomenology defies discrete definition because of the ineffable nature of its transformative outcomes. It is a phenomenology that "transforms and enhances personal life and professional effectiveness" (Psathas 2008). It can be described as the methodology and methods of somatic-hermeneutic-phenomenology put into action in the Lifeworld that can lead to personal, professional, organizational, and systems transformation.

Transformative Phenomenology as described by Rehorick and Bentz (2008) relies on (to varying degrees) the eidetic phenomenology of Edmund Husserl, the social-phenomenology of Alfred Schutz, the bodily-awareness of Maurice Merleau-Ponty, the ontological-existential phenomenology of Martin Heidegger, and the self-reflective hermeneutic methods of Hans-Jorg Gadamer, among other philosophies.

Transformative Phenomenology places a high respect on the phenomenological tradition that values *somatics*, the concept of body. Although it is not as prominent as it is in Merleau-Ponty's writings, phenomenology has always recognized that consciousness is embodied. Husserl critiqued the disembodied attitude of psychology (1954/1970). Both Gadamer and Ricoeur examined the nature of body and incorporated it in their hermeneutics (Derksen/Halsema 2011). Hanna who is grounded in phenomenology brought somatics into a larger setting for practices of healing (1962, 1993). Hanna's work includes the practices such as yoga, meditation, Buddhists' mindfulness that are based on the Asian tradition of body-mind-spirit interconnectedness. Having these lineages in its foundation, Transformative Phenomenology emphasizes the importance of somatic awareness. Transformative Phenomenology also requires researchers to embody or enact the principles, qualities, and attitudes of the methodology in their actual lives. Rehorick and Bentz (2008) have found phenomenology to be transformational when its research engages with human issues and concerns that engage scholar-practitioners. Bringing somatic learning to the forefront intensifies the power of the work of consciousness and social transformation.

Processes like Transformative Phenomenology allow for *truthful* communication to be developed. This is a phenomenology that embraces mindfulness, somatic awareness, and empathy. The process also embraces shared collaborative understanding, healing practices for self and others, deep personal reflection around lived experience, and enhanced consciousness. Practitioners of Transformative Phenomenology recognize how enculturated patterns of learning, working, communicating, and external goal setting that have ignored the body and lived- experience throughout the lifespan can be addressed. They focus on developing leadership for well-being, collaborative relationships, enhanced communities of learning and care, and social and environmental justice.

Transformative Phenomenology is a foundation for embodied acts of reasoning – situationally informed judgments – in response to the technification of the social world (Polkinghorne 2004). Embodied reasoning promotes decision-making in the human realm using approaches that:

> Take place within a shared embodied and culturally informed background; they are mainly derived through processes that operate out of awareness; they are emotionally informed; and they integrate concerns about multiple values and particular needs . . . (this) does not encourage practitioners to ignore scientifically validated knowledge statements that relate to their practice . . . it requires practitioners to think for themselves.
>
> (Polkinghorne 2004, p. 149)

Practitioners who embody phenomenology as a way of being can realize a transformative potential that did not exist before. This is the potential to catalyze transformative learning in support of consciousness change within self, others, groups, organizations, and larger systems. Husserl made a prediction about this potential when he commented:

> Perhaps it will even become manifest that the total phenomenological attitude and the epoché belonging to it are destined in essence to effect, at first, a complete personal transformation, comparable in the beginning to a religious conversion, which then, however,

over and above this, bears within itself the significance of the greatest existential transformation which is assigned as a task to mankind as such. (Husserl 1954/1970, p. 137)

In what follows, we map the potential that can emerge from an "education" in Transformative Phenomenology, as developed, practiced, and embodied by Rehorick and Bentz (2017). Those who choose to engage in this learning process end up realizing that "the deepening of awareness that results from phenomenology is itself a process of transformation" (Rehorick/Bentz 2008, p. 4). Through Transformative Phenomenology we learn how phenomenology can impact one's research and transform one's life and practice.

What indication(s) do we have that phenomenologists are currently acting in the world in ways that foster greater understanding, truth, truth seeking, and moral-rightness, for positive change in consciousness? What process is involved in the development of these qualities? What are the qualities of these agents-of-change? And, how are other people who are not familiar with phenomenological ways-of-being influenced by these phenomenological scholar-practitioners? We answer these questions through an examination of the experience and practice of Fielding Graduate University (FGU) doctoral students, and graduates, who chose to engage with phenomenology.

What is Transformative Phenomenology?

Rehorick and Bentz (2017) provide a retrospective assessment of two decades of phenomenological research carried out at Fielding Graduate University, which attracts experienced mid-career professionals seeking a flexible and customized approach to graduate learning. Scholar-practitioners (scholar-leaders) emerge from the Fielding program.

Former students contributed chapters to the edited volume that outlines the impact of phenomenology on their research, practice and lives. These authors provide rich stories of the diverse practices that embody *truthful* communication to address practical concerns in the Lifeworld from the diverse vantage of the executive coach, human development professionals, leadership specialists, company executives, directors of medical organizations, professional musicians, and community social innovators.

Within the same volume, Rehorick and Bentz (2017) present the results of an empirical study of seventy-six dissertations completed by Fielding scholar-practitioners over two decades that relied on phenomenology to varying degree. They attributed the research studies as being either based upon-, informed by-, or inspired by phenomenology. The seventy-six dissertation topics point to a great diversity of practical human centered topics. Melville posits, "the (Fielding) doctoral program should be judged by the real-world impact of what students learn" (Melville 2016, pp. 114–116). The body of applied research created by FGU scholar-practitioners is provided as a demonstration of the utility of phenomenology and hermeneutics to professional practitioners engaging the world through the lens of Transformative Phenomenology.

George Psathas (2008) reminds us that, "phenomenology is many things to many people" and that "phenomenology can restore, affect, influence, and change persons" (p. xi). "Phenomenology becomes an artful, assimilative experience for those who take it seriously and incorporate its premises, methods, orientations, and perspectives – boldly, affectively, cognitively, and assumptively" (Psathas 2008, p. xi) For the learner, the process of Transformative Phenomenology brings phenomenology to consciousness and offers the opportunity for the learner to incorporate it into their Lifeworld. We believe that phenomenology transforms anyone who cares to engage with it in a deep way:

> Transformative phenomenology may be the way to show how we can experience renewal – through our readings, our study, our interviews, our organized protocols, our hermeneutic exploration, our understandings; in short, through all of the mysteries entailed in the transformative process. (Psathas 2008, pp. xii–xiii)

Husserl reminds us that the phenomenologist engages in a perpetual effort to understand things like a beginner, finding an entry point into the philosophy again and again (Natanson 1973). For the beginner at Fielding, the focus is not on an exploration of a more exclusive, theoretical, kind. Any number of philosophers, methodologies, and methods can serve as entry points into the phenomenological realm – Husserl, Schutz, Merleau-Ponty, Heidegger, Gadamer, Wolff, van Manen, Wagner, and Psathas. Barber (2017b) observes that Fielding scholar-practitioners do not restrict themselves to one version of phenomenology but use phenomenology to explore their interests, through a multidisciplinary lens, to a greater or lesser degree as they see fit:

> As if phenomenology itself precludes any absolutizing of itself . . . these authors are unwilling to abide within the comfortable bounds of phenomenological philosophy itself. Instead, they seek to bring its resources to bear on a variety of practical concerns in such a way that it is impossible to think of them in any other way than as the "Scholar-Practitioners" that they call themselves. (Barber 2017b, pp. 7–8)

It is this openness to finding new entry points to phenomenology that is characteristic of the Fielding scholar-practitioner. Where the past "awaits new interpretations to help reconceive it . . . blocking attempts to predict with any certainty the future the past will yield" (Barber 2017b, p. 7).

Writing, and the interpretation of texts, is central to the process of Transformative Phenomenology. Learners become engaged in their research project from a first-person perspective. They often experience a thoughtful, disorienting, incoherence in coming to phenomenology for the first time through the development of their protocol statements, conducting their interviews, engaging with hermeneutic explorations, and reflecting on lived experience (Rehorick/Taylor 1995). The allure of phenomenology and hermeneutics grows over time. The veiled nature of the taken-for-granted is acknowledged and the "unclouded phenomenological eye" emerges:

> A person's view of the Lifeworld, understandings, and situations of others are clouded by his preconceptions, scientific and popular constructs, and media images and distortions. Over time, these may blind us to what is apparent to the unclouded phenomenological eye, much as cataracts impair one's vision.   (Rehorick/Bentz 2008, p. 21)

The ineffable process of personal learning and transformation is realized with the endless opportunity to return to the philosophy, again and again.

Education and The Emergence of the "Leregogue"

> Leregogy is a term coined to try and bridge the indomitable severing of roles between teacher and learner. It implies a transactional and shifting set of "roles" wherein both people, are at various times and sometimes synchronously, both teachers and learners.[2]
> (Rehorick/Taylor 1995)

Barber suggests that the openness that Fielding phenomenologists exhibit toward their research might be attributed to the leregogic method (attitude) of teaching that Rehorick and Bentz have adopted (Barber 2017b). They offer leregogy as an alternative collaborative learning model to that of the teacher-directed focus of pedagogy, and the self-directed focus of andragogy.

The neologism "leregogy" as conceived by Rehorick describes the guiding and supportive stance between a teacher and a learner that is founded on trust, devoid of power, accepting of faultiness, and conscious of the impact of reward and criticism. A leregogic teacher walks beside the learner as an equal and

---

[2] The conception of leregogy traces its origins to Rehorick and Taylor, "Thoughtful Incoherence." For further development and applications see David Rehorick and Stephen Jeddeloh, *Discovering Leregogy*, (2010); David Rehorick, Stephen Jeddeloh, and Kenzie Lau-Kwong, "Boundary of Transformative Learning," (2014); David Rehorick and Sally Rehorick, "The Leregogy of Curriculum Design," (2016); and Rehorick and Bentz, *Expressions of Phenomenological Research*.

affirms the role of teacher-as-guide. It is a relationship where social distance and dialogue mitigates dependence and spawns creativity. The teacher and learner acknowledge that there are many possible avenues to the learner's destination. In a leregogic relationship, the teacher learns from, and with, the learner as they engage in a unique self-directed journey of scholarship and self-discovery (Marlatt 2017, pp. 45–80).

Whether or not a leregogic attitude is innate to the learner, we contend that such an attitude is a natural outcome of the adoption of qualities (competencies) that arise, implicitly, through an education in Transformative Phenomenology as modeled by Rehorick and Bentz. Students who experience a phenomenological education through leregogic mentorship can emerge as transformative-phenomenologists-in-action, expressing a leregogic attitude that is infused with phenomenological qualities (Figure 1). A leregogic education can lead to the emergence of a phenomenological way-of-being that shows deep respect for the experience of others and is focused on recognizing "inner value." The qualities and attitudes of transformative phenomenologists are presented next.

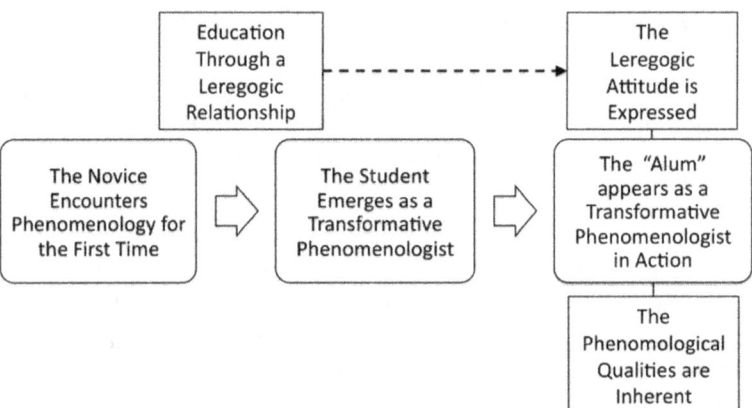

Figure 1: Education Through a Leregogic Relationship and the Emergence of the Transformative Phenomenologist.
Copyright (2019) by Valerie Bentz and James Marlatt. Reprinted with Permission.

Qualities and Attitudes of Transformative Phenomenologists

Transformative phenomenologists seek positive changes in self, Lifeworlds, and professional practice for the benefit of society. They are educated in the principles of Mindful Inquiry – develop a capacity for mindful thought, interpret situations in the context of history and culture, attempt to alleviate suffering by critiquing the sources origins of oppression, and pull back epistemological blinders by going back to the things themselves (Bentz/Shapiro 1998).

Rehorick and Bentz identified ten qualities[3] of phenomenological scholar-practitioners based on their analysis of phenomenological research completed at FGU from 1996 to 2016 (Figure 2). Transformative phenomenologists seek to transcend the reality of everyday lived-experience in service of generating common understanding among others. Over 75 doctoral students were introduced to the founders of phenomenology during this period.

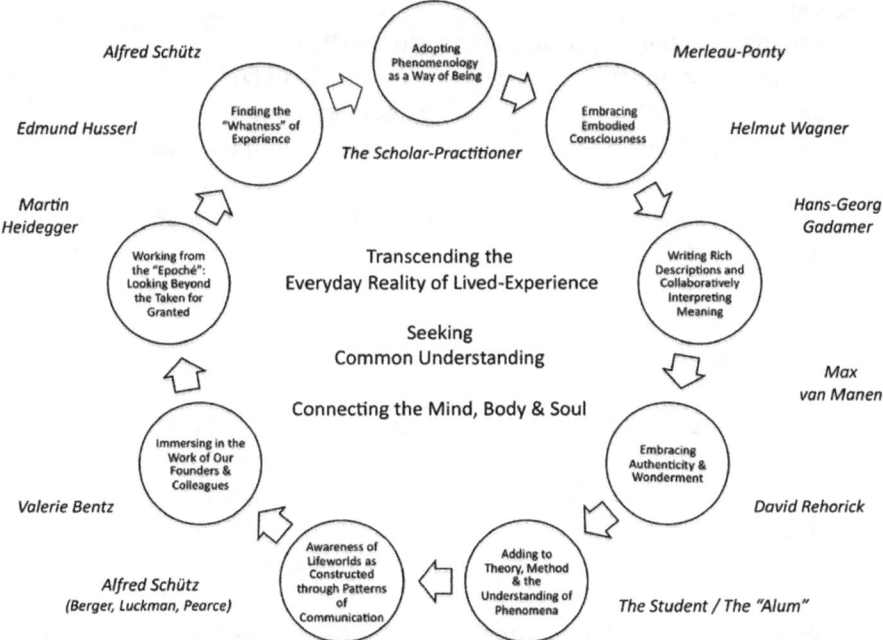

Figure 2: The Qualities of Transformative Phenomenologists.
Copyright (2019) Valerie Bentz and James Marlatt. Reprinted with Permission.

---

3 The authors originally referred to ten "competencies." The term "qualities" was adopted retrospectively as being a more relevant descriptor. The term "competency" is overused and problematic in the world of organization development. Competency frameworks abound and executives try to use them in the belief that they can identify the competencies that will drive productivity, and that Human Resource departments can train and measure people in those hard and soft competencies for the sake of productivity. These attempts are illustrative of what Heidegger calls making persons into "the standing reserve for use."

The Transformative phenomenologist-in-action exhibits phenomenological qualities and adopts "leregogic" attitudes that promote reflection and enhanced consciousness. Some of these qualities and attitudes are listed below, modified after Rehorick and Bentz (2017):

Inherent Phenomenological Qualities

- experiencing phenomenology as a way of being
- approaching life and practice with the "sparkle" of wonder and creativity (openness)
- engaging from the perspective of the epoché (Husserl)
- seeking the "whatness" of experience (Husserl, Schutz)
- embracing embodied ways of knowing (Merleau-Ponty)
- seeking mutual enhanced understanding (i.e. Coordinated Management of Meaning)
- a practical focus on recognizing the natural attitude in the reality of everyday life (Schutz)

Mindful "Leregogic" Attitudes

- being open and mindful of learning from and within relationship (openness, mindfulness)
- embracing doubt and chaos and tolerating incoherence when encountering new situations
- accepting silence as a component of learning in relationship (deep listening, emergence)
- staying open to immediate experience. (letting-go, detachment, releasement, surrender-and-catch) (Heidegger, Wolff)
- understanding that dialogue, empathy, friendship, trust, spirit, hope, and love are important elements in learning, meaning making, change, and transformation (love of humankind, cognitive love, respect, trust)

In the next section, we provide additional insight into the collective potential of Transformative Phenomenologists in the world through the exploration of a phenomenologically inspired community-of-practice as a case example.

Part III: The Surrey Experience – A Case for a Phenomenological Antidote

Fielding Graduate University convened a two-day meeting in Surrey, British Columbia during February 2018 that brought together voices from the Surrey community and the Fielding scholar-practitioner community. The two-day meeting was organized under the theme of *Social Innovation for Leadership in Work and Life* and focused on generating a dialogue about practicing Transformative Phenomenology. Fielding administrators, faculty, graduates, students, city administrators, and members of the Phoenix Drug and Alcohol Recovery and Education Society attended the meeting – including citizens in recovery. The Phoenix Society is a leader in social innovation in the area of homelessness, addiction, crime, unemployment, and poverty in the city of Surrey (Wilson/Wilson 2017). Wilson describes how Transformative Phenomenological inquiry – in – action shaped social innovation across individual, group, organizational, and institutional levels of engagement (A. Wilson 2018). Michael and Ann Wilson refer to their "living practice" of embodied inquiry that "strengthened a focus on our development as scholar-practitioners and the process of becoming embodied in our research and accountable to the Lifeworlds of marginalized citizens we served" (Wilson/Wilson 2017, p. 3).

During the first day of the meeting Fielding scholar-practitioners described their contributions to Rehorick and Bentz's (2017) edited volume *Expressions of Phenomenological Research: Consciousness and Lifeworld Studies*. A Fielding research and practice session was held at the Phoenix Society Rising Sun Social Innovation Centre on the second day.

In what follows, one of the authors of this paper (Ayumi) will write in first person, and reflect what she calls *The Surrey Experience* as an example of the phenomenological antidotes for the Deathworlds. This is a hermeneutic understanding of the Surrey event. In this interpretive analysis, she will interweave her first-person voice, lived experiences of hers and other participants,[4] and Heideggerian philosophy.

---

[4] Some of the presenters of the event wrote short reflections of the event, and I used them as a part of the data for my interpretive analysis for this section.

On the Surrey Experience

I participated in the event as one of the speakers, but I had not had any expectation for the event. I actually had not paid attention to the agenda much as my main interest was to see my professors – Dr. Valerie Bentz (Fielding faculty; co-author of this paper) and Dr. David Rehorick, who had opened the door to phenomenology (Transformative Phenomenology) for me, and deeply impacted my way of life. I just wanted to see them again. On the day I flew to Vancouver, where Surrey is located nearby, the whole Vancouver area was covered by snow, which had not happened for many years. I was welcomed by the crisp air, white falling snow from the light gray sky, beautiful black silhouette of tree branches and birds in the white background, and their deep silence. In retrospect, the magic of the snowy scenery was as if it was preluding the profoundness I would experience during the next two days. I say profound because the Surrey experience was authentic, magical, and sacred. Although I could not articulate my sentiments back then as it had an ineffable aspect, it was a powerful experience for me, and I felt other participants had similar feelings.

With the Heideggerian perspective, humans are a part of the world as *being-in-the-world*, and they are implicated by what is happening around and in them (Heidegger 2008). As such, the Surrey event participants (including me) were implicated and affected by many layers, facets, or a web of various factors that interplayed and synergized each other at that space and time. These layers or facets are intertwined, and the source of the profoundness cannot be explained in a linear fashion. But in what follows, I will delineate them from the perspectives of the setting, the people (the hosts, and the event participants), and the thinking to explicate the essence of the Surrey experience.

The Setting: The Rising Sun Project – Phenomenologically Approached Social Innovation

As we have discussed in the earlier section, the Rising Sun project was approached phenomenologically, and it affected many lives of Surrey citizens. Having the people from this project, both people who lead and support the project as well as the residents who used to be living on streets as homeless, had a deep impact to the attendees of the event. In addition, the second day of the event took place at one of the Rising Sun facilities, and its physical space created an additional meaningful container for us – the event participants – to connect ourselves to the humanity and to have dialogues at the higher conscious level. Some of the participants express it as follows: "While deep dialogue often occurs at Fielding events, this one was special, thanks in part to the graciousness of our hosts and the healing power of what they have created in Surrey with the Phoenix Society." (Fielding alumna) Another alumna said, "The experience raised my consciousness and questions about what makes a civil society, a good community, a home. I sensed that many who participated felt the same." A Fielding student commented, "By far the highlight of the weekend was the time spent and visit to the Phoenix location." Through the talks on the Rising Sun project and the various comments from the local participants (people from Fielding and Phoenix Society), I sensed that they not only attuned to the humanity, but also to the sacred land from the Indigenous people, on which the facilities stand.

The People (The Hosts): Michael and Ann Wilson, Founders of the Phoenix Society and the Rising Sun Project

Michael and Ann Wilson were the connecting point for the event as they are the founders of the Phoenix Society and the Rising Sun project. Michael is a Fielding alumnus, and Michael and Ann wrote a chapter on the Rising Sun project as a phenomenologically-approached social innovation (2017).

Both Michael and Ann embody authenticity, altruism, and the phenomenological attitude, and their warm and welcoming presence was unmistakable. The phenomenological attitude is the orientation or a way of being that one engages to others as a whole person of mental, emotional, bodily, and spiritual self, and at the same time he or she considerers that others are also whole persons. A phenomenologically attuned person heeds one's assumptions and pre-knowledge and does not jump into judgment without reflecting on his or her biases. A phenomenologically attuned person is also not afraid of getting in touch with the deep part of self and one's vulnerabilities, listens to others (and all living and non-living things) deeply, and can have genuine dialogues with self and others.

One of the Fielding students at the event describes her experience of Michael as follows:

> This past weekend appears to generate from a transcendent place. When you look into Michaels' eyes deeply or perceive his aura, he is connected, loving, and firmly grounded in what is happening at the moment . . . As I connect with Michael, across the occupied room, gaze meeting gaze, I feel a sense of joy and communication that itself is addictive. I don't want it to end . . . A being whose transcendence is not subject to the limitations of the physical universe.　　　　　　　　　　　　　　　　　　　　(Fielding student)

At the end of the second day, I was talking with a long-term resident of the Rising Sun facility about Ann, and he was telling me how much he appreciates her and Michael:

> She [Ann] always takes a time for me when I get upset and need to talk to someone. Talking to her calms me down. Ann and Michael, both of them, always sit with me when I need to talk. Actually, they do not even have to say anything. Just being with me, it alone helps me feel better. (Resident of Rising Sun, personal communication, April 25, 2018)

While listening to the resident, I was nodding deeply in my heart about the warm, welcoming, and healing energy that emanates from Michael and Ann. Although my encounter with them was rather limited, I knew what this resident was talking about. I felt I was welcomed, accepted, and loved when I was with Michael or Ann, just like the participant of the above comment. I felt that they consider me as part of *us*. Monroe (2002), political psychologist, concludes from her research that the only explanatory factor for altruism is the perception of self in relation to other human beings, that is the sense of shared humanity or the perception that all the humans are *one*; Monroe calls this *the altruistic perspective* (Monroe 2002). What I sensed from Michael and Ann is the transcendence that goes beyond the limit of the physical self, or using Monroe's term, the altruistic perspective.

The People (The Event's Participants)

It was not only Michael and Ann who manifested or engaged in the phenomenological attitude, and had authenticity and altruism. The whole group, the participants, were engaging with each other in the phenomenological way whether they understood phenomenology as an academic subject or not. Our phenomenological attitude was filling the rooms and the participants' hearts as if they were patterns in music played by different instruments.

As explained, the phenomenological attitude includes being able to dwell in one's deep part of self and share the experience with others, as well as being able to be present with others' inner depths. This attitude deals with one's vulnerability. Vulnerability is something people often try to avoid, but Brown (2012), social science researcher, asserts it is a path to humanity and growth. "Vulnerability is the birthplace of love, belonging, joy, courage, empathy, and creativity. It is the source of hope, empathy, accountability, and authenticity. If we want greater clarity in our purpose or deeper and more meaningful spiritual lives, vulnerability is the path" (Brown 2012, p. 33).

I was touched to see both the speakers and the audience were willing to share their vulnerabilities. I saw that in the topics of their presentations, but also how they delivered the messages. Some of them, including myself, seemed not comfortable talking in front of people, but they spoke from their hearts and their way of engagement stroked the chord of my heart. It was same with the residents of the Phoenix Society, who were willing to ask questions, make comments, and share their experiences with the group. We, the event participants, were very supportive for each other, and developed a safe and sacred space in a joint, gradual, tacit, and embodied manner. It was as if we were writing, sharing, and appreciating personal phenomenological protocols, and then co-created deeper joint protocols as equal human beings.

For example, one of the Phoenix Society residents sensed the urgency to express what she felt from the group and set the tone for the 2nd day by singing an Indigenous song. I did not know the song, but I joined singing after hearing the repeated tune and phrase, although I did not understand the words. While singing together and looking into the eyes of other participants, I became a part of the *one*, and got grounded. Valerie (Fielding faculty; co-author of this paper) caught quickly what people were sensing, and she spontaneously made a human circle by all of us holding hands. At the end of the session, the lady who sang the song showed us her courage again by telling us she needed help, and the rest of the group stayed in the moment with her, being present and sending her both verbal and nonverbal support. This ending again made me feel that I was a part of the one.

Another Fielding student reflected that the Surrey experience was transformational, and stated, "I did not imagine that this conference would have affected me so profoundly. Participating in this conference was an empowering experience." He originally felt very uncomfortable at the event as he thought he was not good enough:

> While at the conference, I was suffering from "impostor syndrome." . . . I felt that I could be asked to leave at any moment. I was in the presence of accomplished social activists, administrators, academics, and authors. Certainly, they would see right through me and know I did not belong. In fact, if I listened closely enough, I am sure I would hear people whispering about me. I had to hide until I could escape.

But as he was participating in the event, he gradually transformed. He continued to reflect:

> Saturday was awesome. I fellowshipped with some amazing people who took a genuine interest in me. As the day progressed, I grew more confident and bold in my conversations . . . As my presentation began, I felt a peace wash over me. Although I was anxious, I knew God was with me. Even when the computer froze up, I was at peace. The words I needed to say so that

> I could understand myself came out. There was power for me at that moment. I cannot speak for anyone else there, but I changed after I was done. I have a better understanding of who I am. I am comfortable with me. Most importantly, I learned I mattered. (Fielding Student)

It is a story of courage, but I do not think his courage would have come to surface without the collective Surrey experience that all the participants were jointly creating. Other participants comment on their experiences as follows:

> There was a magical potpourri of collective intention, shared wisdom and synergy on the Sunday that was something unusual and amazing – beyond the feedback and experiences of the room at the end of the morning, the informal feedback and reflections in conversations afterward had a common theme of how powerful and impactful it was to have that range and mix of individuals in that kind of learning space together . . . it was further intriguing (thanks to the magic of the universe!) that even the topics shared that morning aligned and fit so beautifully into the space and how it was being held. (Fielding student)
>
> On the second day, I was moved by the deeply personal stories of courage, compassion and commitment shared by the presenters and the space that was created with the participants to explore issues conceptually and also to be alive in the room. The experience raised my consciousness and questions about what makes a civil society, a good community, a home. I sensed that many who participated felt the same. (Fielding alumna)

In the following, Jim (Fielding alumnus; co-author of this paper) succinctly summarizes the essence of the Surrey experience:

> Our community came together with the unstated intent of validating our role in catalyzing positive change in the world around us. . . . Our stories came from the heart and, in turn, impacted some of the hearts and souls of others around us . . . Our consciousness was raised toward a tacit acknowledgement of the "goodness" that surrounds us, and an inspired hope for a better world. The energy that we gained from the ephemeral experience of meeting other like-minded people may dissipate, but the ripple effect of those interactions will continue to resonate, as we remain mindful of our collective potential.

The Surrey experience exemplifies that *living or doing phenomenology* as a practice can be a counteracting power to the Deathworlds, not only because of the humanity aspect, but also it challenges the metaphysical understanding of being and the technological understanding of being that people hold since the time of Plato (Heidegger 1977; 2008). The Deathworlds may be more pronounced in the current climate because of the advanced computer generated technologies, but the origin of the technological understanding of being has been the same; it is the frame of mind that people live in, which promotes the continuous advancement of technology and deepens the downward Deathworld's spiral.

Heidegger does not critique technology itself, but he questions the technological understanding of being, and how dangerous it could be. He posits that humans have been pursuing efficiency wanting more for less, and this thinking or culture drives technology even further. Heidegger is concerned people are taken up with technology, and they don't even think about what they might lose by participating in and being consumed by technology (Heidegger 1966a; 1977). Some advanced technologies, such as Singularity, might be easy to grab people's attention and make them question the directions. However, the technological understanding of being is pervasive in people's lives and is often hidden from their consciousness. People may think they are using technology as resources or tools, but the opposite is also true: humans are resources to be used as *standing reserve* and being orderable:

> Everywhere everything is ordered to stand by, to be immediately at hand, indeed, to stand there just so that it may be on call for a further ordering. Whatever is ordered about in this way has its own standing. We call it standing reserve [*Bestand*]. (Heidegger 1977, p. 17)

An airplane on a runway is an object, but it is also a standing-reserve or a cog to be ordered for the whole transportation system (Heidegger 1977). Humans use airplanes as a tool to get to another location quickly, but it is also true that humans are used to fill the airplanes, in other words, they are standing-reserve to be ordered in the system of air transportation (Dreyfus 1993). Likewise, social networks (e.g. Facebook, Instagram, Twitter) make it possible for people to connect with others instantly regardless the locations and time, and to reach out to a large number of people. But at the same time, people are considered as target for the information dissemination, and to be worse, their personal information is used as standing-reserve to be ordered for marketing, politics, and other kinds of statistics. Technology or the technological understanding of being affects people's understanding of being. With this frame of mind – what Heidegger names *Ge-stell* (Enframing) – humans, other living beings, and Mother Nature are mere materials to be used, manipulated, and ordered in the pursuit of efficiency and predictability.

The technological understanding of being is so pervasive and dominates our thinking and actions, while "the splendor of the simple" (Heidegger 2001, p. 7) or insignificant yet profound practices, such as friendship, gathering with people for good conversation, walking in a path in woods, are marginalized because they are not the acts for efficiency (Dreyfus 1993). The Surrey event was a good illustration that how a get-together of people that was phenomenologically lived let the transcendence appear – the transcendence from the individual to the oneness, as well as the transcendence beyond the technological understanding of being.

At the Surrey event, the participants did not try to will out the calculated positive outcome. The goodness of the event organically surfaced through the interplay among the setting, the people, and the non-calculative flow of the event. The event had the agenda (outline) for two days such as who presents what, but the participants attuned to what was emerging throughout the days. It was a different type of gathering from typical corporate training programs that are created by the deductive approach of using the instructional systems design. In such programs, the measurable goals and objectives are identified first, and then designers move onto dividing them into sub-goals and identifying strategies and activities to achieve these sub-goals. Teaching points and learning points are identified and captured in training manuals for instructors, so that there is not much deviation among training sessions delivered by different instructors. I used to work in that kind of environment as the producer of training programs in leadership and human skills. This approach has its own merits, but it is driven by the *Ge-stell* and the technological understanding of being. On the other hand, the Surrey event had *technology* (as *technikon* and *techne*) in the original sense for the ancient Greek and it prompted poiesis in our group as for the Greek, "*techne* belongs to bringing-forth, to *poiesis*, it is something poietic" (Heidegger 1977, p. 13).

The Thinking: Meditative Thinking and Hermeneutic Circle

The event generated the hermeneutic circle in which the participants were positively affecting each other, but the process of reflecting on the event deepened my thinking and insights even further. Our hermeneutic circle or the *fore-structure* of understanding never ends (Heidegger 2008). In the acts of contemplating, sharing our reflections, and musing further, we, the authors of this paper, keep deepening our understanding of the Surrey experience. For example, at the beginning of the reflective stage, I was moved by the participants' attitude for each other, that is, considering each other as equal human beings. But as I kept reflecting, I started to question about my being with others. It was easy at the event to perceive the Rising Sun residents as equal human fellows, and I was touched with the preciousness I felt from each person. But through the continuous process of reflection, I thought of my past, of the times I was walking on streets in San Francisco (where I live), trying to avoid homeless people on the streets. I was scared of them and perceived them as *the homeless* or *the drug addicts*, not as human fellows with their potentialities hidden inside of them. I did not have the same mindset and openness towards the homeless people back then. The reflection on the Surrey experience made me realize not only what I was overlooking but also possibilities of my any other hidden negligence and gave me an opportunity to look the world in a different way.

Thinking about the Surrey experience I shared in this Part III has the nature of *meditative thinking* (Heidegger 1966a) that ponders fundamental yet hidden meanings of being[5] through the contemplative and cyclic movements of reflections. Heidegger laments people are in "flight from thinking" (1966a, p. 45) and avoid or have forgotten to engage in meditative thinking. He observes that people's dominant thinking is *calculative thinking*, that is the thinking in the analytic and linear manner for predicting and analyzing issues, solving problems, or taking actions. The calculative thinking is rooted in the pursuit of efficiency and predictability and goes hand in hand with the technological understanding of being, and it nurtures the downward spiral to the Deathworlds.

The phenomenological attitude and meditative thinking in Transformative Phenomenology bring transformation to the one who engage in them. It made a difference for the Surrey event participants, and it made me look at the world differently.

Part IV: Social Learning – Transformative Phenomenology Communities-of-Practice as an Antidote to Deathworlds

The reflection of the Surrey event in the last section (Part III) highlights the power of the communication and network of people grounded in the phenomenological processes and attitudes. The synergy among the group members amplifies the transformative nature that has been observed by Rehorick and Bentz (2008, 2017) and explained in Part II of this paper. In the following, we will examine the social aspects of Transformative Phenomenology, especially through the lens of communities-of-practice.

Communities-of-practice (CoPs) are groups of people who share a concern or a passion for something they do and learn to do it better as they regularly interact (Wenger-Trayner/Wenger-Trayner 2015). Lave and Wenger introduced the concept as a framework for understanding social ways of knowing and earning (Lave/Wenger 1991). The framework evolved into a social theory of learning (Farnsworth et al. 2018; Wenger 1998). The concept emerged out of a study of apprenticeship that identified that learning takes place through a complex set of social relationships that exists beyond the mentor and novice – where learning is more reliant on journeyman and more experienced apprentices that act as

---

[5] In this case, the hidden meanings of being concerns more of the raison d'être of beings, and it has the *ontic-existentiell* nature than the *ontologic-existential* interpretation of Being that Heidegger (2008) argues throughout his career.

a "living curriculum" for the apprentice who is seeking identity. The Fielding scholar-practitioner community meets the criteria defining a CoP espoused by Wenger: CoPs share a domain of interest, consist of a formal or informal caring community that enables people to learn from each other, and focus on a shared practice (Wenger-Trayner/Wenger-Trayner 2015). The cultivation of these elements by the community is a key activity of its members. Members navigate from the periphery of the community toward more central roles as they gain confidence and revise their identities toward one that values expertise. "The practice of the community is dynamic and involves learning on the part of everyone" (Wenger-Trayner/Wenger-Trayner 2015, p. 4).

Wenger identifies four elements of social learning capability that supports innovation and learning in social systems (Wenger 2009). *Social learning spaces* promote genuine encounters between learners. *Learning citizenship* requires personal engagement and a willingness to learn. *Social artists* provide bold, or quiet, inspiration to learning citizens and are tuned to the social dynamics of the learning space. *Learning governance* focuses on decision processes that optimize social learning capability. All of these elements were evident at the Surrey meeting. New perspectives emerged as voices from two inquiring communities intersected within an empathetic social environment and inviting physical space.

A model of the Fielding Phenomenological CoP provides some insight into the complexity of social learning systems (Figure 3). Participants of the Surrey meeting are depicted as a circle of Schutzian puppets representing dispossessed people (including people in recovery), students encountering phenomenology for the first time, doctoral students, and leregogic graduate scholar-practitioners, mentors, and social innovators. Testimony of consciousness-raising and identity seeking is illustrated through quotations from some of the participants.

The circular construction of the figure suggests that a phenomenological CoP is a learning process, in which a learner takes an on-going journey as a new learning or horizon puts a learner onto a new level of learning process. Just like the hermeneutic circle, it is an upward spiral to deepen the understanding and growth. Conversely, the uncomfortable, the sense of not knowing, and vulnerability are inevitable aspects of the circular learning process as it demands going back to the Novice. The phenomenological CoP as social learning system provides mutual support for the learning process for the members for their growing pain, while it keeps in check for the development of individual and collective hubris.

The circular nature of social learning also suggests that the learning process is always available to *start again* even when a learner gets lost. This is significant in the current epoch of the Deathworlds where people feel their selves are fractured due to the controlling and technocratic thinking that permeates the modern world. The computer assisted social media is driven by and fosters

Chapter 20 Transformative Phenomenology as an Antidote — 343

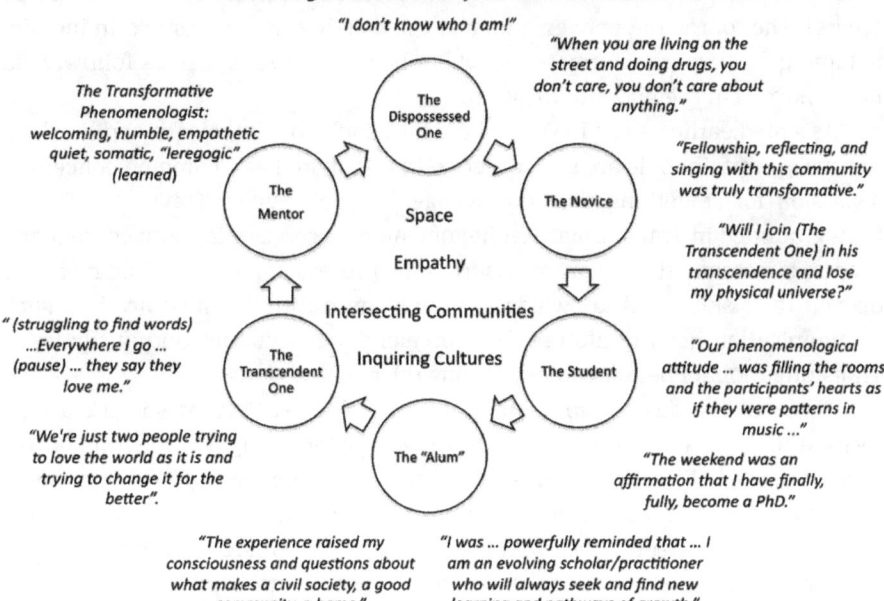

Figure 3: A Phenomenological Community-of-Practice in Action represented as a circle of Schutzian puppets.
Copyright (2019) by Valerie Bentz and James Marlatt. Reprinted with Permission.

the *fast-communication* (*fast* as in fast-food, meaning quick but superficial and not much nutrients), and it fuels further fragmentation in the Lifeworlds and fractured selves. As the participants of the Surrey event experienced, the social communication that embodies the phenomenological qualities and attitudes heals human spirits and unites people. It was a place that Habemas's *truthful* communication existed (Habermas 1979).

Looking at the Surrey event as a CoP grounded in Transformational Phenomenology, the four aspects of truthful communication permeate. Whether it is influenced by Husserlian bracketing or Heideggerian fore-structure, the processes of reflecting, heeding, identifying, and sharing one's assumptions and biases are a part of the thinking, talking, and acting for the participants, which made the conversation *understandable* (speakers share their norms and assumptions) and *truthful* (examine their ideological and experiential distortions). The community consisted of various people in terms of their backgrounds, such as professional, academic, experiential, ideological, social, and economical. Plus, the ways they experience the world – the way they think and feel, and what they think and feel – were all different. Yet the participants of the event resonated with each other and made the communication *true* (assertions are cogent and affirmed by others). The topics and conversations at the meeting were grounded in individual and collective transformations, which held *rightness* (speakers follow valid moral norms) in their communication.

As stated earlier, CoPs in general are for people to jointly learn and in which to develop certain topic areas – content – that is shared as a common concern or a passion for something they do (Wenger-Trayner/Wenger-Trayner 2015). For CoPs grounded in Transformative Phenomenology, concern for both content and process are essential as a way of ensuring the process of growth. While members deepen their skills and knowledge through the truthful communication, such communication itself reinforces the aforementioned qualities and attributes of Transformational Phenomenology among the members.

Thus far, the discussion of the phenomenological CoPs as social learning focused the ones in Fielding Graduate University including the one from Surrey event, but the CoPs grounded in Transformative Phenomenology are not limited to official groups of researchers, scholars, scholar-practitioners, or professional practitioners, nor need to be affiliated to Fielding Graduate University. Anyone who practices Transformational Phenomenology as a research methodology, a way of living, or a learning process is a part of the larger CoP of Transformational Phenomenology. Opportunities to engage and embodiment of its principles, qualities, and attitudes can create truthful communication in their spheres of influences.

Epilogue

The danger is in the near. It is the Deathworld in our post-modern society, where the calculative and technology driven thinking is invisibly dominant, and the extinction of species is visibly happening. While people's selves are fractured and alienated, the need for revitalizing the spiritual reality of mankind and other living species has been growing. A number of philosophers and thinkers call for looking into our consciousness, and Habermas (1979) urges us to engage in *truthful* communication to counter the Deathworlds and revitalize the Lifeworlds.

Processes such as Transformative Phenomenology provide a container or vessel for cultivating truthful communication among us, and act as an antidote to the Deathworlds. Transformative Phenomenology, as an umbrella concept for a phenomenological research methodology and method, a way of living, a learning process, and a community of practice, is grounded in the actions and practices in the Lifeworlds, the somatic, the hermeneutics, and the leregogic attitudes, which leads to transformations both in individual and collective levels. The process of engaging and enacting Transformative Phenomenology in our lives brings *oneness* as the inclusive coherence that transcends multifold realities.

As noted earlier, Gebser (1985) calls for each one of us looking into selves and our consciousness in order to restore healthy spiritual reality. It is a call for getting back the Lifeworlds from the Deathworlds. We, the authors of this paper agree with Gebser: "great demands are placed on us, and each one of us have been giving a grave responsibility, not merely to survey but to actually traverse the path opening before us" (1985, p. 5). A vessel is here, as Transformative Phenomenology, waiting for ones who wish to take a responsibility and traverse the path with us.

References

Barber, Michael D. (2004): *The Participating Citizen: A biography of Alfred Schutz*. Albany: State University of New York Press.
Barber, Michael D. (2005): "If only to be heard: Value-freedom and ethics in Alfred Schutz's economic and political writings". In: Endress, Martin/Psathas, George/Nasu, Hisashi (Eds.): *Explorations of the Life-World: Continuing dialogues with Alfred Schutz*. New York: Dordrecht, Springer, p. 173–202.
Barber, Michael D. (2017a): *Religion and Humor as Emancipating Provinces of Meaning*. New York: Springer.
Barber, Michael D. (2017b): "Forward". In: Rehorick, David/Bentz, Valerie (Eds.): *Expressions of Phenomenological Research: Consciousness and Lifeworld Studies*. Santa Barbara: Fielding University Press.
Barber, Michael D./Dreher, Jochen (2014): *The Interrelation of Phenomenology, Social Sciences, and the Arts*. New York: Springer.
Bentz, Valerie/Shapiro, Jeremy (1998): *Mindful Inquiry in Social Research*. Thousand Oaks: SAGE Publications.
Bentz, Valerie/Giorgino, Vincenzo M. B. (Eds.) (2016): *Contemplative Social Research: Caring for Self, Being and Lifeworld*. Santa Barbara: Fielding University Press.
Bentz, Valerie/Rehorick, David/Marlatt, James/Nishii, Ayumi/Estrada, Carol (2018): "Transformative Phenomenology as an Antidote to Technological Deathworlds". *Schützian Research* 10, pp. 189–220.
Brown, Brené (2012): *Daring Greatly: How the Courage to Be Vulnerable Transforms the Way We Live, Love, Parent, and Lead*. New York: Avery.
Casacuberta, David (2016): "Toward Embodied Digital Technologies". In: Bentz, Valerie/Giorgino, Vincenzo M. B. (Eds.): *Contemplative Social Research: Caring for Self, Being and Lifeworld*. Santa Barbara: Fielding University Press, pp. 276–300.
Derksen, Louise D./Halsema, Annemie (2011): "Understanding the Body. The Relevance of Gadamer's and Ricoeur's View of the Body for Feminist Theory". In: Mootz III, Francis J./

Taylor, George H. (Eds.): *Gadamer and Ricoeur: Critical Horizons for Contemporary Hermeneutics*. New York: Continuum Press, pp. 203–225.

Dreyfus, Hubert (1993): "Heidegger on the Connection Between Nihilism, Art, Technology, and Politics". In: Guignon, Charles B. (Ed.): *The Cambridge Companion to Heidegger*, ed. Charles B. Guignon. New York: Cambridge University Press, pp. 289–316.

Farnsworth, Valerie/Kleanthous, Irene/Wenger-Trayner, Etienne (2018): "Communities of Practice as a Social Theory of Learning: A Conversation with Etienne Wenger". In: *British Journal of Educational Studies* 64. No. 2, pp. 139–160.

Gebser, Jean (1985): *The Ever-Present Origin* (N. Barstad, A. Mickunas, Trans). Athens: Ohio University Press.

H. H. The Dalai Lama (2018): "The Ancient Wisdom the Dalai Lama Hopes Will Enrich the World." *BBC News*, correspondent, Justin Rowlatt. Retrieved from http://www.bbc.com/news/world-asia-india-43208568, visited April 1, 2018.

Habermas, Jürgen (1970): *Toward a Rational Society*. Boston: Beacon Press.

Habermas, Jürgen (1973): *Knowledge and Human Interests*. Boston: Beacon Press.

Habermas, Jürgen (1979): *Communication and the Evolution of Society*. Boston: Beacon Press.

Habermas, Jürgen (1989): *The Theory of Communicative Action, Volume Two: Lifeworld and System: A Critique of Functionalist Reason* (T. McCarthy, Trans.). Boston: Beacon Press.

Hanna, Thomas (1962): *The Bergsonian Heritage*. New York: Columbia University Press.

Hanna, Thomas (1993): *The Body of Life: Creating New Pathways for Sensory Awareness and Fluid Movement*. Rochester: Healing Arts Press.

Harris, Tristan (2016): "How Technology is Hijacking Your Mind – From a Magician and Google Design Ethicist". Retrieved from https://medium.com/thrive-global/how-technology-hijacks-peoples-minds-from-a-magician-and-google-s-design-ethicist-56d62ef5edf3, visited on April 1, 2018.

Heidegger, Martin (1966a): *Discourse on Thinking* (J.M. Anderson, E. H. Freund, Trans.). New York: Harper & Row Publishers.

Heidegger, Martin (1966b): "Only A God Can Save Us: The Spiegel Interview". In: Sheehan, Thomas (Ed.): *Heidegger: The Man and The Thinker*. Piscataway: Transaction Publishers.

Heidegger, Martin (1977): "The Question Concerning Technology". In: *The Question Concerning Technology and Other Essays* (W. Lovitt, Trans.). New York: Harper and Row, pp. 3–35.

Heidegger, Martin (2001): "The Thinker as Poet". In: *Poetry, Language, Thought* (A. Hofstadter, Trans.). New York: HarperCollins, pp. 1–14.

Heidegger, Martin (2008): *Being and Time* (J. Macquarrie, E. Robinson, Trans.). New York: HarperCollins.

Husserl, Edmund (1954/1970): *The Crisis of European Sciences and Transcendental Phenomenology: An Introduction to Phenomenological Philosophy*, (D. Carr, Trans.). Evanston: Northwestern University Press.

Kida, Gen (2013): *The True Nature of Technology*, (M. Emmerich, Trans.). Tokyo: Deco.

Kurzweil, Ray (2006): *The Singularity is Near: When Humans Transcend Biology*. New York: Viking Penguin.

Lave, Jean/Wenger, Etienne (1991): *Situated Learning: Legitimate Peripheral Participation*. Cambridge: Cambridge University Press.

Manning, Chelsea (2018): "Whirling death machines need to be stopped . . .". March 27–28, 2018. Retrieved from www.democracynow.org, visited on April 1, 2018.

Marlatt, James (2017): "The Transformative Potential of Conversations with Strangers". In: Rehorick, David/Bentz, Valerie (Eds.): *Expressions of Phenomenological Research:*

Consciousness and Lifeworld Studies. Santa Barbara: Fielding University Press, pp. 45–80.

McKie, Robin (2017): "Biologists Think 50% of the Species Will Be Facing Extinction By the End of the Century". Retrieved from https://www.theguardian.com/environment/2017/feb/25/half-all-species-extinct-end-century-vatican-conference, visited on April 1, 2018.

Melville, Keith (2016): *A Passion for Adult Learning: How the Fielding Model is Transforming Doctoral Education.* Santa Barbara: Fielding University Press.

Monroe, Kristin R. (2002): "Explicating Altruism". In: Post, Stephen G./Underwood, Lynn G./Schloss, Jeffrey P./Hurlbut, William B. (Eds.): *Altruism & Altruistic Love: Science, Philosophy, & Religion in Dialogue.* Oxford: Oxford University Press.

Natanson, Maurice (1973): *Edmund Husserl: Philosopher of Infinite Tasks.* Evanston: Northwestern University Press.

Oliver, Kelly (2004): *The Colonization of Psychic Space: A Psychoanalytic Social Theory of Oppression.* Minneapolis: University of Minnesota Press.

Polkinghorne, Donald E. (2004): *Practice and the Human Sciences: The Case for a Judgment-Based Practice of Care.* Albany: State University of New York Press.

Psathas, George (2008): "Forward". In: *Transformative Phenomenology: Changing Ourselves, Lifeworlds and Professional Practice.* Lanham: Lexington Press.

Rehorick, David/Bentz, Valerie (Eds.) (2008): *Transformative Phenomenology: Changing Ourselves, Lifeworlds, and Professional Practice.* Lanham: Lexington Press.

Rehorick, David/Bentz, Valerie (Eds.) (2017): *Expressions of Phenomenological Research: Consciousness and Lifeworld Studies.* Santa Barbara: Fielding University Press.

Rehorick, David/Jeddeloh, Stephen (2010): "Discovering Leregogy: A Phenomenological Account of Improvised Collaborative Transformation." *International Human Science Research Conference*, Seattle, WA.

Rehorick, David/Jeddeloh, Stephan/Lau-Kwong, Kenzie (2014): "At the Boundary of Transformative Learning: Empirical, Phenomenological, and Conceptual Insights". In: *Spaces of Transformation and Transformation of Space*, pp. 81–93. XI International Transformative Learning Conference, Teachers College, Columbia University, New York.

Rehorick, David/Rehorick, Sally (2016): "The Leregogy of Curriculum Design: Teaching and Learning as Relational Endeavours". In: Tajino, Akira/Stewart, Tim/Dalsky, David (Eds.): *Team Teaching and Team Learning in the Language Classroom: Collaboration for Innovation in ELT.* London: Routledge, pp. 43–163. (Part of the Routledge Research in Language Education series).

Rehorick, David/Taylor, Gail (1995): "Thoughtful Incoherence: First Encounters with the Phenomenological-Hermeneutical Domain". In: *Human Studies: A Journal for Philosophy and Social Sciences* 18. No. 4, pp. 389–414.

Sassen, Saskia (2014): *Expulsions: Brutality and Complexity in the Global Economy.* Cambridge: Harvard University Press.

Swami Vivekananda (2018): "Southern California Bulletin of the Vedanta Society". March 2018. Retrieved from https://vedanta.org, visited on April 1, 2018.

Schutz, Alfred (1975): "Alfred Schutz on Phenomenology and Social Relations". Helmut R. Wagner (Ed.). Chicago: The University of Chicago Press.

Wagner, Helmut (1983): *Phenomenology of Consciousness and Sociology of the Lifeworld.* Edmonton: University of Alberta Press.

Welton, Donn (1997): "World". In: Embree, Lester (Ed.): *Encyclopedia of phenomenology.* New York: Dordrecht, Springer, pp. 736–743.

Welton, Michael R. (Ed.) (1995): *In Defense of the Lifeworld: Critical Perspectives on Adult Learning*. Albany: State University of New York Press.

Wenger, Etienne (1998): *Communities of Practice: Learning, Meaning, and Identity*. Cambridge: Cambridge University Press.

Wenger, Etienne (2009): "Social learning capability: four essays on innovation and learning in social systems". In: *Social Innovation, Sociedade e Trabalho*. Booklets 12 – separate supplement, MTSS/GEP & EQUAL, Lisbon, Portugal. Retrieved from http://wenger-traynor.com/resources/publications/essays-on-social-learning-capability, visited on April 1, 2018.

Wenger-Trayner, Etienne/Wenger-Trayner, Beverly (2015): "Communities of Practice: A Brief Introduction". Retrieved from http://wenger-trayner.com/wp-content/uploads/2015/04/07-Brief-introduction-to-communities-of-practice.pdf, visited on April 1, 2018.

Wilson, Michael/Wilson, Ann (2017): "Rising Sun: Actioning Hermeneutic Phenomenological Inquiry or Community Based Social Innovation". In: Rehorick, David/Bentz, Valerie: *Expressions of Phenomenological Research: Consciousness and Lifeworld Studies*. Santa Barbara: Fielding University Press, pp. 236–271.

Wilson, Ann (2018): "Social Innovation Summit: Exploring Leadership in Work and Life." *Fielding Graduate University Conference on Social Innovation for Leadership in Work and Life: Expressions of Phenomenological Research*, Society for Phenomenology and Human Studies, Surrey, B.C.

"Yemen: New evidence of U. S.-made bombs; charity warns of starvation on 'unprecedented scale.'" (2018): Retrieved from https://www.democracynow.org/2018/9/19/headlines/yemen_new_evidence_of_us_made_bombs_charity_warns_of_starvation_on_an_unprecedented_scale, visited on April 1, 2018.

James Marlatt and Valerie Malhotra Bentz
Epilogue: The Essence of Collaborative Transformative Phenomenology

> The smallest act in the most limited circumstances bears the seed of the boundlessness... of human interrelatedness... because one deed, and sometimes one word, suffices to change every constellation. – Hanna Arendt, *The Human Condition*, p.189

As we write this afterword, the world is in the throes of the COVID-19 pandemic, an unimaginable calamity just a short while ago. The zoonotic virus presumptively emerged through a singular transmission from endangered pangolins to humans in a wet market in Wuhan. Collectively, it seems like we have never been so wide-awake to our interrelatedness with humanity and vulnerability to a natural phenomenon. We surrender to the Deathworldly news of exponential infection rates, fear, anxiety, suffering, and grief. Death counts, politics, economic fall-out, social-distancing, lockdowns, and the uncontrollable catalyze uncertainty in our social worlds. The hope of recovery to normalcy and stability beckons. Our collective global Lifeworld – our taken-for-granted world of everyday life – has been turned upside down. The frailty of human affairs has never seemed so apparent for many who are now living in the global Petri dish, as the chain-reaction of the spreading virus transcends geographical, political, cultural, and social boundaries, changing "every constellation." But, while affirming that the "smallest act" can lead to Deathworlds, the opposite life-giving potential of the seed of the "smallest act" seems equally possible as affirmed by the authors in this volume that we, perhaps presciently, titled "From Deathworlds to Lifeworlds" long before the outbreak.

In our opening chapter, we sought to answer several questions through our participatory action research project. What is the place and relevance of Transformative Phenomenology in transforming consciousness for a livable world? What is the value of "teaching" phenomenology to people by introducing different ways-of-knowing through "writing phenomenology?" What is it like to be a "stranger" collaborating with others in a global community? Can Transformative Phenomenology act as an antidote to Deathworlds that pervade our Lifeworlds? We believe that we are closer to affirmatively answering these questions through the phenomenological expressions offered by our authors.

The Transformative Potential of "Writing Phenomenology"

We offer Transformative Phenomenology not as a cook-book solution to the challenges of our times, but as an accessible pathway toward a novel stance, a way of engaging the world, to look beyond the taken for granted. In the end, a way to resuscitate and transform the Lifeworld starting with a renewed awareness of self and others, as our contributors to this book relay.

Through the process of "writing phenomenology" our students and authors unveiled a rich array of Deathworldly phenomena, and explored them from individual, social, and ecological vantages in collaboration with others. As the phenomena revealed themselves to our students through their protocols, an enriched awareness of their consciousness emerged, opening pathways toward the recovery of the Lifeworld – and some were transformed as a result.

We asked our students to reflect on the impact of phenomenological writing as part of the process of evaluating the utility of Transformative Phenomenology for raising consciousness. Through their introduction to phenomenology, writing rich descriptions of lived experience, and collaborative interpretation of meaning, students discovered the "whatness" of experience, looked beyond the taken for granted, and embraced new approaches to understanding the Lifeworld. Many were grabbed by the transformative potential of our phenomenological elixir as was poignantly summarized in the following statement by one of our doctoral students:

> Where do I begin with your question about phenomenology having an impact on my life? I don't even recognize myself anymore compared to the person . . . just the other day, I was recounting to a friend the events that have taken place in my life over the past few months, noting the internal transformation that also impacted my Lifeworld.
>
> Of course, life is dynamic and non-linear, so I'm not able to discern one specific *thing* that caused all of the changes in my life. However, without a doubt, phenomenology contributed to the transformation of my consciousness, and the shift in consciousness spilled into my external environment . . . bracketing alone changed how I interacted with people.
>
> When I learned to suspend assumptions, biases, and judgments I became *present* when I engaged in conversations with people. From that *presence,* I discovered authenticity in myself, which resulted in deeper, more meaningful relationships with people.
>
> (self-observation, 2019)

As our alums and students can attest, coming to phenomenology can be a transformative experience for those who choose to engage.

What's Next for Collaborative Transformative Phenomenology?

A key aspect of Transformative Phenomenology is its applied nature. It is a somatic-hermeneutic-phenomenology put into action for change in the Lifeworld (Marlatt et al. 2020). Here, and in the edited volumes *Reflections of Phenomenological Research* and *Transformative Phenomenology*, David Rehorick, Valerie Bentz, alumni, and students provide compelling evidence about how transformative phenomenologists create personal, professional, organizational transformation for a better world (Rehorick/Bentz 2008, 2017).

Our Fielding Somatics, Phenomenology, and Communicative Leadership (SPLC) Community-of-Practice is active and believes that Transformative Phenomenology allows for truthful communication and consciousness-raising to support individual, social, and ecological transformation. Membership of the Fielding SPCL concentration, faculty-alumni-student collaborative writing projects, the development of teaching opportunities, and this action research project confirm that the Silver Age of Phenomenology at Fielding continues to evolve (Bentz et al. 2020). Presentations by Fielding alumni and students at international forums such as the European Sociological Association, the Schütz Circle, and the Society for Phenomenology and Human Studies, and the cadre of scholar-practitioners engaged around the planet are evidence of the influence of Fielding transformative phenomenologists and like-minded people.

Our evolving action research project is focused on raising global consciousness about Deathworlds through the development of the Fielding SPCL community-of-practice, the broader Fielding community, and by connecting with like-minded citizens. We observe that many people are impacted when they become aware of Deathworlds and that they are activated to contribute to efforts leading to a better world. The concept of the recovery of the Lifeworld resonates with people's souls.

One of our community activities is the development of a Deathworlds Mapping Project in the form of a participatory action research project focused on raising global consciousness about Deathworlds for social and ecological transformation. In this context, Deathworlds are human worlds focused on destroying meaning, coherence, we-relationships, and intersubjectivity for humans and other life forms. Once destroyed these worlds become dead zones killing or expelling all life. As the survival of life forms on earth is in question, humans must overcome economic and technological forces leading to Deathworlds (Bentz et al. 2018). We empathize with Saskia Sassen, a public scholar, who calls for these Deathworldly spaces on our planet to be identified and given sustained and heightened visibility as real enlivened spaces and places on our maps and in our minds so that they can become the "new spaces for making . . . local economies, new histories and new modes of membership" (Sassen 2014, p. 222).

Our community members will identify Deathworld themes and localities that have the potential to be developed into on-line "Story Maps" – engaging displays of maps, images, and commentary about our research and practice. And develop a web-based geographical information and publication system using powerful maps as a foundation for information sharing. The call is to continue to sustain our growth from a Community-of-Practice to a Community-of-Action.

References

Arendt, Hanna (1998): *The Human Condition* (2nd Ed.). Chicago: University of Chicago Press. (Original work published in 1959).

Bentz, Valerie Malhotra/Rehorick, David/Marlatt, James/Nishi, Ayumi/Estrada, Carol (2018): "Transformative Phenomenology as an Antidote to Technological Deathworlds". In: *Schützian Research* 10, pp.189–220.

Marlatt, James/Rehorick, David/Bentz, Valerie Malhotra (2020): Transformative Phenomenology. In: Possamai, Adam/Blasi, Anthony J. (Eds.): *SAGE Encyclopedia of Sociology of Religion*. Thousand Oaks: SAGE.

Rehorick, David/Bentz, Valerie Malhotra (Eds.) (2017): *Expressions of Phenomenological Research: Consciousness and Lifeworld Studies*. Santa Barbara: Fielding University Press.

Rehorick, David/Bentz, Valerie Malhotra (Eds.) (2008): *Transformative Phenomenology: Changing Ourselves, Lifeworlds, and Professional Practice*. Lanham: Lexington Books.

Sassen, Saskia (2014): *Expulsions: Brutality and Complexity in the Global Economy*. Cambridge, London: Harvard University Press. (Kindle Version)

About the Authors

Tetyana Azarova, Ph.D.
Tetyana Azarova earned a Ph.D. in organizational development and change. She has professional experience in corporate finance and is also a former professional chess player. Tetyana is currently in transition, shifting her focus to human consciousness evolution, spirituality, personal and organizational development. She was born in Ukraine and has lived and worked in the U.S. for the past 20 years.

Barton Buechner, Ph.D.
Dr. Barton Buechner is a 1978 graduate of the U.S. Naval Academy, serving in the Navy for 30 years in a variety of operational and senior staff positions before retiring as a Navy Captain in 2008. He is presently a senior adjunct professor in the M.A. in Psychology with an emphasis in Military Psychology program at Adler University, and also an adjunct faculty member with the University of the Virgin Islands, co-teaching an online course in phenomenology, somatics, and communication. Dr. Buechner earned an M.A. in Organizational Development at Case Western Reserve University and a Ph.D. from Fielding Graduate University. His phenomenologically-informed dissertation focused on mentoring of student veterans in higher education settings. He currently serves as on the boards of directors of the CMM Institute for Personal and Social Evolution and the National Veterans' Foundation. He lives in Midland, Michigan, where he plays bass guitar in a blues/rock band and supports various veterans' organizations and causes.

Małgorzata Burchard-Dziubińska, Ph.D.
Małgorzata Burchard-Dziubińska is a researcher in the field of economics of natural resources and environmental protection. She holds a postdoctoral degree in economics. Currently, she holds the position as an associate professor at the Faculty of Economics and Sociology at the University of Łódź, Poland. She is an author and editor of papers and books related to issues of sustainable development, economic transition, the economics of natural resources and environmental protection, co-editor of Journal "Ekonomia i Środowisko" (Economics and Environment). Since 2018 she has been the President of the Polish Association of Environmental and Resource Economists and in 2010–2015 she was the President of the Polish Economic Society–Łódź Division. She was a manager in several scientific projects and a scholarship holder, among others: Ludwig Erhard Stiftung (2005 and 2013), and Santander Universidades, The Lauder Institute, Wharton School, University of Pennsylvania (2014). Her fields of expertise are the economics of sustainable development, the economics of natural resources, environmental protection policy, environmental management.

Darlene Cockayne, Ph.D. Candidate
Darlene Cockayne has earned two master's degrees, one in psychology with an emphasis in military psychology from Adler University in Chicago, Illinois and the other in human development from Fielding Graduate University in Santa Barbara California. She is currently a doctoral student at Fielding Graduate University working on her dissertation, which focuses on the reintegration of our veterans from military life to civilian life and their struggle. Darlene homeschools her two beautiful daughters and is the wife of a veteran. She is an Illinois native where she resides with her family.

Lorraine Crockford, Ph.D.
Lorraine Crockford, Ph.D., is a licensed psychotherapist who practices in California. Her practice is focused on trauma & anxiety as well as addictive disorders. Dr. Crockford works with Type-I and Type-II trauma intervening with relaxation and calming interventions in brief and longer-term treatment. Her orientation includes the soma (embodiment experience) providing Progressive Relaxation, (Eye Movement Desensitization, EMDR; and Cognitive Processing Therapy, CPT for post-traumatic stress disorders, PTSD). Dr. Crockford completed her doctoral degree in 2019 at Fielding Graduate University in human development. Her interest in scholarship brings focus to the multiple realities in the work of Alfred Schütz and in particular scaffolding Schützian concepts to deepen the understanding of human experience, whereby one comes to perceive the lifeworld intersubjectively between the self in relation to the constructs of the other in family, work and social systems.

Lori Davidson, Ph.D. Candidate
Lori Davidson, M.S., HS-BCP, is a human services practitioner with experience in counseling, administration, and program development. She has extensive knowledge in several areas of the health and wellness field, including nutrition and exercise. Lori currently works for Montgomery County Community College as an assistant professor, supporting many first-generation college students, inside and outside of the classroom.

Jennifer Decker, Ph.D.
Jennifer Decker is a doctoral student at Fielding Graduate University. She is a fitness trainer who works with both one-on-one clients and small groups in Hershey, PA. Her specialty is women's functional training. In her thirteen years of experience, she has encountered and worked with several women whose primary motivation for fitness was body image. Throughout her career, she discovered that many of these women were concerned with body image to the extent that they would be willing to risk their well-being for the latest diet fad or exercise trend. These interactions inspired her dissertation research on middle-aged women who endanger themselves exercising for body image.

Michelle Elias, Ph.D. Candidate
Michelle Elias is currently a doctoral student at Fielding Graduate University. She earned a master's degree in Psychology with an emphasis on Military Psychology from Adler University and a bachelor's degree in Psychology from California State University, Fullerton. She's taught Special Education for more than 30 years. Michelle is a wife of a retired sailor, mom to two (one an active duty soldier), stepmom to four, and granny to five fantastic female grandchildren. Michelle's interests are centered around military families and the phenomena around military life. Michelle is a California native where she continues to reside with her husband.

Carol Estrada. Ph.D. Candidate
Carol Estrada is a Doctoral Candidate in Human Development at Fielding Graduate University. Her dissertation research centers on the lived experience of young adults with terminal cancer. Additionally, she coaches university students new to phenomenology on the use of phenomenologically based writing protocols as a means of preparing for research. Professionally she is the owner of The Learning Connection Utah which provides 1:1 academic

and coaching services to children, most of whom have special needs or who are struggling in traditional academic settings.

Valerie Grossman, Ph.D.
Valerie Grossman, an educator counsellor founded and is CEO of Health Reach Canada Inc. (www.healthreachcanadainc.org) a fully volunteer, United Way Donor Choice non-profit organization, registered in Canada and the USA, whose purpose is helping people help themselves via health & education programs. Dancing through the Rain, her book, documents one woman's voice as she addresses life's difficult issues with a positive outlook, thereby reframing dark experience to create positive outcome. She resides in Calgary, Canada, but is often overseas helping people understand & resolve presented problems. Valerie loves to hike in nature & practices yoga &meditation.

David Haddad, Ph.D.
David Haddad is an independent researcher and writer in phenomenology. His contribution, "Intentionality as an Instrument in Action Research," was added to Transformative Phenomenology, co-edited by Drs. Valerie Bentz and David Rehorick. He practices a blend of writing phenomenology, Zen Buddhism, and Christianity in Idyllwild, California.

David Jones, Ph.D.
David works in the School of Education at Fresno Pacific University and studies in the School of Leadership Studies at Fielding Graduate University. His research interests include human development within systems, human learning, disability studies, graduate writing, feminist disability theory, and nontraditional student success. His discovery of phenomenology represents a happy accident, one that fostered tremendous personal growth that spilled into other life domains, thus effecting a ripple of brilliant results. His dissertation explores how discourse in creativity research operates to exclude the accomplishments of racialized, gendered, and disabled creators.

Anna Kacperczyk, Ph.D.
Anna Kacperczyk is an assistant professor of sociology at the University of Łódź in Poland. Substantive areas of her research included palliative and hospice care in Poland (2006), the sustainable development of an Amazonian village (2013), the social world of climbing (2016), and trash (2019). She is interested in social worlds' theory, the methodology of social research, especially the problem of the position and role of the researcher in the investigation process. She basis research on the theoretical framework of symbolic interactionism, using ethnography, autoethnography, and methodology of grounded theory during her field research. She is chairperson of the Section of Qualitative Sociology and Symbolic Interactionism of the Polish Sociological Association and the member of the board of European Society for the Study of Symbolic Interaction. She serves as associate editor and cover designer of the journal *Qualitative Sociology Review*.

Krzysztof Konecki, Ph.D.
Krzysztof Konecki is a professor of sociology and works at the Institute of Sociology, Faculty of Economics and Sociology, University of Łódź, Poland. His interests lie in qualitative sociology, sociology of interaction, symbolic interactionism, sociology of the body, methodology of social sciences, visual sociology, communication and intercultural management,

organizational culture and management, and contemplative sociology. He is the editor-in-chief of *Qualitative Sociology Review* and holds the position of President of the Polish Sociological Association and is a member of the Committee of Sociology of the Polish Academy of Science; he was also a member of the Executive Committee of European Sociological Association.

Łucja Lange, Ph.D. Candidate
Łucja Lange is a Ph.D. Candidate at the Sociological Institute, University of Łódź & at the Literary Research Institute, Polish Academy of Sciences in Warsaw. She holds MAs in Theatre Studies (2004) and Ethnology and Culture Anthropology (2015). Her interests include death studies, anthropology of body and senses, marginalization, animal studies, gender studies, theatre, and photography. Łucja is the author of the book "Anthropologist as the Internal Auditor" (2016) and co-editor with Inga B. Kuźma of the books "Homelessness in Łódź" (2016) and "Flat and Home as a Cultural and Social Non-obviousness." In her recent research, she studies the experience of parent's bereavement processes. Another research focus is on cancertainment and metaphors used to describe illness on cancer patient blogs. More information available on her website: www.langel.pl

Natalia Martini, Ph.D. Candidate
Doctoral Student at the Institute of Sociology, Jagiellonian University, Kraków, Poland. Sociologist with a background in cultural studies, who has a strong interest in urban everyday life, as well as creative, transdisciplinary methodological approaches to urban phenomena. Her work cuts across sociology and human geography and favors critical and activist approaches to scholarship.

Tsolmontuya Myagmarjav, Ph.D. Candidate
Tsolmontuya Myagmarjav was born in Mongolia, with experience working in the aviation industry as a flight engineer. She is a Ph.D. student at the University of Łódź, Poland since 2016, researching cost-effective methods for the rehabilitation of land after mining. Her concentration of research is on Mongolian herders who lost their livestock as a result of climate change and mining. Since 1990, Mongolia has become an economic interest for foreign investment in mining. She has a goal of achieving ecological justice for Mongolian nomads.

Ayumi Nishii, Ph.D.
Ayumi Nishii, Ph.D., a Japanese native currently living in California, works in the areas of organizational and personal development, and enjoys playing a role of a catalyst to "connect, collaborate, and create." Her background is in organizational development, leadership training, and human resources in Japan and the United States. She explored the meaning of servanthood with her hermeneutic phenomenological dissertation, *Servanthood as Love, Relationships, and Power: A Heideggerian Hermeneutic Study on the Experiences of Servant-Leaders* (2017). She is currently working on translating McGee-Cooper's *The Art of Coaching for Servant Leadership: A Guide for Coaches, Managers, and Anyone Who Wants to Bring Out the BEST in Others* into Japanese. The areas of her interests include servant leadership, dialogue, Heideggerian philosophy, spirituality, and holistic wellness. She holds a master's degree in organization management and development and a doctorate in human and organizational systems from Fielding Graduate University.

Debra Irene Opland, Ed.D.
A native of South Dakota, Debra Irene Opland has spent most of her life living in the Black Hills, pursuing careers in theatre, photojournalism, business, art, anthropology, and finally, peace education. Debra received her degree from the Educational Leadership for Change Program at Fielding Graduate University; her dissertation is entitled, *Ićhimani Wáȟwala, Journey to Achieve Peace through Self-Understanding When Indigenous Wisdom is Applied to Enculturation and Education for Humanity*. As action-oriented outcomes of the dissertation, she applies Indigenous wisdom to a *Peace Paradigm and Pedagogy* upon which to base *Community and Curriculum for Humanity* – civic/school development projects implemented through the post-doctoral continuation of her work – beginning within reservation communities in Western South Dakota, the poorest counties in the U.S.

David Rehorick, Ph.D.
David Allan Rehorick, Ph.D. is Professor Emeritus at the University of New Brunswick (UNB), Canada where he taught from 1974 to 2007. He is also Professor Emeritus at the Fielding Graduate University, serving as Research Consulting Faculty (1995–2006), then full-time faculty (2007–2012). His research, publications, and editorial contributions encompass the domains of phenomenology and interpretive studies, educational praxis and theory, sociological theory, population studies, the healthcare sciences, and the creative arts. He has served on six editorial boards of academic journals, including Review Editor of Human Studies: A Journal for Philosophy and the Social Sciences. As a developer in higher education, David was appointed Founding Faculty and Fellow in Comparative Culture at The Miyazaki International College in Japan (1994–97). He was also the founder of Renaissance College, the first undergraduate leadership studies program in Canada, and became the first Director of International Internships (2001–04).

Ann Ritter, Ph.D.
Ann Ritter completed both a Ph.D. and M.S. in human systems in the School of Human and Organizational Development/Leadership Studies at Fielding Graduate University. Her firm, Alpha Rho Leadership Communication, is based in metro Atlanta, where she also teaches and practices yoga and yoga therapy under the banner of The Human Nature Bridge. A former marketing communication professional, Dr. Ritter has more than 25 years of management experience in financial services, consulting, manufacturing and non-profits and also has taught in the Robinson College of Business at Georgia State University as both a part-time lecturer and visiting faculty member for business communication programs. She has trained executives for media and presentation skills and coached a highly diverse population of undergraduate and graduate business students on how to prepare for communication and thought leadership roles. Her earliest experience was as a stage performer and storyteller, and she continues to bring that experience to bear on her work. She serves on the board of Atlanta-based Beacon Dance Company and is also an ad-hoc dance company member.

Rik Spann, M.A.
Rik Spann M.A. is a corporate musicologist and independent researcher, specializing in organizational improvisation, mainly from the jazz metaphor. He is the founder of Kind of Blue Improvisation and Leadership Consultancy. He worked professionally in the worlds of music, theatre, film, dance, journalism and visual arts, performing and exhibiting around the globe. He studied musicology, linguistics and human and group development, always working from a

transdisciplinary perspective. His way of applying the jazz metaphor to business programs on leadership, strategy, team development and transformational change led to an internationally acclaimed series of initiatives. Rik published on a wide area of topics, like jazz history, jam structures, generative metaphors, group creativity, liminality, Miles Davis & Gregory Bateson, social constructionism, design thinking, management cybernetics and cosmopolitan communication. Rik works in initiatives of Fielding Graduate University, Santa Barbara. He works for the CMMi (board member), TAOS Institute (associate) and the Change Studio (consultant).

Whitney P. Strohmayr, Ph.D. Candidate
Whitney P. Strohmayr is working on a doctoral dissertation on the phenomenology of women's intuition at Fielding Graduate University. Her experience includes development for a non-profit organization serving adults with severe mental illness and their families, housing coordination for literally homeless individuals with mental illness, and English instruction for speakers of other languages. Her research interests include adult development and social and ecological sustainability.

Dagmara Tarasiuk, Ph.D. Candidate
Dagmara Tarasiuk is an architectural engineer and ethnologist by profession. She is currently a Ph.D. student in sociology at the University of Łódź, Poland, Department of Sociology of Organization and Management. Her ethnological research has focused on the anthropology of the city (in the context of the category of places and non-places), total institutions and self-sufficient communities. She is currently working on a doctoral dissertation in which she is studying taking care of the body in the context of yoga and its transformational aspects. Also, she is a scholarship holder of the project "Experiencing corporeality and gestures in the social world of hatha yoga. Meaning and knowledge transfer in body practice." Privately, she practices yoga.

About the Editors

Valerie Malhotra Bentz, MSSW, Ph.D. (Senior Editor) is a professor of human and organization development at Fielding Graduate University, where she served as associate dean for research. Her current interests include somatics, phenomenology, social theory, consciousness development, and Vedantic theories of knowledge. Her books include *Contemplative social research: Caring for self, being, and lifeworld*, with Vincenzo M. B. Giorgino; *Transformative phenomenology: Changing ourselves, lifeworlds and professional practice*, with David Rehorick; *Expressions of phenomenological research*, with David Rehorick; *Mindful inquiry in social research*, with Jeremy Shapiro, and *Becoming mature: Childhood ghosts and spirits in adult life*. She also authored a philosophical novel, *Flesh and mind: The time travels of Dr. Victoria Von Dietz*. She is a Fellow in Contemplative Practice of the American Association of Learned Societies. Valerie was editor of Phenomenology and the Human Sciences (1994–1998). She has served as president and board member of the Clinical Sociology Association, the Sociological Practice Association, and the Society for Phenomenology and the Human Sciences. She founded and co-directed an action research team and center in Mizoram, India. Valerie was a co-founder of the Creative Longevity and Wisdom program at Fielding. She is the director of the Doctoral Concentration in Somatics, Phenomenology, and Communicative Leadership (SPCL). She has twenty years of experience as a psychotherapist and is a certified yoga teacher and a certified massage therapist. Valerie is a member of the board of the Carpinteria Valley Association, and environmental activist group. She plays bassoon and piano. Contact: vbentz@fielding.edu. Website: https://www.valeriebentz.com

James Marlatt, MBA, CEC, Ph.D., P.Eng. (Editor) is an Institute for Social Innovation Fellow at Fielding Graduate University with an interest in applied social phenomenology. Jim is a certified executive coach and leadership development consultant with coaching credentials from Royal Roads University. He holds a Ph.D. in human and organizational systems from Fielding Graduate University, *where he conducted research on transformative learning through the executive coaching relationship.* Jim's publications include the book chapters: "The transformative potential of conversations with strangers" in Fielding monograph *Expressions of phenomenological research;* "The silver age of phenomenology at Fielding" in *The Fielding Scholar Practitioner: Voices from 45 years of Fielding Graduate University;* and "Embodied awareness: Transformative coaching through somatics and phenomenology" appearing in the Fielding coaching monograph *Innovations in leadership coaching*. He was the research coordinator for the 2019 Fielding international and multi-institutional "From Strangers to Collaborators" participatory action research project led by Professor Valerie Bentz. Jim is also a professional geological engineer, with a long international career in the mineral resource industry, *and a research publication history in the applied natural sciences*. He acts as an international education and training consultant to a United Nations affiliate on matters related to sustainable energy supply. Jim, a proud father of two daughters, lives on Vancouver Island, Canada with his spouse Margaret, where he enjoys wildlife and landscape photography. Contact: jmarlatt@email.fielding.edu

Endorsements

"This unique book brings together 78 participants from 11 countries to reveal the ways in which phenomenology – the study of consciousness and phenomena – can lead to profound personal and social transformation. Such transformation is especially powerful when 'Deathworlds' – physical or cultural places that no longer sustain life – are transformed into 'Lifeworlds' through collaborative sharing, even when (or, perhaps, especially when) the sharing is among strangers across different cultures. The contributors share a truly wide range of human experiences, from the death of a child to ecological destruction, in offering ways to affirm life in the face of what may seem to be hopeless death-affirming challenges."

    Richard P. Appelbaum, Distinguished Research Professor Emeritus and former MacArthur Foundation Chair in Global and International Studies and Sociology at UCSB, and Professor at Fielding Graduate University, where he heads the doctoral concentration in Sustainability Leadership

"*Deathworlds to Lifeworlds* represents a collaboration among Fielding Graduate University, the University of Łódź (Poland), and the University of the Virgin Islands. Students and faculty from these universities participated in seminars on transformative phenomenology and developed rich phenomenologically based narratives of their experiences or others'. These phenomenological protocols creatively modify and integrate with everyday experience the conceptual frameworks of Husserl, Schutz, Heidegger, Habermas, and others. The diverse protocol authors demonstrate how phenomenological reflection is transformative first by revealing how Deathworlds, which lead to physical, mental, social, or ecological decline, imperil invaluable Lifeworlds. Deathworlds appear on Lifeworld fringes, such as extra-urban trash landfills, where unnoticed impoverished workers labor to the destruction of their own health. Poignant protocol-narratives highlight the plight and noble struggle of homeless people, the mother of a dying 19-year-old son, persons inclined to suicide, overwhelmed first responders, alcoholics who through inspiration achieve sobriety, unravelled We-Relationships, those suffering from and overcoming addiction or misogynist stereotypes or excessive pressures, veterans distraught after combat, a military mother, those in liminal situations, and oppressed indigenous peoples who still make available their liberating spirituality. Transformative phenomenology exemplifies that generous responsiveness to the ethical summons to solidarity to which Levinas's Other invites us."

Michael Barber, Ph.D., Professor of Philosophy, St. Louis University, Author of He has authored seven books and more than 80 articles in the general area of phenomenology and the social world. His seventh book, *Religion and Humor as Emancipating Provinces of Meaning*, was published in 2017 by Springer Press. He is also editor of *Schutzian Research*, an annual interdisciplinary journal.

"Moving beyond the social phenomenology carved out by Alfred Schütz, this impressive volume of action-based experiential research displays the efficacy of applying phenomenological protocols to explore Deathworlds, the tacit side of the foundational conception of Lifeworlds. Over twenty chapters, plus an epilogue, readers are transported by the train of Transformative Phenomenology, created during what's been called the Silver Age of Phenomenology (1996 – present) at the Fielding Graduate University. An international amalgam of students and faculty from universities in Poland, the United States, the Virgin Islands, Canada, and socio-cultural locations throughout the world harnessed their collective energy to advance the practical call of phenomenology as a pathway to meaning-making through rich descriptions of lived experience. Topics include dwelling with strangers, dealing with trash, walking with the homeless, the death of a young person, overcoming colonialism, precognition, environmental destruction, and so much more. The research collection enhances what counts as phenomenological inquiry while remaining respectful of Edmund Husserl's philosophical roots."

David Rehorick, Ph.D., Professor Emeritus of Sociology, University of New Brunswick (Canada), and Professor Emeritus, Fielding Graduate University (U.S.A.)

"Deathworlds is a love letter for the planet—our home. By documenting places that no longer sustain life, the authors collectively pull back the curtain on these places, rendering them meaningful by connecting what ails us with what ails the world. They offer powerful stories and ways to take action to re-create life-affirming societies and practices.

Katrina S. Rogers, PhD, conservation activist and author of "Hermeneutics for understanding International Relations, Environment, and other issues of the twenty-first century."

"Recognizing the inseparability of experience, consciousness, environment, and problematics in rebalancing life systems, this book offers solutions from around the world."

Four Arrows, aka Don Trent Jacobs, author of *Sitting Bull's Words For A World in Crises.*

This book helps us notice the Deathworlds that surround us and advocates for their de-naturalization. Its central claim is that the ten virtues of the transformative phenomenologist allow us to do so by changing ourselves and the worlds we live in. In this light, the book is an outstanding presentation of the international movement known as "transformative phenomenology." It makes groundbreaking contributions to a tradition in which some of the authors are considered the main referents. Also, it offers an innovative understanding of Alfred Schutz's philosophy of the Lifeworld and a fruitful application of Max Van Manen's method of written protocols.

Carlos Belvedere, Ph.D., Professor, Faculty of Social Sciences, University of Buenos Aires

"*Deathworlds into Lifeworlds* wakes people up to how current economic and social forces are destroying life and communities on our planet, as I have mapped in my work. The chapters by scholars around the world in this powerful book testify to the pervasive consequences of the proliferation of Deathworld-making and ways that collaboration across cultures can help move us forward."

Saskia Sassen is the Robert S. Lynd Professor of Sociology at Columbia University and a Member of its Committee on Global Thought, which she chaired till 2015. She is the author of eight books and the editor or co-editor of three books. She has received many awards and honors, among them multiple doctor honoris causa, the 2013 Principe de Asturias Prize in the Social Sciences, election to the Royal Academy of the Sciences of the Netherlands, and made a Chevalier de l'Ordre des Arts et Lettres by the French government.

Index

Addiction
– As Deathworld 208f
– Overcoming via weightlifting 208–210
Alternative realities
– Challenge of in Mizoram 300f
Amazon rainforest
– Greed dominates 289
– Oppression and violence 289
– Fires 295
Anxiety disorder 130
Anxiety, ontological
– In Deathworlds 35

Being
– Loss of in Łódź 98
Being with dying 158–160
Body-spirit learning
– Repressed in Dominant Worldview 12
Bracketing (Husserl)
– Of preunderstandings of precognition 103
– Of expectations in Mizoram 302–304
Bribery 127
Burke, Kenneth
– Dramatistic pentad 10
– Motivational experience 137

Chemical plant explosion
– In Zgierz, Poland 2018 39f
Child labor in Łódź industry 56
Collaboration
– Across nations 5
– And co-learning 8, 13
– Challenges in Dominant Worldview 117–118
– Through Jazz metaphor 254f
– Transformative 239–240
– Typifications challenged in 121
– With strangers 144–146
Collaborative inquiry sustained 309
Collaborative Transformative Phenomenology 349f
Co-learning 8–10
– and Self-acceptance 104
– see also Lerogogy

Collectivization of herding in Mongolia 281
Colonization of Mongolian sheepherders 280f
Community of Practice—Surrey experience 333–334f
Consciousness transformation 324

Death of loved one 126–127
– Of father 139
– Of young son 150–160
Death risk for middle-aged women 217–219
Deathworld Making
– Through technologization and mechanization 16
– Capitalism's role 16
Deathworlds
– Addiction 208–210
– Amazon rain forest 289f
– Dead zones 323
– Defined 14–15, 321
– Divorce of parents 126
– Experienced 119
– Famine 296
– water shortage, malaria 296f
– First responders to emergencies 180f
– Garbage dumps 82
– Hidden pollution 35
– History of in Łódź, Poland 56–57
– Industrialized–hunting and meat industries 29
– Loss of self 322
– Mongolian sheep herders 282–287
– Military wife and mother 225f
– Mining industry 282
– Museums in Łódź reveal extreme wealth of few 56–57
– Revealed in photographic focus 31f
– Santa Barbara County, California 46, 60
– Scientific thinking 59
– Self injury 217–219
– Social construction of irrelevance 41f
– Stroniewice Village in Poland 58–59
– Stress/pressure 212–214
– Toxic neighborhoods 83

– Within Lifeworlds 15
Denial of Deathworlds 61
Depression 128–129
Desolation, as an absence of taken-for-granted 59
– Layers in Łódź history 51f
– Outsider experience 45–46
Divided Identity in Lakota reservation 267f
Dominant Worldview 7
– Defined VIII
– Vs. Indigenous Worldview 17
– Challenges of collaboration in 18–19, 46
– See Indigenous Worldview

Ecocide denied 66
Embodied awareness 173
Embodiment
– of Lifeworld 251
– as Somatic practice 10
Emotions devalued 190
Epoche 47f
– as inspirational 214–215
Essential structure
– of Being with dying 155
– of Grief 202–203
Expulsions as dead zones 323
Extrasensory abilities 111

Famine in Mizoram 297
Fear 124–125
– of son's military deployment 236–239
– of veteran husband's suicidal tendencies 233
– in Mizoram, India 296f
First responders to emergencies
– Insecurity and shame in 188–189
– "In-order-to motives" 182
– as strangers 181
– trauma in 181

Garbage dump
– As toxic Deathworld 82f
Gebser, Jean
– Consciousness change needed for the survival of human life 20–21

Grief 201–203
Growing up in North Dakota 264–266

Habermas, Jurgen
– Truth-seeking communication 324–325
Healing
– Through phenomenological writing 140–141
Higher education
– Pressure in 212–215
Homeless
– Walking with in Łódź Poland 91–100
Husserl, Edmund
– and phenomenological protocols 7–8
– essence of experience 137
Hyper-alertness in first responders 187

Indigenous in Amazon rainforest
– European created disharmony 291
– Slave trading 290
Indigenous students at risk 272–274
Indigenous Worldview 17
– And peace educator 263
Injury risk in women exercising 219
Insider/Outsider in Mizoram 300–301
Inspiration 163f
– As transpersonal 165
– Liberation through 174
Imaginative variations
– Overcoming failure experience 140–141
– in precognition 112

Lakota reservation 268–272
Leper Village
– Water shortage in 305f
Leregogy 8–10
– Defined 329–330
Lifeworld
– Built over Deathworld in Lodz 56f
– Defined 8, 28, 231
– Of Being with Dying 156
– Inspired vs. uninspired 168–170
– Image based for women 218–219
– Restoring 135f
Liminality 103, 113–115
– Endless 247f

Jazz 246
– Lifestyle 344–245
– Moral code 247–249
– Transformative 243–244
– Worldwide 249–250
Lived Experience 117f
Living phenomenology 338f
Łódź, Poland 3–101
– Collaboration with Strangers Research 3f
– Deathworlds, insider experience 27f
– Deathworlds, outsider viewpoint 45f
– Trash in 63f
– Homeless in 91f
– Opulence on display 58
Loneliness 129

Majuwa, Nepal, See Leper village
Malaria
– Undiagnosed 310
– Diagnosed and treated in Tanzania 311
Manning, Chelsea
– Whistleblower about Deathworlds of U.S. Drone strikes 319
Materialistic paradigm 166–167
– As taken-for-granted 167
– Lonely and stressful 168
Mautam 297
– Mizo word for famine
Mongolian sheepherders
– Colonization of Lifeworld 280f
– Forced migration 287
Moral Dilemma of researchers
– About Deathworlds 89f
Military Wife and Mother 225f
Mizoram Action Research Team 298–299
Multiple Realities
– Being with dying 156–157
– Of Addicted 211
Museums in Łódź
– Opulence of the wealthy 57
Mystic, practical 255–257
Musical identity 129–130

Natural attitude 47f
Nature disconnection in monotheism 105
Nuclear family as mistake 16

No-place 66–67
Obsessive Compulsive Disorder 128
Opulence on display in Łódź 58
Outsider as Stranger 45f

Panic
– Healing through phenomenological writing 138–139
Participatory action research 296f
Phenomenologist as transformed 252–253, 33
– Ten qualities of 10
Phenomenological descriptions
– And transcendental meditation 8
Phenomenology
– Essential structure of trash 74–78
– Indigenous world view vii–ix
– Mysticism vii
– Precognition 103f
– Through walking 94
– Trash 63–90
– Transformative 3–4
– Writing 118–121
– See also Transformative Phenomenology 252–253
Phoenix Society of Surrey B.C. 335–337, 343
– Rising Sun project 335
Place, insiders/outsiders 20–21
Placelessness
– Of homeless in cities 92
Plastic
– Destroys wildlife 57–69, 87
Poignant experience 135–137
– Of Being-with-Dying 153
Precognition 102f
– Examples 102–103
– In animals 105–106
– 19th century Gothicism 107
– As normal 108
– Beliefs about 108
– In pop culture 109–110
– As gift 113
Protocols 4, 9
– Examples 152–154
– Husserlian 7–8

- Schutzian Lifeworld 8
- Sequence 9–10

Relationship, abusive 200–204
Relevances, imposed 221
Revolution 1905 Street in ódź, Poland 49f
- Foreboding qualities 51–55
Rising Sun Project, Surrey B.C. 334f
Romantic Partnerships 196f

Sassen, Saskia
- Expulsions as dead zones 323
Sch tz, Alfred
- Imposed relevance 320
- Lifeworld protocols 8
- Lifeworld structures 137
- Participating citizen 320
- Provinces of meaning
- finite 61
- Puppets
- cyclist as "culprit," motorist as "grim reaper"
  - In recovery from addiction 209–210
  - Women exercising 219
- Relevances differ between groups 34
- Social worlds of garbage dump 82
  - and trash industry 84
- States of consciousness 183–184
- Stocks of knowledge 82
- Stranger 6, 47f, 181
- Taken-for-granted 170–171
- Trauma 180
- Types
character and habitual 46–47
- Typifications of self 219–220
- Vantage points 82
- We-relationships with Mizo participants 303f
Somatic Practices: yoga, dance, drum circles, Tibetan bowls 11–12
Somatic Mindfulness 250
Spirituality 165

Tanzania
- Diagnosis and treatment of malaria 311
Tension and alcohol 171–172
Technology as deadly force 322
Tlawmngaihna, Mizo practice of selfless caring for others 300
Transformation
- Nature of 122–123
- Signs of 147
Transformative Phenomenology 3–10
- As Antidote to Deathworlds 21, 319, 325–327, 345
- Collaborative 349
- Of precognition 102f, 112
- Survival of life depends on 324
- Ten qualities of phenomenologists 10–11, 330–332
- With Strangers 6, 142–143
Transformative Space
- Of liminality 243–249
Trash
- Communities of pickers 82
- Chemical plant fire trash heap 36
- Essence of 74–77
- Lifeworld of 81f
- Invisible and Visible 87
- In Ecuador 64
- In Poland 64–87
- Toxic neighborhood 83
Trauma 124
- Complex developmental 182–183
- Somatic reaction 184
- Untreated danger of 189

Veterans
- Depression and suicide risk 233
Volunteering 125–126

Wagner, Helmut
- Imposed relevances 320
- We-relationships 198–199
Walking as research method 92–93
Water

– Shortage in Mongolia due to
  mining 283
– Tanks funded in Nepal 307
Weightlifting treatment for addiction 208f
We-relationship
– Between researcher and participants 303
– Courage and trust in 146
– In Being with Dying 159f
– Grief and Unraveling 196–209
Wilson, Michael and Ann 335–336
Worldviews: Dominant and Indigeneous
  viii–ix
Writing phenomenology 118–121
– As transformative 350

www.ingramcontent.com/pod-product-compliance
Lightning Source LLC
Chambersburg PA
CBHW061928220426
43662CB00012B/1841